"Ain't You Glad You Joined the Republicans?"

BOOKS BY JOHN CALVIN BATCHELOR

The Further Adventures of Halley's Comet (1981)

The Birth of the People's Republic of Antarctica (1983)

American Falls (1985)

Thunder in the Dust: Images of Western Movies,
by John R. Hamilton; text by John Calvin Batchelor (1987)

Gordon Liddy Is My Muse, by Tommy "Tip" Paine (1990)

Walking the Cat, by Tommy "Tip" Paine:
Gordon Liddy Is My Muse II (1991)

Peter Nevsky and the True Story of the Russian Moon Landing (1993)

Father's Day (1994)

"Ain't You Glad You Joined the Republicans?" (1996)

"Ain't You Glad You Joined the Republicans?"

A Short History of the GOP

JOHN CALVIN BATCHELOR

Henry Holt and Company
New York

Original manuscript/ w/ Can. Rights
Import/package done solely for Holt w/ Can. Rights

Henry Holt and Company, Inc.
Publishers since 1866
115 West 18th Street
New York, New York 10011

Henry Holt® is a registered
trademark of Henry Holt and Company, Inc.

Published in Canada by Fitzhenry & Whiteside Ltd.,
195 Allstate Parkway, Markham, Ontario L3R 4T8.

Library of Congress Cataloging-in-Publication Data
Batchelor, John Calvin.
Ain't you glad you joined the Republicans? : a short history of
the GOP / John Calvin Batchelor.
p.   cm.
Includes index.
ISBN 0-8050-3267-3 (alk. paper)
1. Republican Party (U.S. : 1854–)—History.   I. Title.
JK2356.B39 1996   95-43639
324.2734—dc20   CIP

Henry Holt books are available for special
promotions and premiums. For details contact:
Director, Special Markets.

First Edition—1996

Designed by Paula R. Szafranski

Printed in the United States of America
All first editions are printed on acid-free paper. ∞

1   3   5   7   9   10   8   6   4   2

All quotations and details, unless otherwise noted, are from
the following newspapers: the Republican *New York Tribune*, the Republican *New York Daily Times,* or, after
1926, the Republican *New York Herald Tribune*, or, after
1966, the *Washington Post.*

Illustrations are from *The National Cyclopedia of American Biography* (New York: James T. White & Co.) unless
otherwise marked. Cartoons and illustrations from the
New York Herald Tribune © New York Herald Tribune
Inc. All rights reserved. Reproduced by permission.

For the Republican heroes in my life,
my father and mother,
Calvin Rogers Batchelor
and
Jeanne Sharlene Batchelor

Contents

"Ain't You Glad You Joined the Republicans?"

"Ain't You Glad You Joined The Republicans?"

1854–1865

At Chicago, the gavel pounded to open the Republican presidential nominating convention at exactly noon, Wednesday, May 16, 1860.

No one came to order. There were ten thousand Republicans inside this tall, vast, turreted meeting hall called the Wigwam; ten thousand more waited outside on a field located between Michigan Avenue and the lake; and everyone was as wild as children as they hollered and signaled that the time for the hard questions was finally here.

Who will be our candidate? Who can whip the Democrats? Who can end slavery? Who can stop disunion? Who's going to be the first Republican president in history?

After six angry years of a revolution at the ballot box that had invented a modern political party out of disgust for the South's slaveholding, the Republicans ached to know: who will lead us to total victory?

Rumors swept the arena like gusts off the lake. In this brand-new building the acoustics were so sharp that everyone could hear the speakers at the podium at the same time they suffered the hammering and sawing from the roof as crews rushed to finish the shell. The interior was arranged in a pecking order: At the center there were seats for one thousand delegates and alternates arranged by states on the wide, low platform. Behind the delegates were chairs for eighty VIP editors, and in the lower gallery directly in back were seats for several hundred more journalists. Squeezed in everywhere else along the upper galleries were thou-

Convention 1860: *The second national convention of the Republicans met in the newly built Wigwam in Chicago, Illinois, where Abraham Lincoln was nominated on the third day, May 18.* Harper's Weekly, *May 19, 1860.*

sands of male spectators, who were flanked by two ladies-only sections overhanging the stage wings.

Such dazzling excitement made folk "orationize" spontaneously and disagree passionately. Seward? Bates? Frémont? McLean? Lincoln? *Surely it will be Seward!*

In the delegate section, no one had bigger ears for the rumors than the most famous Republican editor of all: slight, wan, Ahablike Horace Greeley, then forty-nine, the founding editor of the fundamental Republican Bible, the *New York Tribune.*

Greeley was as deeply Republican as he was bottomlessly antislavery. He had been the critical voice of the party since its sudden birth six years before. Without Greeley's scolding, cajoling, long-striding editorials, there would not have been a Wigwam packed with ten thousand righteous crusaders protesting against the disgraced Buchanan administration and the divided Democratic party. Without Greeley, there plainly would not have been a Republican party.

The gavel pounded out order. The day's business was organization of the convention and housekeeping of the committees. The convention elected a presiding officer. The state delegations presented their credentials. There were only twenty-seven states present: all the North, all the Border states; but only Virginia and Texas from the South. The platform committee retired to its hard work. The credentials committee started arguing about the missing states. There were resolutions from the floor about how to count the votes. Simple majority for nomination? Aye. Two votes per electoral college vote for each participating state? Aye.

The ruthless rumor mill whirred. Seward? Not Seward? Then who?

Greeley nodded over his notes. He had his own edgy opinions, but what he really needed to know was the affections of the three largest delegations, the Empire State of New York, the Keystone State of Pennsylvania, and the Buckeye State of Ohio.

"Everything is confusion," a *Tribune* correspondent filed by telegraph at 1 P.M. "Half the convention are in doubt."

Mighty New York's seventy delegates were solidly for the most august and accomplished Republican of the day, Senator William H. Seward of New York, then fifty-four years old, former attorney, former governor, former Whig, now master of the game of Republican national affairs. Seward had been working toward the presidency since he'd joined the party in '55. Every New Yorker was confident that Seward was going to be the next chief executive—especially the wily Seward himself, who was home in Auburn, New York, tending to the rebuilding of his stables while awaiting word by telegraph from Chicago. Seward would win. Bet on it.

Then again, mighty Pennsylvania's fifty-four delegates held back from Seward just because he was so powerful and so obvious; and they were said to side with their new champion in the Senate, Simon Cameron of Harrisburg, the Republican party boss of Pennsylvania. Not Seward. Certain.

Mighty Ohio's forty-six delegates also held back from Seward, perhaps because he was too conservative on the abolition of slavery for some, perhaps because he was too radical on the abolition of slavery for others. Ohio pushed forward either of its two heroes in the Senate, the awesome abolitionist Salmon P. Chase or the feisty abolitionist Ben Wade. Maybe Seward? Maybe.

Seward was openly favored by the Wisconsin and Michigan delegations and by healthy groups from Massachusetts and the rest of New England. Yet there were several figures who were advanced as sectional favorites. A prominent mention was Edward Bates of Missouri, a former

Democrat and ex-slaveholder, whom Horace Greeley himself recommended in a letter circulated through the convention. Then there was Nathaniel Banks of Massachusetts, the former Speaker of the House of the Thirty-fourth Congress and present Boston darling. Also remarked upon was Justice John McLean of Ohio, an aged member of the Supreme Court who had opposed the Dred Scott decision.

Toward the bottom of the barrel was the favorite of Illinois's twenty-two delegates, Abraham Lincoln, the ex-Whig country lawyer, stump speaker, and "prince of good fellows" from Sagomon County, who had acquitted himself well since he'd been put up for the vice presidency back in '56. Everybody in Illinois liked Honest Abe. He'd taken on the "Little Giant"—Democratic senator Stephen A. Douglas of Illinois, who was sure to be the Democratic party's candidate for president—and Lincoln had talked the Little Giant to a standstill in the Senate race of '58. Lincoln had toured the abolitionist battleground of Kansas in '59 and had even risked speaking at sophisticated New York's Cooper Union in February—always earnest and eloquent for the Republican antislavery cause against the Southern agitators. Abe Lincoln had repeated again and again, whenever he was asked, his famous argument from the summer of 1856, when he first left the dying Whigs and became a Republican, that line from the Bible, "A house divided against itself cannot stand."

True, Lincoln wasn't presidential timber, too little known, too conservative on the demand for immediate abolition, too unfamiliar with the potentates in the Capitol who ruled the country like dukes. But he was well liked. Maybe if the promoters worked hard, Lincoln could win the support of the anti-Seward men for the bottom of the ticket?

Convention 1860: Chicago, Illinois. Harper's Weekly, *May 12, 1860.*

And yet Lincoln, waiting by the telegraph office in the dusty spring air of his hometown of Springfield, Illinois, had instructed his supporters carefully that it would be all or nothing—he didn't want the vice presidency.

The convention adjourned the first day past 10 P.M. The Republican mob, smelling of chewing tobacco and groaning out its hunger, poured out of the giant Wigwam and headed for the hotels off Michigan that were jammed with up to forty thousand visitors. The luxurious Tremont House was the official headquarters of the power brokers, and it was raucous with argument and song. Not a few of the boys slopped their beer and shouted out that chorus first popularized back in '56: *"Ain't You Glad You Joined the Republicans?"*

The newspapermen, dressed like beggars, eavesdropped quietly and then headed for the magnetic telegraphs.

Seward's friends headed for the private bar. How many votes have we got?

At midnight the reports were shaky for Seward. Indiana vacillating; Virginia perhaps not voting at all; Maine unsettled. The only certain delegations for Seward were New York, Michigan, Wisconsin, Minnesota, and Texas.

Seward's lieutenant and moneyman, Thurlow Weed, told the press, "Everything depends upon the obstinacy and union of Pennsylvania, Ohio, New Jersey, Indiana and Illinois."

Elsewhere in the Tremont House, the platform committee scribbled and argued. Slavery must be abolished! No, slavery must be contained! No, we must listen to Seward's own words—that the debate over slavery is "an irrepressible conflict between opposing and enduring forces." No, Seward is too much like the radicals! He can't carry the doubtful Border states!

Friends of Lincoln cannily reminded everyone that Honest Abe wasn't radical at all and could sweep the Border states and the Old Northwest. Since first arriving in the city, Lincoln's friends had been calling on New England delegations and warning them that Seward was weak everywhere out West. Doubts were planted like mustard seeds that if Seward couldn't do it—if Seward was too controversial, too distrusted, simply too famous to be chief magistrate—then someone uncelebrated but most well liked could be.

At 10:40 P.M., Horace Greeley telegraphed New York, "As to the presidency I can only say that the advocates of Governor Seward's nomination, who were much depressed last night, are now quite confident of his success." Greeley added carefully, "Mr. Lincoln now appears to have the next best look."

Convention 1860: The major candidates for the Republican nomination. Note that Lincoln was positioned in the outer ring with Frémont. Seward was the clear favorite. Harper's Weekly, May 12, 1860.

BANKS

McLEAN   CAMERON

JOHN BELL   CASSIUS M. CLAY

The second day in the Wigwam seemed to go Seward's way. The overnight booms for John C. Frémont of California, the presidential candidate in 1856, and for the conservative-choice Edward Bates of Missouri, were shoved aside.

There was also this strong motion by the Stop-Seward forces for the dark horse Lincoln. "Mr. Lincoln is rapidly assuming prominence as the candidate of the opposition to Mr. Seward," said the telegraph to New York City. "Honest Old Abe is now the coming man."

By dinnertime the platform was approved without a nay from the floor. The Republican party had constructed its strength on its antislavery absolutes; however, the economic planks in the platform contained the most innovative commercial ideas of the age: calls for the building of a Pacific railroad and scientific agricultural colleges, support for the improvement of rivers and harbors, and determined support of a high tariff to protect Eastern manufacturers and farmers from cheap foreign goods. Also a most generous immigration plank reassured the suspicious German delegates that the party stood for tolerance and stood against its nativist Know-Nothing element.

Late in the afternoon there had been a presentation of a special new gavel for the podium that was made out of the oak wood of Admiral Perry's flagship, *Lawrence*. The assembly cheered at the reference to the infamous Kansas town of Lawrence, scene of the antislavery battles of "Bleeding Kansas" for the last six years. The motto on the gavel's handle read, "We have not yet begun to fight."

At 10 P.M. Thursday, after rejecting a call to start the presidential balloting, the delegates swung their hats in celebration and filed out for the dining halls and hotels.

Tomorrow was the day to choose the man. *If there was a deal to make, now was the hour.*

The horse-trading was fiercest at the big suites in the Tremont House. Teams of delegates charged from room to room to give or demand commitments for tomorrow's ballots. Offer what? Who? Why?

At 11:45 P.M., the *Tribune*'s correspondent telegraphed New York, "The feeling that Mr. Seward will be nominated has increased all day." Twenty minutes later he added, "The Seward men are full of hope, but cannot give their figures."

Greeley telegraphed his verdict at about the same time, 11:40 P.M., "My conclusion, from all I can gather tonight, is that opposition to Governor Seward cannot concentrate on any candidate, and that he will be nominated."

What neither Greeley knew nor any other observer could confirm for many years, long after the war, was that much later that night, two of

Lincoln's friends sat down with two Pennsylvanians and closed a deal that would swing the convention to Lincoln. In exchange for a seat in the Cabinet for the Pennsylvania boss Simon Cameron, Lincoln would get most of Pennsylvania's votes on the second ballot.

The die was cast for the most surprising rise in the history of the presidency. A prairie giant was about to slay the anointed David of New York. No one knew yet but a handful of hard men.

The next morning at the Wigwam, Friday, May 18, 1860, with eleven thousand inside and twenty to thirty thousand outside, the nominating process began with a contest of demonstrations.

Seward was entered into nomination by the New York delegation to "loud and long applause."

Lincoln was put forward by the Illinois delegation to "perfectly deafening applause," though "some hisses were heard."

Then followed the also-rans: William L. Dayton of New Jersey to "light applause"; Simon Cameron of Pennsylvania to "applause"; Salmon P. Chase of Ohio to "loud applause"; Bates of Missouri to "applause."

The crucial first ballot started, each state delegation rising in place to announce its votes. With every change in the tally, men on the roof of the Wigwam called down the moving tally to the multitude outside. The telegraphs flashed the progress to the whole nation as the weight of the competition went back and forth from Seward to this rising man, Lincoln.

The first ballot count closed. No majority yet of the 466 cast. For Seward, 173½. For Lincoln, 102. The rest of the vote was spread among twelve also-rans, chiefly Bates and Cameron. The first ballot was made official.

Crosscurrents of speculation swept the Wigwam. Seward can't make it now! Lincoln's people must have made a deal! Pennsylvania? What's Cameron going to do?

"Ballot!" they cried. "Ballot again!" they demanded.

The ceremony was repeated. Steady Horace Greeley voted again, for not only was he an observer, he was also serving as a delegate at the request of distant Oregon. Greeley cast a second time for Bates and waited on destiny.

Lincoln picked up a handful of delegates from New Hampshire, from Delaware, from Kansas, from Ohio. Then came the profound turn like a thunderstorm. Cameron and Pennsylvania threw the bulk of the Keystone State's votes to Lincoln.

Results of the second ballot were written in stone. Seward, 184½. Lincoln, 181. Still no winner, but closer, close.

The excitement in the hall was methodical. State delegation chairmen rose for recognition to announce dropouts from the also-rans. The vote tally was in flux. The assembly could feel what was coming. Men were screaming out, "Ballot! Ballot!" Women visitors were waving their handkerchiefs and calling, "Seward!" or "Lincoln!"

The third ballot made history. There was no order to it. Defections from Seward were helter-skelter. Voting for Lincoln was pell-mell. When Ohio gave Lincoln twenty-nine votes, there was a hollow gasp. The count was amazing. For Seward, 180. For Lincoln, 230½, a whisker shy of the 233 needed for majority.

Immediately a man from Massachusetts leaped up and commanded the chair to change four votes to Lincoln.

There was a pause to ascertain the official word from the podium. The rumor mill didn't hesitate. Two six-pound cannons set up on the roof began firing the facts. *Boom!* We have a winner! *Boom!* Lincoln is nominated! *Boom!* Not Seward! *Boom!* Lincoln's our man!

Pandemonium ruled the Wigwam. Dancing delegates waved hats, coats, state flags, the sticks and boards of the delegations, anything they could grab. The roar of the crowd matched each cannon report. A life-sized portrait of rangy and beardless Abe Lincoln was carried bobbing across the stage. The new gavel banged and banged. One hundred cannon reports later they were still cheering for the miracle of a nation of common men who could rise up to secure the future with the simple act of voting.

Greeley was caught in the tumult. *Boom!*

He'd not backed Lincoln, but then again, he'd dreamed something dynamic like this could happen. *Boom!*

He'd struggled for this enthusiasm day and night for the past six years. *Boom!*

Everything in this vast arena, in this hasty, hurtling convention, was Greeley's dream. *Boom!*

This hollering, this madness for victory, this cannonading, this sudden candidate, this profound revolution at the ballot box, this Republican party—all of it was the harvest of Horace Greeley's hard planting.

Boom!

★ 1854 ★

Six years before, the only booming was in Horace Greeley's head when he'd first named the newborn political party Republican in a passionate editorial blast.

The ingenious and ambitious founder of the *New York Tribune* said it was a "simple name." He used the simplicity right away to heave one of his antislavery bombs at the reigning Democratic party—Andrew Jackson's thirty-year-old *Democracy*—during the cataclysmic 1854 debate on slavery.

Greeley, then forty-three and already a muzzle-loaded moralist, wrote in his newspaper on June 16, 1854: "We should not care much whether those thus united *(against the extension of slavery into the West)* were designated 'Whig,' 'Free Democrat' or something else; though we think some simple name like 'Republican' would more fitly designate those who had united to restore the Union to its true mission of champion and promulgator of Liberty rather than propagandist of slavery."

Horace Greeley was writing of the burning controversy of the day— the passage by Congress of the 1854 Kansas-Nebraska Act that aimed to extend slavery into the West as the territories were organized into states of the Union.

Greeley was not inventing the name Republican out of whole cloth; it was an echo from the extinct National-Republican party that had once upon a time opposed Andrew Jackson's Democratic party. The idea of

Horace Greeley (from a photograph by Brady). Harper's Weekly, *September 15, 1860.*

*New York
Tribune tower*

Republicans was in small currency at the time to describe a band of voters from many parties who were opposed to the Nebraska bill. But it was Greeley's editorial talent to choose and popularize the name Republican from among many possibilities for the antislavery cause. And then it was Greeley's genius to attach to this new Republican party a spectacular revolutionary goal: *"to restore the Union to its true mission of champion and promulgator of Liberty."*

Who were the first Republicans? They were everyone and anyone shaken by the Kansas-Nebraska Bill. They were men who were revolted by what was understood as a conspiracy of Democratic politicians and Southern oligarchs to destroy the brittle balance of power between the North and the South. They were angry men who hated the institution of slavery more than they loved the reputation of peace.

For the men who became the Republicans, 1854 was the worst of times, the very worst of times, and their despair moved them to a dissenting blowup against not only the Nebraska bill but also the federal government in the hands of the Democrats and the South in the hands of slaveholding potentates. Republicans were first protesters of Democratic party chicanery before they were campaigners against the Democracy. They were first appalled, betrayed, brokenhearted patriots of the North before they were partisan politicians hammering at the South. They were first ordinary men—for the nation of twenty-five million was then governed by the votes of approximately three million free adult males—before they were the Frémont Clubs of '56 or the battalions of Wide-Awakes of '60 who first paraded for the storybook hero John C. Frémont and who later elected the surprise candidate Abraham Lincoln and the ironfisted Radicals.

The truth was that the birth of the Republican party was a revolutionary rising against the status quo of human bondage.

After a century and a half of partisan struggle, the loud-voiced, glory-bound story of the Republican party has always been the story of liberty in the United States of America—national liberty for the most, civil liberty for the least, private liberty for all.

There was no magical moment when the party was announced; there was no tea party or midnight ride or Bunker Hill. There was only a mighty flow tide of disgust at what slavery was doing to American comity. One year men could tolerate knowing that twelve-year-old children were abducted from Africa and transported like cattle in American ships to be sold into doom at Richmond for fifteen hundred dollars in gold, and the next year they could no longer stomach the facts.

Certainly one of the strangest facts of all is that at the very beginning of the Republican tidal change, there was the pounding editorial piety of loud and clear Horace Greeley.

A poor man's son, a New Hampshire–born, self-taught, endlessly industrious grandson of the American Revolution, Greeley was a successful newspaper publisher in 1854 when, in the flush of his middle age, he took the professional high risk to wave his pen in the air at the outrage of the Kansas-Nebraska Bill and to demand in cut-stone sentences that patriots put aside their busy lives and champion liberty against the traitors of slavery.

To measure the passion behind Greeley's editorial writing, to sense the wrath on all sides and the heartache that created a whole new party like a harvest in the growing season of 1854, it's important to sketch the political landscape of America's struggle over slavery.

In 1776, Thomas Jefferson was obliged to remove a denunciation of the slave trade from his final draft of the Declaration of Independence to appease many slaveholding delegates at Philadelphia, thereby making a lie out of his own revolutionary claim that "all men are created equal." The United States Constitution of 1787 also failed to abolish slavery. However, the Constitution did allow that the slave trade, though not slavery, could be banned in the states of the Union by 1808. And the Constitution did not override the Northwest Ordinance of 1787 that prohibited slavery north of the Ohio River—in the territory that would become Ohio, Indiana, Illinois, Michigan, and Wisconsin.

For the next six decades the Congress, the chief executive, and the courts made sound and fury over slavery, but it all signified nothing. The Missouri Compromise of 1820 was a trade-off in Congress that admitted Missouri as a slave state and Maine as a free state; it also offered the promise that slavery would not spread north of Missouri into the unorganized territories of the West in exchange for the promise that Congress would not prohibit slavery in the Union.

Later congressional tinkering, such as the failed Wilmot Proviso of 1848, the putative compromise of 1850, the Fugitive Slave Law of 1850, did nothing to solve the conflict between the sixteen free states and fifteen slave states at midcentury.

There were periodic flare-ups against slavery—such as William Lloyd Garrison's radical New England Anti-Slavery Society in 1831, or James G. Birney's tiny Liberty party in 1840, or the more sophisticated Free Soil party made up of Conscience Whigs and Democratic Barnburners in 1848, or the splinter antislavery movement out of the Democracy calling

*William Lloyd
Garrison*

itself the Free Democratic party in 1852. None of these cliques lasted longer than a gust of wind in the face of the apologists for the rich and prospering slave business. The cash of the country was invested in land and slaves, and to challenge slavery was to confront wealth itself, North and South. The other sectional-driven economic debates, such as the North favoring (and the South opposing) a Pacific railroad, or a high tariff on farm and manufacturing goods, or the homestead grants for immigrants, or the improvement of rivers and ports, were mites beside the behemoth of slavery.

A booming new nation of bumper crops and Midas gold and silver fields and sprouting railroads was divided as if by a stone wall into two belligerent camps.

The startling introduction of the Kansas-Nebraska Bill in January 1854 by Senator Stephen A. Douglas, Democrat of Illinois, exploded sixty years of hypocrisy and frustration. Douglas, bullheaded and very smart—the Little Giant of Illinois, then forty-six years old—was chairman of the Senate's critical Committee on Territories. Douglas hoped to bring the huge Nebraska territory into the Union in a way that would advance himself for present authority and a future presidential bid. Douglas was a most able politician who did not waver once he set his course. The challenge for him was to finesse the balance of power between the North and the South, since both sides feared the other would gain another state and more congressional and electoral college weight. Douglas moved to make cozy arrangements with the Southern politicians and a quick deal with the weak-willed president Franklin Pierce; then he revealed his Nebraska bill on the Senate floor, January 22. Douglas aimed to organize the Nebraska territory into two states, Kansas and Nebraska, without stipulating beforehand if either were slave or free. Douglas said he'd leave the decision about slavery to the settlers by popular vote, the so-called squatter sovereignty.

What no one had to wait to see was that when the Kansas-Nebraska Bill became law, the Missouri Compromise of 1820 was broken.

The North felt betrayed. The South felt cunning. The abolitionists—radicals of the North—saw the Nebraska bill as a deal with the devil that must be reversed. The fire-eaters—radicals of the South—saw the bill as a wedge that could open up an empire of slavery from sea to sea.

What the introduction of the Nebraska bill did immediately was to

Stephen A. Douglas

break down what concord there was between the North and South over slavery. It also destroyed the stability of the all-powerful Democratic party forevermore.

It wasn't the opposition Whigs who undid the Democrats. The Whigs were the only opposition party in 1854. The Whigs were a fussy stew of prosperous farmers and the proper merchant class that had bubbled up twenty years before to contest Andrew Jackson's Democracy. They had taken a satirical name, Whigs, to mock the imperial instincts of "King Andrew." In two decades the Whigs had won the White House with two generals who both had died in office, and had commanded famous credit for their two congressional stars, Daniel Webster of New Hampshire and Henry Clay of Kentucky. However, the Whig party had not ever seriously challenged the Democracy's local organizations, especially in the South, nor the Democrats' patronage-fattened muscle in the national legislature.

By 1854 the Whig party was sliding into muddled inoffensiveness. The Cotton Whigs of the South usually voted with the conservative Hunker Democrats of the North. The Webster-worshiping Conscience Whigs of the North were too conservative to side openly with the abolitionists. The Whigs fancied themselves to be a national party, that is, nonsectional; yet they had not achieved any viable popularity. The Nebraska bill began Whiggery's last stagger toward extinction.

Salmon P. Chase

What broke up the Democracy was the Democracy itself. The day after Douglas introduced the Nebraska bill, two imperious and aggressive antislavery senators, Salmon P. Chase of Ohio and Charles Sumner of Massachusetts, joined four abolitionist representatives from the North to denounce Douglas and his bill with a profound document called the "Appeal of Independent Democrats."

Written chiefly by the brilliant Chase—then forty-six years old, son of an Episcopal bishop, a cofounder of the minor Free Soil party of 1848—the "Appeal of Independent Democrats"

Charles Sumner

was a bald assertion that the Nebraska bill was infamy at the highest level: "We arraign this bill as a gross violation of a sacred pledge; as a criminal betrayal of precious rights; as part and parcel of an atrocious plot."

The appeal also announced a national emergency: "We warn you that the dearest interests of freedom and the Union are in imminent peril. Demagogues may tell you that the Union can be maintained only by submitting to the demands of slavery. We tell you that the safety of the Union can only be insured by the full recognition of the just claims of freedom and man."

The appeal closed with the dream of a rescue that would soon come true with the birth of the Republican party. "We shall go home to our constituents, erect anew the standard of freedom, and call on the people to come to the rescue of the country from the domination of slavery. We will not despair; for the cause of human freedom is the cause of God."*

Published widely in major newspapers on January 24, 1854, the "Appeal of Independent Democrats" was understood by all as an explosion. Within days the arguments in the document led to spontaneous protests of frustrated Whigs, disgusted Free Soilers, enraged abolitionists, and brokenhearted Barnburner Democrats and Free Democrats across the North and Northwest.

---

*Congressional Globe, 33rd Congress, 1st Session (January 20, 1854), 28, pt. 1, 281–82.

These scrambling protesters didn't at first have a name for themselves other than calling themselves "anti-Nebraska men."

A very early mention of an anti-Nebraska meeting was at Detroit on February 18, when the future Radical Republican senator Zachariah Chandler, then forty-one, gathered with other disaffected Conscience Whigs to debate the crisis of the Nebraska bill. The text for the evening included Horace Greeley's angry anti-Nebraska editorial from a few days before, "Is it a Fraud?"

Zachariah Chandler

"It is our earnest conviction that the bill of Douglas," wrote Greeley, "in so far as it proposes to disturb the Missouri Comprmise, involves gross perfidy, and is bolstered up by the most audacious false pretenses and *frauds*. If we are wrong in this conviction, let it be shown, and we stand condemned: but if we are right in our view of it, who can truly say that we speak of the plot and its contrivers more harshly than they deserve?"

A most famous proto-Republican meeting took place at Ripon, Wisconsin, in a Congregational church in late February and March. After the second meeting, the convener, Alvan E. Bovey, wrote to Horace Greeley that his group had gathered as fifty-three Whigs, Free Soilers, and Democrats and had emerged calling themselves *Republican*.

Through the spring Anti-Nebraska powwows broke out like chicken pox, always marked by small notices in sympathetic newspapers ranging from the *Detroit Tribune* to the *New York Tribune*. Gamaliel Bailey's Washington newspaper *National Era* argued that anti-Nebraska men should set aside their anxiety about sectionalism and go ahead to form a new Northern-based party. In May several anti-Nebraska congressmen met in rooms in Washington and agreed they felt comfortable joining a new party called the Republicans.

Douglas's Kansas-Nebraska Bill passed the House on March 3, with the Southern Cotton Whigs deserting the Northern Conscience Whigs and voting for it. The debate in the Senate was a lopsided contest, with the prominent antislavery senators Chase of Ohio, Sumner of Massachusetts, and Seward of New York well outnumbered by Douglas and his Southern allies from South Carolina and Virginia. The bill passed the Senate on May 22 on its way to becoming law.

In despair at the Senate vote, Horace Greeley published a list of the senators who had affirmed the Nebraska bill. "One million square miles of territory," Greeley wrote in a boxed column entitled, "Be It Remembered": "heretofore shielded forever by a bargain, forced by the South upon a reluctant and struggling North—(and whereof all that part enuring to the advantage of Slavery has been fully secured and enjoyed)—has been opened to slave-holding immigration and settlement and so exposed to be brought in the Union as Slave States. Shall not Free People mark their destroyers?"

Two weeks later Greeley, casting around for a way to bring together the dark antipathy to the Congress and the sly Democrats, wrote his famous editorial of June 16, 1854, that branded the new party with the simple name Republican.

Summerlong the anti-Nebraska protest grew spontaneously state by state and county by county at Whig conventions at so-called people's or fusion conventions from Wisconsin to Illinois to Maine. A few anti-Nebraska partisans were bold enough to label their meeting as Republican. It was in this season of contretemps that Democratic newspapers began derogating the new party as the "Black Republicans." In response the pro-Republican newspapers began decrying the Northern conservative Democrats and Whigs as "doughfaces."

A famous Republican mass meeting of up to ten thousand took place at Jackson, Michigan, on July 6—an often cited official date for the founding of the Republican party. The Michigan meeting was so large and unexpected that the leaders had to move the crowd outside to an oak grove. Eventually the Republicans nominated a complete Republican slate for the Michigan state fall canvass. They also adopted a platform that contained much of what would become the party's foundation planks: calling for opposition to the Kansas-Nebraska Act, demanding the repeal of the Fugitive Slave Act, urging the reestablishment of the Missouri Compromise, hoping for the reconsideration of the Wilmot Proviso for the abolition of slavery in the District of Columbia. There was also a plank calling for the Pacific railroad.

Greeley was encouraged by the Michigan mass meeting and wrote an editorial called "Michigan" days later that set the party's name in stone type again. "The name under which the opponents of the Nebraska Iniquity have enlisted for the war is simply Republican," Greeley suggested, "and this, we think, will be very generally adopted."

The anti-Nebraska campaign gained a profound supporter in October at the Illinois state fair in Springfield when Abraham Lincoln, then a forty-five-year-old local attorney and influential Whig politician—he had served one term in the House in the last days of Webster and Clay—rose to speak against the Nebraska bill. Stephen A. Douglas himself, an old local acquaintance of Lincoln's, was in the audience that day to hear what had been advertised as a rebuttal of Douglas's popular pro-Nebraska speech of the day before.

Lincoln was not speaking as a Republican. He still held himself a traditional Henry Clay Whig—cautious, law-abiding, nonabolitionist—and he still maintained that these new Republicans were too radical for him. Yet according to the much later memories of Lincoln's law partner and promoter, William "Billy" Herndon, Lincoln understood right away that he could ride the anti-Nebraska train to national office.

Young Abraham Lincoln

In his shirtsleeves and baggy trousers in a damp heat, Lincoln rose to a packed audience in the statehouse and made his first great antislavery speech—employing a moral tone similar to Greeley's but also displaying that here was a politician who knew how to advance himself in the middle ground of the debate between the fire-eaters and the abolitionists.

"If all earthly power were given me," Lincoln said of slavery, "I should not know what to do as to the existing institution. My first impulse would be to free all the slaves, and send them to Liberia, to their own native land."

Then Lincoln firmly announced that he opposed the Kansas-Nebraska Act: "The spirit of seventy-six and the spirit of Nebraska are utter antagonisms, and the former is being rapidly displaced by the latter."

However, Lincoln was no abolitionist, nor would he go farther than supporting a return to the standoff of the Missouri Compromise. "Let us turn slavery from its claims of 'moral' right back to the position our fathers gave it," he argued, "and there let it rest in peace."

The next day the fledgling Illinois Republican party met at Springfield in its first state convention. However, Abraham Lincoln deliberately left town beforehand to avoid being labeled a radical. Lincoln's ploy didn't convince the Douglasite Democrats. The local newspaper branded Lincoln a "black Republican" anyway and asserted that "one great Whig had fallen into their [the Republican] fold."*

The 1854 midterm elections were the first test for all anti-Nebraska forces of all stripes. The *New York Daily Times*, a Whig paper that was fervently anti-Nebraska under its founder, thirty-four-year-old Henry Jarvis Raymond, painted the election crisis bluntly just weeks before the New York state fall canvass: "The great issue to be decided a fortnight

---

*Illinois State Register, October 7, 1854.

Henry Jarvis Raymond

hence, is whether New York assents to the repeal of the Missouri Compromise—the indefinite extension of Slavery, and the permznent domination of the Slave-holding interest over all the departments—Legislative, Executive, Judicial—of this great Republic."

The election results were mixed. The Republicans swept Michigan, and the anti-Nebraska forces won many state parochial races. In the popularly elected House of Representatives, the anti-Nebraskans gained over 100 of the 234 seats for the new Thirty-fourth Congress. Still, because there were several factions in the House besides the new Republicans, the Jacksonian Democracy maintained its majority power.

The most potent new protesting group was not the Republicans but a rival political party of nativists, anti-Catholics, and big-city politicians called the "Know-Nothings" or American party. Founded in New York in 1849 as the secret Order of the Star Spangled Banner, the party got the nickname Know-Nothing from the anecdote that when asked about a meeting, a member was supposed to answer, "I know nothing." At its core the party knew very little besides a fear of new immigrants, especially poor Roman Catholics from Germany and Ireland.

Greeley called the Know-Nothings an "epidemic" and a manipulation by discredited politicians, and he predicted the party would not last. He was not instantly correct, because through 1855, as the Democrats and Whigs broke apart, the Know-Nothings gained quickly from the disaffected Democracy. Know-Nothings were most successful in Boston, where they elected a mayor and, to the House from the Seventh District, a cagey ex-Democrat and ex–Free Soiler named Nathaniel P. Banks.

The Republicans were hard-pressed by the Know-Nothing appeal to the dark tempers of the city dwellers. When a Catholic church was dynamited in Rhode Island by Know-Nothing gangs, many anti-Nebraska men in New England cheered silently. For those crucial few months of 1855, there was a hard contest between those who hated immigrants and those who hated slavery extension. But then in June the Know-Nothings made the mistake of publishing a platform that was ambiguously proslavery. The new pro-Republican press remarked of the Know-Nothings with irony, "The Native American Party intends to elect the next President. It has placed itself on pro-slavery ground. The attempt is not a novel one, and has not always succeeded. We shall see how it comes out now."

The Republican party's most important new partisan against Democrats and Know-Nothings was New York's famous Whig senator William H. "Governor" Seward, then fifty-four, a former New York governor and an eloquent writer and orator. Seward was long a nationally popular man, and his conversion to Republicanism brought the prospect of New York's dominating thirty-five electoral votes and the fact of Seward's financier, the infamous boss Thurlow Weed of New York City.

William H. Seward

Seward, speaking at Albany, New York, in October 1855, pronounced his clear position: "Slavery is not, and can never be, perpetual." Seward then declared his future, "The Republican organization has laid a new, sound, and liberal platform. The principles are equal and exact justice; its speech open, decided, and frank. That is the party for us."*

*Frederick W. Seward, *Seward at Washington as Senator and Secretary of State: A Memoir of His Life, with Selections from His Letters, 1846–1861* (New York: Derby and Miller, 1891), pp. 256–57.

John Greenleaf Whittier

John Greenleaf Whittier's verse "Crisis" portrayed the Republicans as the rising party for the awakening republic.

Wake, dwellers where the day expires
  Your winds that stir the mighty
    lake
And fan your prairie's roaring fires—
  They're Freedom's signals!—wake!—
    awake!

★ 1856 ★

The presidential year began with a breakthrough victory for the awakening Republican party. Thanks to off-year election success in 1855, the Republicans controlled a hefty minority in the House of at least one hundred and eight representatives, depending upon how sympathies were counted. Election of a new Speaker of the House required a 117-vote majority, if everyone voted. The Republicans converted

Nathaniel P. Banks

thirty-nine-year-old Nathaniel P. Banks of Massachusetts from the Know-Nothings and advanced him as their fusion candidate. After nine thrashing weeks of rancor and maneuver into the winter of 1856—including a fist-and-cane assault on Horace Greeley outside the Capitol by an enraged Arkansas Democrat—the Republicans managed to change the rules to allow a plurality Speaker. Banks was immediately elected as the fusion Speaker of all anti-administration parties. The Republicans were delighted, and the headlines boasted their tenacity, "Backbone Triumphant."

Greeley saw the Banks victory as a harbinger and asked his readers, "If a speaker can be elected without the aid of a single Southern vote, and in spite of a strong cohort of Northern doughfaces avowed and secret—why not a President be chosen in a like manner."

The Republican revolution gained momentum at its first organizing convention, which was deliberately held on Washington's birthday, February 22, 1856, at Pittsburgh. The Republicans could finally look at each other in a single room. They liked much of what they saw and heard from Greeley, Raymond, Banks, David Wilmot of Pennsylvania, Governor Kinsley S. Bingham of Michigan, and the old Jacksonian Francis P. Blair and his large family. The Pittsburgh delegates called for a nominating convention to gather in Philadelphia on the anniversary of Bunker Hill, June 17.

The Know-Nothings continued to deteriorate when, at their February nominating convention in Philadelphia, they restated their proslavery stance and then surprised many by nominating for president the undistinguished former Whig president and ex-Seward ally Millard Fillmore, then fifty-three and living in New York City.

David Wilmot

The Republicans, entirely a Northern party, now viewed the competing Know-Nothings as spoilers and the weary old-line Whigs as failures. The Republicans saw the way to power was to bypass the weaker vessels and to increase their partisan attacks on the mighty Southern-dominated Democrats.

In the spring two simultaneous outrages—the infamous cane attack on Charles Sumner on the Senate floor and the infamous armed attack on Lawrence, Kansas—provided the Republicans with sensational hammers to wield against the Democrats.

Sumner of Massachusetts, cosigner of the famous "Appeal of Independent Democrats," was an awesome abolitionist voice, a Harvard-educated, self-absorbed bachelor, tall, lion maned, stentorian, a generalissimo of self-righteousness.

Charles Sumner in his Washington rooms.

Over two days, May 19–20, Sumner made the most famous speech in Senate history, "The Crime against Kansas." Sumner was addressing the crisis then building at Lawrence, Kansas, where abolition-supported settlers were besieged by Southern-sponsored "Border ruffians." Sumner's oratory was attended by an overflow crowd of visitors to the Senate gallery, including the dying Webster himself, sage of the dying Whigs.

"It is the rape of a virgin territory compelling it to the hateful embraces of slavery," Sumner declared as he reviewed the history of the anti-Nebraska crisis to the very moment that word was coming from the so-called Bleeding Kansas of an armed attack on the Free-Soilers.

Toward the close of the first day's speech, Sumner delivered a deliberately prepared insult to the absent Democratic senator Andrew Butler of South Carolina and the attendant Stephen A. Douglas of Illinois.

"I must say something in response to what has fallen from senators who have raised themselves to eminence upon the floor in championship of human wrongs," Sumner declared, turning to Butler's empty chair. "I mean, the senator from South Carolina [Butler] and the senator from Illinois [Douglas], who, unlike as Don Quixote and Sancho Panza, yet like this couple, rally forth together in the same course. The senator from South Carolina believes himself a chivalrous knight, with sentiments of honor and courage. He has chosen a mistress who, though ugly to others, is always lovely to him, though polluted in the sight of the world, is chaste to him. I mean the harlot, slavery."

"And the senator from Illinois, like Sancho Panza," said Sumner, looking at the nearby Douglas, "is always eager to do the humiliating services of his masters."

Two days later, on May 22, a humid afternoon in the capital, Democratic representative Preston Brooks, then thirty-six, a dashing, slender, mustached Charleston fire-eater and nephew of the defamed Butler, walked up to Sumner's desk on the Senate floor (the old Senate Room) just as the senator was franking letters hurriedly for the last post. Brooks's accomplice, Representative Lawrence M. Keitt of South Carolina, was standing watch at the narrow entrance of the nearly empty chamber. Brooks addressed Sumner, "I have read your speech twice over carefully. It is a libel on South Carolina, and Mr. Butler, who is a relative of mine."

Sumner did not have a chance to look up. Instantly Brooks smashed Sumner's head with a gold-tipped gutta-percha cane. Brooks proceeded to beat a trapped, helpless man with at least twenty blows. Sumner, in the back row of seats, was trapped beneath the bolted-down desk. He did eventually escape by ripping the desk from the floor and crumpling forward into the aisle. He was smeared with blood from two grievous head gashes.

Other senators cried out at the wickedness, but no one stopped or detained Brooks, who departed, boasting, "Next time I will have to kill him." Within days Sumner had recovered from his wounds sufficiently to begin what would become a troubled three-year convalescence away from the Senate. Within a week Brooks and Keitt had resigned from the

House in a tantrum and gone home to the welcome of South Carolina—from where they were returned to the Congress the next fall.

In the perversity of coincidence, the attack on Sumner came on the same afternoon that the first reports arrived from the West via steamer of an attack several days before on Lawrence, Kansas, by Southern partisans called "ruffians."

The next day, May 23, the nation was stunned by two incredible headlines: "Assault on Senator Sumner" ran alongside "Startling News from Kansas—The War Actually Begun—More Murdering and Pillaging."

Greeley's *Tribune* used a blunderbuss to condemn the South for both events. "Failing to silence the North by threats, notwithstanding the dough-faced creatures who so long misrepresented the spirit of the Republic and of the age, the South now resorts to actual violence."

The appalled and irate Republicans shouted down the roof of the republic for the next three weeks. Righteous and responsible men set their courses for Philadelphia for the first Republican nominating convention, June 17–20, in the City of Brotherly Love's aging neoclassical Musical Fund Hall on Locust Street off Eighth Street.

Mad as they were, the Republicans knew the Democracy was well organized and had to be fought with savvy. Two weeks before at Baltimore the Democrats had discarded the failed Franklin Pierce, and bypassed the ambitious Stephen A. Douglas, in order to nominate for president an ancient, priggish, legalistic diplomat, James Buchanan of Pennsylvania.

Then sixty-five years old, Buchanan was a sincere but ambivalent figure from the antislavery congressional district of Lancaster, Pennsylvania. Buchanan's major advantage as a national candidate was that he had been out of the country as the ambassador to Great Britain during the anti-Nebraska imbroglio. He'd said nothing inflammatory on record either way; and when Buchanan finally did speak of the crisis, he sounded like a frail censor. "Disunion is a word which ought not to be breathed amongst us," he had announced in Baltimore upon returning from Europe, "even in a whisper."

At Philadelphia, in the damp Delaware Valley heat, the Republicans aimed to avoid party strife and find a candidate who could unite the party. After Seward's ally Thurlow Weed arranged a sophisticated alliance with a breakaway faction of the Know-Nothings, the delegates set aside as too abolitionized the obvious choices, such as Chase of Ohio, Seward of New York, or Banks of Massachusetts. Instead they chose the handsome and extremely wealthy John C. Frémont, then forty-three, who had briefly served as a California senator.

Frémont's important credentials were his colorful reputation as the frontier explorer called the Pathfinder, his extreme wealth in the Mari-

John Charles Frémont

posa grant gold field of California, and his marriage to the resourceful Jessie Benton, daughter of an old powerful Democratic senator from Missouri. It also was useful that, because he'd been born in Savannah, Georgia, Frémont was not an inarguable agent of the Boston abolitionists.

The Philadelphia convention also featured the emergence of Abraham Lincoln on the national stage when he was put forward from the floor for the vice presidency. For two years Lincoln had hesitated to leave the Whigs—disputing the Douglasites as plotters against harmony, denouncing the Know-Nothings as corrupters of the Declaration of Independence, yet holding back from the Republicans, whom he saw as too radical, too abolitionized. Then in May, just a month before the convention, Lincoln

The first national convention of the new Republican party was held in June 1856 at Philadelphia's Musical Fund Hall on Locust Street near Eighth Street. Philadelphia Inquirer Library.

had let his law partner Billy Herndon list his name with the Illinois Republican party for the first time.

The party first heard Lincoln's name during the last day's nominations for the vice presidency. A Pennsylvanian stood to nominate Abraham Lincoln of Illinois as a "prince of good fellows." An Illinois supporter said Lincoln was born in Kentucky, was in the prime of life at about fifty-five (he was actually forty-seven), and was "as pure a patriot as ever lived."

When a man from Ohio called out, "Can he fight?" the reply came back, "Yes, sir. He is a son of Kentucky!" The assembly cheered and laughed. An Illinois Lincoln supporter promised delegates, "We can lick Buchanan anyway, but I think we can do it a little easier if we have Lincoln on the ticket with John C. Frémont."

The rude wit worked in some fashion, for Lincoln finished second in the straw poll though few present had ever heard a word he'd said. The delegates did finally choose a former Whig from New Jersey for the vice presidency: mild, polite William L. Dayton, who later was Lincoln's effective wartime ambassador to France.

On that muggy June day, Lincoln was home in Springfield and had reason to feel rewarded for his cautious conversion to the Republican cause.

The Philadelphia platform was built on the promise to undo immediately the Kansas-Nebraska Act and to admit Kansas as a free state. Its philosophical foundation was rockbed Thomas Jefferson: "With our republican fathers, we hold it to be a self-evident truth, that all men are endowed with the inalienable rights to life, liberty, and the pursuit of happiness."

The platform also advanced two progressive commercial ideas, long stalled in Congress because they were perceived as too costly by the Southern politicians: a Pacific railroad "by the most central and practicable route," and a federally financed improvement of the rivers and harbors.

The campaign was feverishly partisan and celebratory. Frémont did not campaign beyond writing letters, according to the contemporary tradition of the presidency. Instead the electioneering was left to surrogates from the party elite. The Republicans dominated the North by using torchlight processions featuring fireworks and mass meetings featuring marathon speakers. Each Republican word or deed was carefully reported in the burgeoning number of Republican newspapers. In the parades, banners defamed the Democrats as dangerous and fractious: "Buchanan and Bludgeon and Bowie Knives—Sectional." Other banners venerated the Republican platform as godly and all-Union: "Frémont and Freedom, Books and the Bible—National."

Early signs of Republican weakness came from several crucial state elections held in September and October. The good news was that in Maine the antislavery Republican Hannibal Hamlin of Bangor, future vice president, won the Senate; and in fertile Ohio, with twenty-three electoral votes, Republicans bested both Democrats and Know-Nothings. Nevertheless, the bad news was that the Hoosier state was lost to the "Slave Democracy." And in crucial twenty-seven-electoral-vote Pennsylvania, Buchanan's home state, the voters stayed with Democratic candidates by a slim majority in the state legislature and a firm majority in the Congress. The Pennsylvania Democracy held the rich industrial counties of Philadelphia, Montgomery, and Schuylkill, while the opposition had to settle for the Pittsburgh and Erie regions.

As election day neared, the Republicans knew they were fighting uphill. "Fellow citizens!" Greeley exhorted at full volume; "Men who love justice and your country! Vote for Frémont—then Liberty and the Union, Kansas and the Constitution, your home and your native land, will be rescued from a fearful peril. Pause and consider!"

The Republicans also excited the citizenry with Frémont glee clubs singing the Republican rallying song to the tune of "La Marseillaise."

> *Arise, arise, ye brave!*
> *And let your war cry be!*
> *Free Speech, Free Press, Free Soil, Free Men,*
> *Fré-mont and Victory.*

The Republicans also sang the rallying song *auf Deutsch* to appeal to the large German Protestant population in New York and across Pennsylvania and the Northwest: "Entzwei! entzwei! / Das Joch der Sklaverei! / Frémont, Freiheuit and Sieg!" And every Republican rally in New York showed banners in two languages: "Kansas belongs to labor, Not to Slavery," and "Kansas gehort der Arbeit, nicht der Sklaverei."

At the most famous abolitionist meeting hall in New York, the Broadway Tabernacle Church in New York City, the sponsor of frequent Republican and Frémont Club meetings, the choral groups serenaded with clever stanzas about "Bully Brooks," and with choruses such as "Buchanan is a used up man!" and "Frémont shall lead the Free." Often there was the partisan boast, "Ain't You Glad You Joined the Republicans?"

On election day the Republicans sounded all alarms. "The Presidential Chair is the last entrenchment of Freedom," warned editor Henry Jarvis Raymond of the *New York Daily Times*, "the election of Frémont is the last hope."

The heroic abolitionist Reverend J. P. Thompson of the Broadway

Tabernacle Church pleaded, "One vote may decide whether Freedom or Slavery shall prevail over this broad domain."

The Republicans lost. More than four million men went to the polls and gave the Republican John C. Frémont eleven states and 114 electoral votes, including New York, Ohio, and Michigan. The Know-Nothing Millard Fillmore took one state and 8 electoral votes. The Democrat James Buchanan won nineteen states and a solid majority of 174 electoral votes, including sweeping the South and taking the critical Pennsylvania, New Jersey, and Illinois.

More negative was the fact that the Republicans lost the House of Representatives to the Democrats; the new Thirty-fifth Congress would show in the House: Democrats 118, Republicans 92, with 26 others, including Know-Nothings. The new Senate would show Democrats 36, Republicans 20, with 8 others.

The Republican party had not been able to overcome traditional sectional partisanship. Also working against the Republicans was the disproportionate number of electoral votes going to the South—since the slaves, though not citizens, were counted as three-fifths of a free person according to Article 1, Section 2 of the Constitution.

The Republicans immediately spoke of the future with revolutionary language and partisan wit.

"We have lost a battle," proposed Greeley. "The Bunker Hill of the new struggle for Freedom is past; the Saratoga and Yorktown are yet to be achieved. A party of yesterday, without organization, without official power, without prestige, and latterly almost without hope, has not overborne the oldest party in the country, with its hundred thousand officeholders, its eighty millions of annual expenditures, its million and a half voters trained by the habits of a lifetime to vote without question or hesitation whatever bears the label."

There was also angry contempt for the Democracy. "The general sentiment is, we apprehend," wrote the *New York Daily Times,* "that now the Union is wholly in the hands of the Disunionists, it is comparatively safe from dissolution."

★ 1860 ★

James Buchanan's presidency failed as soon as he'd sworn the oath of office.

Knocks against the new administration came in waves. Just after the inauguration on March 4, the Supreme Court handed down the inflammatory Dred Scott decision, *Scott v. Sanford,* that supported the Kansas-

Nebraska Bill with law. Not only did Dred Scott make the Missouri Compromise unconstitutional, it also supported the extension of slavery into the territories. Worse for Buchanan, the Republicans smelled a rat. There was widespread rumor that the new president had colluded with Chief Justice Roger Taney (an old Jackson Cabinet member) to arrange Dred Scott in the favor of the South.

A summer Wall Street panic was a second hard knock. The Ohio and Life Casualty Company failed of a sudden. In a chain reaction of bad credit, the failure ripped down the stock market, especially the railroad and state stocks. The dynamic Cleveland and Pittsburgh Railroad fell by 75 percent in a month; even the mighty New York Central declined by 25 percent. The bulls ran and hid; the bears ran wild. By early fall the market demanded cash only for trades, no credit. "Intrinsic value seems no longer to be an element in the price of values," commented a *Tribune* observer, "and the market is as near chaos as possible."

Trouble came soon again in December 1857 in "Bleeding Kansas." A cabal of Southern partisans aimed to take advantage of Douglas's "squatter sovereignty" policy in the Kansas-Nebraska Act. The plan was to pack a meeting in Lecompton, Kansas, in order to fashion a state constitution that protected slaveholders and excluded free blacks. It was called the Lecompton Constitution, and it was so fraudulent that a territorial election rejected it in January 1858. Amazingly, Buchanan in Washington chose to treat the Lecompton document as if it was the will of all Kansans. The North howled. The South picked its teeth.

For the Republicans, the Lecompton scandal proved a boon for recruiting. In anti-Lecompton mass meetings that echoed the anti-Nebraska sensation, the party gained important converts from big-city Know-Nothings, prideful Whigs, and disgusted Northern Democrats.

Stephen Douglas thought the Lecompton Constitution a lie and broke with his party over it. The Republicans in Congress joined with Douglas and other anti-Lecompton Democrats to block the Buchanan administration's scheme to admit Kansas as a slave state. Suddenly Douglas was seen as a potential convert to the Republicans.

At just this moment Abraham Lincoln of Springfield stepped forward to challenge Stephen Douglas of Springfield for the Illinois Senate seat.

Douglas was the favorite to succeed the weak Buchanan on the 1860 Democratic ticket. Lincoln, an active Republican for two years, saw that taking on the nationally known Douglas was a main chance to pull himself up by his bootstraps and walk onto the national stage. Lincoln also knew that his best strategy against Douglas was to appeal to the middle ground of voters—to present a *conservative* antislavery voice.

In June Lincoln addressed the cheering Republican state convention in Springfield with a prophetic speech that would stand for all time as his most pungent remarks on the slavery crisis before the war—his "House Divided" masterpiece.

Lincoln accused Douglas, President Buchanan, Roger Taney's Supreme Court, and the whole of the Democracy with a conspiracy to disable and destroy the Union unless they got what they wanted—the extension of an empire of slavery across the continent. Lincoln warned his audience with Jesus's famous remark about the devil, *"A house divided against itself cannot stand."* Then Lincoln proclaimed a threatening formula: "Either the opponents of slavery, will arrest the further spread of it, and place it where the public mind shall rest in the belief that it is in course of ultimate extinction; or its advocates will push it forward, till it shall become alike lawful in all States, old as well as new—North as well as South."*

Abraham Lincoln in 1858

In late summer Lincoln and Douglas agreed to meet in a series of face-to-face debates across the state of Illinois. The seven contests, staged with cannon salutes, special trains, and fireworks, became heroic performances of intellect and endurance. Each man spoke for ninety minutes on the pros and cons of slavery, and then there was lengthy rebuttal—to the frequent cheers of crowds of up to twelve thousand.

Lincoln's cause was boosted profoundly when the *New York Tribune* featured every word and audience reaction of the first debate at Ottawa, Illinois.

"I do not question Mr. Lincoln's conscientious belief," baited Douglas, accusing Lincoln of Black Republicanism, "that the negro was made his equal, and hence is his brother, but for my own part, I do not regard the negro as my equal, and positively deny that he is my brother or any kin to me."

Lincoln's reply remained the core of his argument all summer. "I hold that there is no reason in the world why the negro is not entitled to all the natural rights enumerated in the Declaration of Independence, the right to life, liberty and the pursuit of happiness. I hold that he is as much entitled to these as the white man. I agree with Judge Douglas, he is not my equal in many respects—certainly not in color, perhaps not in moral or intellectual endowment. But in the right to eat bread, without

*Henry Steele Commager, ed., *Documents of American History,* (New York: Appleton-Century-Crofts, 1962), pp. 345–47.

the leave of anybody else, which his own hand earns, he is my equal and the equal of Judge Douglas, and the equal of every living man."

After Ottawa, Greeley blessed Lincoln by declaring that this self-educated and homespun lawyer had "the decided advantage" over Douglas, who was believed the greatest orator of the day.

Lincoln lost. Election day 1858 gave the Illinois state offices to the Republicans but left the state legislature with the Democrats. Because the legislature then chose the U.S. senator, Douglas was returned to the Congress.

The gleeful Douglas began immediately to politick for the White House. Lincoln was disconsolate and bitter, complaining of the expense of the campaign. Lincoln did rouse himself enough to think about the next turn. "The fight must go on," Lincoln wrote a supporter in November. "The Democratic strength is waning. There will be another 'blow up' in the Democracy."

Lincoln's prediction was deadly accurate. Eighteen fifty-nine was a year for stacking grievances like muskets.

In the U.S. Senate, the strong abolitionists such as Sumner and Ben Wade of Ohio gained strength from newcomer Republicans and new converts such as Zachariah Chandler of Michigan, Simon Cameron of Pennsylvania, Preston King of New York. In the House, the Republicans stood behind fervent abolitionists such as the temperamental South-hater Thaddeus Stevens from Buchanan's own district in Lancaster, Pennsylvania, and the former slaveholder Henry Winter Davis of Maryland. The push and shove in the aisles was ruthless. The Re-

Benjamin F. Wade

publicans blocked the Buchanan administration's attempt to buy Cuba and extend slaveholding to the Caribbean. Then Buchanan blocked the Republican-sponsored Homestead Bill meant to encourage immigrants to settle the free territories. Baiting and defamation were so constant in the Capitol that senators Chandler, Cameron, and Wade boasted they would duel with anyone who crossed them. Ben Wade carried a sawed-off shotgun. There were no more canings.

The gunfire came in October with John Brown's infamous raid on Harpers Ferry, Virginia. Brown had achieved a Republican celebrity for his 1856 antislavery violence in Kansas. Now Brown began a bizarre crusade to free the slaves by establishing a free state in the Virginia mountains. Brown made an inept attack on Harpers Ferry that was meant to signal the uprising. The brief battle to subdue Brown, featuring

Colonel Robert E. Lee's ground assault, was an instant national sensation.

John Brown's raid rocked the Republicans. The first worry was that the autumn victories in Ohio, Pennsylvania, and Iowa would be stained by the fact that the party's Boston elite had for years funded and feted this same insurrectionary John Brown. Would the party be branded as one of treasonous agitation?

John Brown

At Charlestown, Virginia, Brown's last written message just before his execution spooked everyone in the country. "I John Brown am now quite <u>certain</u> that the crimes of this <u>guilty, land:</u> will never be purged <u>away;</u> but with Blood."

The executioners let Brown's body swing for thirty-seven minutes. Greeley was outraged: "Slavery has killed John Brown. . . . Let us be reverently grateful for the privilege of living in a world rendered noble by the daring of heroes, the suffering of martyrs—among whom let none doubt that History will accord an honored niche to Old John Brown."

The Republicans in Congress were not so free to eulogize John Brown. They hardened their hearts and turned away from the corpse, condemning Brown as a madman and traitor.

The damage was done to the party. The first setback came right away, during another lengthy struggle to elect a new Speaker of the House. The nominal controversy was over the wide Republican endorsement of a tendentious anti-South book, Hinton Rowan Helper's *The Impending Crisis in the South: How to Meet It;* the underlying issues, however, were the Brown fiasco and the open hatred between the North and the South. After an angry exchange on the floor, the Republican party had to shelve its premier candidate for the Speakership, the new abolitionist star John Sherman of Ohio, younger brother of William Tecumseh Sherman, and later a major player in several Republican administrations. In a demonstration of patience and pragmatism, the party then joined with Know-Nothings and anti-Lecompton Democrats to blunt the Buchanan administration's candidates and instead elect a mutual compromise—the aged, old-line Whig William Pennington of New Jersey.

John Sherman

The Republicans hadn't won, but

neither had the Democrats. John Brown had wounded the cause. The cause had survived to launch a new campaign for the president's house.

The year 1860 opened with a Republican party that was ready to soar on two mighty wings. One wing was the abolitionist princes who now described themselves as the *Radicals*.

The other wing was called the *Conservatives*. They were mostly ex-Whigs, and were definitely anti-Nebraska and anti-Lecompton, but they held back from urging immediate abolition of slavery. The Conservatives included men as diverse as the shrewd Lyman Trumbull of Illinois (Lincoln's ally) and the brilliant jurist William Pitt Fessenden of Portland, Maine.

William Pitt Fessenden

Lyman Trumbull

Both wings claimed Seward of New York; they both also suspected Seward: too conservative for the Radicals, too abolitionist for the Conservatives.

There were also minor factions in the party that drew their strength from moral issues other than slavery. These included the temperance men preaching against the rum shops, the prosperous German Protestants distrustful of former New York Know-Nothings, and the Massachusetts ex–Know Nothings who were contemptuous of the party's intellectuals and their tolerance for the Irish Catholics.

In May all the party's elements traveled to Chicago with a hard determination to nominate a man who could cap the Republican revolution by taking the presidency from the hated Democracy.

Earlier that month the Democracy had blown up again at its nominating convention under thunderstorms at Charleston, South Carolina. The delegates had hoped to nominate Stephen A. Douglas for president; but the convention collapsed when a Southern faction walked out. Simultaneously at Philadelphia the remnant of the Know-Nothings and

Whigs had cobbled together a flimsy construction called the Constitutional Union party. The ticket was the aged Tennessee senator and slaveholder John Bell and the garrulous Harvard president Edward Everett. The tiny Bell-Everett platform avoided the slavery question and offered a bland endorsement of the Constitution, the Union, and law enforcement.

With the opposition scatterbrained, the Republicans bent their backs to unite behind a single candidate. Seward was the clear favorite, but everyone came to the table ready to give up anything but Old Glory to get the job done. A *New York Times* headline predicted, "Expediency to be the law governing the nominations."

The Chicago convention was all expedience. Each man conducted himself with the decorum of a knight-errant in the Holy Land. A strange consequence of such unusual chivalry was that only cooperation and generosity were permitted on the floor of the Wigwam. The horse-trading and hard-drinking were left to the fifteen hundred guests packed into the Tremont House like seals in a rookery.

From the podium several speakers flattered the convention for its manners even as they railed against the Democrats as poisoners of the Union. "The stern look which I see on every face," declared a first-day orator, "and the earnest behavior which has been manifested in all the preliminary discussions, show that all have a true and deep sense of the solemn obligations which are resting upon us."

On the second day the Wigwam was crammed heel-to-toe for more of the same sober partisanship. The platform was read and argued and accepted with a dutiful dispatch. Beside the critical planks opposing the extension of slavery, and the planks calling for a restoration of the Missouri Compromise, was a passionate fury at what the Democrats and the Buchanan administration were doing to the country. "We brand the recent re-opening of the African slave-trade, under the cover of our national flag, aided by perversions of judicial power, as a crime against humanity, a burning shame to our country and age, and we call upon Congress to take prompt and efficient measures for the total and final suppression of that execrable traffic."

The third day was a date with destiny. No one knew beforehand which way the balloting would go. The Seward friends had their head count and deals; so did the Lincoln friends, the Chase and Wade and Bates friends. Not until those thousand delegates and alternates came together on the floor Friday morning and cast the first ballot was there a hint that the world was going to turn upside down. When Seward failed to win outright on the first go, the assembly knew a new horse was coming on. With the second ballot came the Lincoln deal with Pennsylvania

William Maxwell Evarts

that opened the way. The third ballot changed the United States of America forever. Lincoln was the new prince.

"I move, Sir, as I do now," proclaimed the famous attorney William Maxwell Evarts of the New York delegation, overcoming the disappointment at Seward's failure, "that the nomination of Abraham Lincoln of Illinois as the Republican candidate for the suffrages of the whole country for the office of Chief Magistrate of the American Union be made unanimous."

Within the hour the abolitionist Senator Hannibal Hamlin of Maine was chosen as the vice presidential nominee. The word went out to the world on magnetic telegraph, and the next morning dominated the *New York Tribune*:

Hannibal Hamlin

**The Chicago Convention
Naming of Candidates
Intense Enthusiasm
The Struggle Between Seward and Lincoln
Lincoln Nominated.
Only Three Ballotings Had.
The Vice-Presidency
Hon. Hannibal Hamlin Nominated
How the Nominations Are Received
Salutes, Bonfires and Pyrotechny
Great Joy and Enthusiasm**

At the Springfield telegraph office Lincoln read the offer of the nomination. He soon excused himself to go home to tell his wife, Mary Todd Lincoln.

The immediate response of the Democratic papers was ominous. In the North the *Albany Atlas and Argus* declared, "The Republican party has committed suicide in order to escape from justice." In the South the *Richmond Daily Dispatch*, a paper that routinely published tales of the murder of slave owners by slaves, declared the Republican platform "the same nigger business it was four years ago."

The campaign was all foreshadowing. For the first time in American history there was a fair-equal four-way race. The Democracy, after failing

at Charleston, had cracked in two. At Baltimore the reconvened delegates nominated
Stephen Douglas of Illinois on the regular Democratic ticket, laying claim to the Northern
Democracy. At Charlestown the Southern
slaveholders nominated Buchanan's slave-
holding vice president John Breckinridge of
Kentucky on the rump Democratic ticket, laying claim to the Southern Democracy. Meanwhile the Bell-Everett Constitution Union
ticket appealed to the Border states.

Mary Todd Lincoln

With an electorate awash in characters and
promises, the Republicans knew they could
triumph by winning the North's electoral votes, especially New England,
the Hudson River valley, and the Ohio River valley.

Following custom of the office, Lincoln did not campaign aggressively; however, his supporters pressed their strategy to sweep the North
with aggression and enthusiasm. Young men sang partisan lyrics with a
martial air:

> *March forth to the battle,*
> *All fearless and calm;*
> *The strength of your spirit,*
> *Throw into your arm;*
> *With ballets for bullets,*
> *Let this be your cry;*
> *With Lincoln and Hamlin,*
> *We'll conquer or die.*

The Republican newspapers produced detailed accounts of each party
meeting and speech of the canvass.
Notable for perhaps the earliest use
of the elephant as a Republican
symbol was the *Illinois State Journal*'s coverage of a Springfield rally
for candidate Lincoln himself: the
next day's paper displayed an elephant symbol at the top of the column on the event.

Rail splitter

There was early controversy
over Lincoln's unusual nickname
"rail-splitter," and eventually there

Grand procession of the Wide-Awakes for Lincoln and Hamlin on Broadway in New York City during the campaign of 1860. Harper's Weekly, October 12, 1860.

was a clever explanation that used class envy to the Republican advantage. "The title of 'rail-splitter' given to Mr. Lincoln," wrote Greeley, "is merely an emphatic way of stating that he rose from the class of men stigmatized by slave-holding Senators as the 'mud-sills' of society. . . . It is simply saying to the mass of the voters, here is a man who can be trusted to uphold the great interest of labor. He must know and understand those interests; he must sympathize with them, for he once was a laborer himself."

In Northern cities the Republican torchlight processions and mass meetings of tens of thousands were led by a Republican phenomenon of the campaign, the Wide-Awake Clubs—cavalcades of young men and women wearing liberty caps, flowing capes, and colored sashes who danced through the streets in zigzags. The Wide-Awakes inspired the faithful with their trademark cheer, *"One-two-three-four-five-six-wide-awake! Wide-awake!"* Also:

> Who is shouting "Free Homesteads? Free Soil!" in a tone
> To shake every slave-oligarch down from his throne!
> Wide-awake! Wide-awake!

John Greenleaf Whittier's verse "The Eve of the Election" praised the Republican zeal and especially the work of the youthful Wide-Awakes.

> To party claims and private aims
> Reveal that august face of Truth
> To which are given the age of Heaven
> The beauty of immortal youth.

Early fall elections showed the Republicans in command in the North. Maine, Pennsylvania, Ohio, and Indiana went for Republican state and congressional candidates with what Greeley called a "hurricane sweep." Banners were raised from Bangor to Lawrence in hopes of victory. The American eagle appeared on banners promising, "United We Stand, Divided We Fall." The black flag appeared on banners recommending, "Down with the Black Flag of Disunion."

Election day the tireless campaigner Horace Greeley summarized six years of the party's climb to a revolution at the ballot box: "Republicans! The repudiation of the Missouri Compromise, the brutal bludgeoning of Charles Sumner, the wanton outrages that so long desolated Kansas, the infamous Lecompton outrage, and all the long series of plots and crimes by which Kansas and Nebraska were temporarily subjugated to Slavery, all come up for review Today!"

Lincoln lampooned as an acrobat crossing over the rapids at Niagara Falls during the campaign of 1860. Harper's Weekly, *August 25, 1860.*

Four and one-half million free men voted. Lincoln won a firm plurality victory with nearly 40 percent of the popular vote. Lincoln carried all of the North except New Jersey, which he divided with Douglas, and secured a clear electoral college majority of 180 electoral votes.

The South split its votes in a waste of shame. Intrepid Douglas, despite 29 percent of the popular vote, won only one and a half states for 12 electoral votes. Breckinridge, with 18 percent of the vote, won twelve Southern states for 72 electoral votes. The spoiler Bell won only three states for 39 electoral votes.

Most important, the Republicans won the new Thirty-seventh Congress with clear majorities in both houses. The Republican party was now the ruling party of the world's only democracy.

★ 1864 ★

War between the North and the South followed the Republican victory with a merciless drumbeat.

No one was shocked by the peacock march to battle that started a month after the election. In December, South Carolina's congressmen, including the now deceased Brooks's accomplice Keitt (Brooks had died of a sudden illness in the winter of 1857), walked out of Congress in a contemptuous pout. Late in the month South Carolina declared the union between South Carolina and the United States was dissolved.

In January, Kansas was finally admitted to the Union as a free state. At the same time the slave states of Mississippi, Florida, Georgia, Louisiana, and Texas left the Union. Everyone understood that war was coming. Prominent New Yorkers Thurlow Weed, Governor Edward Morgan, and Horace Greeley begged President-Elect Lincoln to seek a compromise.

In February, Buchanan, who had argued that "if [the Union] cannot live in the affections of the people, it must one day perish," did nothing when longtime Democratic senator Jefferson Davis of Mississippi was elected president of the hostile Confederate States of America.

In March, Lincoln, now officially the president, rejected any compromise that did not restore the Union. The president showed that he and his seasoned administration—Seward at State, Chase at Treasury, Cameron at War, Bates at Justice, young Francis P. Blair at the Post Office—were ready to fight. The shrunken Congress stood with the president.

Lincoln also entreated the Southerners to relent. "We are not enemies, but friends," he argued in his first inaugural address. "We must not be enemies. Though passion may have strained, it must not break, our bonds of affection."*

In April, the South took the first shot of the war with a contrived display: a sinister cannon barrage directed at Charleston's helpless federal Fort Sumter.

Through the spring, the posturing was deafening. The two sides armed steadily and approached each other like wild stags. The first mass gun battle the summer of 1861, twenty-five miles from the White House at a Virginia creek called Bull Run, was choreographed in the press right up to the time the guns fired, the blue line ebbed and broke, and the casualty lists were proof that war was murder and civil war was suicide.

Lincoln sought to show unity of purpose, first by choosing a Cabinet from both wings of his party and then by naming a general staff of prominent Republicans such as Frémont and Banks as well as loyal Dem-

*Henry Steele Commager, ed., *Documents of American History,* pp. 387–88.

Lincoln's first cabinet: State, William H. Seward; Treasury, Salmon P.
Chase; War, Simon Cameron; Attorney General, Edward Bates; Post-
master General, Montgomery Blair; Navy, Gideon Welles; Interior,
Caleb Smith.

ocrats such as Ben Butler of Massachusetts and George B. McClellan of
Pennsylvania.

Once war started, the Radical Republicans were not content to co-
operate with Lincoln or the disgraced opposition. Led by Chase in the
Cabinet and by Chandler, Sumner, Wade, and Thaddeus Stevens in the
Congress, the Radicals insisted on the immediate abolition of slavery by
fiat and on the immediate prosecution
of the war to the extreme, including ar-
resting and destroying traitors. They
also insisted that the seceded states be
held to a strict loyalty test before they
could rejoin the Union.

The war was a futile shoot-out that
bled the nation as if it were a slaugh-
terhouse. Battles such as Bull Run,
Shiloh Church, Antietam, Fredericksburg, live in infamy as the murder of
frightened boys by terrified boys on
worthless killing fields where nothing
was achieved but rage and pandemic.

Thaddeus Stevens

What was accomplished on Capitol Hill was a steady radicalizing of
the country. Lincoln still saw himself as a Conservative, and he resisted
the Radicals; yet failure on the battlefield forced Lincoln's hand. The

president's signature on the 1861 Confiscation Act and the 1862 Emancipation Act were gradual steps toward outright abolition by constitutional amendment. The Radicals demanded more. Following the December 1862 disaster at Fredericksburg, there was an attempted Cabinet coup against Seward led by Chase and his allies in the Senate. Lincoln outmaneuvered the Radicals with candor and wit, but he recognized his weak hand.

"If there is a worse place than Hell," the president confessed after Fredericksburg, "I am in it."

Not only did the Radicals intimidate the president, the Cabinet, and the party, they also belittled Congress and the army and navy when they formed a Joint Committee for the Conduct and the Expenditures of the War in order to manage the nation like a fiefdom.

The Radicals did achieve an admirable legislative record. Crucial to the country's progress was the 1862 Homestead Bill that granted a free 160 acres to settlers of certain territories. The 1862 and 1864 Pacific railway acts financed a transcontinental railroad and telegraph. The 1862 Morrill Act granted lands to states to build agricultural and industrial colleges and advance national education. Also, just prior to the war Congress had passed the Morrill Tariff that had raised the protective tariffs. The war's demand for revenue accelerated the trend to protectionism—the beginning of a seventy-year Republican tradition in support of a high protectionist tariff both to protect American industry and to fill the public till.

A special Radical achievement was congressional passage of the 1864 National Banking Act, which was designed by Treasury Secretary Chase. The act established a system of nationally chartered private banks that could issue currency backed by the federal treasury—a financial innovation of necessity that served for fifty years until the Federal Reserve System was created under Woodrow Wilson.

Lincoln did work to push back against the Radicals' demands. The president's most effective way to control the Radicals wasn't legislative but rather a sleight-of-hand political ploy. In the first year of the war Lincoln encouraged the formation of an expedient hybrid called the National Union party. The idea was that the Union party could attract both Republicans and Democrats without the divisive rhetoric of the last decade. In truth the Union party was completely a prettified Republican instrument that made a halfhearted effort to recruit wayward Democrats by talking more about saving the Union than about abolishing slavery.

The Radicals fumed at the masquerade. Horace Greeley was worried that the war was being fought only to return to the standoff of 1859. Greeley was no certain Radical—sometimes he was with them, most times he was all alone on a solitary charger—but Greeley was distinctly for final abolition. He published a famous editorial in the *Tribune*, "The Prayer of Twenty-Millions," that argued the war must be fought to end slavery forever. "The Rebellion, if crushed out tomorrow, would be renewed within a year if Slavery were left in vigor," Greeley reasoned. "Every hour of deference to Slavery is an hour of added and deepened peril to the Union."

Lincoln replied to Greeley in an equally famous letter, of August 1862, that appealed for moderation and pleaded for time and understanding. "My paramount object in this struggle," Lincoln wrote, "is to save the Union, and is not either to save or destroy slavery. If I could save the Union without freeing any slave I would do it, and if I could save it by freeing all the slaves I would do it; and if I could save it by freeing some and leaving others alone I would also do that. What I do about slavery, and the colored race, I do because I believe it helps to save the Union; and what I forbear, I forbear because I do not believe it would help save the Union."

Greeley was persuaded by Lincoln's clarity and threw his support to the Union party.

On election day 1862, Greeley condemned the Northern Democratic opposition. "They want to buy the traitors back into the Union by new concessions to slavery; we hope to see the Rebels put down by a permanent widening of the area of Freedom. Let the loyal judge between us."

The midterm election results were disheartening. The Republicans surrendered their majority in crucial states such as New York, Illinois, Ohio, and Indiana. The party did hold on to the leadership in Congress—one hundred and two Republicans to seventy-five Democrats with nine Democrat-leaning uncommitted in the House—but this meant the party had just a narrow control of the dictatorial Committee for the Conduct of the War.

Eighteen sixty-three started with more slaughter on battlefields such as Murfreesboro and Chancellorsville. The party's name change would not solve the political crisis. Only a decisive military victory over the Confederacy could reverse the trend away from the Republicans. The bowels of the problem was the generalship. In spite of all the North's advantages in population, wealth, industry, naval mobility, and army firepower, neither Lincoln nor the Radicals were able to settle on a general staff that could engage and defeat the South's paladins.

Lincoln became an isolated, morbid figure, his celebrated sense of humor a poor mask. The newspapers' casualty lists were a daily horror. In the Eastern theater of war, the celebrated Robert E. Lee of Virginia, West Point '29, achieved a reputation of brutal mastery in the Shenandoah

Valley. In the Western theater of war, the unknown Ulysses Simpson "Sam" Grant of Illinois, West Point '43, achieved a reputation for brutal determination along the Mississippi. Europe toyed with the prideful Confederacy. Secretary of State Seward feared England or France would recognize the rebellion as a sovereign state. The guns answered the fears. Miraculous blood-soaked Union victories at Vicksburg, Mississippi, and Gettysburg, Pennsylvania, followed by a swift suppression of the Draft Riots in New York City, scared off the conniving Europeans. The administration and Lincoln's Union party staggered erect through the autumn's state elections.

As the presidential year 1864 began, the Republicans knew they were holding on to power by the tip of bayonets. In February at Willard's Hotel in Washington, Lincoln met Grant for the first time and told him he was the new commander in chief of all the armies. Grant was determined to lock with Lee's army and wreck it. However, through the spring, at the disastrous Wilderness, Spotsylvania Courthouse, and Cold Harbor, Grant's losses were so heavy he was labeled Butcher Grant. Lincoln was now cursed for winning battles, too.

Lt. Gen. Ulysses S. Grant

The slaughter deepened the political dissent. The North's so-called Peace Democrats, mocked as snakelike Copperheads, found a wide audience for their defeatism. The Copperheads condemned Lincoln as a tyrant. At the same time the Radicals were back to plotting with the high-minded Chase, this time to replace Lincoln on the upcoming presidential ticket.

The truth was that everyone was brooding about discarding Lincoln. The Radicals had put doubts in the country's mind that Lincoln's conservative voice was not strong enough to shout down the traitors. The Republicans found the president wanting as a revolutionary. The Democrats found him wanting as a leader. The Rebels found him wanting as a human being.

In Ohio, the future Republican president General James A. Garfield of the Western Reserve wrote a friend, "We hope we may not be compelled to push Lincoln four years more." In New York Thurlow Weed wrote in the pious *Independent*, "The ship of state tosses upon a rough sea; who shall take the helm?" The Democratic *New York Herald* said of Lincoln, "He has been tried and proved a failure. . . . His administration has thus been a broad and continuous farce."

In June the Republicans met in a National Union Convention at the ornate Frontstreet Theater in Baltimore, Maryland. The chamber was cramped like a coffin in comparison to 1860's windy Wigwam. Also modest was the convention's aim to renominate Lincoln without a floor fight and to write a nondivisive platform.

There were very few Radicals present. A week earlier the most extreme members of the clique had met in a rancorous convention at Cleveland. They had set aside the booms of the spring for Chase, Grant, Banks, even Ben Butler. Instead they had nominated a battle-chastened John C. Frémont to run against Lincoln on a severe abolitionist platform that called for a one-term president and for the Monroe Doctrine to be enforced with guns against the interfering France and England.

At the Baltimore convention, the delegates wrote a platform meant to appease the Radical temperament, calling for slavery's "utter and complete extirpation from the soil of the republic." The single question for the delegates was who Lincoln would choose for a running mate. Lincoln tinkered from the White House. He moved the convention away from the able vice president, the Radical Hannibal Hamlin of Maine, and toward a loyal Democrat. The choice was either the respected Daniel Stevens Dickinson, a sixty-four-year-old jurist from the potent New York Democracy; or the controversial Andrew Johnson, then fifty-five, the former Democratic governor and senator from Tennessee, who had sided with the Union and since 1862 had been fortified in the state capitol at Nashville as the military governor.

The delegates recoiled from giving power to Dickinson and the Copperhead-riven New York Democracy. They chose instead Andrew Johnson as an open advertisement that there was a place in the Union for loyal Southerners.

The campaign was silent dread. Lincoln understood he faced sure defeat in the fall. His own party was fractured by doubt and bitterness, and in July the division deepened when Lincoln pocket-vetoed the ruthless Radical Wade-Davis Act on reconstruction.

Andrew Johnson, 1864

Lincoln also knew his most significant threat was from the surging and resourceful Democrats, who were preaching cease-fire with the wing of the party called the Peace Democracy, while also promising military supremacy with the wing of the party called the War Democracy. In August at the Chicago Wigwam, the aroused Democrats nominated for president the popular Democratic general, thirty-eight-year-old George B. McClellan, former commander of the Army of the Potomac whom Lincoln had twice dismissed for poor results. Copperheads wrote the Democratic platform and, if elected, promised an armistice, which meant surrender.

All summer Lincoln felt the hatred. Chase quit the Cabinet in high dudgeon and entertained his new opportunities with the Radicals. Grant struggled with the siege of Petersburg; Sherman struggled with the siege of Atlanta. Greeley wrote in July, "There is danger of social convulsions; but courage, countrymen, it is but the darkness before the dawn." In August Lincoln conceded that his presidency was doomed and with it the Union. The president wrote a confidential memo to the Cabinet that de-

Abraham Lincoln, 1864

clared, *"This morning as for days past it seems exceedingly probable that this administration will not be re-elected."*

The darkest hour was when an embassy of Republican champions, including Greeley and the young editor Whitelaw Reid of the *Cincinnati Gazette* (who would eventually succeed Greeley at the *Tribune)*, visited the White House to urge Lincoln to withdraw his nomination in favor of a new ticket to be named at a new convention in late September.

Exhausted, abandoned, condemned, Lincoln was faced with a futile choice. Defy the party and lose the Union. Obey the party and lose the Union.

The accident of battle saved the republic. First, Sherman outmaneuvered and defeated Joe Johnston and took Atlanta. Second, Grant sent his cavalry genius Philip Sheridan to outride and defeat Jubal Early in the Shenandoah Valley. Put together with David Farragut's storybook heroism to run the gun batteries and capture Mobile, Sherman's and Sheridan's dashing victories gave Lincoln the ammunition he needed to counter the doubters.

Gen. William Tecumseh Sherman, 1864

Gen. Philip H. Sheridan, 1864

Adm. David E. Farragut, 1864

In October the campaign parades in New York showed Republican-Union banners that told the tale: "Farragut, Sherman and Sheridan—*Our Campaign Managers.*"

Lincoln won reelection in an invalided Union. His electoral college victory of 212 to McClellan's 21 did not hide the fact that the great Union states of New York, Pennsylvania, and Ohio gave the president most narrow majorities. Lincoln actually lost wealthy New York City.

Lincoln had a mandate to finish the job if he hurried. Sherman cut the heart out of the Confederacy from Atlanta to Savannah to Charleston to Columbia. Grant strangled the hopeless defenders of Richmond and Petersburg. The final gunfight at Appomattox Courthouse closed quickly when a tireless corps of "colored troops" double-timed all night to overwhelm the last butternut line. "Unconditional Surrender" Sam Grant, wearing a muddy plain tunic coat, accepted Lee's unconditional surrender on a very still Sunday afternoon, April ninth.

The Republican party had outlasted the war. The president had outlasted his own party. Yet within moments of the celebration the victors were back at odds. The Thirteenth Amendment that ended slavery had passed the Congress in January. Emancipation and even restoration of the Union no longer appeased the Radicals. They wanted reconstruction built upon a foundation of iron righteousness; they wanted revenge.

Lincoln recognized the gauntlet ahead. In his second inaugural address in March, before the guns stopped, he was pleading with the Radicals when he said, "With malice toward none, with charity for all, with firmness in the right as God gives us to see the right, let us strive to finish the work we are in—"

In April, after the guns stopped, Lincoln spoke more bluntly to his Cabinet about reconstruction: "I hope there will be no bloody work after the war is over. None need expect me to take part in the hanging or

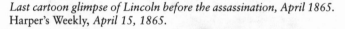

Last cartoon glimpse of Lincoln before the assassination, April 1865.
Harper's Weekly, *April 15, 1865.*

killing of men. We must extinguish our resentment if we expect to have harmony and union."*

Then Lincoln was gone like a snuffed candle flame. Horace Greeley's shock was total. The telegrams of the simultaneous attacks on Lincoln and Seward started coming into the *Tribune*'s Park Row office after midnight. Greeley suffered the bulletins like barrages all night.

To read Greeley's April 15 column on Lincoln's death was to feel the broken heart of an age. *"God, in his inscrutable Providence,"* Greeley closed, *"has thus visited the Nation; the future we must leave to him."*

Lincoln's monument at Springfield, Illinois

New York City says good-bye to Lincoln at City Hall, April 1865. Harper's Weekly, May 6, 1865.

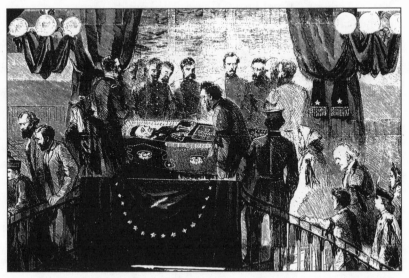

*William E. Dodd, "Lincoln's Last Struggle—Victory?" in *Lincoln Centennial Association Papers* (Springfield, Ill., Lincoln Centennial Association, 1927), p. 98.

☆ **2** ☆

The Fall of the Radicals—
The Rise of the GOP

1866–1894

Awesome Salmon P. Chase, chief justice of the United States, stood abruptly from his throne chair at the fore of the Senate chamber of the U.S. Capitol.

"Mr. Anthony," Chief Justice Chase called out the first senator on the alphabetical roll.

Henry B. Anthony

The senior senator of Rhode Island, the conservative Republican Henry B. Anthony, sprang from his chair.

It was time to vote on the impeachment bill: Saturday noon, May 16, 1868, a spectacular spring day under the blue skies of the District. The sunshine cascaded through the central skylight and illuminated the grim faces of the assembled fifty-four senators and most of the interested guests from the House of Representatives.

The business at hand was passing verdict at the first trial by Senate of a president of the United States. Today was the climax of a long-drawn-out constitutional crisis that pitted the Congress against President Andrew Johnson. This particular episode had fallen like a meteor in late February, when the president had deliberately defied his enemies in the Republican party and fired Lincoln's second war secretary, Edwin M. Stanton. The quick re-

52

sponse in March was that the Republican
scold Thad Stevens, the representative from
Pennsylvania, had forced through the Re-
publican-controlled House an impeachment
bill against President Johnson.

After a six-week trial before the Senate,
most of it in secret session, there were eleven
charges of impeachment to vote on. The first
few dealt with the fact that the president
had fired Stanton against the will of the
Congress; others dealt with the president's
bad temper and big mouth. All the articles

Edwin M. Stanton

proceeded from the same root cause: Johnson had defied the Radical-
dominated Congress for three years, and now Johnson had to go.

By prior agreement, today's initial vote would be on the eleventh article of impeachment, which claimed that it was a high misdemeanor
when Johnson had denounced Congress as a tyranny in August 1866.
Since no one denied that the president had said it, the impeachment managers aimed to win a conviction on the count right away.

The Senate room was as silent as the shallow breathing of hundreds.

Mr. Justice Chase's hand trembled as he held out a paper before him.

What a twist that it was Chase who must call the roll—Chase the
primeval Radical Republican, Chase who had been tempted more than
once to unseat Lincoln, Chase who must now supervise a trial he didn't
believe in and a verdict he thought a reckless coup d'état.

Chase's voice quivered as he addressed Anthony. "How say you? Is
the respondent, Andrew Johnson, president of the United States, guilty
or not guilty of a high misdemeanor as charged in this article?"

"Guilty," Anthony replied.

A muttering cut across the packed Senate floor. Anthony's vote had
been doubted by some of the Radicals, but now he'd done right and
voted to throw "His Accidency" Andy Johnson out of the White House.

The correspondents in the gallery marked their tally sheets as a single
man. The Constitution required a two-thirds majority for conviction—
meaning the impeachment managers of the House and their Radical allies of the Senate needed thirty-six out of fifty-four votes from the
twenty-seven states of the Union. The unreconstructed Southern states
had no voice.

Chase called out for the Democratic senators James A. Bayard of
Delaware and Charles R. Buckalew of Pennsylvania, and they voted as
expected—not guilty.

All twelve Democratic senators would be voting not guilty, so the bat-

Impeachment: The U.S. Senate as a court of impeachment for the trial of Andrew Johnson, May 1868: Chief Justice Salmon P. Chase presiding. Harper's Weekly, *May 30, 1868.*

tle to convict by two-thirds majority would be among the forty-two of the Republican ranks.

The general public, seated in the encircling galleries overhead, also marked their sheets; but they were sure not to utter an offending sound. Chase had warned the gallery beforehand that at the first upset the room would be cleared by the armed police.

Now came Simon Cameron of Pennsylvania, the absolute boss of the Keystone State. Tall, cool, long-necked Cameron, operating for decades from his base at Harrisburg, was back in the Senate for a third tour. Chase started to pose the ceremonial question, but before he could finish, the impatient Cameron declared, "Guilty!"

Chase moved down the alphabet: Radical Alexander G. Cattell of

Roscoe Conkling

New Jersey, "Guilty." Then the famous Radical Zachariah Chandler of Michigan, cofounder of the party out West, "Guilty." The Radical Cornelius Cole of California, "Guilty." The young and ambitious Radical Roscoe Conkling of New York, future absolute boss of the Empire State and the Grant-worshipping Stalwarts.

"Guilty, yes," Conkling declared.

Conkling wanted to get this over with so he could move on to next week's nominating con-

Impeachment: In March 1868, the sergeant-at-arms of the Senate summoned Andrew Johnson to his trial by Senate. Harper's Weekly, March 28, 1868.

vention at Chicago, where he aimed to deliver the mighty New York delegation to the savior of the Union, General of the Army U.S. Grant.

The truth was that the Republicans were removing Johnson today for spite. They'd then put in the thick-hided Radical Ben Wade of Ohio as an interim. They fully intended to elect Grant in the fall election.

Moreover, this whole constitutional battle was a vain demonstration of naked partisan power, the Radical Republicans versus everyone else in the world, and destruction to anyone who resisted the Radical desire. The Radical-led Republicans had controlled overwhelming majorities in the Congress since the landslide election of 1866, when the voters had rejected Johnson's argument that he be permitted to engineer a gradual

Reconstruction in the South. The Radicals wanted revenge in the South, and today they wanted revenge on Johnson.

The Capital had not always been so angry at the president. Johnson had started his sudden tenure with lockstep support by the Radicals, regardless that he was a lifelong Democrat; they had stood beside him that black Sunday after Lincoln's death and watched him sworn in as the seventeenth president by Chase himself. Johnson had at first pleased the Radicals by making radical, anti-Confederate statements, such as, "Their great plantations must be seized and divided into small farms, and sold to honest, industrious men." Yet within a year of Lincoln's death, Johnson had dared to veto the Radical-designed 1866 New Freedmen's Bureau Act and 1866 Civil Rights Act, meant to enforce Negro suffrage in the former slave states. Worse, Johnson had spoken against the holy Radical tablet of the Fourteenth Amendment.

In rebuke, Congress had overridden easily all of Johnson's vetoes and had demanded the Fourteenth Amendment be accepted by the Southern states before they could rejoin the Union. Congress had declared war on the president, denouncing him as a liar and traitor and corrupt, pardon-selling, fork-tongued devil. The whole country had recoiled from Johnson's loudmouthed antics. "The President—chief barnacle on the ship of state" read a protest banner in September 1867. Even the effete, ambivalent *Atlantic Monthly,* brain trust of the country's Boston intellectuals, had published articles debating the efficacies of impeachment.

Johnson had not accepted his condemnation without a fight. He had embarked in the summer of 1866 on a fiery speaking tour from Maryland to New York to Michigan to Missouri, called "a swing around the circle," in order to warn the people that the Radicals were tyrants. What Johnson had received for his energy was mockery wherever he traveled. "When the wicked are in authority," read one anti-Johnson banner on the tour, "the people mourn—Isaiah." What Johnson had received at the polls in 1866 and 1867 was complete repudiation, with a Congress now so filled with Johnson haters that he could only hope to survive this day, not ever to get back any genuine authority.

"Mr. Fessenden," Chase continued the roll call. The score was now twelve Republicans voting guilty and five Democrats voting not guilty. "How say you, is the respondent, Andrew Johnson, president of the United States, guilty or not guilty of a high misdemeanor as charged in this article?"

The stern William Pitt Fessenden of Portland, Maine, then sixty-one, took his time getting up. He was the author of the profound 1866 Fourteenth Amendment that defined citizenship to include former slaves (but not American Indians) and demanded that all enjoy "equal protection before the law." Fessenden knew that his own work had been undercut by Johnson's devious behavior. Fessenden knew that the 1866 race riots in Memphis and New Orleans, and the 1867 rise of the murderous Ku Klux Klan hatemongers from out of Tennessee, were all direct consequences of Johnson's unwillingness to enforce the Fourteenth Amendment. Fessenden also knew that the newly passed 1867 Reconstruction Acts that had garrisoned the South with Union troops were all that Congress could think to do, first to protect the crushing of the freed Negroes by the South's "black codes," and second to force the Fourteenth Amendment and the new Fifteenth Amendment on the unrepentant South.

In all, Fessenden knew that Johnson had brought this calumny down on himself by aiding and comforting the ex-Confederates and their race-hating kindred of Cain. What Johnson was most guilty of was intolerance and cynicism, convicted by his own words with remarks such as, "It would not do to let the Negroes have universal suffrage now; it would breed a war of races."

Nevertheless, Fessenden had already announced that he refused to go along with his own party's tantrum to remove a president simply because he was a quarrelsome bigot.

Fessenden looked over his colleagues and voted firmly, "Not guilty."

The galleries breathed deeply. Here was a crack in the kingdom of Republicanism. A major senator from a major solid state had defected to Johnson for reasons of conscience. No matter what the Radicals had threatened, Fessenden had turned away and voted for the South's lackey Johnson.

In later decades it would be argued that Fessenden's "not guilty" marked the high-water mark of the Radical power.

Chase called on Joseph S. Fowler, then forty-eight, the junior Republican senator from Andrew Johnson's own Tennessee, who was regarded a Radical. Not only did Fowler represent the birthplace of Andrew Jackson's Democracy, which had remained stoutly Union during the late war, he also represented the birthplace of this new horror, the hate-based paramilitary Ku Klux Klan of ex-Rebel soldiers, who ranged across the South terrifying and subjugating the freedmen.

Fowler rose to make a little speech. "As long as we shall fail to do our duty," he started, adding out of context, "and to impeach and remove Andrew Johnson from office is not our duty." He finished oddly, "The blood of loyal men slain in the South will rest upon our souls."

Chase was impatient with this meandering. It was too late for persuasion. "Mr. Fowler?" Chase asked.

The living Radical statue Charles Sumner was disgusted by Fowler's whining. Fowler had long boasted he would rid the nation of backsliding

Johnson, but just recently he'd made remarks that chided the impeachment trial as "more of sectional prejudice than of patriotism." Sumner meant to mock Fowler when he said, "We do not hear the senator."

"Not guilty," Fowler replied.

Frederick T. Frelinghuysen

The count moved down to the stout Radical Frederick T. Frelinghuysen of New Jersey, "Guilty," and then to the doubtful James W. Grimes, conservative Republican of Iowa.

There was a delay. Grimes, sixty-two, a longtime antislavery orator, was mortally ill. During the impeachment trial, he'd suffered a half-paralyzing stroke that was believed to have been brought on by the strain of the debate. He had arrived late to the proceeding today, and now struggled to stand.

Chase said, "Mr. Grimes need not rise."

Grimes, clutching the desk, straightened up and spoke, "Not guilty."

There were several invalid senators, some weakened with an outbreak

James W. Grimes

of bad water that made the partisans suspicious of poisoning by Johnson's forces; however, everyone—ill or not—had pulled themselves to the trial today.

The correspondents in the press galley above Chase's head were making quick assessments of the voting so far. Because so many had announced their votes ahead of time, the newsmen could skip ahead of the actual vote to concentrate just on the doubtful senators.

The impeachment managers also concentrated on their worries for a handful of the remaining Republican senators. Over the last few days the margin of victory had whittled down to one or two. Would the doubtfuls hold on for conviction?

The other side, composed of the friends and attorneys of the president, was worrying about a similar list of doubtfuls. There were reports that the president had a secret list of names of men who would vote for him if they were needed. Fessenden's preannounced defection to Johnson was notorious, but would Fessenden's infamous act of principle bring along other wavering conservative Republicans?

The day came down to the fact that no one was sure until the vote was done. After all, Grimes might not have made it into the vote. And the changeable Fowler, whom many had counted on the president's side, might have been frightened back to the Radical side.

When Fowler had voted "not guilty," the telegraph had flashed out to the large crowd of Johnson sympathizers who were at Willard's Hotel readying a celebration or a wake. The telegraph had also flashed up Pennsylvania Avenue to the White House, where the president was meeting with the Cabinet, less Stanton, while awaiting the outcome. With Fowler's vote, the president started to feel confident.

Chase continued his call. Another doubtful conservative Republican defected, John B. Henderson of Missouri: "Not guilty." The following fifteen votes went along party lines, including the conservative Republican Edwin D. Morgan of New York, who voted, "Guilty."

Now the tally was twenty-four for conviction and fourteen for acquittal. The newspapermen could see that it was going to come down to a surprisingly shaky vote, conservative Republican Edmund G. Ross of Kansas.

John B. Henderson

Ross, fifty, had come to the Senate in '66 to take the seat of the suicide James H. Lane. Ross was a servant of the railroads. He had always voted with the Radicals and was counted as a vote for conviction as late as the night before, when he had let on that he was with Sumner and the rest. However, in the procedural vote prior to the roll call, Ross had voted with the Democrats. Ben Wade had smoked trouble. ("Ross is gone," Wade had said to the air.)

Also, all during the roll call vote, Ross had been behaving bizarrely— sitting with his head down while he tore a white piece of paper into strips that he let fall around him.

"Mr. Ross," Chase called. "How say you?"

Ross refused to look up at Chase or anyone else. He kept tearing paper and making a snowy field at his feet. The *Baltimore American* had predicted twenty-four hours earlier that Ross would hold fast. Every New York paper, Republican or Democrat, believed he would vote Kansas for conviction.

Now it was time for decision. Ross rose. "Not guilty," he said.

Sumner ground his teeth. Thad Stevens slapped his chair. Bold Ben Wade, who as the president pro tempore of the Senate was just a twist of fate away from the White House, looked away from the light.

The newspapermen counted quickly ahead. From Ross on down,

there were thirteen Republican votes to go. Twelve were needed for conviction. Lyman Trumbull of Illinois, Lincoln's old colleague, had preannounced that he would vote for acquittal, "Not guilty"—another vote on principle. This meant that the impeachment managers needed everyone else. The doubtful were the two senators from the Civil War–created state of West Virginia, Van Winkle and Waitman T. Willey.

Everything went swiftly. All eyes went to Peter G. Van Winkle of West Virginia. "Not guilty," Van Winkle said.

It was over. When the Democrat George Vickers of Maryland voted "not guilty," there were nineteen for acquittal—twelve Democrats and seven Republicans—just enough to block the conviction by two-thirds majority.

The room whirled in sighs. The finish of the vote was quick because it was meaningless. Hardly anyone noticed when Ben Wade of Ohio voted "guilty"—a decision that later was chided as improper, since he was voting for his own presidency and was clearly not an impartial juror.

The final tally was written in stone. For conviction, thirty-five. For acquittal, nineteen. After some delay for procedural matters, the Senate voted to adjourn for ten days before it would take up the vote on the other ten charges in the bill of impeachment.

No one expected anything to change. The real purpose of the adjournment was to race to the Republican convention in Chicago to elevate General U.S. Grant to U.S. savior.

Immediately following adjournment the so-called Republican recusants who had voted against the Radicals—Fessenden, Fowler, Grimes, Henderson, Ross, Trumbull, Van Winkle—were denounced in telegrams flung to the corners of the globe. Not one of them would ever win election again.

One of those telegrams went to the president and his Cabinet. The president did not disguise his cool pleasure.

In the corridors of the Capitol the reaction was heated.

"To think we should have lost by the vote of a miserable poltroon and traitor as Ross is humiliating" was the Radical sentiment.

Johnson-hater Thad Stevens limped out of the Senate room in a crouch and was lifted in his chair and carried back to the House side. Stevens looked pale, emaciated, faint. He would not live out the summer.

Johnson-hater Benjamin Franklin Butler, Democrat representative from Massachusetts, who had led the prosecution of the case from March 30, came out into the hall to denounce the seven recusants as bribe takers. Butler accused them of "the detestable hunger of gold." This was the Butler style of hyperbole. During the prosecution, the rotund and portentous Butler had waved a bloodstained old shirt in the

Senate chamber and claimed it was from the
back of a carpetbagger who had been horse-
whipped by unrepentant Rebels. Ben Butler's genius for melodrama had invented a
partisan figure of speech—"to wave the
bloody shirt" —that the Republicans would
use against the Democracy for the next
twenty-five years.

Across the corridor the president's defense attorneys, led by the best defense
counselor of the age, William M. Evarts

Benjamin F. Butler

of New York, gathered at the exit of the Senate room to accept the praise
of female admirers. Soon Evarts was joined by a Tennessee ancient, and
they went out to the president's waiting carriage to be rushed to the
White House.

Within the half hour newsboys were outside Willard's Hotel and the
National Hotel, screaming "Extras!" "The acquittal of the president!"

The president's supporters called at the mansion all day. Late into the
night the chandeliers were kept brightly lit as well-wishers arrived to
drink and hoot. Later there was a sober meeting at Secretary of State Seward's house to talk through the day's critical events. Seward, despite his
considerable accomplishments since the war to negotiate France out of
Mexico and purchase Alaska to rid North America of Russia, was hated
by the Radicals as much as Johnson, and today had been his vindication
as well.

No one on any side believed there was any advantage to the day. The
trial was not a victory. It was a crucial turn in the road of the Republican party: Away from the Radicalism of the war years and toward what
would become known as the Stalwarts of Grant. Away from confrontation between the Congress and the Executive and toward a monolithic
cooperation between party bosses and the president's patronage power.
Away from the depredations of the war and toward the wealth of what
would be celebrated as the Gilded Age.

In subsequent years there would be much talk that the Senate vote
had been fixed, that Johnson had arranged with just enough Republican
senators to vote "not guilty" so that he could have had Willey of West
Virginia or Sprague of Rhode Island if he'd needed them.

There would also be charges, never proved, that Johnson had pur-
chased the votes he needed by promising the patronage power to those
who supported him. When the patronage was given to Ross soon after,
the charge gained credibility.

But in the end, what came of the drama of May 16, 1868, was

demonstration that the Republican party was willing to attack and destroy anyone or any institution in order to force its will. A party that had launched a million troops against Richmond was not reluctant to launch the Senate against a sloppy president or five military districts against the prostrate South.

And why? The candid answer was that the Republican party was in muscular and ruthless pursuit of its ideal of liberty for all.

Astute Horace Greeley declared as much two days before the verdict, when he wrote in the *Tribune,* "Of all the false dogmas which incited and upheld the late frenzied war of Disunion, the assumption that 'This is a white man's government,' wherein political rights and franchises are the rightful monopoly of a single race or caste, alone remains to be overthrown.

"This last enemy of our peace," Greeley closed, looking toward the November election of Grant, "this fomenter of intestine feuds, of hostility and bloodshed, alone remains to be overcome; and the first Tuesday of November must see it unhorsed and put at rest forever."

★ 1868 ★

Ulysses S. "Unconditional Surrender" Grant was the hero who rode to the rescue of the Republican party the first Tuesday of November, 1868.

The election was never in credible doubt from the moment that the Republicans met mid-May in convention at Chicago's Crosby Opera House to nominate the world-famous Union General of the Army by unanimous acclamation. The delegates—nastily singing "Old Grimes is dead!" for crippled Senator Grimes, the impeachment defector—were determined like bees for a summer swarm. Grant and his vice presidential nominee, Speaker of the House Schuyler "Smiley" Colfax of Indiana, were praised as "both in the prime of their manly vigor, and in the fullest maturity of their powers." At the convention close, the delegates boasted, "Today the canvass opens. Let the word be: 'Grant and Victory.' "

An unusual puzzle about Grant's nomination was that he might not have wanted to leave the ceremonial and plush job of General of the Army (at twenty-five thousand dollars per annum) for the demanding and argumen-

Schuyler Colfax

General-of-the-Army Ulysses S. Grant at Army Headquarters.
Harper's Weekly, *June 6, 1868.*

tative job of chief executive (at twenty-five thousand dollars per annum). Days before the convention, when the impeachment was in the balance, Grant had hinted at his reluctance: "I have allowed the use of my name by the Republicans for months and months, and it would be unsoldierly and ungrateful for me to desert them now when things look gloomy."

Once he was nominated, Grant sounded no less ambivalent. His acceptance remarks on the front porch of his Washington home poignantly illustrated his candor, sincerity, veracity, and also his complete absence of glamour, fluency, cunning, or heart for plain-dressed politics. "Being entirely unaccustomed to public speaking," Grant said on May 22, "and without the desire to cultivate that power (laughter from the audience), it is impossible for me to find appropriate language to thank you for this demonstration. All that I can say is, that to whatsoever position I may be

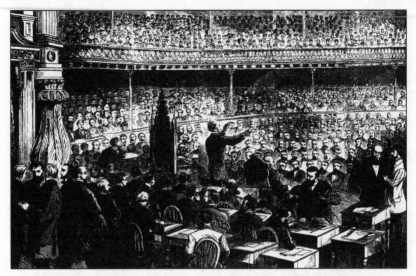

The Republicans nominate Grant and Schuyler Colfax in Chicago. Harper's Weekly, *June 6, 1868.*

called by your will, I shall endeavor to discharge its duties with fidelity and honesty of purpose. Of my rectitude in the performance of public duties you will have to judge my record before you."

The strange irony of Grant's troubled, graft-ridden, scandal-scarred administration over two terms was that he really was a magnificent soldier and gifted battlefield commander—fearless, self-confident, determined—who was happily worshiped for saving the Union on the desperate fields of Mississippi and Virginia; however, none of his skills of generalship—delegation of authority, serenity in the face of chaos, plainspokenness—mattered one whit when it came to the duplicitous battles of party politics.

The truth was that Grant had no partisan politics, neither Republican nor Democratic nor any other. He was a soldier who did his duty and

Julia Dent Grant

rode to the sound of guns. He'd been the same man since the day he entered West Point in 1839. Prior to becoming president he had voted only once for the presidency—for Buchanan in 1856, "because," he joked with a bite, "I knew Frémont."

Most telling, Grant told no one why he wanted to become president, not even his beloved wife, Julia Dent Grant. Nor did Grant take time to explain how he regarded the lengthy, thoughtful 1868 convention platform that, besides condemning Johnson as a scoundrel, called for the suffrage for all loyal men, a guarantee of the national debt, a fostering of immigration, a belligerence toward meddling European powers, and the total support of the widows and orphans of veterans.

Grant made no motion to campaign, not even to make a speech other than the cryptic remark "Let us have peace." Like a modest Cincinnatus, Grant let the furious outpouring of affection for him in song and paean do all the work.

"Republicans all, and ye brave boys in Blue," sounded one ditty, "We've chartered a train, and she's waiting for you; / The steam is all up, and we cannot delay; / For Grant's on the engine, and we must away!"

Alfred E. Street's popular verse "We Vote as We Shot" preached the point that any vote other than for Grant was dishonoring the fallen: "The quick and the dead, all loud sounding this chant / 'We vote as we shot' for Flag, Union and Grant! / Off traitors and Copperheads! back to your haunt! / Hurrah for the banner, the Union, and Grant!"

The day before the election, proud and rugged General Philip Sheridan, Grant's eventual successor as General of the Army, announced, "Say to the Boys in Blue that it is as essential to have a political victory this Fall as it was to have an Appomattox in '65, and that every man who loves his country should vote for Grant."

The wild autumn squalls of election eve gave way to a perfect cool sunshine day in New York City when the Union went to the polls to restore peace to the White House.

More than five and a half million males voted. Grant won solidly. The surprise was that, despite all the "bloody shirt" waving that accused the Democrats as Rebels and traitors and Ku Kluxers, Grant did not crush the Democracy's halfhearted Copperhead nominee, former New York governor Horatio B. Seymour.

Grant gained twenty-four states and 214 electoral votes; however, he took only 53 percent of the popular vote, including all of the half million freedmen voting in the South for the first time. But for the fact that the deeply Democratic but unreconstructed Texas, Virginia, and Mississippi did not participate, the Republican victory might have slipped away. Grant actually lost New York and New Jersey to the power of the Tammany Hall Democratic machine. The Democracy was wounded by Johnson's shenanigans, but it was not wasting away.

Grant finally spoke out in his inaugural address, March 4, 1868. The first striking detail was that he underlined his ambivalence about his new assignment: "The office has come to me unsought; I commence its duties untrammeled." Like a good general, however, he turned to security and confidence, especially guaranteeing the soundness of the dollar (greenbacks to be repaid with hard gold money) and promising that "a prostrate commerce is to be rebuilt and all industries encouraged."

Striking in the inaugural address was that Grant did not make much of Negro suffrage other than to say it was a source of agitation that should be settled. Grant was chiefly concerned with the morale of his new charges, just as if he were a generalissimo assuming a new command. "The young men of the country," he emphasized, "—those who from their age must be its rulers twenty-five years hence—have a peculiar interest in maintaining the national honor. A moment's reflection as to what will be our commanding influence among the nations of the earth in their day, if they are only true to themselves, should inspire them with national pride."

Grant's administration immediately plunged into a tale of weak men, bad money, and slapdash policies that undermined everyone's belief in Grant's goodness and eventually led to national shame.

The Cabinet was an immediate source of embarrassment when Grant chose sycophants and army pals who would leave him alone. Then came the infamous Wall Street gold corner on Black Friday, September 24, 1869, when Grant's own brother-in-law tried to prevent the U.S. Treasury from selling gold in order to help two speculators, Jay Gould and

The Gold Room in New York, scene of the gold corner, September 24, 1869. Matthew Hale Smith, Bulls and Bears of New York with the Crisis of 1873 and the Cause *(Freeport, N.Y.: Books for Libraries Press, 1972).*

"Jubilee Jim" Fisk of New York, dominate the New York City gold market and "bull" prices up. Grant's quick decision to sell Treasury gold restored the market to credibility and wrecked the speculators' attempt at a money coup; however, the president was left looking like a sneak thief.

The scandals and failures tumbled apace. In domestic affairs the rotten patronage system led to loud calls for a professional civil service from strong-minded thinkers such as the *Nation*'s eloquent editor E. L. Godkin and also from high-minded senators such as Carl Schurz of Missouri. In foreign affairs Grant's able secretary of state, Hamilton Fish of New York, did maneuver an 1871 treaty with Great

E. L. Godkin

Britain that avoided armed conflict over a farrago of issues; however, Grant's 1870 ploy to annex Santo Domingo failed badly and led to a final break with the cranky Charles Sumner.

Grant's administration failed worst in the South, where the Ku Klux Klan told the stupid lie that it had disbanded itself in 1869. No one believed it, but the Congress had lost heart to enforce the Fourteenth and Fifteenth Amendments or the 1870–71 Ku Klux Klan Acts. The cowardice rebounded on the president. The dreams of the Republican party to free the slaves and grant suffrage to all loyal men deteriorated into futile congressional investigations of the Klan's power, sensational newspaper headlines about the Klan's cruelty, and a grunting fatalism by the federal occupying

Hamilton Fish

forces that the South was ungovernable because it had become little more than the way of the Klan. Was the cancer of the Ku Klux Klan incurable? No one knew for certain, and Grant did not ask.

The Republicans denied Grant's aimless wreck of half-witted greed and sinister cronyism until it was too late. At the midterm elections of 1870, the Republicans held on to the Senate but lost the House to the Democrats for the first time since Buchanan's administration. Yet Greeley's *Tribune* could still write of Grant, "He is Abraham Lincoln's lineal successor, and the popular heart breaks in unison with his aspirations and his efforts."

By 1872 Greeley had quit denying. The old rumors of Grant's drink-

The Grant Administration's Indian policy delivered by Secretary of War and later General of the Army William T. Sherman. Harper's Weekly, *August 15, 1874.*

ing, and the president's careless habit of going to lunch with lobbyists and accepting spans of gift horses from the wealthy, were advanced as proof that a second term would lead to a Babylonian monarchy.

★ 1872 ★

The revolt against Grant and his maladministration was led not by the Democracy but by some of the Republican party's strongest thinkers.

The dissenters called themselves the Liberal Republican party. The leaders included Prussian-born war hero and senator Carl Schurz of Missouri, also Lincoln's former secretary of the navy Gideon Welles of Connecticut, and diplomat Charles Francis Adams of Massachusetts. Chief among them was the crusading Horace Greeley of New York.

The Liberal Republicans met in a break-away convention in May 1872 at Cincinnati's vast, untidy Convention Hall. The delegates were careful to speak against Grant's policies but not against the reputation of the ever popular president.

"What the people now most earnest demand," argued Carl Schurz, one of the admired orators in the age of oratory, "is, not that mere good intentions, but that a superior intelligence, coupled with superior policies,

Carl Schurz

should guide our affairs, not that merely an honest and popular man, but that a statesman be put at the head of our Government."

Seven thousand anti-Grantites in the hall agreed with cheers. The delegates wrote a platform that called for a cleaned-up civil service, a low tariff for the Southern and Western farmers, a sensible system of taxation, the ceasing of land giveaways to the railroads. A plank also asked for some small gesture of amnesty toward the ex-Rebels.

In all, the Liberal Republicans advanced an articulate and sound plan for their movement and for the United States. The peculiar surprise of the convention was that the Liberal Republicans couldn't advance a

Charles Francis Adams

credible candidate. The gifted Chancellorsville and Gettysburg hero Schurz was bypassed. On the sixth ballot the convention also bypassed the sagacious descendant of presidents Charles Francis Adams and instead chose the world-famous but amateurish politician Horace Greeley.

The magnetic telegraph news stunned the nation. The cunning Democratic press praised Greeley as a saint in the hope that his candidacy would weaken the Radicals. "No man has labored harder since the war," wrote the *Richmond Dispatch,* "to restore peace, equality and a good feeling among the people [and to] expose the prolonged misrule of ultra-Republicanism."

The Republican press loyal to Grant did not hide its derision. "The first tendency of most people, yesterday," wrote the *New York Times,* "when they heard that the Cincinnati Convention had nominated Horace Greeley, was to laugh. . . . If any one man could send a great nation to the dogs, that man is Horace Greeley. His candidacy may serve to enliven the gloom of politics; and supply the jokers with new themes; it will take no part in the practical affairs of men."

"In Congress there was 'laughter on all sides,'" commented the Republican *Hartford Courant*. "Senator Trumbull said Greeley's nomination would be 'received with mirth all over the country,' and if the ticket should not be destroyed by the 'waves of laughter,' it might run."

The Republican *Boston Advertiser* judged, "The Liberal Reform goose is cooked [with a candidate who is] hallowed by the prestige of disaster."

Silent Grant moved steadily to counter the Liberal Republican complaints by lowering some tariffs and signing the Amnesty Act that forgave all but about five hundred ex-Confederates. In Philadelphia under pastoral June skies, the Republican party rallied around Grant for a second term at a singing convention in the Academy of Music. The most popular speeches were "John Brown's Song" and "Marching through Georgia" and a Montana tenor's rendering of "Red, White, and Blue."

Henry Wilson

For the bottom of the ticket the Philadelphia convention chose the old Radical Henry Wilson of Massachusetts to replace the undistinguished Schuyler Colfax. The Philadelphia delegates also affirmed a platform that contained the best social thinking of the day, including opposition to discrimination by "race, creed, color, or previous condition of servitude"; opposition to land grants to corporations; opposition to the income tax left over from the war; opposition to the patronage system and the franking system; opposition to violent and treasonable organizations (the Klan); opposition to any repudiation of the public debt.

Most interesting in the platform was careful language that encouraged rapprochement between capital and labor, and that noted the party was aware of "its obligations to the loyal women of America for their loyal devotion to the cause of freedom."

In other words, the Republican party had discovered the new intellectual notions of socialism, trade unionism, and feminism without knowing what to do about them.

For the first and last time in history, the Democratic party did not propose candidates for president and vice president at its Baltimore convention in July. Instead the Democracy endorsed Greeley and the utopian Liberal Republican platform.

The summer-long campaign was a contest between the tireless Greeley and the silent Grant. Greeley crisscrossed the country speaking for good government and speaking against Ben Butler's now infamous "bloody shirt" argument—that the South was a pack of treasonous Democratic dogs. Greeley preached reconciliation between the North and South and said that he was "eager to clasp hands across the bloody chasm" of the late war.

Dignified Grant hated what was said against him and despised Greeley's betrayal. The president stayed away from the campaign, driving his swift gift horses and summering outside the capital. In September the Credit Mobilier scandal broke over Washington. The central charge was that a wide menu of major Republicans had been bribed by the Union Pacific Railroad. Everyone believed that Credit Mobilier was all true, and that the sitting vice president, Schuyler Colfax, was likely guilty of complicity if not bribe taking. It didn't signify. Nothing could weaken the country's devotion to "Flag, Union, and Grant." The farcical campaign closed with prominent Democrats like the pompous, cynical Horatio Seymour making speeches for Greeley, despite the fact that Greeley had spent the last twenty years bombarding Seymour in New York.

Election day was a tangle of solid voting by the Republicans and scattershot voting by the Democrats. Grant won a landslide with more than 55 percent of six and a half million votes, sweeping the North and West, along with six states in the South, for 286 electoral votes. Grant's coattails also brought back both houses of the new Forty-third Congress to the Republicans.

Heroic, hard-charging, honorable Horace Greeley took nearly 44 percent of the vote but no electoral college votes, when the electoral college system broke down in contretemps and castigation and electors cast 80 electoral college votes for candidates other than Grant or Greeley.

Greeley lost more than the election. The week before election day, Greeley's adored, invalid wife, Mary, died in his arms, and he buried her in the family mausoleum in Brooklyn's Greenwood Cemetery with a dark solemnity that alarmed his friends. When Greeley mentioned to friends that he was "the worst beaten man who ever ran for high office," he wasn't talking about politics, he was describing his broken heart and mind.

Greeley soon started back to work at the *Tribune,* only to find that the young and brilliant Whitelaw Reid, who had supported Greeley at the Cincinnati convention, had assumed the practical powers of the editorship. Greeley puttered at some editorials, then one day in mid-November he put down his pen and pushed away in despair. "There is an idea worth using," Greeley remarked to the flummoxed staff, "but I haven't felt able to work it out properly. You had better put it in shape." Greeley went home to his farm in Chappaqua. He swiftly withered with what his doctor called "extreme nervous prostration" and "inflammation of the brain." Friday, November 29, Greeley descended into delirium. At noon he suddenly cried out, "I know that my Redeemer liveth!" At 3 P.M., he pronounced, "It is done!"

Horace Greeley died insensate that evening, attended by one of his two daughters and many stunned friends. He was sixty-one years old.

Statue of Horace Greeley in New York City

The next day a heartbroken *Tribune* staff raised a black flag in front of the offices. Written on the flag were Greeley's last words, "It is done! Horace Greeley." Whitelaw Reid wrote in memorium, "We leave his praise to the poor whom he succored, to the lowly whom he lifted up, to the slave whose back he saved from the lash, to the oppressed whose wrongs he made his own."

Tuesday next, the closed coffin lay in state at City Hall. On Thursday, December 5, Grant and all imaginable dignitaries and potentates attended the funeral in New York. The procession was so long, it took two hours to travel from the solemn crowds in front of the church at Forty-fifth Street and Fifth Avenue down Broadway to the Battery. Only the family and the *Tribune* staff joined the ferry ride to Greenwood Cemetery to inter Greeley's remains with those of his wife and five lost children.

★ 1876 ★

At Greeley's death, the Radical zeal in Congress faded, too, soon to be replaced by the Grant loyalists called the Stalwarts.

Similarly, the Radical dream of universal suffrage was replaced by the earthy and expensive work of winning elections against the Democrats. Electioneering didn't need preachers and philosophers; it needed tireless partisans who were willing to pound the Rebel-stained, Klan-poisoned Democracy every day, no surrender.

Grant needed right away the devotion of his loyalists—men who were sealed to him by the power of the presidential patronage—because his second administration was battered by financial crises like a cornfield in a hailstorm.

First, the Congress frightened many in the country by demonetizing silver and making gold the lone monetary standard. The Fourth Coinage Act of February 1873 was called "the crime of '73" and began two decades of hysteria about a conspiracy against silver and the Western mining states' "silverites" by the gold-hoarding elite in the East.

Second, the Congress raised the salaries of everyone in Washington with the so-called Salary Grab Act in March. The public outcry against the giveaway forced repeal of the act the next year. President Grant did get to keep his raise to fifty thousand dollars per annum.

Third, the panic of 1873 started with the sell-off in railroad stocks and quickly led to the failure of railroad financier Jay Cooke's bank and the ruinous closing of the stock exchange on September 20. When the market reopened, the damage was catastrophic. What followed was a numbing bear market in credit and equity markets worldwide. The government made it worse by flooding the currency with greenbacks. Business failures by the thousands began a five-year deep depression.

Other blunders and plain plundering—the war secretary took kickbacks from post traders in the Indian Territory—drove the Republican party to wide defeat in important state elections in 1874. The Republicans held the U.S. Senate, but the Democrats took back the House. Importantly, the Democrats swept New York with the much admired Tammany Hall reformer Samuel J. Tilden for governor.

The birth of the Republican elephant by Thomas Nast in Harper's Weekly, *November 7, 1874.*

Of note, the famous Republican elephant was born during the '74 mid-term elections in two editorial cartoons by the prominent *Harper's Weekly* cartoonist Thomas Nast. The background for the cartoon was a circulation war between the Democratic *New York Herald* and its broadsheet rivals. To attract readers, the *Herald* fabricated a story about the mass escape of animals from the Central Park Zoo, the sensational "Central Park Menagerie" scare. At the same time the *Herald* was maintaining its drumbeat editorial charge against Grant that he was planning to abolish the Constitution and grab a third term for himself as the new American Caesar. Nast was an ardent Republican, and he worried that the Democratic smear of ceasarism against Grant was hurting the Republicans in the canvass. On November 7, the week of the elections, Nast combined the menagerie hoax with the ceasarism smear in a cartoon he called "Third-Term Panic."

The scene is Central Park. The Republican vote is pictured as a stampeding elephant. The *New York Herald* is pictured as the traditional Democratic jackass (from the 1833 cartoon that had put Andrew Jackson's head on a jackass) with the important alteration that the jackass is wearing a lion's pelt labeled with the ceasarism charge. The *Tribune* is shown as a giraffe with its head above the crowd; the *Times* is a utopian unicorn; the *World* is a hooting owl. The caption reads, "An ass, having put on a Lion's skin, roamed about in the forest, and amused himself by frightening all the foolish Animals he met in his wanderings"—Shakespeare or Bacon.

The cartoon was meant as a warning that the Republican vote was being spooked into abandoning the Republican party. The fear was that the out of control elephant would fall into a pit of troubles. In the foreground the Democratic party is pictured as a sly fox watching the elephant stumble over the flimsy issue planks such as inflation that were covering the pit.

After the Republican disappointment at the polls, Nast published the

Andrew Carnegie

follow-up in *Harper's,* November 21, 1874, showing the Republican elephant falling upside down into the pit of political chaos: "Caught In A Trap—The Result of the Third-Term Hoax."

The notion of the Republicans as a runaway pachyderm was immediately popular, and within a few years Nast was using the elephant without labels to represent the party in all its moods.

Grant's frantic reign was the birth of Mark

The new-born elephant takes a tumble by Thomas Nast in Harper's Weekly, *November 21, 1874.*

Twain's Gilded Age. It was a time of such spectral tales of greed that many of the fortunes excavated under Grant would become the pantheon of American wealth: Andrew Carnegie, John D. Rockefeller, Jay Gould, Cornelius Vanderbilt, Philip Armour, Leland Stanford, Phillip Frick, George Westinghouse. These new fortunes were ready to purchase whatever they wanted from the government. The only check on rampant individualism then as well as later was rampant competition—the survival of the fittest at the marketplace. This selling of favors cost the Republicans expensive respect.

Leland Stanford

A lone moment of decency came in early 1875, when the fading Charles Sumner shepherded through Congress a new Civil Rights Act that aimed to fight discrimination. The legislation had no teeth, but it would remain on the books in the face of jim crow laws until it was enhanced with new civil rights laws in the 1960s.

By late 1875, Grant and his supporters had so alienated the public and press that the Democrat-dominated House passed a nonbinding resolution against a third term for Grant. Most House Republicans joined in the majority, 233–18.

The Grant loyalists were unshaken and earned their nom de guerre as the Stalwarts. Led by the New York boss, Senator Roscoe G. Conkling, the Stalwarts had the power of the patronage, especially in rich New York, where the collector of the port was future vice president and president Chester A. Arthur. What Conkling and the Stalwarts wanted was a third term for Grant. The rumor was that Grant wanted it, too. Yet the Stalwarts were practical partisans, and they approached the Republican convention by biding their time and hoping for a deadlock.

James G. Blaine

All spring, the Republican press advanced as party savior the former Speaker of the House James G. Blaine of Maine, forty-five, who had earned a national reputation for eloquence and leadership. Blaine also had an unhappy reputation for independent wealth based upon the payoff of a failed railroad and other bribe taking. A tall, dapper, St. Jerome–looking sophisticate, well educated and well married, Blaine was extremely well liked by New England and by the influential big-city press. Blaine inspired the sort of loyalty that could fend off the Stalwarts with his own coterie called the Half-breeds. He also was an astute politician, and the month before the convention he survived a House Judiciary Committee attack on his mysterious finances by fending off the allegations with expedient remarks. By June, the Blaine boom looked to be the favorite for the nomination.

Suddenly, James G. Blaine showed himself to be star-crossed—a man who would dominate the Republican conventions and nominations for

Grant burdened by the Gilded Age. Harper's Weekly, *October 24, 1872.*

the next twenty years but who would not ever be able to land the prize of the White House. What happened was that on Sunday, June 11, as the delegates were gathering at Cincinnati for the convention, word came from Washington that Blaine had collapsed. It was only heatstroke: Blaine had been on his way to church and had fallen down at the church door. However, in the vast "Four-Acre" Convention Hall at Cincinnati, the bulletins about Blaine's condition mixed with worries about Blaine's mysterious wealth. Gradually, the momentum for Blaine was broken.

The Blaine friends fought on. In the most famous nominating speech ever given, the Illinois politician Robert J. Ingersoll (who had already aroused the convention by waving the bloody shirt—"Every man that shot Union soldiers was a Democrat! The man that assassinated Lincoln was a Democrat! Soldiers, every scar you have got on your heroic bodies was given you by a Democrat!") now ignited the Blaine-loyal Half-breeds with stellar hyperbole. "Like an armed warrior, like a plumed knight," Ingersoll shouted from the podium, "James G. Blaine marched down the halls of the American Congress and threw his shining lance full and fair against the brazen forehead of every defamer of his country and maligner of its honor."

Rutherford B. Hayes

The balloting on Friday, June 16, was as unpredictable, contentious, and surprising as any since Lincoln's nomination. Blaine held a big lead for six ballots over a gaggle of Stalwart choices. But then, as Conkling's Stalwarts shifted their support around to lesser Grantites, there was a boom for a complete newcomer, the popular governor of Ohio, Rutherford B. Hayes.

The friends of Hayes elbowed out Blaine on the seventh ballot and won a majority. The party turned to meet its new star. "Old Granny" Hayes, fifty-three, was a smart, experienced, much-admired war hero who had fought with Sheridan in the Shenandoah Valley. "His friends say he can jump any fence upon which he can place his hands," boasted the first report, "that he is a splendid horsemen and a capital shot, and that he can cut a swath in any Granger's meadow."

Hayes proved a responsible and blameless candidate. He announced ahead of time that he would only serve one term, a shrewd strategy aimed to appeal to the doubtful states of New York, New Jersey, and Indiana. New York was a primary concern, because the popular reform governor Samuel J. Tilden was soon the revived Democracy's presidential candidate.

Hayes also ran on a savvy platform that promised bold civil service reform to end the patronage, and also pledged the vote-winning issues of support for the veterans, support for "equal rights for women" (a suffragette had addressed the Cincinnati convention), and continued support for a high tariff. The platform also appealed to the nativist element by speaking against Chinese immigration in the Pacific states and rejecting public funds for Roman Catholic schools. The platform was keen to "deprecate all sectional feeling" because the Republicans now understood that the Democracy was counting on a "unified South" to recapture the presidency.

In the end, all platform arguments were beside the point. The election was stolen by the Republicans at the direction of Grant and the Stalwarts and the complicity of Southern Democrats in the House and Senate.

On election day, nearly eight and a half million men gave Tilden more than 50 percent of the vote. At first it appeared that Tilden had won a majority of the electoral college. However, within days it was clear that there had been tomfoolery among the Republican-appointed electors of South Carolina, Florida, Louisiana, and Oregon. The election was thrown into the House while commissions investigated obvious irregularities. Within weeks, it was clear that outrageous shenanigans at all levels of the government aimed to steal the election for the Republicans. The parliamentary battle dragged on through the winter. The partisans were shameless on both sides. The climax was left to three days before the inauguration.

In the early hours of March 2, 1877, the Democrat-controlled House sealed the deal with the Republicans and, finally battering down Tilden filibusters, voted by majority to approve Hayes's electors. Twenty minutes later the Senate was in session to receive the count of the thirty-eight states of the Union.

"At 4:10," reported the *Tribune* correspondent in the morning's paper, "the President of the Senate announced that Rutherford B. Hayes had received 185 votes for President and William A. Wheeler 185 votes for Vice-President, and that therefore they were respectively elected." The reporter added, "One solitary hiss was heard. With this exception the announcement was made in the midst of the most profound silence."

"One solitary hiss" marked the end of the Radical cause. After 4:10 A.M., March 2, 1877, the Republican party was in the hands of practical men who would do what was needed to win, no rules, no surrender—stand toe-to-toe with the Democracy and just slug it out, devil take the hindmost.

Every Republican voter in the country suspected that a brutal deal had been made by the outgoing Grant administration. The price was the Radical Reconstruction. In exchange for the votes of those Southern Democrats in the House, the Hayes administration agreed to withdraw the last of the military garrison in the South, agreed to put a Southerner in the Cabinet, agreed to support Southern railroad interests.

The verdict of history was that the wrong man became president. The hard truth was that the Fourteenth and Fifteenth Amendments, the documents the Radicals had fought the war to write, the law of the land that took the lives of six hundred thousand to ratify, were put away in a drawer. Civil rights was not enforced in the South again until the Earl Warren Supreme Court decision *Brown v. Board of Education* in 1954

The Thomas Nast elephant after the stolen 1876 election and Hayes's electoral college victory. Harper's Weekly, *March 24, 1877.*

and the Eisenhower administration fight in Little Rock, Arkansas, in 1957.

In disgust at the sellout, the Democracy's Tammany Hall in New York groaned that Hayes's election was "a Conspiracy of Force and Fraud." The Republican response was to charge that Tilden had lost because "idiocy and proclivity to suicide are Democratic peculiarities."

What peculiarity the Democracy had actually discovered was a way to beat the Republicans. Nominate a popular and reform-minded Northern politician, all the better if he was the governor of New York, and then bank on the support of the electoral might of the "unified South."

★ 1880 ★

President Hayes's pledge to serve only one term meant that he could act on many controversial issues while holding public confidence for his principles.

Hayes dealt with the open wound of the ex-Confederacy by turning the South over to Southern Democrats. The Radical favorite of the helping-hand Freedman's Bureau was dismantled. The Radical-funded troops were sent out of the South. The "colored" Republican politicians were sent to defeat. The opportunistic carpetbaggers were sent to blazes. Soon enough, the Democracy learned to speak of "the Solid South" as a weapon more powerful than all the guns from Shiloh Church to Five Forks.

Hayes dealt with the withering business depression by sorting out the debate over bimetallism. The Republican party wanted to undo "the crime of '73" and make silver as well as gold negotiable currency, at the ratio of 16:1. The hope was to answer the complaints and hold the votes of the "silverites" of the Western mining states. Hayes opposed the 1878 Bland-Allison Bill to restore silver at 16:1 as inflationary, but the president's veto was overridden. The threat of inflation was avoided by having the Treasury purchase a fixed rate of silver coinage each month, not the free and unlimited supply the silverites dreamed of. Hayes thereby had not only satisfied the mining states but also undercut the raw energy of the hectoring Greenback Labor Party—the nascent socialist, inflationist faction—that wanted silver redeemed on a parity with gold.

Hayes's treasury secretary was the famous old Ohio Radical John Sherman (who had been the chief Republican agent in fixing the Southern electoral votes for Hayes). Sherman was equally deft in fixing the nation's finances by resuming the redemption of species out of the $200 million gold reserve.

Hayes also challenged the patronage system of Roscoe Conkling's Stalwarts by firing the collector of the port of New York, future president Chester A. Arthur.

Hayes's good management was not quick enough to slow the Democrats. Ten thousand business failures in 1878 left the Republicans vulnerable in the midterm elections. The Democrats won both houses of the new Forty-sixth Congress and began the rebuilding of the Democracy.

Hayes's and Sherman's attention to sound money and sincere civil service reform did build national confidence. Bull markets in railroads and mining stocks returned in the summer of 1879. The autumn off-year state elections went the Republican way in the North and gave the party hope. Hayes's annual message to Congress was cautious, well argued, and dominated by the good news of the financial recovery. The South was gone to the Democracy. The North was Republican and growing again.

With Hayes out of the race, the Republicans prepared for the convention by choosing between the two hostile camps, the Stalwarts and the Half-breeds.

The Stalwarts were sincere in wanting Grant for an unprecedented third term. Since leaving office Grant had traveled around the world to

The seventh Republican convention at the Chicago Exposition Building in June 1880. Harper's Weekly, *June 19, 1880.*

gain the applause of kings and courts. Now he was wealthy, rested, and ready.

The Half-breeds were just as stout for their "plumed knight," the now senator James G. Blaine of Maine.

Seven hundred and seventy-eight delegates met in balmy June in Chicago's spacious Convention Hall in the Exposition Building on Adams Street. The delegates were locked immediately in fierce rumor-mongering and deal making.

The platform was an afterthought, meant not as a social design but rather as a barrage at the Democracy. "We charge upon the Democratic party the habitual sacrifice of patriotism and justice to an insatiable lust for office and patronage," the platform declared, "that to obtain possession of the National Government, and control of the place, [they have] crushed the rights of the individual, advocated the principles and sought the favor of the Rebellion against the Nation, and endeavored to obliterate the sacred memories of the war."

The platform did affirm the Republican faith in a protectionist tariff, an honest civil service, and a sound dollar, backed by silver and gold at 16:1. The platform cited long statistics to prove the stunning new prosperity in the country. There were also planks opposing Chinese immigration, public aid to Catholic schools, and the railroad monopolies then suspected of spreading like wildfire.

The nomination process was a true trial by fire. The first ballot on Monday showed Grant and Blaine each just short of the majority, trailed by State Secretary Sherman, the popular jurist Senator George F. Edmunds of Vermont (one of the men who had helped steal the Hayes election), and a scattering of others.

The balloting continued with much deal making but little change through Monday and Tuesday. The surprise came on Wednesday, on the thirty-fourth ballot, when a handful of

George F. Edmunds

Eastern delegates changed their votes to the popular new senator from Ohio, James A. Garfield.

Garfield was on the floor at the time, a delegate from Ohio who was doing his best to support his mentor, John Sherman. Flabbergasted by the attention, Garfield, forty-eight, a quick-witted parliamentarian, called for the chair's attention.

"I rise to a question of order!" Garfield called out. He argued that no one had a vote to cast votes for a man not asked. "I refuse!" he declared.

James A. Garfield

At Republican conventions, humor always worked wonders. Garfield was immediately rewarded for refusing by attracting fifty unwanted votes on the thirty-fifth ballot. The arena could feel the boom for the new man and a way out of the impasse.

Then came the hot thirty-sixth ballot. "[Garfield] was struck by Presidential lightning," wrote the *Tribune* supporter, "while sitting in the body which was to nominate him."

On that thirty-sixth ballot, the Stalwart forces held fast for Grant. However, Blaine's Half-breeds joined Sherman's friends to rush to Garfield.

The word was to Stop Grant by any means necessary. The balloting continued down the alphabet. With West Virginia's nine votes and Wisconsin's twenty votes, the stunned Garfield won the nomination by the whiskers on his face.

Chester A. Arthur

In a calculated maneuver to appease the Grant loyalists, the convention then gave the vice presidential nomination to a good Stalwart: Chester A. Arthur, forty-nine, long active in New York City politics and a survivor of the Hayes attempt to clean up the civil service.

The presidential canvass kept up the energy of the surprising nomination. Garfield was an honest, thoroughly likable man, a genuine war hero who had served under Hayes. The Democrats helped the Republicans when they nominated an amateur politician, the war hero General Winfield Scott Hancock of Pennsylvania, who ran on the fundamental Democratic planks of a low tariff, constitutionally guaranteed states rights, and antimonopoly legislation.

Garfield did make speeches for a high tariff and good government, but he never left Ohio, still yoked by the tradition that candidates did not campaign. The Republicans were rich with surrogates, including Grant himself, who was most worried that the Southern Democrats would regain the White House behind Hancock's camouflage; as well as the famous Negro orator Frederick Douglass, who regarded the Democracy as a creature of the South's reactionaries.

Frederick Douglass

Grant, appearing in October in doubtful New Jersey, warned, "I believe the present hour to be as important as any since 1865. The mission of the Republican party is not ended until a free ballot can be cast throughout this land without endangering the life, prosperity or social position of the voter."

Blunt, tireless Douglass, appearing in October in the doubtful New York at the Cooper Union Hall, warned, "Friends we must take no step backward. We must resolve that not Hancock and [William Hayden] English be the president and vice-president, but that deep-chested, large-hearted, three-story headed man (laughter) James A. Garfield (applause). And I will tell you why I am opposed to Democratic Rule. When the South gets ready and has a mind to behave herself it may have this government; but until every man can walk to the same ballot box in Charleston with the same freedom that he can in the city of New York, we intend to hold this government."

The Democrats fought hard to the end, accusing Garfield with the infamous Credit Mobilier bribery of the Grant years. Election day, Greeley's inheritor at the *Tribune,* handsome and righteous Whitelaw Reid, blasted the Democrats: "For the first time in our political history, a whole party [has] turned blackguard and sought success by making Billingsgate take the place of logic."

The voting was a dead heat. It divided so evenly between the parties that less than ten thousand out of more than ten million votes cast gave Garfield the popular victory. Significantly the newborn third party, the Greenback Labor party—an amalgam of anti-Chinese, pro-silver, and pro-labor forces—took a critical three hundred thousand, mostly in the West: the initial stirrings of the labor movement had reached in and changed an election for the first time.

The victory was decided in the ultimate election battleground of New York State. This time New York gave its electoral votes to Garfield and the tempestuous Republicans, for a total of 214. Hancock and the Democracy took all the South and New Jersey, for a total of 155.

The House swung back to the Republicans for the first time since '74; while the Senate remained Democratic by one vote. From now until the

Republican national headquarters in the Fifth Avenue Hotel, New York City. Harper's Weekly, *November 6, 1880.*

rise of McKinley and the GOP, the Congress would seesaw back and forth between the two parties, always vulnerable to the squally success of splinter parties, always vulnerable to the legislative flood of the moment—and most cantankerous toward the White House.

★ 1884 ★

Garfield's fate was wretched. Yet his murder was a direct consequence of the Republican party factionalism that had raised him up to the White House.

Immediately after the March inauguration, Garfield moved to break the Stalwarts by challenging and humiliating and driving out of office the two New York Stalwart senators, boss Roscoe Conkling and his pal Thomas Platt.

In retaliation, on July 2, 1881, Garfield was shot down at close range by a lone gunman while walking with his new secretary of state, James G. Blaine, at the Baltimore depot.

Garfield collapsed. Blaine cried, "My God, he has been murdered! What is the meaning of this?"

A policeman named Kearney pursued the gunman outside and arrested him without a struggle. "In God's name," Kearney demanded, "what did you shoot the president for?"

The gunman was Charles Guiteau, a tormented second-rater who had corresponded with the White House for months in hope of a patronage job. Guiteau's infamous answer to the policeman at the scene was, "I am a Stalwart, and want Arthur for president."

In truth, Guiteau acted alone, without any conspiracy of Stalwarts. His naming of Arthur was just devilry. Yet it was also understood at the time that Guiteau had done the bloody work that was in the guilty thoughts of tens of thousands of displaced Stalwart office seekers.

Garfield lingered horribly for ten weeks with doctors helpless to extract the groin shot. Inventor Alexander Graham Bell designed a listening probe to try to find and remove the bullet; he failed. Robert Lincoln called at the White House and reported, "Now I can tell you he has been and continues to be a very sick man." In September Garfield was moved out of Washington's malaria zone in hope of a miracle. The nation went on deathwatch. In the end the sad, brave Garfield died of exhaustion at enduring the pain and infection. "A Shudder and Painless Death," claimed the report. "A severe pain in the heart was followed by death at 10:35 P.M. [September 19]."

Fortunately for the nation and party, Arthur, taking the oath of office on September 20, turned out to be a responsible administrator and earnest reformer despite his spoils-rotten backers. Arthur did veto a hate-filled bill to restrict Chinese immigration; he did sign a treaty of commerce with Korea; he did support Blaine's takeover of the Hawaiian Islands; he did authorize the Tariff Commission to adjust some of the

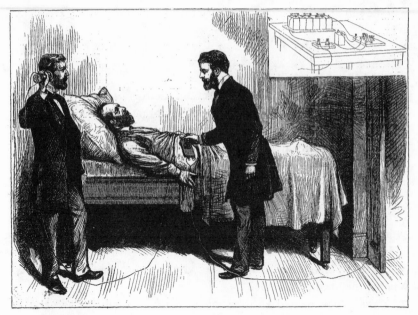

Alexander Graham Bell's listening probe was used to search for the bullet in the dying President Garfield. Harper's Weekly, August 13, 1881.

most inappropriate tariffs; he did sign the Pendleton Civil Service Reform Act to redress the worst of the patronage system by establishing the Civil Service Commission; and he did begin the reconstruction of the dilapidated American fleet by laying the first keels of America's steel navy.

Booker T. Washington

At the same time, Arthur could only watch as the population exploded past fifty million and followed the railroads across the continent. Industrial development was moving so swiftly—Rockefeller's Standard Oil Trust, Booker T. Washington's Tuskegee Institute, the first Labor Day parade in New York, Alexander Graham Bell's first long-distance connection between Boston and New York, Thomas Edison's incandescent electric lighting in New York—that the pontificating politicians in Washington and the state capitals were most harried to catch up.

Public disgust at Republican squabbles opened the door for the Democrats again in the 1882 midterm elections. The Democracy swept back into control of the House while shaving the Republican hold on the Senate to a splinter. In crucial New York, the

Democracy advanced a friendly, reform-minded sheriff from Buffalo named Grover Cleveland, who took the governorship easily and laid claim to the mantle of presidential contender.

The accelerating growth and slapdash political corruption raised a whirlwind that helped crash the economy again in the presidential year 1884.

Ulysses S. Grant lost everything but his name when his stock exchange firm failed on May 6, 1884. The panic that followed closed more than ten thousand banks and plunged Wall Street into another wasting bear market.

Grover Cleveland, the only Democrat to defeat the Republicans between the Civil War and WWI.

In the face of widespread business failure, labor strife, and public anger, James G. Blaine of Maine, now a private citizen, aimed for the presidency one more time.

What blocked Blaine was the sitting president Arthur, who wanted to keep his job, and the deep bitterness between the Stalwarts and the Half-breeds, who blamed each other for the rotten civil service, the general despair, and the murder of Garfield.

" 'I am holier than thou' has become nauseating to all Republicans, whether Stalwarts [Grant and Conkling Republicans] or Half-breeds [Garfield and Blaine Republicans]," wrote the *Tribune*'s Whitelaw Reid, a Blaine man, on the eve of the nominating convention.

The early June convention, again at Chicago's comfortable Convention Hall on Adams Street, was quick to establish Blaine as the solid choice of the young and ambitious members of the party.

"I am for Mr. Blaine," said a weighty new voice from Canton, Ohio, Representative William McKinley, forty-one, "because I think he is the strongest candidate in the country at large and that the people, having asked for his nomination, should be recognized in the Convention."

There was a nostalgic boom for beloved "Tecumseh" Sherman, the "grand old hero of Kenesaw Mountain and Atlanta." There was the novelty of the first Negro voice to chair the con-

William Tecumseh Sherman, 1884

vention, John R. Lynch of Mississippi. Then the delegates got to the business of approving a lengthy, quilt-patch platform.

There were traditional planks for trade protectionism and appropriate tariff reform, for bimetallism supporting the currency, for antimonopoly and antirailroad regulation, for labor reform, civil service reform, and veteran support. There were new twists—such as support for sheep husbandry, then in depression. There was an aggressive plank for the quick buildup of "a navy which takes no law from superior force."

The platform closed with a blast at the Democracy's sadism in the South: "We denounce the fraud and violence practiced by the Democracy in Southern States, by which the will of a voter is defeated, as dangerous to the preservation of free institutions."

Balloting was swift. From the first, Blaine held the solid lead over Arthur and the also-rans George F. Edmunds of Vermont, John A. Logan of Illinois, and John Sherman of Ohio. On the fourth ballot the withdrawing candidates gave their votes to Blaine, putting him over the top to tremendous cries of enthusiasm, "Blaine, Blaine, James G. Blaine! O-O-hi-O!" War hero John Logan settled for the vice-presidential nomination.

Theodore Roosevelt, 1884

Commenting on Blaine's victory was astute young New York assemblyman Theodore Roosevelt from the New York delegation. Roosevelt, twenty-six, had backed Edmunds of Vermont until the end. "I must decline to say anything about the result," he said. Then he found his bearing. "I will say this—that there are scores of people in my assembly district in New York who desire the nomination of Mr. Blaine." Later, Roosevelt was able to get an item printed back in New York stating that "Roosevelt the young New York reformer [had] a brilliant smile lighted by electrically bright teeth, unrimmed glasses over manly eyes, and a dark straw hat, with the straightest of brims"; moreover, he wore "No. 34 undershirts and No. 32 drawers."

What Roosevelt was discreet not to say was that Blaine's nomination had alienated the reform element in the party, headed by the old Liberal Republican breakaways Senator Carl Schurz of Missouri and editor E. L. Godkin of the *Nation*. The reformers now called themselves the Mugwumps—from the Massachusetts Indian word *mugquomp,* meaning "great personage." Mugwumpery was so disgusted by Blaine that its intellectuals and fellow travelers left the Republican party in order to support the Democratic nominee, Governor Grover Cleveland of mighty and crucial New York.

The 1884 campaign was splenetic, endlessly tactical, and most expensive. At the time it was called the dirtiest election in American history—overlooking the stolen electoral college of '76. The Blaine versus Cleveland battle was certainly unbridled when it did not hesitate to slander both candidates and their families.

Blaine was castigated by the Democrats for his well-documented selling of favors to the railroad interests and for his *spoilsmanship*—his willingness to look the other way when Republicans were caught at graft.

The Republicans counterattacked by charging that Cleveland had fathered an illegitimate child in Buffalo, a fact that Cleveland promptly admitted to regardless of the scandal.

Henry Ward Beecher, the aging abolitionist preacher in Brooklyn who sided with the Mugwumps, defended Cleveland's indiscretion with wit: "If every man in New York who had broken the Seventh Commandment would vote for Mr. Cleveland, we would elect him by 200,000 majority."

Henry Ward Beecher

The Republicans defended Blaine with adoration—boasting of his Scotch-Irish stock, his grandfather the commissary officer at Valley Forge, his dignified public service and savvy diplomacy. "O, thou desire of the nation, loved from the sea to the sea," crooned a campaign song to Blaine. "High above stain as a star, still upward thy path be."

Both parties knew the contest turned on New York's thirty-six electoral votes. The last weeks were ceaseless noise. "Here's to James G. Blaine!" called out the Republican clubs marching in the tens of thousands on New York's Whitehall Street. "He's the sort they raise in Maine! / Slander's tongues have wagged in vain, / Still he stands without a stain!"

Blaine defended his own wealth and the wealth of the party at an excessively splendid dinner of French cooking for two hundred potentates at New York's Delmonico's (which was later joked about as the "soap" dinner): "The Republican Party, gentlemen, cannot be said to be on trial. The Republican party in its twenty-three years of rulership has advocated the interests of this country far beyond that of its predecessors in

The 1884 Delmonico dinner for Blaine lampooned in Harper's Weekly, *November 15, 1884.*

office. It has increased its wealth in a ratio never before realized, and I may add, never before dreamed of."

On election eve, the Republican clubs waved the bloody shirt in verse with more South-bashing lyrics:

> *Blaine and Blue begin with B*
> *Gray and Grover, too, agree*
> *And blue can beat gray again*
> *With leaders like our Blaine of Maine!*

Over ten million voted. The early results showed Blaine ahead in the electoral college as long as he held on to New York's thirty-six votes. The vote dragged on through Wednesday, November 6. While the Republican party waited on fate, the *Tribune* exhorted the faithful with paeans: "Honor to the grand Republican party and its glorious leader. Honor to the steady veterans, whom the treachery of free traders made more devoted to the cause, who ignored personal differences, treated with contempt the filth and Chinese gongs with which the foe carried on the barbarous warfare, and who appealed to the reason and conscience of the people, not in vain."

New York slipped away to Cleveland. At 2 A.M. on Thursday, November 7, the Associated Press reported that Cleveland had gained a plurality victory in New York of just over one thousand votes out of more than one million in the state.

Those one thousand votes made Grover Cleveland the new president. Cleveland had taken nineteen states for 219 electoral votes, including the Solid South's 127 votes. Blaine had taken all the North except Connecticut, New York, and New Jersey, and all the West but Indiana for 182. Of note, the Greenback Labor party and the Prohibition party each gained enough votes in New York to have materially affected the result.

The Republican postmortem was sour. Singled out for an excuse was a bizarre incident just days before the election. Calling on Blaine at the party's Fifth Avenue Hotel headquarters was an embassy of Protestant preachers, including a troublemaker named the Rev. Dr. Samuel D. Burchard. After leaving Blaine, Burchard told the reporters outside that the Democracy stood for "rum, Romanism and rebellion." The Democratic press picked out this strange slander and used it on campaign posters labeled "R-R-R" to drive the Irish vote toward Cleveland.

Samuel D. Burchard

The Burchard incident was turned into a clever postelection verse entitled "RRR—1884—GOP."

> Blind, Blundering Burchard bluntly blurted out
> A bit of bigotry that blasted Blaine.
> R-um, R-ome, R-ebellion—rash reflecting R's
> 'To R is human,' we are taught again!

Blaine later reflected on the "RRR" scandal. "Oh, I had thousands upon thousands [of Irish votes]," he told the reporters. "And should have had many more but for the intolerant and utterly improper remark of Dr. Burchard which was quoted everywhere to my prejudice and in many places attributed to myself." He emphasized, *"But a lie you know, travels very fast, and there was not time before election to overtake and correct that one, and so I suffered for it."*

Young Theodore Roosevelt also reviewed the election. "What caused the defeat?" Roosevelt remarked to a reporter while on his way to his cattle ranch in the Dakotas for hunting and riding. "A combination of untowardness. If the Conkling wing of the Stalwarts had been true, if Burchard's alliteration had not been sprung so late in the campaign, if that 'soap' dinner at Delmonico's had not come off, if the Prohibitionists had been as loyal as they claim, Blaine would have won." Roosevelt added with a sharp tongue about the party battles of the past decade, "I am glad Roscoe Conkling, that flatulent pouter-pigeon in politics, is out of the Republican party at least."

It was also the Republican party that was out of the White House and the patronage power for the first time since the Civil War.

★ 1888 ★

Broad and boisterous Grover Cleveland turned the jokes about his overweight into public admiration when he courted and won the heart of the darling debutante Frances Folsom, whom the president married in the White House.

Cleveland was not as popular with his own supporters in office or in the press. Known for his independent decision making and aloof manner, he supported controversial civil service reform, which irked the purist Mugwumps. The president also dared controversial vetoes of pensions, which angered the veterans.

Cleveland's most dangerous step was to take on tariff reform in his 1887 annual message to Congress. What Cleveland wanted was to lower the tariffs to make goods cheaper for the South and West, leaving just enough revenue to satisfy the government's spending needs. What the president got was the immediate enmity of Northern manufacturers, Republican and Democrat, who did not want to be squeezed by cheap European imports.

The major successes of Cleveland's first term were corrections of past congressional abuses: these included the passage of the Electoral Count Act, which made each state responsible for its own electoral votes, and the repeal of the Tenure of Office Act, which had handcuffed presidents since Johnson by allowing Congress to dominate the appointments process. Also to Cleveland's credit was the encouragement of a rapid construction of a steel navy by an aggressive Navy Department.

The Cleveland presidency was the high-water mark of congressional meddling with the chief executive. In 1885 a monograph entitled *Congressional Power,* by young professor Woodrow Wilson, made a strong case for enhanced presidential power.

Cleveland's worst first-term mistake was to stir up the powerful lobby of the Grand Army of the Republic by offering to return the Confederate battle flags to the Southern states. In reaction the GAR declared Cleveland an enemy of the fallen heroes of the war.

There was little Cleveland or the Democratic House could do about bad weather. It was Cleveland's bad luck to be in office when a series of droughts cursed the Great Plains states and crushed the agricultural prices. A low tariff combined with no rain to plunge farmers from Ohio to Iowa into famine.

The presidential year 1888 opened with the perennial James G. Blaine still first in the hearts of Republicans.

The surprise was that Blaine appeared to have no tolerance for the battle. He departed for a European tour and, from Britain, wrote two unambiguous letters to the Republican press that he was not a candidate. Did he mean it? The result was that the press announced in May, "Mr. Blaine Ends All Doubt / He Cannot Accept Nomination / Letter to Whitelaw Reid, Esq."

Whitelaw Reid, a Blaine diehard, wrote in admiration that Blaine's withdrawal was "an act of magnanimous self-abnegation rare in political history."

The party was left to sift for a popular candidate to match the lordly Blaine. Everyone felt stumped. "No parallel since Lincoln's time" was the word.

Fortunately, the Democrats were no better organized. The Democracy renominated Cleveland without energy at St. Louis just two weeks before the Republican convention.

The Republicans mocked Cleveland's clumsiness and obesity in a verse entitled "White House Reveries / 2 A.M."

> *And so I have received the nomination;*
> *I, Grover Cleveland, late of Buffalo*
> *And somehow it now brings me more elation*
> *Than when they chose me first, four years ago*
> *For then it dazed me by its suddenness;*
> *This time I won it by my—my finesse!*

The Republicans returned to Chicago's Convention Hall. As the delegates gathered in mid-June—in a withering heat wave—the leading

The ninth Republican convention at the newly built Auditorium building in Chicago, Illinois in June 1884. Harper's Weekly, *June 23, 1888.*

names for the nomination were an uninspiring melange of Western men, Governor Russell A. Alger of Michigan, Senator John Sherman of Ohio, Senator William B. Allison of Iowa, and former senator Benjamin Harrison of Indiana.

Early on, a pundit spoke shrewdly about a dark horse candidate. "In case Sherman is beaten," he said, "I am confident that Harrison will be nominated."

The platform was devoted to high tariffs. "We are uncompromisingly in favor of the American system of protection," the document declared. "We protest against its destruction as proposed by the President and his party. They serve the interests of Europe; we will support the interests of America. The protective system must be maintained."

Other planks included familiar support of the bimetallism of gold and silver as money, and assurance of generous pensions to veterans. There was opposition to taxes on tobacco and liquor, to Chinese immigration, to trusts and monopolies, to railroad landgrabs. New details included support of the organization of the territories into eight more states of the union (North and South Dakota, Washington, Montana, New Mexico, Wyoming, Idaho, and Arizona) and condemnation of the Mormon Church as a polygamous menace.

On foreign policy, there were planks calling for a steel navy, a big merchant marine, and new coastal fortifications. There was also a demand that the country push ahead for the Nicaragua Canal in the Isthmus of Panama.

To attract the Prohibition party, which had made the difference in New York in '84, the platform closed piously, "The Republican party cordially sympathizes with all wise and well-directed efforts for the promotion of temperance and morality."

Before the balloting, the delegates were balanced between John Sherman of Ohio and Benjamin Harrison of Indiana. Then a telegram arrived from Blaine at the Scottish border at Newcastle stating that he refused to lend his support to any boom. Was this a last-moment attempt to get the draft? It didn't work, for on the first three ballots on Friday, June 23, the enthusiasm was for Sherman of Ohio, who was followed by a long list of also-rans from a long list of states. Blaine was near the bottom of the count.

After a steamy night of deal making, the convention was back at work on Saturday afternoon. The deadlock was maddening in the heat wave. The break came when New York's popular Chauncey M. Depew withdrew his own name from nomination and threw New York's vote to Harrison.

The next day the Republican *Chicago Tribune* charged that Depew's move to Harrison and away from the another major contender, Allison of Iowa, was made because Allison was antirailroad and Harrison was prorailroad. Chauncey Depew rejected the idea with less than convincing rhetoric: "[These] statements are most unqualifiedly false. Railroad interests had nothing whatever to do with it. We found that we could agree on Harrison."

It took another sweaty day of bargaining among the party bosses (such as Senator Matthew S. Quay of Pennsylvania, industrialist Mark Hanna of Ohio, and former senator Thomas C. Platt of New York) until all the friends-of-Blaine forces concentrated their votes—on the eighth

Matthew S. Quay

Thomas C. Platt

ballot on Sunday—to nominate the little-known dark horse Benjamin Harrison of Indianapolis, Indiana.

The Republican genius was that Harrison, fifty-four, a full-bearded war hero, was now a candidate for the same job his famous grandfather had held briefly. That grandfather was Whig president William Henry Harrison, the war hero of the 1811 Battle of Tippecanoe, who had died suddenly in office a month after the inauguration in 1841.

In New York the reaction to Harrison was bittersweet. Blaine loyalists distributed little slips of paper decorated by a spread-eagle design that read, "We'll vote this year for Tippecanoe / And for James G. Blaine in '92." Wall Street, bulling up the prices in anticipation of a Republican victory, was more blunt about why it favored Harrison. "Never mind that the prices are up," said a broker. "I have been living on beer and sandwiches for several years and I'm going to vote the Republican ticket and live better the next four years."

Another trader, a Georgian in New York, said, "I was named for this young fellow's grandfather and I think I shall vote for him."

Levi P. Morton

Boosting the Republicans in critical New York State was the choice of Harrison's running mate: the confident New York banker Levi Parsons Morton. Morton, sixty-four, was living with the irony that in 1880 he had declined the offer of the vice presidential spot on the doomed Garfield's winning ticket. Morton's brown stucco house at 85 Fifth Avenue displayed a portrait of Garfield in the hallway and a portrait of Arthur in the library.

The Republicans opened the campaign with witty songs that laid out the twin issues of personality and tariff.

> *O Cleveland, you must face defeat—*
> *Put up that old bandanna,*
> *You cannot Cannot CANNOT beat*
> *This man from Indiana*
> *That flies the Union banner;*
> *With Harrison we'll win the day*
> *As sure as comes election*
> *Down with the wipe that's stamped Free Trade—*
> *We'll give it no protection.*

Benjamin Harrison's acceptance letter from Indianapolis made the Republican demand for high protectionist tariff the central debate of the contest: "The Republican party holds that a protective tariff is constitutional, wholesome and necessary. . . . We believe it to be one of the worthy objects of tariff legislation to preserve the American market for American producers, and to maintain the American scale of wages, by adequate, discriminating duties upon foreign competing products."

Benjamin Harrison

Harrison followed the tradition of staying at home during the campaign, but he did speak frequently to all comers, emphasizing his support for working men and women, for Negro rights, and especially for his railroad friends. Meanwhile, the Republican national chairman, Senator Matthew S. Quay of Pennsylvania, camped at party headquarters at the New York Fifth Avenue Hotel to raise a huge campaign chest from the manufacturers, as much as three million dollars. Wall Street turned out in parade the last week before the election, the William B. Seward Club crying out for Harrison and taunting Cleveland: "Grover, good-bye!" and "Put Grover in the cold, cold ground."

Campaign verse pounded the point that Cleveland's position against tariffs and supporting foreign trade was bad for American business.

> All is over with Free Trade Grover
> Adieu, Dear Grover, taking leave of thee,
> We use the sad initials R.I.P.
> Don't mourn him, friends, why would you be dejected?
> Because a free-trade head lies unprotected!

The last days of the campaign Republicans tried a campaign trick that may have swayed the Irish vote in New York. A Republican agent named George A. Osgoodby pretended to be a naturalized British-American named Murchison when he wrote a bogus letter to a British lord, Sackville-West, asking for advice on how to vote. Sackville-West was duped and wrote back that he favored Cleveland and the Democrats. The Sunday before the election the *New York Tribune* reproduced a facsimile of Sackville-West's letter across the front of its second section under the inflammatory headline "Lord Sackville's Interference." A fair assumption was that whomever the English approved of, the Irish should hate.

The Republican return to power in the canvass of 1888. Harper's
Weekly, *August 18, 1888.*

Twelve million voted. The Sackville-West dirty trick might have made
the difference in New York City, which went for Harrison, bringing
along the state's 36 electoral votes. Harrison swept the North and West
for a total of 233 (201 needed). Cleveland took Connecticut, New Jersey, the Border states, and the Solid South.

The Republicans also gained back the House. For the first time since
Grant's administration, the Republicans now controlled Washington.

Wall Street celebrated its bet on the Republican protectionists to end election week by closing firm: brassy New York Central at 109, innovative Pullman of Illinois at 170.

The Republicans celebrated their relief by speaking of the party with elevated language. For the first time *Grand Old Party*—used ten years before about the Southern Democracy—entered the lexicon of electioneering as a pet name for the Republican party.

"Let us also be thankful that under the rule of the *Grand Old Party,*" read the *Tribune* editorial the day after the victory, "which has helped the country to become more honored and powerful, richer and more prosperous, happier in its homes and more progressive in its institutions, than any other country on earth, these United States will resume the onward and upward march which the election of Grover Cleveland in 1884 partially arrested."

★ 1892 ★

Benjamin Harrison proved good to his word on protectionism, and he made the 1890 McKinley Protectionist Tariff the watchtower of his pro–Wall Street administration.

Harrison also delivered on the Republican platform promise of civil service reform, when the president named young New York assemblyman Theodore Roosevelt as civil service commissioner. Harrison kept his promise to the veterans by signing the 1890 Dependent Pension Act, which established the service pension, and he aimed to preserve public lands by elevating the Interior Department to Cabinet level and by passing the 1891 Forest Reserves Act.

Harrison also tried to keep his promise to support Negro rights by advocating, though not getting passed, young Massachusetts congressman Henry Cabot Lodge's Force Act, meant to protect Southern Negro suffrage.

In the Senate, veteran John Sherman of Ohio pushed through two more campaign promises. First was the 1890 Sherman Anti-Trust Act (written by George Hoar of Massachusetts and George F. Edmunds of Vermont), the first federal action to restrain or control business monopolies such as Rockefeller's Standard Oil Trust. Second was the 1890 Sherman Silver Purchase Act, which delivered on the bimetallism plank's promise to support the price of Western silver by increasing the mandated monthly federal purchase to 4.5 million ounces of silver at the prevailing price. This silver policy was an update of previous legislation (1878 Bland-Allison Act; passed over Hayes's veto) that had hoped to satisfy the Western silverites in Congress. Sherman was now making a direct payoff to the mining state interests: in exchange for Western support of protectionism, the Republicans would support the silver mines. The danger not faced up to at the time was that artificially propping up the price of domestic silver—which had no overseas market—would lead to two serious troubles, both paper currency inflation and a run on the federal gold supply. Sherman took the long-term risk for the immediate gain of votes for the McKinley tariff.

The tariff platform promise was the most immediate cause of pain for Harrison and the Republican party. The battle was between the so-called revenue tariff advocated by the Cleveland Democrats, and the so-called protectionist tariff advanced by the Republicans. In 1890 the popular chairman of the House Ways and Means Committee, William B. McKinley of Canton, Ohio, shepherded through a stern protectionist tariff that was meant to keep foreign goods out of the United States and to keep prices high for American manufacturers.

Prices climbed, punishing the South and West especially. The Democrats were quick to blame the McKinley tariff for a sharp trade decline in 1890 and for rising unemployment. McKinley defended himself, "What boots it that the products of the great West find their markets in New York and Chicago rather than in Europe?"

Thomas B. Reed

In the 1890 midterm elections, the public's angry response to the economic downturn was to turn McKinley out of office in Ohio and the Republicans out of power in the House. The election was a landslide for the Democracy, leaving the new Fifty-second Congress in the House: Democrats 235, Republicans 88, and 9 others who sided with the Democrats. The able Republican Speaker Thomas B. Reed of Maine was replaced by a Solid South Georgian. The Republicans retained control in the Senate only by counting on eight vacillating mining state votes.

Secretary of State James G. Blaine, more imperial than ever as Harrison's prime minister (this was Blaine's second tour at State), was not visibly bothered by the party's 1890 whipping. "I do not mean to imply, gentlemen," he said in Philadelphia, "that the results of the election for Congress will in any degree affect the Republican Party. From the time of John Quincy Adams to Abraham Lincoln (cheers), with one exception, every Administration lost its second congress. [It] is easily recovered."

Wall Street was not sanguine. The markets sold off sharply at the defeat, helping push the nation into a debt crisis of bank failures at home and in Europe. (Barings Bank failed in mid-November.) "Wall Street is so sensitive at this time," reported a financial correspondent for the *New York Tribune*, "that a whisper of 'take care' has more influence than volumes of favorable facts. The cry now is 'there can be no market till time loans are available again.' "

Out of office, Grover Cleveland struck a blow by declaring in the winter of 1891 that the Republican policy of bimetallism was a "dangerous and reckless experiment of free, unlimited, and independent coinage."

The Sherman Silver Purchase Act—which degraded the price of gold by insisting the government purchase 4.5 million ounces of silver each month—was a bomb that did not go off for two more years. Meantime, the Republicans were knocked by the fickle financial men for their stubborn devotion to protectionism and opposition to the so-called free trade of cheap imports from Europe.

Despair at weak prices and labor troubles was widespread across the country. The swift rise of the People's Party of the U.S.A., calling itself the Populist party, was a sign of new competitors at the polls. At a July 1892 convention in Omaha, Nebraska's cozy Convention Hall, the Populists wrote a scathing platform on the state of the Union under Harrison: "We meet in the midst of a Nation brought to the verge of moral, political, and material ruin. Corruption dominates the ballot-box, the legislative, the Congress and even touches the ermine of the bench."

The Populists wanted an end to the exploitation of labor by the protectionist capitalists. "Wealth belongs to him who creates it," declared the Populists. "If any will not work, neither will he eat."

In June, at Minneapolis's Convention Hall by the Falls of St. Anthony, the Republicans gathered at the nominating convention to answer the charges of congressional mismanagement and presidential lassitude.

One more time James G. Blaine was advanced as the savior of the party. This time Blaine wanted the crown. He resigned from the Cabinet just days before the convention to make clear he was a candidate against Harrison. "The ex-Secretary has been made a candidate by the will of his people," claimed the *Chicago Tribune*.

Harrison supporters did not retreat from the plumed knight. The delegates immediately divided into two hostile camps. Both candidates, Harrison at the White House, and Blaine at Bar Harbor, were in constant communication with their managers to encourage deal making.

Banners hanging from the rafters tried to remind the convention that the real challenge of the convention was to maintain protectionism—"American Wages for the American Working Man." Speakers tried to re-

Press Room at the Exposition Building in Minneapolis for the tenth Republican convention. Harper's Weekly, *June 16, 1892.*

mind the convention that the real adversary was the Democracy and the likely opponent of good old Grover Cleveland. "We face 156 electoral votes out of the Solid South," declared a delegate at the podium, "out of 444 total. We must fight together!"

A New York delegate spoke to the future of the party: "Sometimes we are told that the mission of the Republican party is ended; we have met our destiny and fulfilled it. But the destiny of a progressive party is never fulfilled in an advancing and expanding National life. So long as there remains a wrong to be redressed—just so long will this be a mission for the party."

The platform detailed the party's mission: the protection of the tariff, bimetallism to satisfy the silverites, building of the navy and merchant marine, demand for the Nicaragua Canal, support for veterans' pensions, and continuation of the reforms of the Civil Service under Commissioner Roosevelt.

There was special attention to the Ku Klux Klan horrors in the South, now masquerading as justice by Judge Lynch law or by open massacre of olive-skinned European immigrants: "We denounce the continued inhuman outrages perpetrated upon American Citizens for political reason in certain Southern States of the Union."

The permanent chair of the convention was the newly elected governor of Ohio, William B. McKinley, the man who once had taken the blame for the tariff controversy. "Major" McKinley gaveled the floor to order at noon on Friday, June 10, to begin the balloting. The contest was surprisingly swift, with Harrison sweeping to nomination on the first ballot: Harrison's 585 to Blaine's 182 and McKinley's 182.

The delegates sought to counter the powerful New York Democracy by nominating yet another popular New Yorker for the vice presidency: this time the *Tribune*'s champion, handsome Whitelaw Reid, fifty-five, who had served for the last three years as minister to France.

Whitelaw Reid

The future of the party was not overlooked. As McKinley left the hall to take a streetcar back to the West Hotel, several delegates addressed him, "Well, you'll be nominated by acclamation in 1896, anyway." McKinley was too loyal and too wise to look ahead. "Gentlemen," he answered, "what voice I have left is for Harrison, and wherever he is, my heart follows."

Reaction to Harrison's renomination was eager. "The Republican party is as solid as a cube," wrote the *New York Tribune*. "Every side of it squares with patriotism and American interests."

Andrew Carnegie, the richest man in America, who was also denounced by many for the brutality of his Pinkerton agents against strikers in Pittsburgh, telegraphed the president, "The American people know a good thing when they got it. Heartiest congratulations—you deserved this triumph."

New York Central president Chauncey Depew closely analyzed Harrison's win over Blaine: "Harrison has three elements of great strength. He was strong with the business men. Nine-tenths are for Harrison. Also the working men dependent on the manufacturers. And the 'solidity' of the old soldiers—four hundred and fifty thousand voting veterans."

In the presidential campaign, Harrison's strengths were not obvious. The president remained largely at the White House, permitting his surrogates and Whitelaw Reid to tour the country. On the other side, Cleveland was a crafty speaker, and Democratic vice presidential nominee Adlai Stevenson of Illinois was a major asset on the stump in the old Northwest.

Protectionism remained the issue that caused the trouble for the Republicans. Popular Republican congressman Galusha Grow of Pennsylvania, a veteran campaigner at sixty-eight, tried a joke to explain the high tariffs on produce and goods: "The Irishman who was boasting to the marketman on the

Galusha Grow

An early combination of the Republican elephant and the GOP nickname, after the Minneapolis convention. New York Tribune, *June 18, 1892.*

price of his potatoes," Grow related with a smile, "said to him that he could buy as good potatoes in Ireland for 10 cents a bushel. The market man replied, 'Why didn't you stay in Ireland, then?' 'Ah, sure,' said Pat, 'I didn't have the ten cents!' "

Governor McKinley of Ohio campaigned hard and far afield for Harrison. "Free trade builds the factories of Europe," McKinley argued in Brooklyn. "Protection builds the factories of the United States. Free trade lights up the furnaces of Europe, and puts out the fires in the furnaces of America."

Three young Republican stars, Theodore Roosevelt of New York, Elihu Root of New York, and Henry Cabot Lodge of Massachusetts, spoke for Harrison at a rally of Harvard men at Cambridge. Roosevelt slapped at the Democrats, "To pretend that all tariffs are unconstitutional is worthy of the Dark Ages of Nullification and the Montgomery Convention." Forty-seven-year-old Root, Harrison's secretary of war (and Roosevelt's future prime minister and eventual betrayer), remarked that he was sure these young men would make good Republicans: "Youth is nothing if it has not the spirit of progress." Congressman Henry Cabot Lodge of Massachusetts, forty-two years old, future lord of the Senate, said this was his forty-seventh speech on the campaign trail, and his tired voice could only add that the Harvard men should remember, "This is a meeting of young men of the same kind of young men who went to the front in 1861. The Republican Party is the same to-day as then."

Election eve, the party was most confident, trusting the citizenry understood that protectionism was patriotism. In New York, the Republican national chairman Thomas H. Carter (later senator of Montana) closed the campaign by promising victory of at least 229 electoral votes. Wagering at New York's plush Hoffman House favored Harrison 4–3. On election day on the floor of the New York Stock Exchange, there was wild betting at three o'clock at the Lackawanna post to take one thousand dollars even on Harrison and give 2–1 odds on the Empire State going Republican.

Thomas H. Carter

The Republicans were shocked to lose the election. At first report the results were close, but by 2 A.M. Wednesday, November 9, the word was in by telegraph that Cleveland had taken New York State by a fifty-five thousand plurality. Along with a Solid South, a near sweep in the West, and shocking wins in Illinois, Indiana, Ohio, and Wisconsin, Cleveland piled up a massive 277 electoral votes to Harrison's weak 145 electoral votes.

The popular vote was closer. The nation was now at sixty-two million. Twelve million men voted. Forty-six percent went for Cleveland, over 43 percent for Harrison. Populist candidate James B. Weaver of Nebraska gained 8 percent (one million votes) for a pro-labor, pro-inflationist, anticapitalist platform that captured four states and 22 electoral votes out of longtime Republican strongholds in the Great Plains states. The zealous Prohibition party gained a quarter million votes, including thirty-eight thousand in New York.

Wall Street capitalism marked the return of Free Trade Grover by selling off. "The market was weak," said the *Tribune* correspondent. "A feeling of uncertainty and distrust prevailed." Of note, the new industrial trust company stock General Electric of Schenectady, New York, closed 1892 at 109 on the precipice of the worst bear market of the century.

★ 1894 ★

The legend of the Grand Old Party grew like topsy after the defeat of '92.

It was notably Governor McKinley of Ohio who chose to speak of the *Grand Old Party* whenever he regretted the loss of Republican power. "This Grand Old Party we love," McKinley would say to his neighbors at the state capital of Columbus. "Our Grand Old Party," McKinley would offer to visitors on his famous front stoop in Canton.

The term *"grand old party"* had first been used as far back as 1878 by a Georgia politician to refer to the Southern Democracy as the "grand old party" that he loved from before the war, when men were Democrats and dogs were abolitionists. However, through the magic of rhetoric and bombast, the pet name was completely transformed through the bitter Blaine-Cleveland election of '84, the desperate hope of the Harrison-Cleveland victory of '88, and then the shock of the Harrison-Cleveland defeat of '92 to emerge as a Republican euphemism.

By *Grand Old Party,* McKinley meant more than romanticism. He was speaking to the longing of men his age and temper for the glory of the righteous anti-Nebraska days, for the tattered dreams of the veterans of '63. With this careful turn of phrase, McKinley and the Republican press that echoed him were helping to create a new way of looking at Republicanism. Not just the party that beat Douglas and broke the Rebellion, not just the Radical scolds who reshaped the Constitution and reconstructed the South, not just the hard campaigners who waved the bloody shirt and worshiped Grant and outfoxed Tilden and survived the Stalwarts, but also the party of lost greatness, hallowed tradition, bottomless sentiment. *The Grand Old Party.*

As McKinley reminisced, Cleveland's big victory was sliding into catastrophe.

Cleveland was a hard-luck president, and his second term began rocky in the spring of 1893 with a shocking panic in the markets. The ticking Silver Purchase Act bomb finally went off in mid-April. The rumor spread that the U.S. Treasury might stop redeeming silver with gold. Meantime, the Western silver producers compounded the worry by declaring they would not accept Treasury notes for their silver if the paper was backed only by the same silver.

A gold run started like a thief in the night. On Thursday, April 20,

The New York Tribune *tower and building, flanked by the* New York Sun *and the* New York Times *on Newspaper Row, New York City.* Harper's Weekly, *October 27, 1888.*

1892, two big foreign banks, including Lazard Frères, withdrew enough gold to push the U.S. Treasury holding below $100 million (against $155 million in 1890). The next day the run took wing, and there was a $4.5 million gold withdrawal from the Treasury. The reports from Washington were that Cleveland and the Cabinet were divided on whether to honor all redemptions. By the end of April the U.S. gold reserve had fallen to $93 million. The stock market was weaker and weaker. "The root of the evil indisputably is the compulsory purchase every month of 4,500,000 ounces of silver bullion," reported the *Tribune* financial correspondent. "To accomplish the repeal of the Sherman law of 1890 almost any means would seem to be justified."

On Monday, May 1, with Cleveland serenely in Chicago to open the World's Columbia Exposition, the industrial stocks fell out of bed. General Electric sank on Monday from 101 to 97. On Tuesday GE led the industrials down to 95; on Thursday to 91.

Then on Friday, May 5, the market cracked at the opening. When the chairman of the exchange swung the gavel at ten o'clock, traders sold madly, pushing General Electric to as low as 60. The carnage was indiscriminate. Even proud Pullman of Chicago, master of the railroad cars was pushed through 200 to as low as 175.

Trading floor at the New York Stock Exchange on Broad Street the way it looked in the 1880s and 1890s. Harper's Weekly, *September 10, 1881.*

"More menacing than at any period since the days of '73," the *Tribune* correspondent declared the next morning, which scared everyone, since '73 had been a black depression. A trader whistled out in the dark, "The worst is probably over."

The worst was just beginning—a bear market much darker than the panic of 1873, a sell-off in stocks and a run on gold that drained the federal gold reserve to $82 million by the end of '93 and to a shocking $62 million by the end of '94. General Electric went below 30, Pullman below 154. Liquidations swept the country from the high-and-mighty Union Pacific to tens of thousands of banks and businesses. Along with the credit crash and stock plunge came devastating inflation and grinding unemployment. Dread spread like typhoid fever. There was no dole, no charity. The dark face of famine walked across the country.

Grover Cleveland did the worst thing possible and vacillated indecisively and crudely. At first he listened to the Western and Southern silverites in the Democracy and let the markets alone. Then he listened to the Eastern gold men in the Democracy and moved against silver. In desperation Cleveland forced the Democratic Congress to repeal the trouble-causing Silver Purchase Act by November 1893. Meanwhile, the Democratic Congress tried to tinker and fudge a new kind of tariff bill (e.g., farm implements would not be taxed) that was hated by all sides as a mishmash. All of it was too late to stop the depression.

Federal leadership was adrift. Hundreds of thousands were on strike. The gold reserves were in free fall. The winter of '94 saw Populist politicians transform the jobless into so-called armies of protest led by so-called generals of dissent. The most infamous "general" was Jacob S. Coxey of Ohio, who led Coxey's Army on a march from Ohio to Washington in the spring of '94 to demand a public works relief program for the unemployed and a sharp increase in tender notes to pay off debts. Cleveland ordered the leaders arrested.

By summer 1894, Cleveland alienated all that was left of his support when he sent troops against the famous Pullman Company's strikers in Chicago.

The Republicans campaigned for the '94 midterm elections with a dead-shot eye at the disgraced Democracy.

In November former president Benjamin Harrison came to New York City to speak for his old vice president, Levi P. Morton, who was now running for New York governor. "I have wondered why our Democratic leaders should hate an American smokestack," Harrison argued, still hammering on the protectionist plank. "And yet they have in their campaigns described the American manufacturer as a thieving robber-baron."

Harrison added that he'd just come from the labor unrest at the Fall River, Massachusetts, mill, where the strike had been broken by desperation. "I walked through the lines of workmen from some of their shops, bearing on their hats this legend, 'Wages 22 and ½ percent off.' So it is—down, down, down. My countrymen, let us stop this [Democratic] war on American industry."

A vindicated and vindictive Harrison put his case bluntly: "We were told that the rich were getting richer and the poor poorer; and to cure that imaginary ill, our political opponents have brought on a time when everybody is getting poorer."

On Tuesday, November 6, 1894, the Republicans won everything in sight north of the Mason Dixon line. "Looks Like a Landslide / *Republicans Sure of Victory,*" boasted the early headlines. The later ones got better:

A Universal Triumph
The Nation Redeemed
A Republican Congress Elected

The new Fifty-fourth Congress was solidly Republican. And in the House there was a two-thirds majority for veto power: Republicans 244, Democrats 105, with 7 others. In the fall state elections, too, excepting the Solid South, the verdict was *"A Republican Tidal Wave."* Even better for future prospects, the Western silverite Democrats had been so angry at Cleveland that many had gone over to the Populists.

Railroader and later New York senator Chauncey Depew called the November election a *revolution*—deliberately using the word that reached back to the early days of the party's victory over the Democracy. "The primary cause of this *revolution,* I have no hesitation in assessing," said Depew, a man who had been a Republican loyalist since his youth in the 1850s, "was the unheard of condition of the number of men out of employment, not alone in this city and over the state, but over all the states of the Union, as the direct outcome of Democratic rule."

The reawakened Grand Old Party could feel that this was a sea change of its fortunes. The party felt its confidence surge like a bull market. Congress was safely back in Republican hands, the state legislatures of powerful New York, Pennsylvania, and Ohio were firmly Republican, and everywhere was the confidence of revolutionaries at the ballot box.

The panic of '93 and the Republican landslide of '94 turned out to be a profound turn in the dance between the two great American political parties: the mother Democracy and the promising child of the Republicans.

In the crucible of unemployment, strikebreaking, inflation, gold runs, spasmodic and nearsighted legislation, there emerged a rhetorical debate that would color the political contest for the next century. On the one hand, the Republicans accused the Democracy of alienating the working man from his employer. On the other hand, the Democracy accused the Republican party of cynically becoming a creature of thieving robber-barons.

Chauncey M. Depew

Both charges were tactical; both had merit. A generation before, the Republicans had broken with the Democracy as the party of the Southern slaveholders. Now the Republicans hammered the Democracy as the party of Southern backwardness and Northern unemployment.

The Republican party had stubbornly found its up-to-date theme, and it would tenaciously make it work for another generation. Once it had saved the Union. Now it saved the nation's economy. Once it had turned itself into a Radical promulgator that fought for the liberty of men. Now it turned itself into a conservative arbiter that fought for the liberty of the American marketplace. Once it had been angry and revolutionary and earnest and liberty-loving. Now it was angry and revolutionary and earnest and the friend of the boundless liberties of the marketplace.

A vote for the Republicans was a vote for the American smokestack, for the American farm, for the American fireside, for all American profit.

Ready to sing this ballad for the looming twentieth century was that champion of Republican protectionism and Republican sound money and Republican railroad and industrial interests, the handsome, homespun governor of Ohio, William B. McKinley, now fifty-one and as well-meaning a politician as the nation had seen since Lincoln—the savior who would gather all the luck of end-of-the-century prosperity and make a joyful noise for the *Grand Old Party*.

"That Damned Cowboy!"— The Amazing Accident of Teddy Roosevelt

1896–1919

President McKinley reached down his right hand to pat the head of a brown-headed girl who had waited an hour to greet her hero.

After a moment her mother beckoned her away from the crush of the crowd. There were hundreds waiting in the receiving line here at the daz-

The Temple of Music at the Pan-American Exposition at Buffalo, New York: site of the 1901 assassination of McKinley. New York Tribune, *September 17, 1900.*

zlingly modern American Exposition, the new American showplace of the new American age—in Buffalo, New York.

It was Friday, September 7, 1901, and the late afternoon sun was bright in the tall, clean windows of this opulent octagon of the Temple of Music, a vast music hall built to serenade and satisfy hundreds of thousands of visitors.

The president bent his knees to ease his back. He was worn down after a day's excursion to Niagara Falls, yet he would not retreat. These thousands had come for him alone. William McKinley was the most popular American president in memory, as famous in office as Lincoln was in martyrdom. Twice elected president by healthy pluralities in 1896 and 1900 over the silverite Democratic Populist William Jennings Bryan, McKinley was five months into his second term and splendid in his mastery of American politics.

William B. McKinley

Darling of Wall Street's financiers, swift victor over the degenerate Spanish Empire, liberator of the slave colonies of Cuba, the Philippine Islands, and Puerto Rico, commander of the swiftest steel navy at sea, unchallenged ruler of the freshest world power of the fresh century, McKinley stood that day among ferns and palms and easy organ music at the zenith of his career. He had come to Buffalo three days before on a serendipitous holiday with his wife and close family in order to open the fantasy architecture and fountain-strewn grounds of the exposition. "Expositions," he'd declared, "are time-keepers of progress."

Besides, it was lazy summertime, the nation was still on extended Labor Day holiday, and the president was having fun.

Next in the receiving line there was a small, pale young man dressed in black. Why was the young man's right hand wrapped in a white handkerchief?

McKinley smiled, bowed, and reached down for the young man's good left hand. Two feet away. The young man thrust out his bandaged hand.

It was not yet 4 P.M. The destiny of the United States of America was about to change course forever.

Crack! Crack!

At the first shot, the president grabbed his chest and trembled; at the second shot, McKinley bent forward and lurched backward against his personal secretary George B. Cortelyou at the left.

Before the assassin could fire again, two Coast Guard artillerymen, privates O'Brien and Neff, hurled themselves at the shooter and dragged him to the ground. The handkerchief on the assassin's hand was afire. One soldier got the .32-caliber pistol away. Another private jumped on the pile. A secret serviceman charged into the mayhem. The shooter was small, frightened, and whining. He'd later say they hurt his head. His name was Leon Czolgosz, his age, twenty-six, and he was from a large, hardworking Polish Catholic family in Cleveland, Ohio. He was not insane. He said he was an anarchist. He had seven weeks to live.

The huge crowd was now alert to something strange and scary. Those closest to the trouble reeled backward from the smell of gunsmoke.

Is it the president? Is he hurt? Were those shots?

George Cortelyou

McKinley, supported by George Cortelyou and the president of the exposition, John Milburn, retreated stiffly and slowly from the chaos, one step, one more. The president pawed under his overcoat at his waistcoat. There was a chair. McKinley sat down and took off his hat. His face was the white of death.

"George!" McKinley said to Cortelyou.

"Mr. President, what is it?"

"Be careful about my wife," said McKinley "Do not tell her."

"My God!" cried out a nearby dignitary, the ambassador of Mexico Manuel Azpiroz. "Mr. President, are you shot?"

The president watched the pile of soldiers struggling to hold the shooter. "Let no one hurt him," McKinley told Cortelyou.

"This hurts very much," McKinley told Cortelyou.

Cortelyou looked at the president's face and felt terror. Panic swept the men around McKinley. The president kept talking. He told them to remain calm; he repeated that no one should tell his wife, that no one should hurt the attacker.

This measured stoicism was classic gallant McKinley, who was the same square-jawed and brave man he'd been at twenty, when he'd served his commanding officer Colonel Rutherford B. Hayes of the Twenty-second Ohio Volunteers. Hayes had called the baby-faced second lieutenant McKinley "exceedingly bright, intelligent and gentlemanly—one of the best." Veteran of the Shenandoah Valley, veteran of the Radical politics of Reconstruction, veteran of the labor battles of Ohio that had established him as a politician of the people, this honorable, dignified, God-fearing man began his final ordeal by asking for calm.

Cortelyou argued, "You are wounded, let me examine you."

McKinley tried to deny the fact. "No, I think not." The president could hear the screams of panic from the crowd. He added, "I am not badly hurt, let me assure you."

The president brought out his hand. He couldn't deny the blood, nor the spike of pain in his gut. He felt the cold. Shock. He fainted in the chair. He opened his eyes. He felt himself lifted into an automobile.

The president was taken to the exposition's clinic, which was just across the promenade. Surgery began at 5:30 P.M. with standard ether anesthetic. There were two bullet wounds. The breast wound, below the right nipple, was judged harmless: the missile had exited through the flesh.

The stomach wound was sinister, four inches to the left of the nipple, four below it. Dr. Roswell Parke made the incision at the entrance of the wound. The missile had penetrated the anterior wall of the stomach. The doctor turned over the organ and found the exit wound. The pulse was a high 130. The doctor probed for the bullet and could not find it. He did find a small piece of the president's clothing that had been punched into the path of the shot. It was 6:12 P.M. The president was given thirty-five minims of brandy with a hypodermic. The intestines were examined and wrapped in moist towels. Still no bullet to be found. Time to get out. The abdominal cavity was flushed with salt water. Where was the bullet? The doctors sutured shut all the wounds with double rows of silk. The surface wound was given seven deep silkworm sutures with catgut in between. At 6:50 P.M. the anesthetic was discontinued.

The doctor admitted he had failed to find the bullet. The best hope was that the missile had lodged in the back muscles. The immediate dangers, he said, were peritonitis and septicemia.

Dr. Parke said, "The next forty-eight hours will tell the crisis."

It was a pastoral evening in the United States but the crisis was just beginning for another man, several hundred miles away, Vice President Theodore "Teddy" Roosevelt of New York—the young man who was second in line by accident, the young man whose sensational personality would see America through the week-long dying of the revered McKinley and then launch America like a cavalry charge into the twentieth century.

Theodore Roosevelt, 1900

The first Associated Press report moved on the telegraph wire two or three minutes after the shooting.

At that moment Roosevelt was at a huge outdoor banquet at the summer home of Nelson W. Fisk—on the gorgeous Isle of La Motte in the middle of Lake Champlain.

This was the famous annual celebration of the Vermont Fish and Game League, and there were fifteen hundred people on the lawn at generous tables under gay awnings. The vice president had just finished his remarks. Roosevelt was the most sought-after public speaker in the United States now. It was his fate to have been maneuvered by party bosses out of his first-term New York governorship and onto McKinley's ticket. The vice presidency was a well-known dead end. Since the inauguration, "Teddy" Roosevelt had worked ceaselessly to make his vice presidency a worthwhile office. Still, he was said to be frustrated and thinking of studying the law, thinking of a future without public office.

Roosevelt grinned mightily with his well-known cameo of an electric grin, gleaming teeth, brush mustache, small pince-nez. Then he sat down beside his companion and old mentor, former war secretary and now Republican senator from Vermont Redfield Proctor. It was time to eat.

Just then host Nelson Fisk was called to the telephone inside his house. It was a call from the wife of the president of the New England Telephone Company.

Moments later Nelson Fisk hurried to his friend Senator Proctor and told him the president was reported gravely wounded at Buffalo.

Grandfatherly Proctor took Roosevelt inside the house before he reported the news.

Roosevelt was overcome and speechless with the shock. When he recovered, he went outside to tell the celebrants the news and that he must leave them immediately. The crowd was in tears. No one could believe it. McKinley? Why?

Roosevelt had to wait eighty minutes on the island until the yacht *Elfrida* arrived to take him across the water to Burlington. Before embarking, he telegraphed ahead to Buffalo, "I shall not stop in Burlington, but shall proceed at once. . . . Buffalo is about 450 miles, and it will be well along in the day tomorrow when I arrive."

At 8:30 P.M. Roosevelt arrived in Burlington and boarded a specially made up fast train to connections at Albany for Buffalo. The press was on the platform at Albany demanding an interview. "No, I am not prepared to give out any interviews," said Roosevelt. "The awfulness of the calamity is appalling, and it would be a desecration to talk of the future plans at this time. I shall think this matter over seriously."

The whole nation was just beginning to think over seriously what had happened. The omnipotent Republican party—now in control of every state in the North and all branches of the federal government—was pressed specially to respond with authority and certainty.

At Cleveland, McKinley's mighty mentor, the pink-cheeked industrialist and Republican national chairman Senator Marcus Alonzo "Uncle Mark" Hanna of Ohio, was at the Union League Club when a reporter told him the news.

"I don't believe it," Hanna answered, starting immediately for the door. "I can't believe it. No, I won't believe it. There's no use talking to me about it. I cannot believe anything like it." Hanna mounted one of his trust company's streetcars to get to his office.

Marcus A. Hanna

How could he believe it? Hanna, sixty-three, was a dignified and ruthless politician who had devoted his hard-won wealth and Quaker wit to the career of his friend William McKinley. Hanna had been first to help elect McKinley governor of Ohio, then to secure for McKinley the '96 Republican presidential nomination by acclamation and the presidency by majority, then to take John Sherman's seat in the Senate for himself (Sherman became secretary of state). Since then Hanna had stood by his president through the Spanish War and the triumph of 1900. McKinley was Hanna's champion, his Apollo, his sunshine.

Later, when Hanna had seen undeniable news of the shooting, he shared his darkest thoughts. "It is horrible, awful! McKinley never had any fear of danger from that source. Of course, I never talked to him about such a subject, but I know he never dreamed of anything like this happening." Hanna then spoke ominously, "I only hope that he is not seriously injured, but I am afraid that my hope will be in vain. I do want to reach the president before he dies, if he is going to die. Nobody can be safe from the works of a insane man, it seems. It is terrible."

Hanna started by special train for Buffalo. Friday evening, the whole government was in motion as the terrible drama at Buffalo took on a formal schedule.

The first lady was at the presidential party's living quarters at John Milburn's fine Delaware Avenue house. Ida S. McKinley had been an invalid for many years, ever since the deaths of her two children. She had been with her husband that morning on the excursion to Niagara Falls and had come back to Delaware Avenue to rest. She was kept from the truth for many hours. At dark she asked, "I wonder why he does not come?"

Soon after the surgery, the sleeping president was moved by automobile to the Milburn house and settled in the main bedroom on the second floor. Guards appeared outside. The neighborhood was hush-voiced with dread. At the corner of Delaware and Franklin Street, the press took up a deathwatch.

Through the night and into a bright Saturday, Cabinet members still on extended Labor Day holiday (Congress was adjourned) entrained for Buffalo. Agriculture Secretary James Wilson arrived with his wife Friday evening. War Secretary Elihu Root—"I cannot talk. What is there to say?

Ethan Allen Hitchcock

This is terrible, terrible!"—came from Southampton, Long Island. Interior Secretary Ethan Allen Hitchcock—"I am too terrified to make any expression whatsoever"—came from Dublin, New Hampshire. State Secretary John Hay at Newbury, New Hampshire, could not be immediately reached. However, the news quickly traveled to as far as half a world away at Manila, where the future president William Howard Taft, then governor-general of the conquered Philippines, and General Arthur MacArthur, the commander of the occupying forces, cabled, "Greatly shocked by report that President has been shot. Anxiously await exact information."

The president's beloved brother, Abner McKinley, was reached with his family at a ranch at South Platte Canyon, and he started from Denver by special train.

Elihu Root

John Hay

William Howard Taft, 1901

Gen. Arthur MacArthur

Saturday morning, the Republican party chronicler, the *New York Tribune,* chose a headline that sounded the worst: "President's Condition Grave." The bulletins from the sickbed were not promising. The temperature was 102. No sign of blood poisoning. Two doctors and two nurses used digitalis to quiet his pulse. No food, only water. When the president awoke, Mrs. McKinley was able to visit him once. She broke down when he asked her to be brave for both of them. The president had seen gut-shot men die. He knew he was likely doomed. He aimed to hold out until the Cabinet arrived and last details were resolved.

Saturday the gloom settled on Wall Street's weekend session, and the prices plunged, GE down 6½ percent to 253. When the financier J. Pierpont Morgan had been told the news on Friday night, he'd grabbed his companion's arm and gasped, "What's that? Is it serious?" and then he'd gone into a meeting with other bankers to plan how to stem a market panic. On Saturday night, a broker admitted, "Without the slightest wish to rank Colonel Roosevelt below his chief, a general impression among people of means and substance, is that the vice-

J. Pierpont Morgan

president does not possess the poise which is conspicuous in Mr. McKinley's make-up. *Uncertainty* is the worst thing that the Street fears."

The only certainty on Saturday was that the shooter, Czolgosz, was a complete cipher. He called himself an anarchist. "I never had much luck at anything and this preyed on me," he wrote in a confession about his crime. He confessed that he had stalked McKinley for days through the exposition grounds. "I got to the Temple of Music the first one," he wrote with revealing self-pity, "and waited at the spot where the reception was to be held. Then he came—the President—the ruler—and I got in line and trembled until I got right up to him, and I shot him twice through my white handkerchief. I would have fired more, but I was stunned by a blow in the face—a frightful blow that knocked me down—and then everybody jumped on me. I thought I would be killed, and was surprised at the way they treated me."

Czolgosz was asked if he'd meant to kill the president. "Yes I did." Czolgosz added, "I am an anarchist. I am a disciple of Emma Goldman. Her words set me on fire."

Sunday morning brought a bright hope. The Cabinet was checking in one at a time, including the imperial John Hay, and the news was good. The president was rallying. He had better color. His pulse was consistent.

Hanna and Roosevelt (the vice president was staying at the Delaware Avenue home of a friend), attended church together and then hurried to the Milburn house afterward to enjoy the good news. Roosevelt gave out a rosy statement to the press that he would not assume the president's duties. "The President's able and loyal secretary, Mr. Cortelyou, is fully competent to perform any routine duties until the president is able to resume his labors."

Hanna told the reporters, "He's still a sick man. But when a man like the president makes up his mind and says, 'I will not die,' the old one cannot knock him out."

From overseas the telegrams were still flooding in from London, St. Petersburg, Berlin, Stockholm, because after the smashing 1898 victory of the United States over ancient Spain, Europe was respectfully intimidated by the all-popular leader of the Americans.

The good word got out by Sunday evening. "Extra!" the newsboys barked at 6 P.M., "The President will live!"

Monday morning's headlines answered the nation's prayers: "President Better / Hope for Recovery Grows Strong."

The doctors felt confident of their miraculous patient, and on Monday they ordered nourishment, beaten eggs administered through the rectum. The wounds looked to be healing. Midafternoon, the temperature was 101 and the pulse a moderate 113.

The lingering concern was the missing bullet. The speculation was that it was in the back's lumbar muscles, where it would stay encysted and harmless. In Orange, New Jersey, Thomas Edison had hurriedly assembled one of his new X-ray machines and rushed it north with two technicians to show the doctors how to use it to locate the bullet. Yet no one moved to try some new Edison gizmo on a mending president.

Roosevelt was buoyed by the improvement and on Monday evening was overheard in a conversation with a Negro yardman on Delaware Avenue.

"Kunnel, kin I shake yo han'?"

"You certainly may," said Roosevelt.

"Kunnel, ain't you kind of skeered to be stopped on de streets dese days by strangers?"

"No, sir," said Roosevelt, grinning. "And I hope no official of this country ever will be afraid. You men are my protection, and the foul deed done on that afternoon will make you the more vigorous in the protection of the lives of men whom you elect to office."

Roosevelt commented about McKinley, "I believe the bulletins being issued are none too sanguine. In fact, I know they are not. . . . I believe the illness will be a brief one and the recovery will be rapid. I had two men shot in the same manner in the Cuban campaign. They lay in the marshes for some time without attendance, and both recovered."

Later Mark Hanna announced to the reporters, "Just glorious, my boy!" The Associated Press had set up a mobile telegraph cabin at the crossroads, and Hanna was given to drifting there to visit the reporters. "Just glorious! The president is doing splendidly. Why, he'll be asking for a cigar next. He wants to talk, and does so whenever the doctors let him!"

Tuesday morning the president was declared past the crisis, with a temperature at 100.4 and a pulse at 118. "The little piece of lead in the muscles of the back," read the report, "is giving the physicians no concern whatsoever. Once encysted, it can do no harm. The X-Ray machine is ready for use."

Tuesday evening, Roosevelt was so confident that he made plans to depart for his home in Oyster Bay, New York. At 9:30 P.M. at the train depot, Roosevelt was asked if this might turn into a Garfield tragedy. "Ah, but you forget twenty years of modern surgery, of progress," Roosevelt answered. "From what I can learn, also, the Garfield wound was much more serious than the wound of President McKinley. I believe that the president will recover, and I believe it so thoroughly that I will leave here tonight."

Roosevelt said he was puzzled about the assassin. "What has disturbed me has been to find a reason for even anarchists to attack a man like President McKinley. Here is the one country where the anarchists are allowed perfect freedom of speech. Here the ruler is a man descended from farmer stock, self-made. . . . Why shoot him?"

Meanwhile, the anarchist Emma Goldman was arrested at Chicago on suspicion of conspiracy. Then thirty-two, and fierce-faced in her pince-nez, she was equally puzzled by Czolgosz. "Am I responsible," she asked, "because some crack-brained person puts a wrong construction on my words?" On Tuesday the news from Washington was a Senate bill that was introduced to throw out and keep out anarchists. (Goldman was detained for three weeks and then released without charges.)

Wednesday brought the best news of the week. The president was alert and in control of his famous compassion. "How are the people all over the country taking it?" McKinley asked his secretary, George Cortelyou, who was now his interlocutor to the press. "I sincerely hope that nothing that happens to me will distress the people of this country."

The president was moved to a new bed. One doctor said, "He is a very sick man, but his condition under the circumstances could not be better."

Another doctor mentioned that he had reopened the stomach wound that morning in order to clean it because it had not healed properly and quickly. "No suggestion of pus around the wound," the doctor added, calling his work a "secondary operation."

Still, no one moved to use the X-ray machine to locate the bullet.

Edith Roosevelt

Meantime, Roosevelt had reached Albany on Wednesday morning to rendezvous with his beautiful wife, Edith, six children, and many house servants. At 7 A.M. the Roosevelt entourage departed on a train north to the Adirondacks hunting resort of the Tahawus Club, ninety-three miles north of Saratoga, near Newcomb Lake. Roosevelt was in a good mood. He and his family rode buckboards the final thirty-five miles to the resort, arriving at 7 P.M.

Thursday, at Buffalo, rain and gloom descended on the Milburn house and the president. Something was wrong.

The immediate problem was said to be intestinal toxema. The president was suffering severe cramps. A doctor announced, "The president should not have been allowed to take any food through the stomach. The president has not had a natural bowel movement since he was shot."

The hope was that this was just a gaseous stomachache. All afternoon the president sank as his pulse raced. There was still no sign of peritonitis or septicemia.

"I am so tired," the president complained in the evening. "I am so tired."

McKinley intimates gathered quickly, Attorney General Hitchcock and Agriculture Secretary Wilson arriving at 9:35, Abner McKinley ten minutes later.

Outside, the sentries in their ponchos paced their beats in the downpour, bayoneted guns at reverse. The newspaper tent and telegraph hut were alight with moment-to-moment bulletins. The word was out that the doctors were panicky. There was big trouble.

Friday morning the president's pulse had raced to 122. McKinley was in and out of consciousness, and the stomach pain was intense and merciless. The team of physicians stood helpless.

By breakfast there were special dispatches sent out to Roosevelt in the Adirondacks and to Mark Hanna who had gone back to Cleveland. The Cabinet members who had stayed on in Buffalo called at the Milburn house all afternoon.

The storm outside was cataclysmic, lightning flashes and rolling thunder. George Cortelyou often went out in the rain to the curbside to tell the press there was nothing new to report. Then, toward evening, Cortelyou announced, "Gentlemen, we have kept faith with the people. We must continue to do so." Then he told them the president was dying.

Mark Hanna arrived by special train at 6:49 and raced in an automobile to the Milburn house. Root, Hitchcock, Knox, and Wilson greeted Hanna downstairs. He asked to go upstairs immediately. Hanna saw McKinley's pain-twisted face and collapsed in tears. Cortelyou helped the senator from the sickroom. Hanna begged, "I'm all right now. I'm all right again. I must go in and see him again."

At the bedside again, Hanna tried, "Mr. President, Mr. President, can't you see me? Don't you know me?" Hanna was terrified. "William, William, speak to me." In sobbing groans, Hanna was helped from the room.

The doctors knew the president could die at any moment. Before 8 P.M., the doctors used oxygen to revive the president so his wife could say goodbye.

The first lady moved close to her husband.

McKinley was hallucinating. He hummed a hymn. "Good-bye, all," the president is reported to have said to his wife. "Good-bye. It is God's way. His will be done."

The president's extremities were al-

Ida McKinley

ready cold. At 8:30 he became alert enough to beg the doctors to stop the pain and let him die.

What was the pain? The autopsy would show that the missing bullet had destroyed the pancreas. Wednesday's surface infection had been the clue. McKinley died of gangrene that spread up the path of the bullet. One doctor put it bluntly, "Death was by slow rotting." McKinley's stomach was so badly gangrenous that it was perforated.

The last five hours were horror. Sturdy George Cortelyou's health was weak for years from the strain. Abner McKinley soon after collapsed with paralysis and died within three years. At 10:55 the back of the Milburn house was suddenly lit up, but it was premature. Bulletins came every ten minutes. Death was officially set at 2:15 A.M.

In the flood of grief, a few like Root and Knox asked, Where's Roosevelt?

Roosevelt had gone camping for the weekend. Friday morning, ignorant of the president's decline, he had left his family at the Tahawus Lodge and ridden out with guides to find game off the Adirondacks Trail.

Messages from Buffalo had gone to Saratoga, then to North Creek, where the telegraph agent telephoned as far as possible to a house ten miles south of the Tahawus Club. Couriers rode off to the lodge. Not finding the vice president, the alarm was sounded—all available horsemen to the search.

At 5:30 P.M. riders found Roosevelt just making camp on Mount Marcy. His first reaction was stunned disbelief. Then he became the Theodore Roosevelt of the legends. Mounting up, Roosevelt set out into the fading light to cover the thirty-five rugged miles to North Creek. He rode in darkness by dim moonlight as the storms approached from the west. Reaching the upper clubhouse of the Tahawus Club at 1:15 A.M., he changed horses and charged onward to North Creek. Delaware and Hudson superintendent C. L. Hammond had brought up a special train to North Creek: Engine No. 362, the fastest on the road, along with executive coach No. 200 and a special dining car carrying cooks and porters. Roosevelt reached North Creek at 5 A.M. and jumped onboard. At daybreak he boarded another fast train at Albany, where he read the *New York Tribune*'s morning headlines.

The President Dead
He Expired at Buffalo at 2:15 o'clock
The end peaceful and painless
The President's Life Slowly Ebbed away

An apocalyptic rainstorm hit Buffalo. All Saturday mourners called at the Milburn house to leave their cards. Every half hour there were telegrams from the road as a sleepless Roosevelt crossed the Empire State at top speed.

At 1:50 P.M. Roosevelt reached the Terrace Station and was motored to Delaware Avenue and the house of his friend, Ansley Wilcox. The Wilcox house was put under guard by a mounted army unit. Soon after, Roosevelt slipped out the back of the house with Wilcox and boarded a carriage for the short ride to the Milburn house. Half a block on, Roosevelt, showing his tension, leaped out of the carriage and ordered a mounted escort to withdraw. A private visit, he said.

Roosevelt did not see Mrs. McKinley, nor did he view the body. He stayed a few minutes with the members of the Cabinet, especially his longtime friend Elihu Root, and then he returned to the Wilcox house.

Despite their shock, the officials were trying to make up a dignified way to pass power from the dead to the living.

At 3:15 several carriages bearing the Cabinet arrived at the Wilcox house, a large colonial manse from the early days of the city. All crowded into the dining room. Roosevelt and Elihu Root stood on one side. The other Cabinet members arranged themselves on the other side. Twenty newspapermen were ushered into the room as witnesses.

The house was silent, people bowing their heads and whispering, as if death was present. It had stopped raining.

Root stepped away from Roosevelt. "Mr. Vice-President," Root said, "I have been requested by all the members of the Cabinet of the late President McKinley who are present in the city of Buffalo, being all except two (John Hay and Treasury Secretary Lyman J. Gage), to request that for reasons of weight affecting the administration of the government you shall proceed without delay to take the Constitutional oath of office as President of the United States."

Roosevelt's face was rigid. He was about to become living history. He spoke directly into Root's eyes, "Mr. Secretary, I shall take the oath at once, at the request of the members of the Cabinet, and in the hour of deep and terrible national bereavement, I wish to state I shall continue absolutely unbroken the policy of President McKinley for the peace, prosperity and honor of our beloved country."

A federal judge stepped forward with a Bible. Roosevelt took the oath in a strong voice and then signed the document that certified his office.

There were no congratulations. Immediately Roosevelt asked the Cabinet to stay in the dining room for the first official meeting. The newspapermen filed out, and the doors were closed. Presently Senator

Hanna arrived and went into the meeting. Two hours later Theodore Roosevelt emerged as the twenty-sixth president of the United States.

"Let us take a little walk," Roosevelt said to Elihu Root, "it will do us both good." The two started out the door. Soldiers fell in behind. Roosevelt turned around and gave an order, "I do not want to establish the precedent of going about guarded."

With that declaration, Roosevelt, who would spend the rest of his life as either president, or president maker, or presidential candidate, strolled off arm in arm beneath the dripping elms and coloring oaks with Elihu Root, his present secretary of war and future secretary of state and eventual betrayer.

Behind them was the catastrophe of a murdered old hero, the last of the American presidents who'd fought in the foundry of the Civil War.

Ahead of them was the challenge of preparing America as a world power suited to the mysterious twentieth century.

And it was all an accident of Republicanism.

"Now look!" Mark Hanna later told New York Republican boss Thomas C. Platt, who'd forced Hanna to put Roosevelt on the McKinley ticket the year before, *"That damned cowboy is the President of the United States!"*

★ 1896 ★

Five years before, in the presidential year 1896, Theodore Roosevelt had been happy to have a political job at all, as the energetic and ingenuous president of the board of police commissioners in New York City.

The big Republican news that year was not in New York, where a nonpartisan mayor was bold enough to hire the ambitious Roosevelt, but rather in Ohio, where Governor William B. McKinley was being groomed as the new savior of the party.

President Grover Cleveland still ruled in Washington, to the disdain of the Republicans and the disgust of his own party's radical wing, the silverites. The silver controversy now pushed aside every other controversy of the last thirty years. Few noticed the Supreme Court's momentous *Plessy v. Ferguson* decision that gutted all civil rights advances since Lincoln's administration with its "separate but equal" concoction and entombed the Southern Negroes in the jim crow laws. And few cared about debating the tariff issue that had dominated the last four campaigns. Just a handful made noise over the U.S. Marines landing at Nicaragua to put down a revolution, or argued about the United States' ambitions in mediating between Cuba and the Spanish Empire.

Rather, every disagreement was overlooked for the supreme debate over the free coinage of silver. For four years Cleveland had struggled to double-talk his way around the bimetallism problem. The question was whether silver was as good as gold to support the currency in the world markets where the gold standard was law. The Democratic party was dominated by inflationary, insurrectionary silverites. The silverites' demand was for a return to the free and unlimited coinage of silver at the fixed rate of 16:1—a policy that had just been overturned by the Congress in hopes of easing the panic of '93. Not only did the silverites want the restoration of the old Sherman law, they also wanted the Treasury ordered to buy all the silver produced with gold-backed certificates.

McKinley, campaigning craftily from his front porch in Canton, Ohio, was clearly identified with the gold standard as the sole foundation of the dollar—what was then called the sound money policy of the Grand Old Party.

McKinley presented a clear vision of his party. "The American people want an opportunity—and they want it early—to return to power that *Grand Old Party* in every branch of government."

McKinley continued, "Here in this country we are all dependent upon each other, no matter what our occupation may be. All of us want good times, good wages, good prices, good markets, and then we want good money always. When we give a good day's wages to our employers, we want to be paid in good, sound dollars, worth 100 cents and no less."

The debate over silver and gold was actually a sign of the much hotter new national issue of class warfare. Growth, industrialization, labor strife, trust and railroad booms had all come together to create an American landscape where the rich and the poor, the lucky and the tragic, those with advantages and those without advantages, all entered into a political debate that would dominate the twentieth century. As early as the election of '96, two decades before the Bolshevik Revolution, the Republicans and Democrats were arranged into warring camps that changed little for the following one hundred years.

In the winter of '96, Whitelaw Reid's *Tribune,* looking to McKinley's campaign, articulated the class-warfare lines that were already drawn. The editorial was entitled "American Silver Communists":

"Mad and blind hatred of property, hatred of those who appear more fortunate and seem to have easier lives, notions that all men ought to be equal in income and expenditure and tastes and engagements, as well as legal rights with a passionate desire to tear down the existing state of things if it cannot be made to suit such a fanaticism—that is the desperate and dangerous force which only uses the silver issue as a means of striking at all property and all the prosperous.

"Does anybody ask how such a brainless craze came to exist in this free country?

"The Democratic party cultivated it laboriously and patently for twenty-five years, especially in all the Western and Southern States, as its only hope of defeating the Republican party.

"Every day and every night it appealed persistently to the mean hatred of success by those who do not succeed, of property by those who have none, of employers by employed, of capital by labor, and contrived at last to create a communistic spirit in free America which is as ignorant, as stupid, as vindictive and madly destructive as that which lighted the torch and danced around the corpses in Paris."

Kindly, gentle, smart, accomplished McKinley put the best face on the Republican argument that the Democrats were destructive cynics. However, the campaigns of '96 and afterward can all be read for the rhetoric. "Silver" and "Democratic" were said to be violent and communist, just as "gold" and "Republican" were said to be elitist and Wall Street.

From the day in February 1896 that former president Benjamin Harrison withdrew his name from active candidacy for the convention, the party was committed to McKinley. Cleveland industrialist Mark Hanna used his wealth and cunning to line up Southern Republicans to add to the phalanx of supporters from the Northwest and solid Ohio.

The McKinley men marched through Republican state conventions all spring. By May the *Tribune* was routinely using headlines such as "The McKinley Tide / General Confidence that He Will Be Nominated," and "McKinley's Victory Sure / Complete Rout of His Foes."

Nonetheless, the New York boss Senator Thomas Platt and the Pennsylvania Republican boss Matthew Quay did try to offer an alternative to McKinley by booming popular governor Levi P. Morton of New York. The electoral college was still a paramount concern, and everyone knew that to avoid another Democratic victory like Cleveland's, New York must be won.

In June the Republican delegates traveled to tornado-devastated St. Louis to gather in the electric-arc-lit and rectangular Convention Hall built for fourteen thousand. Thirty thousand McKinley soldiers were said to be in town, sounding cocky: "The man who talks now of defeating McKinley's nomination is nothing less than a lunatic," said one McKinley man, "and he should be in an asylum instead of a political convention."

McKinley managers industrialist Mark Hanna and railroad man Chauncey Depew of New York camped at the Southern Hotel to entertain all the McKinley friends on the Republican National Committee.

The most stubborn holdout in town was the cadaverous party boss (and soon to be senator) Thomas Platt of New York, who announced with indignity, "Notwithstanding the action of the packed National Committee, Mr. Morton [governor of New York] will have 60 of 72 votes from the New York delegation."

The highest-minded McKinley doubter in town was Senator Henry Cabot Lodge of Massachusetts (whom Roosevelt envied and admired greatly), who backed for nomination Speaker of the House Thomas B. Reed of Maine. "Enterprise has folded its wings," Lodge spoke against the Democrats, "and mopes and blinks in the market place."

McKinley's lead was insurmountable—built up by the maneuvers of Mark Hanna (who saw to it that several Southern delegations included Negroes for McKinley). On Thursday, June 18, McKinley was nominated with 661½ votes out of 906. The celebration that ignited at St. Louis spread by telegraph wire to a whistle-blowing, brass-cannon-blasting celebration back at Canton for the cherished Major McKinley.

Suddenly the party was united again, and no negative voices were heard. Gone with Blaine, who had died in 1893, was the acrimony of the Stalwart and Half-breed and Mugwump years. When Blaine's name was mentioned at the podium, he received a greater cheer in death than he ever had in life.

Cheers for the deceased James G. Blaine at the St. Louis convention in June 1896. New York Tribune, June 18, 1896.

Gone too were any platform struggles. Protectionism was listed up front with its twin call for reciprocity trade treaties. Sound money was the platform's foundation. There was no debate about the failed policy of bimetallism from the last twenty years. Gold was king. "All our silver and paper currency must be maintained at parity with gold," the platform declared.

Well down on the list of planks—after an assertion of the Monroe Doctrine, demands for a Nicaragua canal, a bigger navy, and enforced immigration law—was all that was left of civil rights. The Republican party condemned the "barbarous practices" of lynchings in the South— the only sign in either of the major party platforms of the Klan and its horrors.

Also at the end of the platform was a plank for women's suffrage. "We favor the admission of women to wider spheres of influence."

Garret A. Hobart

McKinley could run safely throughout the North on the whole platform of protectionism, sound money, and a big navy. To be sure of the East, McKinley and Hanna urged the convention to name for the vice presidency Garret A. Hobart of Paterson, New Jersey, a round-faced, walrus-mustached, dark-eyed fifty-two-year-old who had served the party ably since the Civil War and who was a solid gold man.

Preparing for a slugfest of campaign, the Republican National Committee chose Mark Hanna as the chairman of the party. "My loyalty and my love for our candidate," Hanna said of why he worked so hard for McKinley. "All I've done is that I gave the plain American people a chance to voice their sentiments in regard to their favorite presidential candidate, and their answer was, 'William McKinley, American.' "

McKinley and Hanna's campaign was helped measurably by the fracturing of the Democratic party in July at the Chicago convention. Driven to surrender by Cleveland's shilly-shallying and the crushing depression, the Democracy quit the conservative North and lurched toward the radical ideas of the South and the silverites. Favored for the presidency at the outset was Senator "Silver Dick" Bland of Indiana. Yet coming from out of nowhere was a phenomenon in American politics, ex-congressmen William Jennings Bryan, thirty-six, of Nebraska.

Tall, swarthy, stentorian, and handsome, Bryan stood up on July 9,

1896, to make a platform speech in support of the free and unlimited coinage of silver—the silver communist plan. What happened instead was that Bryan's astonishing oratory got him nominated for president by acclamation.

"We are fighting in defense of our homes, our firesides, our families," Bryan argued against the Republicans. "Our petitions have been scorned, but now we have no petition to offer, for we are strong in our might and we defy them. They ask us if a Robespierre will arise. No, instead of that the people need an Andrew Jackson." Bryan closed his spectacular philippic with a declaration of class war on McKinley and the GOP, "We shall answer their demand for the gold standard by saying to them, '*You shall not press down upon the brow of labor this crown of thorns. You shall not crucify mankind upon a cross of gold.*' "

Three days later in Canton, Ohio, McKinley stood on his famous front porch and answered Bryan's rhetoric with a history lesson of the battle between the parties. "Then it was a struggle to preserve the government of the United States," McKinley recounted. "Now it is a struggle to preserve the financial honor of the government of the United States. Then it was a contest to save the Union. Now it is a contest to its spotless credit. Then section was arrayed against section—Now men of all sections can unite, and will unite, to rebuke the repudiations of our obligations and the debasement of our currency."

McKinley never left his front porch. By November, McKinley's optimism had overwhelmed Bryan's tireless traveling and speechifying for silver and labor and Populist leveling. To buoy the GOP, Mark Hanna raised a giant campaign chest by calling in the bank and railroad and oil trusts and telling them each how much he wanted them to contribute. Hanna didn't have to ask more than once. Wall Street was committed to McKinley's campaign speeches calling for a "full lunch pail" and an "honest day's work" and "sound money."

On October 31, Flag Day in New York, the Republicans staged a triumphant parade from Wall Street up Broadway. Behind banners such as "Our National Honor Must Be Maintained," and "McKinley Is a Peach," twelve dozen bands blared out the "Star-Spangled Banner," "Three Cheers for the Red, White, and Blue," and the party favorite, "Marching through Georgia."

The Tobacco Leaf Trader Sound Money Club featured an Uncle Sam figure on stilts who was flanked by two toy elephants branded with the letters GOP. The Columbia University Sound Money League showed three lines of students dressed in white beavers, white sweaters, and gold trousers and stockings. The dominant color of the parade was yellow for the gold plank—yellow slouch hats, yellow coats. And everyone was

The Sound Money parade for McKinley and Hobart on Broadway, New York City in October 1896. New York Tribune, *November 1, 1896.*

chanting: "Left—Left—Bryan will get left." Or a putdown of the sil-verites: "1-2-3-4-5-6 teen Nit! / Rah! Rah! Rah! Mac!" Or the taunt:

"Little Billie Bryan / Sitting in the sun / Wishing—how he's wishing / 'Lection Day Was Done!"

On Tuesday, November 3, McKinley spoke confidently from his front porch, "There is no safer jury in the world to sit upon American interests and American honor than the American people themselves."

Fourteen million men voted. McKinley gained 51 percent of the popular vote, making him the first majority Republican president since Grant; he took a huge 271 electoral votes. Bryan held the Solid South and several mining states for 176 electoral votes. The two splinter parties, the National "Gold" Democrats and the Prohibition party, ran far behind.

The Republicans also retained control of both houses of Congress and dominated the state elections.

From Cleveland a joyful Mark Hanna telegraphed McKinley, "The feeling beggars description. The boys at the Union Club send love and hearty congratulations."

The next day, with the Republicans in command, the bear cave of a stock market celebrated with a brave rally. "Tens of millions of capital only await[ed] the signal," remarked a trader. Even crushed General Electric climbed above 30. The country was in a feisty mood. A week after the election, the *Tribune* headline was superb foreshadowing for the battles ahead: "Spain Would Be Easily Whipped / Her Navy No Match."

In the first American campaign battle of class warfare, the Republican verdict was "Anarchy and Repudiation Tramped Under Foot." The score was GOP 1; the Democracy (mocked as the Same Old Party and the *Popocracy*) 0.

★ 1900 ★

William McKinley's first administration had a golden touch and a fist of a steel navy.

Republican achievements were well trumpeted. Immediately after inauguration in March 1897, McKinley called a special session of Congress, and, with Speaker Thomas B. Reed's muscle and Chairman of the Ways and Means Nelson Dingley, Jr.'s hard work, pushed through the protectionist Dingley Tariff Act.

State Secretary John Sherman moved to annex the Hawaiian Islands (over the protest of Queen Lilioukalani) and then to paint Spain into a corner over its rebellious Cuban colony. Meanwhile, the markets continued to rally on the sound money policies, helped considerably by the

USS Maine *at its commissioning.* Harper's Weekly, *May 26, 1888.*

bountiful gold strike in Alaska that brought in fresh supplies to the gold reserves beginning with the summer of '97.

In the winter of 1898, the mysterious sabotage on the battleship USS *Maine* in Havana harbor and the loss of 260 men brought the nation together for the strange, gleeful little Spanish-American War fought on two oceans.

Theodore Roosevelt had left New York for a Republican patronage post at the Navy Department. He used his position to demonstrate a spontaneous talent for innovation. Immediately after *Maine* sank, Roosevelt cabled Commodore George Dewey to tell him to prepare for an attack on Manila Bay in the event of war with Spain. By mid-April, McKinley and Congress had declared war. By Mid-June, Roosevelt had left the Navy Department in order to raise a volunteer mounted rifle regiment, the Rough Riders, and had landed his unit with the American army at Santiago, Cuba. By mid-July, Roosevelt was a much publicized hero for the Battle of San Juan Hill. ("You can fall back if you want to," Roosevelt remarked under fire on the critical day of his combat, on July 1–2, 1898, "but my men will hold it till the last man dies!")

By mid-October, Spain had agreed to surrender Cuba, the Philippines,

Rough Riders

and Puerto Rico to a U.S. delegation at Paris that included Whitelaw Reid. And by mid-November the war hero Theodore Roosevelt, after a whirlwind campaign wearing his Rough Rider hat, was elected the Republican governor of New York.

McKinley fanned out the American navy across the Pacific. Insurrections in the Philippines were met with force and eventually with tact by Governor-General William Howard Taft and General Arthur MacArthur. The European adventurism in China was met with the Open Door Policy dictated by new secretary of state John Hay (Lincoln's recording secretary) and then with U.S. military action during the Boxer

Rebellion. The Congress supported the American foreign enterprise by authorizing expenditures for a dozen new steel capital ships, ammunition, sailors, and generous expansion of Annapolis.

The presidential year 1900 opened with the capstone of the administration's sound money policy in the passage of the Gold Standard Act, fixing the gold dollar at 25.8 grams, nine-tenths fine. Gold was king, and the markets celebrated with more buying.

McKinley was so popular that the only question in his administration was who would be his vice president—because the amiable and harmless Garret A. Hobart had died suddenly the previous fall.

Immediately the party's favorite son for the vice presidency was Governor Theodore Roosevelt of New York. But not because Roosevelt coveted the job. In fact, Roosevelt said he didn't want the job. "Under no circumstances!" Roosevelt declared. However, the New York party boss, Senator Thomas C. Platt, wanted to get rid of the troublesome Roosevelt, who had crossed the bosses by imposing a franchise tax on the Traction Trust, that is, the streetcar companies, which were controlled out of Philadelphia by the Pennsylvania boss, Matthew Quay, and which shared their income with the Platt New York City Republican machine.

The problem with Platt's cynical plan to dump Roosevelt on the vice presidency was that McKinley and his mentor, national Republican chairman and Ohio senator Mark Hanna, let it be known that they did not want Roosevelt on the ticket. They thought "Teddy" Roosevelt impudent, naive, unpredictable, unreliable, and just generally a fast-talking, scene-stealing show-off.

The cunning Platt and Quay aimed to play the McKinley and Hanna disapproval against the Roosevelt refusal to get what they wanted in the end. Before the June convention, Platt told the press, "All I know about it is that the governor [Roosevelt] says he will not take it. . . . He has told me that the inactive life he would have to lead in Washington as Vice-President would kill him."

But then, as the delegates gathered at the ornate new Great Convention Hall in Philadelphia on the shore of the Schuylkill River (near the University of Pennsylvania), Platt told the reporters that he wanted Roosevelt on the ticket because he wanted the best for the party. Platt also mentioned that he appreciated why Hanna didn't want to force Roosevelt onto the ticket—because the president didn't think it right to push anyone into such a difficult national service.

Roosevelt understood Platt's game and declared, "My decision is irrevocable." Roosevelt even sent out his longtime friend Senator Henry Cabot Lodge to the reporters to make sure they heard that Roosevelt was

New York party boss T. C. Platt aims to sideline a Roosevelt train onto the do-nothing vice-presidency. New York Tribune, *June 20, 1900.*

sincere. Lodge told the press he planned to nominate Navy Secretary John D. Long to the second spot.

The new junior senator Chauncey Depew of New York told the press that he thought Roosevelt was the man for the job. "For the last forty years within my memory of national conventions," Depew observed, "the vice-presidency has always been a matter of political expediency or dicker."

The dickering continued as Roosevelt, a New York delegate to the convention, took his room at the Walton Hotel. "I have nothing to say," Roosevelt told the delegates who started petitioning him even before he finished breakfast. Later Roosevelt sounded his exasperation: "Well, these fellows have placed me in an awful position. I want to be governor of New York for another term at least, and I do not care to be nominated for the vice-presidency. But they are forcing the matter on me on all sides, and it is going to be very difficult to decline it. If I refused it, people will say that 'Roosevelt has the big head and thinks he is too much of a man to be vice-president.' "

The night before the first gavel, Hanna, Lodge, and Roosevelt held a spontaneous powwow at the Walton Hotel that revealed the total confusion in the party.

"I think we can nominate someone besides Roosevelt," Hanna said.

Roosevelt blurted, "For God's sake, go ahead and do it."

"That's right," Lodge said, "let's go ahead and nominate some other man."

Hanna asked, "What is the matter with [Secretary John D.] Long?"

"Nothing," Lodge said. "Go ahead and nominate him."

Hanna was frustrated. "Well, what is the matter with [Indiana senator Charles W.] Fairbanks?"

"Nothing in the world," said Lodge. "Go ahead and nominate him. *Nominate anybody you can.* We're all standing ready to help you."

The platform was a solid gold, steel navy document. The gold standard, protectionism, and reciprocity treaties were leading planks; so were promises to maintain enlightened governance of the conquered territories of Cuba, the Philippines, and Puerto Rico. There was a plank that condemned the trusts and "combinations" on Wall Street—what would be the first round of decades of Republican struggle to regulate the capitalists who heavily financed the party. There were standard Republican promises to support veterans, to restrict cheap labor immigration from Asia, to reform the civil service, to promote the Isthmian canal, to develop the annexed Hawaii, to grant statehood to New Mexico, Arizona, and Oklahoma.

Significant new planks addressed civil rights. The party, unsure how to respond to the push for women's votes, noted the bravery of the female nurses in the late war and yet refused to promise women's suffrage. Another plank denounced the epidemic of lynchings in the South.

On Thursday, June 21, a mild overcast day, Roosevelt was scheduled to speak in order to second the placing of McKinley's name into nomination. Roosevelt marched toward the podium to the overwhelming roar of the sixteen thousand in the arena. He kept his face stern, waiting for quiet, but then sunlight shot through the giant skylights and lit up his beautiful wife, Edith Roosevelt, seated in the gallery in a pink summer gown and black hat trimmed with white bows and feathers. Roosevelt smiled and waved to her. He then stole everyone's breath with a spectacular speech that ranged over the history of the party and closed with his trademark aggressive language—an eloquence that defined his nature:

"We stand on the threshold of a new century," Roosevelt argued, "a century big with the fate of the great nations of the earth.—Is America a weakling to shrink from the world work that must be done by the World Powers? The young giant of the West stands on a continent, and clasps the crest of an ocean in either hand. Our nation, glorious in youth and

The reluctant Theodore Roosevelt. New York Tribune, *June 20, 1900.*

strength, looks into the future with fearless and eager eyes and rejoices as a strong man to run a race. We do not stand in craven mood, asking to be spared the task, cringing as we gaze on the contest.

"*No!*" Roosevelt shouted. "*We challenge the proud privileges of doing the work that providence allots us, and we face the coming years high of heart and resolute of faith that to our people is given the right to win such honor and renown as has never yet been granted to the people of mankind.*"

McKinley was nominated on the first ballot. Roosevelt was named second on the ticket by acclamation.

The campaign was one-sided. In July, the Democrats again nominated William Jennings Bryan of Nebraska, now forty, with Adlai Stevenson of Illinois as vice president. Bryan campaigned again on class-warfare issues, for silver and against gold, for labor and against Wall Street, for the poor and against the trusts, for free trade and against McKinley's protectionism and overseas imperialism.

McKinley never left the front porch of the White House. Roosevelt campaigned as ceaselessly as Bryan and proved popular even in the South. By November a Republican landslide was so obvious that the joke was that Grover Cleveland himself would skip voting to go duck shooting.

Roosevelt closed his electioneering by reviewing a giant sound money parade in New York on the rainy Saturday before the election. He stayed all that raw afternoon in the viewing stand near Washington Arch in Greenwich Village. "I don't think I'll go to lunch at all," he remarked— as men went by cheering "All Right!"—"I'm like the stork," he said, "I can eat at any time or go without."

Afterward an exhausted candidate dined at his sister's house at 500 Madison Avenue and then took the ferry to Long Island City for the train to his home, Sagamore Hill in Oyster Bay.

Sagamore Hill

On election day, Roosevelt was serenaded on his front lawn in Oyster Bay. McKinley was entertained by the Grand Army Band on his front lawn in Canton, Ohio. "This is not a year I am making speeches," McKinley said from his front porch. "Tomorrow, from one end of this vast country to the other, the American people will speak."

Election night, a great crowd gathered in New York on Park Row to watch the national returns projected by a large lantern slide projector against the face of the *New York Tribune* building. Cartoons, cameos of personages, and even motion pictures were mixed in to keep the evening enthusiastic. The final election numbers were thrilling.

Fourteen million men voted. McKinley's majority was the same as in '96, but this time he gained 292 electoral votes, including winning Roosevelt's New York by 145,000. Bryan held the Solid South for 155 electoral votes. Of note, the new Socialist party's forty-five-year-old presidential candidate Eugene V. Debs of Indiana ("I am in this fight until the end of my life") made a strong debut behind the Prohibition party's usual solid splinter presence.

The Congress emerged as an exclusive Republican fiefdom. In the Senate of the new Fifty-seventh Congress, there were now 55 Republicans to 31 Democrats and 4 Populists. In the House, there were now 197 Republicans to 151 Democrats. In the battle of class warfare, the score was GOP 2, Democrats 0.

On Monday, November 12, Wall Street celebrated McKinley's second victory with the heaviest trading day in its 108-year history, climbing steadily on 1,603,620 shares traded.

★ 1904 ★

McKinley's murder placed a mournful nation of seventy-six million into the hands of the popular but untested Theodore Roosevelt, who, at forty-two, was the youngest person ever to take the presidency.

Roosevelt was all spontaneous tests, youthful challenges, and plain aggression. His motto was "Aggressive fighting for the right is the greatest sport the world knows." His two favorite modifiers were *manly* and *strenuous*.

Roosevelt tested the country right away by dining with Negro polymath Booker T. Washington at the White House three weeks after the Roosevelt family moved in.

Roosevelt challenged the nation with an exhausting annual message to Congress three months after he took charge. He promised action to regulate the trusts, to advance forest and water conservation, to build the Isthmian canal and lay the trans-Pacific cable, to develop the acquired territories of Cuba, Puerto Rico, the Philippines, and Hawaii, to treat the Native American "as an individual—like a white man," to create a commerce department in the Cabinet, to expand the merchant marine.

Most vigorous was Roosevelt's language for the regulation of business—for which he would soon be celebrated as a "trustbuster"—and for expansion of the navy and army—for which he would soon be celebrated as the author of the "Speak softly and carry a Big Stick, and you will go far" policy. On regulation of the trusts, Roosevelt argued, "Great corporations exist only because they are created and safeguarded by our institutions, and it is therefore our right and our duty to see they work in harmony with their institutions."

On military strength, Roosevelt argued, "The American people must either build and maintain an adequate Navy or else make up their minds definitely to accept a secondary position in international affairs." Roosevelt closed, "It has been well said, that there is no surer way of courting national disaster than to be opulent, aggressive and unarmed."

Roosevelt dazzled the nation with the range of his plans and the well-armed conduct of his administration. His personality was unstoppable, whether starting the process in the Panama Canal, or settling the Philippine insurrection, or solving the coal strike between the United Mine Workers and J. P. Morgan's coal trust. He embraced every new piece of technology that entered commerce, such as the automobile, the airplane, the motion picture, and the Marconi wireless.

Roosevelt was happy on the attack. He took his battle against the trusts on a speaking tour in the summer of 1902 when he announced he

The Republicans "stand pat" on the high protectionist tariff. Harper's Weekly, *June 11, 1904.*

wanted a *square deal* for every American—a shibboleth that became his battle cry. Roosevelt's second annual message was aimed directly at the corporations: "We are not hostile to them; we are merely determined that they shall be so handled as to subserve the public good."

Roosevelt's vision of the United States was so large that there were no politicians in either major party or in the European powers who could stand up to his wit and energy. He could turn any quote to his advantage. For example: During an 1892 hunting trip to the South at the time of the fall midterm elections, the presidential train stopped at Ootewah Junction, Alabama. A local guide boarded the train to tell the president there were no bears about. *"Perhaps they were Democratic bears,"* Roosevelt joked, *"and took to the woods upon my arrival."*

Roosevelt won everything he touched. In the midterm elections the Republicans increased their majority in the new Fifty-eighth Congress and in state legislatures. In the courts, Roosevelt's Justice Department won the critical *Northern Securities Co.* (railroad trusts) *v. U.S.* that put muscle in the Sherman Anti-Trust Act and earned Roosevelt his nickname of trustbuster. Overseas Roosevelt used his Big Stick Policy to get what he wanted in Panama, where he took the land to begin the canal; in Alaska, where he rejected the British claim against the Panhandle; and in the Caribbean, where Roosevelt let Europe know that regardless of the provocation of debtor nations such as Venezuela or Santo Domingo, there would be no interference by foreign forces—the Monroe Doctrine and the American navy were supreme in the Western Hemisphere.

The presidential year 1904 was devoted to Theodore Roosevelt. Republican party boss Mark Hanna had died suddenly in his sleep during the winter of 1904, and gone with him was the last man in the country who could have dared to stop Theodore Roosevelt.

Charles W. Fairbanks

By June the only question left was the vice presidency as the delegates gathered at the vast depotlike Coliseum in Chicago. But even that drama was reduced by the obvious front-running of mild-mannered Senator Charles W. Fairbanks of Indiana. The single credible VP boom for someone else was for War Secretary William Howard Taft of Ohio, then forty-seven, who was admired for his pacification of the Philippines. The word was eventually passed that "we should save Taft for 1908."

By tradition the president didn't attend the convention. With the convention in session, Roosevelt did entrain to Pennsylvania to dedicate the Washington Chapel at Valley Forge with observations on the greatness of Washington and Lincoln that were meant to be heard by his friends meeting in Chicago.

"I think you will find that the fundamental difference between our two great national heroes," Roosevelt offered on Washington and Lincoln, "and almost any other men of equal note in the world's history, is that when you think of our men, you think inevitably not of glory, but of duty—not of what he did for himself in achieving name or fame or position, but of what he did for his fellows."

What the great Roosevelt did for his fellows at Chicago was to provide them with supreme confidence. For three days the delegates were giddy with their celebration of everything about Roosevelt, and they sang: "Teddy Roosevelt, he'll be there / The gallant Rough Rider / With his jug full of cider / Teddy Roosevelt, he'll be there."

The platform reproduced Roosevelt's annual messages concerning domestic trust-busting and tariff prosperity and overseas liberation of the Philippines, Cuba, Puerto Rico, Panama, and Hawaii. The platform was blunt about the power of the GOP: "The Republican Party entered upon its present period of complete supremacy in 1897." The praise for Roosevelt was boundless: "This administration has been throughout vigorous and honorable, high-minded and patriotic."

It is important to note that the platform also emphasized the Republican disgust for the Southern Democracy's crimes against the Negro. On the women's suffrage plank, there was a sharp protest by a woman from Ohio for how the platform committee was avoiding taking a stand. "We are not asking anything very hard," said Harriet Taylor Upton, "and if this committee was composed of real citizens, you would jump right out of that window to do our hearing."

The single excitement of the convention was a foreign affairs drama. In Morocco, an American citizen named Ion H. Pedicaris had been abducted for ransom by a desert brigand named Raizuli. By the second day of the convention, everyone in attendance knew that State Secretary Hay had sent a cable to the American delegation at Morocco, "We want Pedicaris alive or Raizuli dead," and then had dispatched warships to show Roosevelt's big stick.

The campaign was a Roman triumph. The Democrats bypassed the incendiary genius Bryan for a weak-voiced fellow from the New York Democracy, Chief Justice of the Court of Appeals Alton B. Parker. Parker, fifty-four and dutiful, supported the gold standard and so deprived the Democrats of the sharpest contrast with the Republican prosperity.

Roosevelt was so popular that Parker's efforts were like throwing stones at a battleship. In the closing week of the canvass there was a squabble over campaign financing. Judge Parker charged that Republican national chairman George Cortelyou was secretly selling influence to the wealthy men on Wall Street, chiefly J. Pierpont Morgan. Parker dared the Republicans to list their backers.

Cortelyou, now one of Roosevelt's right-hand men, responded defensively, "Everybody knows there are good substantial reasons why the honest people who contribute national campaign funds don't want the publicity."

Days later Roosevelt responded, "The statements made by Mr. Parker are unqualifiedly and atrociously false. . . . I shall go into the Presidency unhampered by any pledge, promise or understanding of any kind, sort

Roosevelt rides the GOP against the Democratic field. Harper's Weekly, *June 4, 1904.*

or description, save my promise, made openly to the American people, that so far as in my power lies I shall see to it that every man has a square deal, no less and no more."

Election day, Republicans sang out for their hero:

We are coming, Teddy Roosevelt
For we admire a man
Who is brave, sincere and honest
Who can act as well as plan;
. . . Like a purifying cyclone,
With its deep and muffled roar,
We are coming Teddy Roosevelt
Eight million men and more.

Roosevelt won the largest Republican victory to date, with 56.4 percent of the vote and an awesome two and a half million plurality to gain all the North and West for 336 electoral votes. Parker held the 140 electoral votes of the Solid South and nothing more. Eugene Debs expanded his Socialist party fourfold. The tireless Prohibition party won its usual smidgen.

In Congress, the Republican share in the House grew to the largest majority ever, 250 Republicans to 136 Democrats. The Republican majority in the Senate remained the same under the stern leadership of four prominent Republican conservatives: Nelson W. Aldrich of Rhode Island, William B. Allison of Iowa, Orville H. Platt of Connecticut, and John C. Spooner of Wisconsin. These four senators called themselves the "Stand-Patters'" after a speech by their deceased inspiration, Mark Hanna, who'd once recommended that Ohio "stand pat and continue Republican prosperity."

Roosevelt stood pat for nothing. Bypassing the conservatives and Stand-Patters, the president turned his energy to what would soon be called by the impressive name *the Progressive movement*—but which is better understood as plain old impertinent, irrepressible, innovative, and fearless "Teddy" Rooseveltism.

★ 1908 ★

Roosevelt's first act after election was to say that he would not run again, a promise that would eventually tear apart the Republican party.

"On the fourth of March next I shall have served 3 & ½ years," Roosevelt wrote to the public on November 9, "and these three and a half constitute my first term. The wise custom that limits the President to two terms regards the substance and not the form, and under no circumstances will I be candidate for or accept another nomination."

The crisis Roosevelt's promise would create was eight years in the future. For the present, Roosevelt invented the Progressive Era—a period marked by federal activism, an angry public distrust of the "malefactors of wealth" on Wall Street, a worldwide explosion of military violence without end, and the machine-gun mouth of the amazing President Roosevelt.

Roosevelt's second administration was more successful than his first. In foreign affairs, Roosevelt won the Nobel Peace Prize for achieving a peace treaty between Japan and Russia at Portsmouth, New Hampshire. The president also directed the preparation for the building of the Panama Canal by shepherding the necessary acts through Congress. And

Roosevelt waves the big stick to get the Panama Canal finished by William Howard Taft & Co. Harper's Weekly, *February 17, 1906.*

he carefully advanced the expansion of his Big Stick with the steel navy—including the laying of keels of Dreadnought-class battleships.

In domestic affairs, Roosevelt carried on the battle against the railroads and the many industrial trusts with noisome bluff and slapdash regulation. The president wanted more enforcement than the Sherman Anti-Trust Act provided, and mechanisms such as the Railway Labor Board were years away. Under Roosevelt special attention was given to the corrupt beef trust (the Pure Food and Drug Act and the Meat Inspection Act) in hopes of solving the nightmare exposed in Upton Sinclair's muckraking book about the stockyards, *The Jungle.* It was Roosevelt who coined the term *muckrakers* to characterize the investigative reporting of lawless business practices.

Roosevelt's excellent Cabinet included very active secretaries, such as

Roosevelt-intimate Elihu Root at State, Roosevelt loyalist George Cortelyou at Treasury, and the admired William Howard "Big Bill" Taft at War. Twice Roosevelt tried to elevate Taft to the Supreme Court only to have Taft say he wanted to finish his work as the administration's jack-of-all-trades.

The 1906 midterm elections expanded the GOP majority in the Senate: sixty-one Republicans to thirty-one Democrats. Roosevelt immediately used the election boost to have his Justice Department sue John D. Rockefeller's gargantuan Standard Oil of New Jersey in order to dissolve it under the Sherman Anti-Trust Act. The *Tribune* commented on the suit, "Lynching is swifter, but it will hardly commend itself to a people with any capacity for self-government."

Also right after the election, Roosevelt embarked for Panama to visit the elephantine works at the canal and to display his trademark enthusiasm for American labor by operating a giant steam shovel.

(In Panama, the president was able to read reports from New York that his last old nemesis in the party, ancient Thomas C. Platt, was humiliated and enfeebled by his wife when she discovered him in his mistress Mary La Monte's house on West Thirty-eighth Street. "It's all lies, lies, lies," Platt declared as he agreed to a quarter-million-dollar divorce settlement.)

Roosevelt's 1906 annual message was the usual spirited call to action by the trust-busting, canal-building, peacemaking, and big-stick-waving president. His newest aims included writing campaign reform laws, abolishing child labor, permitting free trade with the Philippines, granting citizenship to the people of Puerto Rico, protecting the rights of naturalized Japanese-Americans, safeguarding Americans abroad. He also warned Cuban dissidents to curtail their violence.

Roosevelt offered a prophetic warning to Wall Street: "Only reckless speculation and disregard of legitimate business methods on the part of the business world can materially mar this prosperity."

Also in the message, Roosevelt faced up to the American horror of lynching. "Every lynching represents by just so much a loosening of the bands of civilization," Roosevelt argued. "No man can take part in the torture of a human being without having his own moral nature permanently lowered. Every lynching means just so much moral deterioration in all the children who have any knowledge of it, and therefore just so much additional trouble for the next generation of Americans."

As Roosevelt predicted, speculation led to two panics on Wall Street in 1907. In mid-March the stock exchange plunged on a two-million-share volume: "I began selling stock six months ago," remarked one millionaire short-seller, "because the bond market was steadily declining while stocks were advancing." Then in the fall the Street panicked when the ponderous Knickerbocker Trust bank closed its doors Wednesday noon, October 22, and started a run on the gold supply. The mighty J. Pierpont Morgan, who ruled the pre–Federal Reserve institution called the Clearing House, told the press of his alarm at the bank run. "We are doing everything we can as fast as we can, but nothing has yet crystallized." Treasury Secretary Cortelyou pumped cash from customs receipts into weak banks and permitted banks to use government-loaned bonds as collateral. Cortelyou countered Morgan's alarm: "This is a time for coolness and prudence, not for alarm."

The fall panic was the worst since 1893, but it too passed. The presidential year 1908 opened with Roosevelt admired at home and feared abroad. To rattle his steel navy sword, Roosevelt dispatched a "Great White Fleet" of sixteen battleships on an around-the-world cruise that impressed the world powers with U.S. military readiness.

Roosevelt chose War Secretary William Howard "Big Bill" Taft to be his successor and to carry on what Roosevelt called "my policies."

Charles Evans Hughes

The Republican party blinked and obeyed. At state conventions and in the states that had popular primaries, the party voted to support Roosevelt's choice of Taft. The single note of dissent was a tiny boom for Charles Evans Hughes, the popular full-bearded governor of New York who would someday carry the party standard against Woodrow Wilson. But this early on, Hughes cautiously showed no interest in challenging Roosevelt's temper.

By mid-June and the Republican convention at Chicago's Convention Hall, "Big Bill" Taft was a shoo-in—all three hundred witty, energetic, golf-playing, mule-riding, diet-conscious son-of-Eli pounds of him.

Taft's certainty gave party fathers in town for the convention an opportunity to philosophize as they celebrated the GOP supremacy.

"I used to resent the assertion that the Republican party was a party of one idea," observed retired senator John C. "Stand-Pat" Spooner of Wisconsin, then sixty-three and in law practice in New York City. "The declaration filled me with bitterness. But, my friends, I have outgrown all that. The Republican party is a party of one idea—an idea that is as broad as the universe and as high as heaven itself. The one idea of the Republican party is the conception of human liberty. As for this talk of the Republican party's dying, there is nothing to it. It can no more die than the concept of human liberty which is implanted in the hearts of mankind for time and eternity. . . .

"But, my friends," Spooner added, "the Republican party is not afraid to die. It has no fear of that account which it will be called upon to render in the hereafter, and that is not true of the Democratic party. In fact it is only the fear to die that keeps the Demo- cratic party alive, and I assure you

John C. Spooner

that the fear is the most creditable thing about the Democratic party."

The platform repeated Roosevelt's ambitious aims. Big capital was promised a tariff reduction. Big labor was promised that antistrike in- junctions would not be used promiscuously. Conservation and wise land management were concerns, as was the need for a bureau of mines and mining. The platform emphasized the party's "unalterable devotion to a policy that will keep the Republic ready at all times to defend her tradi- tional doctrines."

The platform philosophized about the party's class-warfare battle with the Democracy: "The trend of Democracy is toward socialism, while the Republican party stands for a wise and regulated individual- ism. Socialism would give to each an equal right to take, Republicans would give to each an equal right to earn. Socialism would offer equal- ity of possession, which would soon leave no one anything to possess.— The Democratic party of to-day believes in government ownership, while the Republican party believes in government regulation."

On the second day of the convention, senator Henry Cabot Lodge of Massachusetts gave a celebrated keynote speech that continued the Re- publican history lesson: "Recall the cries which have sounded from the lips of these two parties during the last half century. One the one side: Slavery, secession, repudiation of the public debt, flat money, free trade, free silver, the overthrow of the courts and governmental ownership. On the Republican side: Free soil, free men, the Union, the payment of the debt, honest money, protection to American industries, the gold stan- dard, the maintenance of the law, of order and of the courts and the gov- ernment regulation of great corporations."

Lodge's speech triggered a huge demonstration for Roosevelt. Just as Lodge called the president "the most popular and most abused man in the United States to-day," the convention ignited into a forty-six-minute demonstration. *"Four, four, four years more!"* the galleries cried. A large toy "Teddy Bear" appeared on the podium and was thrown from delegation to delegation on the floor until finally a California delegate held on to it to prevent a riot of enthusiasm. The band struck up the "Star-Spangled Banner" to quiet the noise, but still they cheered for their hero.

The next day there was a report that there were rudimentary microphones in the hall that were hooked up to telephone lines that communicated to the White House. The president had listened in on earphones to the convention cheering his name. Roosevelt was said to have smiled at the din, then to have gone horseback riding at Rock Creek.

James S. Sherman

Taft was nominated on the first ballot to the Taft delegates singing "O-H-I-O" to the tune of "Roll, Jordan, Roll" while parading with a stuffed elephant. Representative James S. "Sunny Jim" Sherman of Utica, New York, was named on the second spot. The GOP presented the same Hudson River valley / Ohio River valley axis that had worked so well since Harrison's campaigns.

In Washington, Taft responded to the nomination that evening when he arrived at his house at Sixteenth and K Streets. "I thank you, gentlemen, for your good fellowship," Taft told a crowd of five thousand youthful serenaders. "I thank you on behalf of the real ruler of the family, the lady, who, I hope, is nearby looking on and listening. For those who conduct themselves properly in their family life, no greater need of approval could be needed."

The next day Taft resigned the Cabinet and went home to Cincinnati to organize himself. Taft's credentials were impressive: lawyer, judge, governor-general of the Philippines, provisional governor of Cuba, supervisor of the Panama Canal, and round-the-world traveler. Few men could have been better prepared to run the nation; few men were as skilled in both foreign and military affairs. He had calmed the Philippines, Cuba, Panama; he had crossed Siberia to call on the tsar with Roosevelt's well-wishes. After twelve years of Republican rule, there was not a single credible complaint against "Big Bill" Taft.

Roosevelt certainly believed Taft was the right man. As he departed the White House for a summer vacation, he told the weepy White House staff saying good-bye to their chief, "Do not waste sympathy on me. I have enjoyed every minute of my time here, and my thanks are due to the

American people and not theirs to me for the opportunity I have had to serve them: I have had a perfectly corking time."

The campaign was just as much fun for Roosevelt. Taft started the race ahead and stayed there. The fumble-finger Democrats once more nominated the oratorical William Jennings Bryan to tilt at Rooseveltism.

Taft broke the tradition of Republican candidates and traveled the nation on a special train to campaign for himself. He was smart, funny, energetic, and authoritative, blessed with a huge grin, bright eyes, and a gifted ability to make fun of his famous appetite. He was also willing to fight hard on the campaign trail, especially against Bryan's class-warfare negativism.

"Now some ordinary, cheap common liar has devoted himself to running around the country and saying that I am in favor of paying a man a dollar a day,"

William Howard Taft

Taft said of Bryan while at a campaign stop in Nebraska, "and that I have said that is enough. I was at the head of the Panama Canal for four years, and we may pay steam shovel men down there $250 a month. As I figure that out that makes a little more than a dollar a day."

Labor did favor Taft. "Personally I am going to vote for Taft," said an American Federation of Labor official, "because as secretary of war he did more to enforce laws in favor of organized labor than any of his predecessors."

The final days of the campaign were fought entirely in and for New York in order to help the beleaguered and much admired Charles Evans Hughes of New York hold off a strong Tammany Hall–backed challenge to his governorship. On the last day of October, Taft was in New York City, Governor Hughes was in Fredonia, vice presidential candidate James S. Sherman was in Albany, Republican chairman Ethan Allen Hitchcock was in New York City, Treasury Secretary Cortelyou was in Murray Hill—and William Jennings Bryan was in Utica speaking to support the Tammany Hall candidate who was in Plattsburg.

The Republican parade that closed the campaign included an incident with eight suffragettes who were protesting near the Waldorf-Astoria. The paraders were amused. "Go home and cook your husband's supper," a Republican called.

"We haven't any husbands," the women called back. "And wouldn't marry the best man living—no, indeed."

"Boys," teased the Republican, "I'm going to give every one of them old dames a kiss. Yes, I am. That's what they want—kisses—not votes."

A late scandal erupted when the Democratic press accused the Unitarian Taft of being a secret Roman Catholic. Roosevelt countered the offense, "I believe that the Republic will endure for many centuries. If so, there will doubtless be among its presidents both Protestants and Catholics, and very probably, at some time, Jews."

Nearly fifteen million men voted. Taft won nearly 52 percent and all the North and West for 321 electoral college votes. Bryan held only the Solid South and his own Nebraska and three mining states. The GOP retained huge operating majorities in the Congress and held on to the big states easily, including Governor Hughes's victory in New York of seventy-nine thousand plurality.

Following the election, Bryan was deeply blue and highly philosophical: "My heart has never been set on holding office, but I wanted to do

Roosevelt moon over a triumphant William Howard Taft. Harper's Weekly, *June 8, 1908.*

certain work, and it looked as though the presidency might offer the opportunity to do that work."

Wall Street was deeply golden and highly speculative. The railroader E. H. Harriman and deceased (1892) financier Jay Gould properties were said to have assembled a ten-million-dollar pool with Pennsylvania interests to bull up stocks. The vast trusts were voting with cash. Gone was the swift and cranky Roosevelt. Hail the measured, conservative and reliable Taft.

E. H. Harriman

Jay Gould

★ 1912 ★

Big Bill Taft spent the first half of his administration fighting for the Roosevelt agenda—and the last two years fighting off Roosevelt and the Roosevelt-fueled Progressive party.

Who were the Progressives? They were Theodore Rooseveltites. What was Progressivism? It was whatever Theodore Roosevelt said it was. The Republican party broke apart under Taft; it was Roosevelt who broke it; and the party was not put back together again until after Roosevelt had died of a broken heart in 1919 at the horror of world war and the loss of a beloved son in combat.

Perhaps Roosevelt didn't mean to undermine Taft and the Taft-loyal party bosses; perhaps it just happened that way. Yet from the very first of Taft's years, Roosevelt kept the spotlight on himself. In time Roosevelt spoke out again on how he wanted the country administered, and when he did—calling his ideas "progressive" and "the new nationalism"—Roosevelt's famous voice overwhelmed Taft like a bull moose overcalls a calf.

Two weeks after the inauguration Roosevelt sailed for Africa on a

Taft on the links—the first golfing president. Harper's Weekly, *May 15, 1909.*

two-year safari. The press and public were at the pier, sending off Roosevelt as if an emperor was leaving his children home alone. Every step Roosevelt took in Africa with his son Kermit, from Mobasa in German East Africa to Khartoum in the British Sudan, was followed so closely in the United States that it was as if the Republican heart had gone on safari, too. The expedition has no equivalent in American partisan politics. Roosevelt's record of the trip, *African Game Trails: An Account of the*

African Wanderings of an American Hunter-Naturalist (Charles Scribner's Sons, 1910), is a dumbfounding document, part fantastic voyage, part self-promotion, all epic of a continental-sized personality. At the close of the book is a list of game shot by Theodore and Kermit Roosevelt with rifle and shotgun, including nine lions, fifteen zebras, thirty-four hartebeest, seventeen gazelles—and eight elephants.

"Then the biggest cow began to move slowly forward," Roosevelt wrote of elephant hunting, "and we walked nearly parallel to her, along an elephant trail, until from the slight knoll I got a clear view of her at a distance of eighty yards. As she walked leisurely along, almost broadside to me, I fired the left barrel of the Holland into her head, knocking her flat down with the shock; and when she rose I put a bullet from the left barrel through her heart, again knocking her completely off her feet; and this time she fell permanently."

Back in Washington, Taft was making deals with GOP elephants such as the obstreperous, beefy, and bald-pated Illinois boss and Speaker of the House Joseph Cannon, seventy-five, and the reigning Stand-Pat senator and Rhode Island boss, the white-haired, rock-jawed Nelson W. Aldrich.

In 1909, following ambitions voiced by Roosevelt, there was long debate in the Congress before approving the long-promised tariff revision with the Payne-Aldrich Tariff Act. There was almost no debate before sending to the states for approval the Sixteenth Amendment on the graduated income tax, that which was meant to inhibit the wealthy. In 1910, the Taft administration and Republican Congress gave attention to interstate trade, to campaign reform, to a postal savings bank, to immigrant limits, to further civil service reform.

Taft's record was dutiful and judicious. The president was frustrated that he faced uncertain 1910 midterm elections against a feisty Democratic party that felt cocky since it no longer had to fight uphill against bully-preacher Roosevelt in the White House.

Roosevelt was now returned from Africa, and he threw himself into the campaign as the most official plain Republican citizen in the country. The press called him Colonel Roosevelt or just the Colonel. He called himself a Progressive Republican.

Visiting coal fields in Pennsylvania ("Give us your fist, Teddy!" the miners called), or calling on farm fields on Long Island ("I think now that the best citizen is the kindergarten teacher who becomes a farmer's wife"), and then entraining west on the Roosevelt special, the Colonel talked nonstop for his party and himself.

Roosevelt made a famous campaign speech in late summer, at the dedication of the John Brown battlefield at Osawatomie, Kansas. Roo-

Roosevelt in Africa, 1909. "He could have touched me with his trunk," Roosevelt said of this scene. (Theodore Roosevelt, African Game Trails *[New York: Charles Scribner's Sons, 1910].)*

sevelt ranged over the problems deviling the country and then called for a *new nationalism.* "The new nationalism puts the national need before sectional or personal advantage," Roosevelt argued. "This new nationalism regards the executive as the steward of the public welfare." (What Roosevelt had in mind with his new nationalism was to boost the powers of the presidency in order to bypass Congress and take on the trusts and combinations and "the interests" of Wall Street; Roosevelt had entered the class-warfare battle closer to William Jennings Bryan than to Taft.) Roosevelt closed his speech by linking his new nationalism to Progressivism: "The prime problem of our nation is to get the right type of good citizenship: and to get it we must have progress and all our people must be genuinely progressive."

Back home in New York, Roosevelt charged into the New York canvass for the governorship, backing his young protégé Henry L. Stimson against the New York Democracy's state chairman, John L. Dix. Roosevelt's best weapon was his rapid-fire wit. When asked what he would do about the might of the trusts, he said, "Change the rules." When asked how he was going to defeat the New York Democrats, he said, "We will knock them over the ropes. We will beat them to a frazzle. They have got the money, they have Tammany Hall behind them, but we have got the votes. We are going to knock them over the ropes."

Nationwide the Republicans lost the elections badly. The Democrats captured both houses of Congress by potent majorities for the first time in twenty years. The Democrats also gained the critical state of New York (where Roosevelt's candidate Stimson lost by sixty-five thousand) as well as winning the governorships and legislatures in Massachusetts, Ohio, and New Jersey. The surprise Democratic victor in New Jersey was the big-jawed, squint-eyed president of Princeton University, Woodrow Wilson. The Republican bright spot in the country was the election of the popular Progressive governor Robert La Follette of Wisconsin to the U.S. Senate.

The *Tribune* editorial page was philosophical about the Republican defeat. "It was probably due to a feeling that the Republican Party had been too long uninterruptedly in power. There comes at intervals a year when the majority of people think or imagine that they want a change of government."

Roosevelt took the defeat personally. "It means, in my opinion, a drift back to Democratic principles," he said in Oyster Bay. "It is a pronounced approval of a cry for tariff revision and a protest against Rooseveltism and all that term applies." Roosevelt made no mention of the small but auspicious Roosevelt victory of election day, when the Colonel's young cousin Franklin Delano Roosevelt, of the Democratic

Roosevelts of Suffolk County, entered elective politics as a state senator from his home in Hyde Park.

Taft's response to the defeat was to sail for an inspection tour on the Panama Canal. When he returned, Taft struggled through the next twenty months against a hostile Democratic Congress that aimed to reform the tariff and embarrass the Republicans. The president was also pestered by the National Republican Progressive League headed by the upstart senator La Follette of Wisconsin. Taft dealt effectively with border troubles in Mexico, with gunboat diplomacy in Nicaragua, with Democratic challenges to the tariff, with the court to control the trusts. Yet Taft could not satisfy Roosevelt, who regarded Taft a servant of "the interests" on Wall Street and the conservatives in Congress.

By the opening of the presidential year 1912, Roosevelt had told intimates that he aimed to win the Republican nomination and a third term. In February La Follette wrecked his own boom when he attacked the Republican press before the Periodical Publishers' Association in Philadelphia. Within a week seven Republican governors wrote to ask Roosevelt to challenge Taft and the conservative Republicans. On February 24, Roosevelt replied, "I will accept nomination for President if it

Roosevelt pursues the GOP for a third term; Taft objects, and Abe looks daggers. Harper's Weekly, *February 24, 1912.*

is tendered to me, and I will adhere to this decision until the convention has expressed its preference."

Through the spring Roosevelt challenged Taft in every state convention and the nine presidential preference primaries in the nation, accumulating delegates by the carload. The battle was personal and bitter as only a family feud can be.

"When in February I had made up my mind to enter this fight," explained Roosevelt about his primary campaign, "it was after long and careful deliberation. I had become convinced that Mr. Taft had definitely and completely abandoned the causes of the people and had surrendered himself wholly to the biddings of the bosses and the great privileged interests behind them."

Taft fought back. He condemned the Progressives as emotionalists and neurotics, and he decried Roosevelt as an egotist. "In every statement he makes," Taft said of Roosevelt, "you would think he was the whole show and that there wasn't anybody else in the country. It's 'I' 'I' 'I'. . . . Mr. Roosevelt likens himself to Abraham Lincoln more, and resembles him less, than any man in the history of this country."

The war of words moved on to the hot-under-the-collar theme of class warfare. Taft was owned by the wealthy interests! Roosevelt was a socialistic rabble-rouser! A London observer tried to figure out the rhetoric: "The only thing that seems certain now is that Roosevelt wants to thump something. . . . To read what he says one would imagine he was going to drive every millionaire into the sea."

The Chicago convention, in mid-June, was a fistfight to the finish. The delegate count was the heart of the tale. Roosevelt had won every important popular primary all spring, especially a big victory in California with the support of the maverick Progressive Republican governor Hiram W. Johnson of Sacramento.

A preconvention straw poll of delegates yielded the following count: Roosevelt, 458½; Taft, 439½; and unassigned, 110. Needed for the nomination was 539. Because so many of the 110 uncommitted delegates were the boss-named at-large delegates, or were those from Southern states that were under pro-Taft control—the so-called *rotten boroughs* of the party—the best and only way Roosevelt could win was bluster and bombardment.

Roosevelt aimed to intimidate everyone: delegates, bosses, the president, and his administration. "Mr. Taft's nomination at Chicago," Roosevelt said in Oyster Bay, "can only be brought about by nullifying the will of the people, and by fradulently seating a sufficient number of boss-picked and boss-controlled delegates in the place of those who have been legally picked by the people themselves."

The Party tears itself in two over Roosevelt and Taft. Harper's Weekly, *June 22, 1912.*

Taft maintained haughty silence at the White House. The president permitted his managers and surrogates, including Senator Elihu Root of New York and the former Ohio lieutenant governor Warren G. Harding, to do the hard work of amassing delegate pledges. Meanwhile, at the convention there were random potshots at Roosevelt: "He is a law unto himself," one delegate remarked, "and will doubtless do just as he pleases."

Off to the side of the fray was the autonomous voice of La Follette of Wisconsin, the former farmboy with a fiery tongue, then fifty-seven, who had been bickering with Republican party orthodoxy since Cleveland's time, and who saw himself as more genuinely Progressive than Roosevelt. La Follette controlled Wisconsin's delegates, and what he said he wanted before pledging his delegates was an anticorruption plank in the platform. What La Follete really wanted was to replace Roosevelt as the star of the Progressive movement. Disappointed, La Follette remained unpersuaded by the battle between Taft and Roosevelt (and would later back the Democratic candidate, Wilson).

Roosevelt was all operatic energy. The weekend before the convention opened, he stole attention by spontaneously starting for Chicago on a Friday evening Lake Shore Limited—charging to the crisis one more time. Saturday evening he plunged into cajoling and bedazzling the delegates who visited him at Chicago's Congress Hotel. Roosevelt was greeted as a hero-king, not a politician. The crowds sang "Theee-o-o-o-dooreeee!" to the tune of "Maryland, My Maryland!" The twenty-eight delegates from New Jersey cheered: "Rah! Rah! Rah! / We are the delegates from New Jersey / Are we in it? Just you wait / Till we give Teddy twenty-eight straight!"

Estimates on the delegate count changed hourly. A fight for delegates began at the national committee meeting and then exploded at the credential and organizing committees, where the Taft forces controlled the process. The worst blow to Roosevelt was that his old friend and ally Elihu Root, now senator from New York, accepted the permanent chairmanship of the convention for the Taft forces. A photograph of Root speaking on the dais amid the teeming delegates was a picture of betrayal to the Roosevelt years.

The platform committee finished its work and delivered a document that both Taft "Stand-Pat" conservatives and Roosevelt "New Nationalist" Progressives could easily approve. Tariff revision, antitrust legislation, and currency laws were the traditional concerns. There were several conservation planks such as calls for Mississippi flood reclamation and Alaska coal leases. There was a new worry about the rising cost of living: "When the exact facts are known," the party promised, "[we] will take the necessary steps to remove any abuses that may be found to exist."

Roosevelt was losing to Taft's bosses. On the second day "T.R." buttons plunged in price from ten cents to a nickel to six for a quarter.

Roosevelt would not quit. Before the balloting, he ordered his delegates to bolt the convention. The Taft forces went on with the ceremony, including an impish, alliterative nominating speech for Taft by the little known Ohio politician Warren G. Harding: "Progressivism is not proclamation nor palaver." Taft won the nomination on the first ballot. There was a smattering of votes for La Follette of Wisconsin, and for Associate Supreme Court Justice Charles Evans Hughes of New York, the future party darling.

At the White House, Taft received the news in a sober mood.

At Chicago, Roosevelt remarked, "I am in this fight to win." He then gave orders to his son Kermit and other loyalists to form a third party based on the new nationalism and Progressivism. The Republican party was broken in half.

In August, again at Chicago, the Roosevelt forces met in convention to form the Progressive "Bull Moose" party—named for an operatic quip by Roosevelt, "I feel like a Bull Moose!"

"We stand at Armageddon and we battle for the Lord!" Roosevelt told the roaring convention. The Progressive platform mirrored the Re-

The Bull Moose takes on the Republicans and Democrats. Harper's Weekly, *July 7, 1912.*

publican program with vital additions. Roosevelt called for a department of labor in the Cabinet, for supervision of Wall Street by a federal commission, for the streamlining of the constitutional amendment process— and for equal suffrage for women. The Progressives wanted women to vote, and they wanted the Republican Negro vote to be a fact and not the invention of the bosses from the South's *rotten boroughs.*

Roosevelt explained his new party by revealing his contempt for his opponents: "The deliberate betrayal of its trust by the Republican party, the fatal incapacity of the Democratic party to deal with the new issues of the time, have compelled the people to form a new instrument of government."

The campaign was a popularity contest between Roosevelt and the rest of the world. Taft ran silently by comparison. And the surprise Democratic nominee in July—the scholarly, Virginia-born, and Protestant-forthright governor of New Jersey, Woodrow Wilson, who had been sponsored by the Democratic bosses in 1910—gained the benefit of a three-way race. Whenever Roosevelt popped off, the Democratic press led by the press lord William Randolph Hearst made certain the nation heard the Republican party wrecking itself.

Roosevelt was enormously popular, like a stage star, and every day he shot from the hip at Taft, Wall Street, the Democrats, anything that crossed his path. By September the Republicans were reduced to stunts such as removing Roosevelt's portrait and bust from the New York Republican Club. Wilson's forces imitated Roosevelt's New Nationalism with a program called New Freedoms. The Democrats also tried to smear the Bull Moose with a congressional investigation into the fact that J. Pierpont Morgan had given the Roosevelt campaign $150,000 in 1904. Roosevelt countered, "We never had any [such] communication," and the flap passed.

Fate came for Roosevelt in Milwaukee on Monday, September 14. As Roosevelt emerged from the Hotel Gilpatrick, an assassin fired a pistol right at his heart. A bodyguard tackled the shooter, John Schenk of New York. Roosevelt just stood there with a bullet in his chest. The crowd screamed at the shooter, "Lynch him! Kill the brute! Get rope."

Roosevelt ordered, "Stop! Stand back. Don't hurt him." Still standing, Roosevelt reached under his overcoat and felt the blood. He did not do anything normal. He told his friends, "Let me alone. I'm all right." Then he said, "I will make this speech or die, one or the other."

Roosevelt walked on to the Auditorium, where he took the podium and addressed the audience. "I'm going to ask you to be very quiet, and please excuse me from making a very long speech. I'll do the best I can, but you see there is a bullet in my body. But it's nothing. I'm not hurt badly. But it takes more than that to kill a Bull Moose."

Roosevelt continued the strangest speech in Republican history, "But, fortunately, I had my manuscript, so you see I was going to make a long speech. And, friends, the hole in it is where the bullet went through, and it probably saved the bullet from going into my heart. The bullet is in me now, so that I cannot make a very long speech. But I will try my best."

Roosevelt spoke for eighty-five minutes, then he boarded the night train to Chicago. He did think to telegram to his wife, who was at the Casino Theater in New York when she was told.

"I hope he is all right," Edith Roosevelt remarked, "but I was there and saw McKinley when he was shot, and the doctors said he was all right, too."

Roosevelt finally collapsed into a hospital bed the next day. The doctors treated him with an injection of tetanus antitoxin. They left the bullet inside his chest cavity.

The reaction from the world was speechless worry and an avalanche of concern. Woodrow Wilson's amazing response was to say that he was suspending his campaign until Roosevelt recovered.

Meanwhile, the shooter, Schenk, told the police, "I had a dream several years ago in which Mr. McKinley appeared to me and told me that Mr. Roosevelt was his real murderer, and was not Czolgosz or whatever his name was." Later Schenk said, "I'm sorry I shot."

A week later a grim-faced Roosevelt stepped off the train at Oyster Bay. He was wearing the same overcoat he'd been shot in. There was a patch over the bullet hole.

At the end of October, fate struck the campaign again when it was revealed that Taft's vice president, James S. Sherman of New York, had been dying of Bright's disease, heart disease, and general failure all year, especially since his renomination in June. The Taft forces had concealed the facts for fear they might have helped Roosevelt at the convention. Sherman died within forty-eight hours of the public first learning he was ill. Taft chose not to replace Sherman on the ticket before the election.

The last weekend of the campaign, the silent Taft went to Sherman's funeral. Roosevelt on Friday and then Wilson on Saturday held huge rallies at Madison Square Garden in New York. Roosevelt's shrill speaking voice—a falsetto like a fife—delighted his wild fans as he sang of a revolution at the ballot box, and the bands played the "Battle Hymn of the Republic" and "Onward Christian Soldier." Wilson's preacher's voice—he was the son and grandson of Presbyterian ministers—promised even-handedness, kindness.

After the election the elephant blames the Bull Moose. Harper's Weekly, *November 16, 1912.*

The electorate was as confused as the richest man in the world, Andrew Carnegie, who spoke weakly for Taft. "I have never voted for any but the Republican ticket since the party was formed," said Carnegie. "My first vote was for Lincoln and my next vote will be for Taft, who richly deserves the customary second term."

Election eve in Cincinnatti, Taft was exhausted. "I am not here to make a political speech," he told reporters. "Your minds are already made up, I doubt not."

More than fifteen million voted. Wilson won a mountain of 435 electoral votes despite the fact that he had won only 41.8 percent of the vote, the smallest percentage obtained by any Democrat since Stephen A. Douglas. Roosevelt had torn the Republican party in half. Roosevelt won 27.4 percent for 88 electoral votes. Taft won 23.1 percent for only

8 electoral votes. The tireless Eugene V. Debs and the Socialists achieved the high-water mark for their party: nine hundred thousand votes for 6 percent.

In the new Sixty-third Congress the Democrats expanded their majority in the House, 291 Democrats to only 127 Republicans and 17 unaligned Progressives. The Senate remained Democratic, 51–44, with one uncommitted.

The Grand Old Party was headless and lost. In the class war, the party had just defeated itself. Taft accepted his defeat quietly and planned to go back to Yale to teach law.

Roosevelt returned to *Outlook* magazine, where he had been writing loud editorials since 1909. He still could not use his right hand. He remarked stoically, "I never felt better—just bully. My wound doesn't bother me."

★ 1916 ★

Woodrow Wilson set out to undo the long Republican ascendancy and ran directly into the pit of world war.

"The great government we loved," Wilson said in his inaugural speech of March 1913, "has too often been made use of for private and selfish purposes, and those who used it had forgotten people."

Wilson also warned of class war: "There has been something crude and heartless and unfeeling in our haste to succeed and be great. Our thought has been 'let every man look out for himself, let every generation look out for itself' while we reared giant machinery which made it impossible that any but those who stood at the levers of control should have a chance to look out for themselves."

Woodrow Wilson

Wilson's early program was designed to undo the Republican protectionism and to review and revise Republican foreign and domestic policy. William Jennings Bryan was appointed secretary of state to satisfy Bryan's antiestablishment constituents, not to make policy. Wilson's strong mind quickly tangled with Mexico, where he would struggle for years with prickly dictators.

At home Wilson followed an agenda remarkably similar to Roosevelt's Progressive agenda. (Roosevelt gave Wilson room to maneuver when he sailed on a Brazilian safari.) The agent behind the Wilson first-term policy was the president's extraordinary adviser Edward M. "Colonel" House of Texas, who once had written an ambitious novel, *Phillip Dru, Administrator,* that read like an H. G. Wells dystopian romance. The Wilson theme was good government by benevolent fiat. Wilson's surest domestic success was when he pushed Congress to deliver the 1913 Glass-Owen Federal Reserve Act, which reorganized the creaky national banking system into the independent Federal Reserve System.

The sudden outbreak of mass war in Europe in August 1914 did not obviously affect the midterm elections. No one on the national scene was sure how to interpret the war. Was it mass regicide? Tyranny? Economic determinism? Even Roosevelt was willing to go along with Wilson's policy of neutrality. ("I am not now taking sides," Roosevelt wrote.)

Nevertheless, election day, 1914, was foreboding. The headlines warned of a major battle in progress at a town called "Wipers" (Ypres). The English propagandist Hillaire Belloc claimed that the Germans had so far suffered 1.75 million casualties. The German general Paul von Hindenburg declared, "The war will not end until all the nations who are fighting against us have become subordinate to our rules and desires."

At the polls Wilson and the Democrats gave back much of what they'd gained in 1912. Roosevelt's wayward flock of Progressives returned home to the GOP, and the reunited Republicans improved their minority numbers in both houses of the new Sixty-fourth Congress. The House pickups were most striking in the major industrial states of New York, Pennsylvania, and Illinois. Even Wilson's own Fourth Congressional District in New Jersey went Republican.

At the same time, Roosevelt's Progressive party lost half their seats in Congress and polled badly everywhere. Roosevelt sounded his bitterness at the apparent shrinking field for his ideas: "I have nothing to say."

Within the year Roosevelt and the Republican minority in Congress had much to say about the war. On April 30, 1915, the Germans published a warning in American newspapers that all ships in the war zone were "now liable to destruction." A week later the United States woke up to a nightmare: "1300 Die As *Lusitania* Goes To Bottom / 400 Americans On Board Torpedoed Ship / Washington Stirred As When *Maine* Sank." Instantly the country was furious for retaliation against the Germans. Roosevelt made the Republican case on *Lusitania:* "This represents not merely piracy, but piracy on a vaster scale of murder than any oldtime pirate ever practiced."

Wilson stumbled. First he issued a call for calm deliberation. Then he

Roosevelt vs. Secretary of State Bryan, Uncle Sam arbitrates. Harper's Weekly, *August 14, 1915.*

made a pacifist speech at Convention Hall, Philadelphia, that was meant as a rebuke to Roosevelt's militance: "There is such a thing as a man being too proud to fight; there is such a thing as a nation being so right that it does not need to convince others by force that it is right."

Roosevelt roared back that "150 babies" were drowned on *Lusitania;* then he declared, "Let us as a nation understand that peace is of worth only when it is the handmaiden of international righteousness and of national self-respect."

Wilson disregarded Roosevelt and the public anger and proceeded to exchange warning notes with the Germans that satisfied no one.

By now Roosevelt had determined he was against the Germans, and he spoke out with a pious voice that overwhelmed every other Republican figure. "The most important thing that a nation can save," Roosevelt preached, "is its own soul." What Roosevelt the ex-president chiefly wanted was American military preparedness to go to war with Germany; what Roosevelt the Rough Rider also wanted was to have a military role; and so he supported Wilson as the United States began the training of a large regular army.

The presidential year 1916 began with a growing prosperity in the American markets and a failing civilization in Europe. Wilson, while maneuvering to be a peace negotiator, cautiously urged further military preparedness. Suddenly the Mexican fiasco rocked Wilson again, when

Pancho Villa attacked a New Mexican town, causing Wilson to send General John J. Pershing on a futile raid to capture Villa. What the Mexican raid also did was to make Wilson look indecisive and the country seem vulnerable.

By June Roosevelt was back on his national war horse, this time not only as a Progressive party candidate but also as the likely Republican nominee again. Wall Street bankers encouraged a Roosevelt boom despite his years of Progressive rhetoric against "the interests." Soon the odds on Roosevelt's Republican nomination were 6–5.

The backdrop for the sixteenth Republican convention was the war catastrophe of the Battle of Jutland, which resulted in a murky standoff

Charles Evans Hughes speaks to his daughter's graduating class about his views on the war. New York Tribune, *June 8, 1916.*

between the British and German fleets. There were loud calls for dread-noughts and for Roosevelt. Did Roosevelt want to lead the GOP again?

The Republicans did have an alternative in former New York gover-nor and now Supreme Court justice Charles Evans Hughes, a handsome, full-bearded man with a fine family and many loyal friends. However, Hughes had maintained his silence the last year while his supporters praised his high-mindedness and calm. What did Hughes make of the Germans? What did Hughes make of the German-American demands that the Republican platform not mention "hyphen-Americans"? Bluntly, what did Hughes say to the charge that he was pro-German?

Early June, the Monday before the convention met at Chicago, Hughes finally spoke out at a most unusual event for presidential de-bate—his daughter's graduation ceremony from the National Cathedral School for Girls in Washington. Hughes's remarks were flowery and eva-sive; however, when he said that the American flag "means America first," it was understood that he was signaling he was anti-German and sympathetic to Roosevelt's war talk.

At Chicago, the Progressive National Committee convened the day before the Republicans in hopes of booming Roosevelt again as a Pro-gressive contender. The delegates cheered their man for ninety-three min-utes, crying, "If Teddy had been President, Where Would Villa be?" and "TR a leader, not a trailer!"

As the Republicans convened in Chicago, Roosevelt warned Hughes and his delegates not to weaken toward German aggression. "The pro-fessional German-Americans are seeking to terrorize your convention," Roosevelt wrote from Oyster Bay, "for they wish to elect in November a man who shall not be in good faith an American President, but the viceroy of a foreign government."

The Republican party bosses did not want Roosevelt on the ticket, but they knew to obey his recommendations. The platform imitated the Progressive platform, including promising that the Mexican bandit Villa would be punished, that the U.S. Army would be fully expanded, and that the party would pass a women's suffrage amendment. The platform underlined the party's new patriotism: "In 1861 the Republican Party stood for the Union. As it stood for the union of states, it now stands for united people, true to American ideals, loyal to American traditions, knowing no allegiance, except to the Constitution, to the government and to the flag of the United States."

The cautious Hughes kept quiet in Washington while sending word to Chicago through his boosters that he was definitely not pro-German. On Friday, the first two convention ballots showed Hughes in a firm lead out

Hughes wins the nomination; Roosevelt approves; the Kaiser frets.
New York Tribune, *June 29, 1916.*

of a large field that included Roosevelt and Roosevelt's old adversaries Elihu Root and Charles W. Fairbanks. The party bosses retired to the hotel suites to decide that the party would not suffer a floor fight. On Saturday, Hughes was nominated easily, and Charles W. Fairbanks of Indiana was the vice presidential nominee.

Also on Saturday, the Progressives nominated Roosevelt in the hope of splitting the Republican party again. This time Roosevelt astonished everyone by refusing the party he had raised up. Roosevelt said he was satisfied that Hughes had the right attitude about the Germans. Roosevelt offered his old friend Senator Henry Cabot Lodge as a substitute candidate for the Progressives. Lodge deferred, and the Progressives did not offer a presidential candidate.

At Washington Hughes accepted his nomination with antique reluctance: "I have not desired the nomination. I have wished to remain on the bench." He then resigned the Supreme Court and prepared for the campaign, declaring, "I am for an Americanism that knows no ulterior purpose."

The campaign was entirely about the war. Wilson ran on the simple slogan "He kept us out of war."

Hughes traveled the country tirelessly. "We have not been kept out of the war," he argued at every stop. "We have not enforced our rights. We have sacrificed our honor. We have intermittent peace without honor."

Roosevelt campaigned for the Republicans as hard as Hughes did. After a U-boat sank nine merchantmen off the Nantucket lighthouse, Roosevelt attacked Wilson hard: "The time for the ostrich—the elocuting ostrich—has passed. The war stares at us from just beyond the three-mile limit, and we face it without policy, plan, purpose or preparation."

Roosevelt also condemned Wilson on the *Lusitania*. "Instead of speaking softly and carrying a big stick, President Wilson speaks bombastically and carries a dishrag. At the murder of 1,394 men, women and children on the *Lusitania,* his corpuscles did not shout; they did not even whisper. Apparently, all they did was to suggest to him that it was a happy occasion for his classic remark about being 'too proud to fight.' "

During the last days of the campaign, the rhetoric became ruthless. Hughes and Roosevelt battered Wilson's mishandling of foreign affairs. Henry Cabot Lodge caused controversy when he charged that Wilson's first *Lusitania* protest note to Germany had included a "weasel" postscript that had tried to appease the kaiser. Hughes seized on the *Lusitania* flap in Rochester, New York: "We do not elect Presidents to dispense with American rights." Cranky La Follette contributed a roundabout dismissal of everyone, calling Wilson a weasel, calling Taft the "big, fat, obliging president who did something for Pierpont Morgan," calling Roosevelt "the president who sent the fleet around the world."

At the Republican torchlight parade in New York that closed the campaign, sixty-five thousand marched behind Hughes and a large model of the White House that was marked "Exit Wilson—Enter Hughes." Hughes said of the flag, "It will not be coerced by threat from any quarter. It will not be deflected by any alien machination."

The same night in Bridgeport, Connecticut, fifty thousand cheered Roosevelt "from the River of Doubt to Mount Zion."

Election day brought cool weather and anxious spirits in critical New York. Democrat Thomas Edison said in Orange, New Jersey, that he was "not so sure [who would win]."

Nearly eighteen and a half million men voted (the last presidential election without women). The results were in doubt for three days, first Hughes with 247 electoral votes, then Wilson with 251 electoral votes.

The victory came down to California's 13 electoral votes. The count continued by hand. Wilson won California by 3,773 votes and all of the South, giving him the victory with 49.3 percent of the vote and 277 electoral college votes. Hughes won the big states of Massachusetts, New York, New Jersey, Pennsylvania, Ohio, Illinois, Michigan and still lost the election with 46.1 percent of the vote and 254 electoral college votes.

Wilson learned of his victory while he was sailing up the Hudson on the presidential yacht *Mayflower* on Thursday evening, November 9. Hughes learned of his loss at the same time in Manhattan after returning from the theater.

The new Sixty-fifth Congress remained Democratic, though slimly in the House. The market had already taken into account Wilson's second term, and there was little immediate reaction. Within a month, Wall Street entered a severe bear market in stocks and bonds as investors correctly anticipated the nation's increasing struggles with the war in Europe.

The year 1917 was a march to the trenches. In January Germany announced unrestricted submarine warfare. In February Roosevelt visited the White House to beg for the command of an army division to lead the charge and was flatly turned down. In March Germany tried to seduce Mexico to make war on the United States (and urged Japan to do likewise). In April Wilson called a special session of Congress and pushed through a war resolution against the Imperial German Government. In May the Selective Service Act began the draft of American men between the ages of twenty-one and thirty-one. In June Pershing and the first American troops landed in France. In July the high-minded Wilson did nothing to solve the race riots in St. Louis, Missouri, instead concentrating his energy on Europe's darkness and the million soldiers Pershing asked for. The U.S. Army descended into trench warfare in October. Americans again started reading the horror of the weekly casualty lists.

All the while Roosevelt kept talking, a ceaseless booster and phrasemaker. "We Americans are children of the Crucible," Roosevelt said of the German submarine threat.

"It is worthless to make promises about the future unless in the present we keep those we have already made," he lectured the vacillating Wilson.

"Let us wage war on Germany with all our energy and courage and regain the right to look the whole world in the eyes without flinching," he said of his demand that the country go to war.

The midterm elections of 1918 were Roosevelt's last hurrah. Few knew that Roosevelt's health was breaking down slowly all year—abscesses, sciatia, inflammatory rheumatism. In August he sank into morbid grief at the death of his youngest son, Quentin, in Europe. Roosevelt still found the strength to campaign in November, and he appeared for the party on the steps of the Union League in New York along with Yale law professor William Howard Taft.

"This seems like old times, doesn't it, Theodore?" Taft asked.

"Indeed, it does, Will."

The two then issued a warning against Wilson's "Fourteen Points" plan for making peace in Europe. This was a first salvo in the Lodge-led Republican effort to block Wilson's idea of the League of Nations. "It is not safe to entrust to one man such unlimited power," the two presidents said. "It is not in accord with the traditions of the Republic."

The voters turned the Democrats out of Congress against the strange backdrop of Pershing's army overrunning the Germans and the influenza epidemic in New York growing at the rate of 719 new cases a day. Since the 1913 Seventeenth Amendment, the Senate was popularly elected like the House, and the GOP took the Senate majority, 49–47. New Senate faces included the Taft-loyalist Warren G. Harding of Ohio. Henry Cabot Lodge of Massachusetts took the chairmanship of the Senate Foreign Relations Committee.

Afterward Roosevelt waved the bloody shirt and showed his anger at the Germans who had killed his son. "The entire pro-German and pacifist vote was behind the Wilson Democratic ticket," Roosevelt remarked. "I regard this result as much more a victory for straight Americanism than Republicanism."

The Monday after the election, the world celebrated armistice day. "Germany Has Surrendered / World War Ended at 6 A.M." Wilson was in church when he heard of the armistice signing at ten o'clock Washington time, and he made no comment. Future major players were on the move: Warren Harding, the newly elected senator to Washington; Calvin Coolidge, the newly elected governor of Massachusetts to Springfield; the millionaire engineer Herbert Hoover of California, who had been Wilson's skilled food administrator, to Europe to help feed the starving in Russia.

Roosevelt went quietly into Roosevelt Hospital. He didn't return home until Christmas Day. His three living sons were in Europe; his wife, Edith, was at home with him. There was a dark worry for his health. On Friday evening, January 6, 1919, a cold night at Oyster Bay in the rambling family cottage, Sagamore Hill, Roosevelt dined with his doctor and wife and then wrote a letter to his son Kermit. Later he complained of a pressure in his lungs. Edith watched over him until 2 A.M. and then went to her own bed. Roosevelt's butler, James Amos, listened to Roosevelt breathing shallowly and evenly until just after 4 A.M.

Roosevelt was dead in his sleep of a blood clot in the lungs. He never woke up. His last words had been to James Amos, *"Turn out the light, James."*

The next day the world shook with the news that the most ambitious, curious, temperamental, troublesome, patriotic, compassionate, and unstoppable American politician of his age was gone.

The silence was awful.

☆ **4** ☆

Boom! Bust!—FDR Buries The GOP

1920–1944

October 13, 1929, that last chilly Sunday before the world according to Wall Street came to an end, New York real estate magnate Charles F. Noyes announced a plan to erect a 150-story office building on Broadway at Worth Street, just up from City Hall.

Charlie Noyes's behemoth would dwarf the reigning giant of the 840-foot Bank of Manhattan building at 40 Wall Street, and it would stand twice as high as the masterpiece that was planned for Thirty-fourth Street and Fifth Avenue by former governor Al Smith's Empire Construction Company.

The Republican broadsheet *New York Herald Tribune** took Noyes most seriously. The staggering cost estimate was one hundred million dollars, which was said to be available from unnamed "banking interests." Noyes was a city kingpin who already operated a potent real estate empire, including the most luxurious office building in the city, the squat brute 120 Wall Street.

Financiers licked their lips at the fantasy of raising the world's greatest monolith. "It is characteristic of Noyes to do big things," said one. "He has been doing them for years, and he will give New York 150 stories, since he has said he would."

"A building of that height is feasible," said a former Democratic New

---

*The *New York Tribune* took over the *New York Herald* in 1926 and became the *New York Herald Tribune*.

York mayor. "From an economic point of view I think it will be one of the outstanding buildings of the city."

An Englishman at the New York Athletic Club observed, "The angels will need red lights on such a building to keep them from colliding on foggy nights."

No one said what was obvious from a glance at the drawing of what 150 stories would look like.

Just like the Tower of Babel.

Readers had a laugh—what would they think of next?—then turned the pages of the newspaper.

The proposed 150 story Noyes Building on Broadway. Just like the Tower of Babel. New York Herald Tribune, October 13, 1929.

The World Series was at the climax between Connie Mack's mighty Philadelphia Athletics and the hard-luck Chicago Cubs. There was also a striking notice for a new novel by Southern writer William Faulkner, *The Sound and the Fury*, about an idiot named Benjy.

Finally it was time for the business section and sober study of the weekly recommendations from the brokerage houses about the eight-year-old raging bull market on Wall Street.

By 1929, according to President Herbert Hoover, there were seventeen million investors in various markets now, up from two million under the pinched, failed, duplicitous Democrat Woodrow Wilson.

All sorts of Americans were in the market, kings and knaves, generals and newsboys, anarchists, Republicans, Democrats—even Governor Franklin D. Roosevelt of New York, who had made a failed bid for the vice presidency in 1920, and former governor Charles W. Bryan of Nebraska, William Jennings Bryan's younger brother, who had made a failed bid for the vice presidency in 1924.

The national mania didn't stop at the borders. Ships at sea were rigged with radio hookups to the floor of the stock exchange so that passengers could get quotes while at cocktails. The Dow Jones Company's stock tickers—tall, candy-machine-like typewriters—were installed in every major city on the North American continent. Also, there were satellite stock markets in cities such as Boston, Buffalo, Cincinnati, Chicago, San Francisco, Toronto, Montreal that were tied by wire to the mother of all trading floors, the New York Stock Exchange at the corner of Broad and Wall Streets.

Each morning at 10 A.M., six days a week, an electric gong sounded another day on the Exchange floor at the American game of *trading:* buying and selling the thousands of stocks and bonds listed on the big board as well as on the less liquid curb market, or over-the-counter market. You could feel the moment-to-moment excitement on the floor. Specialists in each issue stood at the numbered posts in order to take buy and sell orders from clerks and runners. Each time there was a price change, the new number was flashed on the huge moving electronic ticker above the floor. Meanwhile, telephone operators handled thousands of inquiries a day for the latest quotes. The only delay between the trade on the floor and the price listing on the big board was how fast a human being could run. The asking and bidding continued for five unbroken hours. Three million shares a session were traded on the big board and half that on the curb. The noise on the floor was the hum of a very busy railroad depot at rush hour, and the roaring din continued until the 3 P.M. electric clangor. Within moments of the close, the virile crowd dispersed quickly to drink and eat, leaving the wooden plank floor itself heaped with a trail of paper slips that represented billions of spent and earned dollars.

Most everyone in the market was rich and getting richer. The New York stock markets had been a centerpiece of American politics since the railroad boom just before the Civil War. Yet never in history had the stock markets climbed to these heights, like mountaineers ascending a mountain of gold, up and up and up without breakdown since the postwar recession of 1921. Up and up and up. A 600 percent increase in eight years.

True, there was plenty of scandal and horse-thieving. A few stole very big; many got very hurt. The wisdom was not to waste your time complaining about scoundrels. Don't bother licking your wounds in public. Just borrow some more cash and go trading. The wit was that a man wasn't really rich unless he lost at least one fortune on the way up.

This bull market produced fortunes like cow chips. Look at the numbers. In September 1919, the day Woodrow Wilson's stroke wrecked his presidency, the markets had been hibernating in a deep bear cave. That month the muscular General Electric of Schenectady, New York, had traded as low as 95. Now, ten years later, GE had reached 400. In mid-October it was trading most actively at 355. GE paid a 6 percent dividend and, in October, was just about to report sensational quarterly earnings of $6.65 per share.

Buy GE! Or buy the supremely solid United States Steel, that most Republican of stocks, now trading most actively in the 220s. Or buy General Motors at 66, up from 13 the day Calvin "Silent Cal" Coolidge was nominated in 1924. Or buy the technological genius of Radio Corporation of America, called Radio, trading at 86. All these companies were solid earners; all were seen as the bluest of the blue chips; all were stuffed into the portfolios of the richest men on the earth.

The rich men said the market would never go down. The rich men also said that the way to get rich was to buy low and sell high; others said that the way to get rich was never to buy at the bottom and always to sell *too damned early*. Yes, the market averages had topped on September 3. Yes, there was spottiness in basic industries: steel and autos and copper were soft, sugar was depressed, aircraft was overbuilt, coal prices were weak, and the building industry was clearly overextended (so why a 150-story building on Broadway?). However, the price of all this was already in the averages. Up and up and up.

Just like the Tower of Babel.

"Rails best," advised E. F. Hutton & Company on Sunday, October 13.

"Temporary interruption in the major upward trend," said J. S. Bache & Company on October 13.

"The storm clouds have disappeared," said Baer, Cohen & Company on October 13, "and we are again favored with a ray of sunshine."

On Monday, October 14, New York City shivered in the coldest October sunshine in memory as the markets started trading dull and slow. President Hoover was at Philadelphia to see the Athletics beat the Cubs 3–2 and win the World Series. All was well. The next day, Tuesday, October 15, trading was dull again on both the big board and the curb, with the beaten-up ten motor stocks moving up an inch, then sliding a half inch. One professional commented at day's end with what would become the next day's headline: "Stock Market Nervous With Prices Lower."

Wednesday, October 16 at 2 P.M., yet another windy, cold afternoon in New York City, with the world at peace and glamorous America at the speakeasies, was the very moment a tear opened in the fabric of well-being on Wall Street. With an hour to go on the big board, volume swelled abruptly as bears pushed blocks of equities onto the market and plunged prices of blue chips.

This dumping at market close was an old trick to manipulate the market one way or another. The word was that today's sudden plunge was a bear raid by a pool of sharpies, hoping to force down prices by selling stocks they didn't own, then buying them back cheap before the market closed and pocketing the difference.

If true, the bears profited and the bulls lost, for at the 3 P.M. gong, all markets were off sharply. Utilities were especially hard hit, with American Telephone & Telegraph, called Phone, down 5 percent. The industrials also suffered; for example, mighty GE was down 3 percent and popular Radio off 8 percent.

The loudest warning of that last hour of Wednesday trading was that the widely held U.S. Steel was pushed down as far as 206 before it recovered to close at 213.

Market professionals looked at this company's performance and frowned. A secondary U.S. Steel offering had been heavily subscribed at 210. Big players had been buying Steel the last week whenever it neared 210 intraday. But now Steel had dipped below support level, called its floor. Technically, this move was called a breakdown. And if Steel was rotten within, then—?

Wednesday evening, the surprise market sell-off was much discussed across the nation. The pundits said that the day had looked a lot like the "dynamiting" break on Thursday, October 4 that had followed the shocking news that loans on Wall Street had swelled to $8.5 billion. On October 4 the market had contracted in fright of all that unpaid debt—an all-time high—but then over the next week the market had stabilized. Perhaps this break too would pass. Perhaps this break would just become more of the volatility that had weighed on the averages since August, when the Federal Reserve had raised the rediscount rate.

What the Federal Reserve bankers had hoped to do in August was to rein in the bull market by making money more expensive to borrow. They had raised the rate charged the best customers from 6 to 7 percent. Yet the Federal Reserve didn't want a crash. They just wanted to sop up the extra cash, like a sponge on spilled milk.

The next day, Thursday, October 17, after a ragged first four hours, the market rallied in the last hour of trading, gaining back some of what had been lost. The pros relaxed with a loud sigh. Maybe everything was okay. Maybe the investment trusts were buying. Maybe we're trying to find the bottom of a new trading range.

After market close Thursday, longtime treasury secretary Andrew W. Mellon of Pennsylvania, seventy-four years old and famous as a banker and aluminum king, hinted at a possible bullish tax cut soon because, he said, "there has been a considerable increase in [federal] receipts from individual incomes in the last year, traceable directly to stock market profits."

Mellon also mentioned that his Treasury Department did not anticipate any continued selling waves. However, Mellon, who had helped engineer the American prosperity with tax reform and debt reduction for three Republican presidents, Harding, Coolidge, and Hoover, said he was watching closely.

The powerless Democrats were watching the markets, too. John Nance Garner of Texas, the Democratic minority leader of the House, promised a timely tax cut.

Even the reform-minded Democratic governor of New York, Franklin D. Roosevelt, was eager to help. Roosevelt, a cousin of the deceased TR, had recovered from the ashes of his failed vice presidential bid in 1920, and then had risen from the personal tragedy of polio, to win Albany the year before. The governor had recently proposed the largest budget in state history. He was ready to bolster New York State's economic slowing with heavy capital spending.

Friday, October 18, was a darker story. The last hour of trading saw more selling in utilities. All blue chips gave up Thursday's increases on low volume. In market parlance, it's called a dearth of buyers. Low-volume decline was a sure sign for trouble ahead.

Friday evening, the market's continued weakness and scary volatility were a puzzlement in American salons. The debate even reached the prestigious home of Mrs. William Randolph Hearst at 137 Riverside Drive in New York City. Here on Friday evening, at the precipice of the collapse of all that wealth could buy, Mrs. Hearst was welcoming the first

families of New York, including the Vincent Astors, the William K. Van-
derbilts, the Goulds, the Condé Nasts, and twenty-five other prominent
socialites, including Mrs. Cole Porter, all gathered to meet the guest of
honor, the Honorable Winston Churchill, former chancellor of the
British Exchequer. The guests dined in Mrs. Hearst's flower-strewn Tap-
estry Room. After dinner there were newsreels in the library. Several of
the newsreels included Churchill or the Astors. Then there was dancing
in the ballroom with Rudy Vallee and his orchestra. All night, amid the
tinkle of champagne glasses and clouds of Virginia tobacco, there was
small talk of the soft stock markets in London, Paris, Berlin, and New
York. Buy, sell, hold?

Not one of Mrs. Hearst's guests, not Astor, not Vanderbilt, not
Gould, not Nast, could know what was coming. All of them lifelong Republicans (except the Hearsts), all of them as well-informed as powerful,
and yet they were as much in the dark as the least of the earth.

Saturday, October 19's two-hour market session, 10–12 P.M., spooked
market insiders again. Selling waves at the opening and panic liquidations throughout sent price averages to the lows of early October on the
second heaviest Saturday volume in history. The tape ran eighty-four
minutes late. Perhaps a public shakeout, the traders said. Perhaps another bear raid, traders guessed. There was also talk that one infamous
bear, Jesse L. Livermore of New York, was said to be most active in the
selling in a struggle with an infamous bull, Arthur W. Cutten of Chicago.

On Sunday, October 20, the brokerage houses did not disguise their
worry about the prospects. "A stopped clock is right twice a day," Morgan, Davis said of the bearishness. "Brokers loans are the problem," said
Merrill, Lynch. "Current unraveling," said E. F. Hutton. "Speculative ex-
cesses," said J. S. Bache.

What frightened everyone was that Steel had closed at 209. The backbone of the market, Andrew Carnegie's infamous steel trust, was broken.

The oldest traders understood what they read in the averages. Tech-
nical breakdown. Floor collapsing. Market correction. Deluge.

Monday morning, October 21, *general panic* was the president of the
United States as traders dumped blocks of stocks on the market at the 10
A.M. gong opening.

At the very same time, the other chief executive, Herbert Hoover, was
out West on his first whirlwind speaking tour since the election. The
Californian Hoover was a popular figure, familiar to the public since the
Wilson administration. He'd been educated at the Republican-built Leland Stanford University as an engineer and had become a millionaire in
mining. He was not ever comfortable as an orator or a politician on the
stump. The presidency was his first elective office. Hoover was his most

confident at his job whenever he got to talk about how men and machines really worked. He arrived at Dearborn, Michigan, that morning to be squired around by two of the richest workers in the United States, billionaires Henry Ford and Thomas Edison. The president inspected an ancient American village built by Ford; then there was luncheon in Detroit and a review of the Edsel Ford Airshow. The entourage dined that evening at Edison's Menlo Park to the music of 1879 by the Ford orchestra. Afterward Dr. Albert Einstein at Berlin called greetings by an international radio hookup.

While Edison, Ford, and Hoover fiddled with dials, the Monday stock markets had burned down on very heavy volume, six million shares on the big board. The curb market list was also hit hard with dumping of bank stocks—a warning that investors were failing their margin calls, so that the banks holding the portfolios as collateral were suffering sudden asset decline. The most worrisome sign was the breadth of the decline. Out of 1,200 traded stocks, 920 fell, with 80 new annual lows.

The infamous bear-raider Jesse L. Livermore warned of the danger ahead. "If anyone will take the trouble to analyze the selling prices of different stocks," argued Livermore, "as for instance the United States Steel, which is selling around eight to ten times its current earnings, many others must look, and have looked for a long time, as selling at ridiculously high prices."

The bull camp wouldn't surrender so easily. Yale University economics professor Irving T. Fisher countered Livermore's warning. "I believe the breaks of the last few days have driven stock down to hard rock."

Fisher also defended the Republican regime. "Under the Coolidge and Hoover administrations," he said at New Haven, "business has been allowed to build up that which was held down by the 'trust-busting' policies of Roosevelt and Wilson."

Tuesday morning, October 22, the bulls seemed to have the confidence of investors as the averages mounted a sharp rise. There was hope that the markets would stabilize despite the fear of a "prolonged bear."

Boosting market confidence was the voice of Charles E. Mitchell, governor of the New York Federal Reserve and chairman of the $8,000-per-share National City Bank of New York. Mitchell was a most unpopular man in both New York and Washington, since all players blamed him for the confusion over the borrowing rates. In the spring and summer, with the market in a trough, Mitchell had resisted raising federal borrowing rates in order to ease a credit bubble. In response, the market had taken off. Mitchell had finally agreed to raising rates in August, and now the August tightening of credit was regarded as too little and too late.

Mitchell had arrived from Europe the previous Tuesday and had immediately started arguing with the Washington Federal Reserve Board. Mitchell wanted to calm Wall Street by cutting the rediscount rate the 1 percent that he had gone along with adding in August.

The Federal Reserve governors argued back: Wouldn't a cut only encourage the speculation that had swelled the Street loans and the six hundred thousand margin accounts? Wouldn't a panicky rate cut create another bubble?

The answer was yes. Mitchell didn't care about excess. He had his eye on market confidence. He had his eye on the shocking fact that, despite the slight Tuesday market boost on strong volume, Steel had sold off again and closed at 207.

Tuesday night, the lights stayed on at Charles F. Noyes's massive beauty 120 Wall Street until 5 A.M. as clerks had to stay up again trying to organize the accounts. Margin accounts required 40 to 50 percent collateral, and the recent volatility was always threatening to wreck accounts unless they were refinanced.

All night at 120 Wall the small talk was about a rate cut. Could Mitchell deliver? And what about Steel? What about all these bargains here? Are the trusts coming in? Who's buying?

Wednesday afternoon, October 24, Wall Steel suffered the severest break in history with 6.3 million shares traded on the big board.

The selling came like an attack. From 10 A.M. to 2 P.M., the market was weak and ragged. GE traded as high as 341, GM as high as 61, Radio as high as 81. Steel was flat and weak.

Then, with an hour to go, there was a sudden dumping on the market of more than 2.5 million shares. No bear raid this time; this was liquidation. Blue chips were flung down for sale, uncovering stop-loss orders (mandatory execution prices) and forcing more distress selling. The slaughter was just as bad in the curb market and the over-the-counter market.

"The good ones go down with the bad ones in a market like this," said a trader.

The selling was accelerated by a chain reaction in the margin accounts. As stock prices plunged, collateral against margin accounts sank, and unless the accounts were reinforced immediately, the holdings were offered at market (minimum bid price), a process that pulled prices even lower.

Before the close, rumors hit the market that some houses were bankrupt, or some big investors were in distress, and this kind of rumor became self-fulfilling. At the close, the averages were at the day's bottom. So were the best issues on very heavy volume. Radio down 13 percent;

GE down 7 percent; Telephone down 6 percent; GM down 5 percent; and Steel down 5 percent.

The best of the best were thrown down like losers.

Wednesday evening, the chorus was loud in many directions. New York Federal Reserve chair Charles E. Mitchell wanted the Washington Federal Reserve governors to cut the rediscount rate immediately. Mitchell complained at the delay, "It is hardly probable that a lower discount rate would cause another speculative outburst in the market."

A true bear, William H. Danforth of Brookline, Massachusetts, who had made five million dollars that day shorting Steel, GE, and Montgomery Ward, commented, "It was just the sawing off of another limb."

Meanwhile, the bullish economist Irving Fisher of Yale gave assurances that all remained well "unless we experience a panic or there is a radical change in market psychology." He also promised that "we will never return to pre-war levels," and that "on a basis of expectations we are not overvalued."

President Hoover spent Wednesday on the Ohio River enroute to Kentucky. (A wild river storm had swept over the president's boat on Tuesday night, while the president slept.) Wednesday evening Hoover dined at Louisville's Brown Hotel, then made a speech from the deck of his ship. At no point did he speak to the press about the market troubles. There was no evidence at the time that he even noticed what had happened. He boarded a train for Washington at ten o'clock in the evening without remarking on the market news then clicking out on the wire.

Could anyone have stopped Black Thursday? Could a rate cut, or a bully speech from Hoover, or a collective rush of cash from the bankers, or a closing of the markets, have stopped the catastrophe?

At 10 A.M., October 25, the gong sounded and the tape told the tale.

The selling was in shock waves. Word of the breakdown spread. Crowds quickly gathered outside at Wall and Broad Streets to watch for trouble. Mounted police tried to control the situation, but this made it worse. When an ambulance arrived midday to fetch a collapsed clerk from a brokerage house, word went around that there were mass suicides inside the stock exchange. Wild reports of men leaping from windows were cheered. At one point the crowd rushed in pursuit of galloping mounted policemen, only to be disappointed by the fact that it was just a skittish horse.

In the brokerage offices along Wall Street the selling didn't cause excitement, rather a strange hush—men and women walking around in hunched poses and speaking in low tones, as if there was a funeral in progress.

The crash of 1929. New York Herald Tribune, *October 26, 1929.*

The day's liquidation had three stages. From 10 A.M. to 1 P.M. the prices were crushed on ruinously heavy volume.

Then at 1 P.M., with the market at the lows, a rumor hit the market that the bankers were meeting. Prices paused, stabilized, and bounced on short-covering. There truly was an emergency meeting at the J. P. Morgan bank that included the younger Morgan himself (son of the deceased J. Pierpont Morgan, d. 1913) and New York Fed boss Charles E. Mitchell.

Was there going to be a rate cut?

When nothing happened, the third stage started a flood after 1:30

P.M. What made the panic even worse was that the telephone operators on the floor couldn't handle the demand of price inquiries, and inaccurate or slow prices added to the fear. At trading post 8, where AT&T was traded, there were 13,400 inquiries in sixty minutes. Scare selling created a whirlpool after 2 P.M.

Another cause of fright was the rumor that the market was closing. A young clerk ran back to his big wire house to report, "They've put a big sign saying that they've closed, and there's a big crowd and a thousand cops yelling."

The truth was that a small sign had been hung on the Broad Street entrance to announce the visitor's gallery had been closed because of the crowd.

At the close, twelve million shares had traded on the big board, the biggest day ever. Every sector had been massacred. Across the continent all the satellite exchanges had followed New York down: there were descriptions such as "collapse" in Chicago; "wild scenes" in Philadelphia; "near panic" in San Francisco; and "crash" in Montreal.

Thursday night, the trains leaving Wall Street were half-empty as the brokerages and law offices stayed open to settle accounts. One hotel loaded one hundred cots in the lobby for overnight guests. Waiters from uptown restaurants crisscrossed the streets pushing food carts for men dining at their desks. In every office and hotel, exhaustion was matched by a giddy sense of doom.

On the wire was not only the news of the panic but also the cries of officials. Washington senators blamed "Mitchellism" and speculation. New York bankers countered that the blame was on the Federal Reserve's lack of action.

The radio news just said, "Crashed."

That night, the ominous word across the nation was that Washington expected that this sudden "deflation" on Wall Street would aid industry by clearing out the speculative loans. Indeed "deflation" was coming, but it would rip down everything.

Friday, October 25, the markets plunged again at the opening but then recovered midday, closing slightly up in composite averages on a heavy big board volume of five million.

That evening the puzzle again was whether this was the time to buy or get out. Prices were cheap. Would the investment trusts buy here? There was gallows humor on the Street. Men who had not been home for two days joked that there was now going to be an easy excuse to your wife for staying out too late. "Honey, the crash!" Others said to buy restaurant stocks so you'd have a place to eat if the market crisis worsened.

President Hoover had finally commented on the crisis on Thursday afternoon. He read a statement to newspapermen that was printed Saturday morning, October 26. "The fundamental business of the country that is the production and distribution of commodity is on a sound and prosperous basis."

Other commentators on Saturday were not so obtuse or reassuring: "We are in the midst of a financial panic," remarked a New York professional, "based entirely on mob psychology and not in any way related to the present condition of America's fundamental industries."

Saturday, October 26, fooled everyone who wanted to be fooled. On two million shares on the big board and a million on the curb, the averages bounced slightly. The word was that investment trusts were buying some blue chips while still dumping others that were "overbulled." The ticker tape closed orderly only thirty-seven minutes late.

The warning was still there, however, with GE off eight dollars and Steel left flat at 202½.

The Sunday, October 27 papers collected the usual brokerage house advice, all for caution. There was one true doomsayer, the legendary Yankee businessman and market pundit Roger W. Babson of Wellesley Hills, Massachusetts, who blamed the investment trusts for the havoc and predicted that the market was hopeless. Writing in the *Herald Tribune,* Babson argued, "Stocks today in Wall Street are in the same position as land was in Florida the week after the Florida boom collapsed in 1924. The sun continued to shine in Florida and has shone ever since. Crops continued to grow after the collapse of the land boom and each succeeding year has given Florida greater crops than ever before. More people visited Florida last year than during any previous year and the hotels did a record business, but you simply could not sell any land in Florida. Speculative interest in Florida land had been killed, and it has not yet come to life."

Monday, October 28, saw the follow-through on the selling-panic that topped out Wall Street for thirty years.

From the opening, the selling was heavy and steady. Today, there was no more carnival spirit outside the exchange. The messengers came and went with their heads down. A rumor hit that a large wire house had lost fifty thousand customers in the last ten days. Margin accounts blew up like firecrackers. The action at post 8 illustrated the selling. At 10 A.M., Phone opened at 263. Thirty minutes later it was at 252. Until 2 P.M. it hung in a tight range around 249, waiting for yet another bankers' meeting at J. P. Morgan. At 2:30, when no rate cut was announced, Phone plunged to 240. The last half hour was surrender, so that at the close, the widely held AT&T was at 232 on 130,000 shares. *Down 12 percent on the day.*

View from the gallery of the New York Stock Exchange during the capitulation sell-off on Tuesday, October 29, 1929. Note the oval-shaped trading posts and the electronic ticker tape in the background. Milwaukee Journal, *October 31, 1929.*

Monday night was silent as a tomb on Wall Street. All the lights were on. All the clerks, traders, and lawyers were at their desks, trying to settle the thirteen million shares traded on the exchanges. There was no joking this time. No rate cut rumor.

Tuesday, October 29, was the capitulation session. The selling was ruthless, pointless, violent. One wire house closed ninety-eight margin accounts at the opening, and every wire house was frightened at the prospect of keeping open accounts they should have closed. The first selling hour saw banks selling their holdings to support their crumbling loan portfolios. The second selling hour saw deaths in New York as well as across the country. In Providence a man collapsed while watching the ticker tape. In Kansas City a man shot himself twice, saying, "Tell the boys I can't pay what I owe."

At the Steel trading post, specialist Major Oliver Bridgman wielded his pencil like a saber as he recorded the furious sell orders in his book. Bridgman was writing the doom for the nation's steel industry. Steel tried to rally when a rumor hit that the company was raising its dividend by one dollar immediately in hopes of bolstering the price. The dead cat did not bounce as Steel dipped as low as 166$\frac{1}{2}$.

Other rumors colored the trading day. Twice there was said to be more bankers' confabs at the Morgan bank; another report mentioned an emergency meeting at the Federal Reserve building in Washington.

Whatever the truth, no rate cut came. None was promised. Indeed the opposite was rumored. "There is a fear among several board members," it was reported later, "of a new era of expansion should precipitate action in the direction of easing money be taken."

The selling was wild liquidation. Mob psychology, it was called, which meant men tore open their safe deposit boxes and pulled out their stock certificates in order to fling them onto the market for sale at any price.

In the first hour three million shares were dumped on the market. At noon, eight million more were thrown out. Another two million were dumped at the close. The final volume was sixteen million on the big board, seven million on the curb. The ticker tape ran nearly two hours late and was badly inaccurate.

Standing in the midst of the paper trash at the final gong, the traders were shell-shocked. All averages were at the day's bottom. The ten motor stocks were particularly destroyed, with GM, the most active stock on the day, closing at 40. General Electric was down 12 percent on the day to close at 222. AT&T sank another 10 percent to close at 204.

Yet the destruction had not been just the hyperextended blue chips. This bear was monstrously hungry. On the big board, out of 1,200 traded on the day, there were 561 new lows and not one stock was recorded up on the day. Crashed.

Just like the Tower of Babel.

Immediately after the gong, the explanations and rationalizations started on the radio news.

"The stock market is not the major barometer of business," said Dr. Julius Klein, assistant secretary of commerce.

"I believe there are wonderful bargains," said the president of American International.

"The absolute necessity of taking the long view," said Moody's Investors Service.

"The Chrysler Corporation is in exceptionally sound financial condition," said Walter P. Chrysler of his company, which had closed at 28¼, after a year high of 135. "We have every reason to look forward to a normal and profitable business in 1930."

"The peak of selling has been reached," said an aluminum executive.

From the White House? From President Hoover, who had been in Cabinet session all day Tuesday while the wealth of his country was reduced to trash? What did he say? Silence.

The next day, Wednesday October 30, the day after the worst day in market history, the markets began all the other worst days. The physical law that bodies in motion tend to stay in motion applied to the markets, too. What crashed those two weeks in October did not stop crashing for nearly three more years. Not 1929. Not 1930. Not 1931. Not until August 1932, exactly three years after the Federal Reserve rate rise that started the selling, did the stock market composite averages bottom out.

By then the United States was dying in a depression that was like a worldwide pandemic. What started falling on Wall Street ripped every market in Europe down with it.

How scary? In 1932, with 50 percent of Americans out of work, with

Absent confidence, there is no economy. New York Evening Post, October 26, 1929.

banks falling like mayflies, with the Western Hemisphere facing severe famine by winter, General Electric traded as low as 8½, and United States Steel as low as 21¼.

Just like the Tower of Babel.

Who did this awful thing? How had it happened? Where did it begin? Who first dared to build a tower of speculation on Wall Street? Who was to blame?

The answer was the people who had raised the United States into the most prosperous nation in history—a 150-story republic by October, 1929.

The answer was the men who'd had all the power, all the glory, since Woodrow Wilson had collapsed in his railcar with a stroke in 1919. The answer was Harding, Coolidge, Hoover, Mellon, Lodge, Hughes, Kellogg, even Chief Justice Taft, and all their dutiful, ambitious, hardworking protégés.

The answer was the Republican party—that was who was to blame. The country did blame. And blame and blame and blame. Blame until the Republican party would have to spend six full decades on its knees in disgrace for that chilly October of 1929, when the world according to Wall Street came to an end.

Did the Republicans deserve the blame? Yes. The party on watch gets the blame and deserves the blame. On watch for every day of the runaway bull market of the Roaring Twenties was the Grand Old Party.

★ 1920 ★

Woodrow Wilson's second administration marched off to war in Europe and then, after the November 1918 armistice, straggled into battle with the Republican Senate over the peace.

Wilson won the war by turning a democracy into a command economy directed by a dictatorial War Cabinet; then Wilson lost the peace by refusing to barter with partisanship.

In May 1919 Wilson and the allies signed the Treaty of Versailles, which condemned and flattened Germany for the war—a cranky one-sidedness that cooked the stew that Hitler's Third Reich would feed upon for twenty-five years. Russia, then suffering civil war under the Bolshevik coup, was frozen out of the negotiations as if Mother Russia didn't signify—a stupidity that isolated Lenin and Stalin and cooked the stew that the Communists would feed upon for seventy years.

Attached to the treaty was the Covenant of the League of Nations, which aimed to establish an international legislative and police body.

Immediately, the Republican-majority Senate challenged the Treaty of Versailles. Critics pointed at Article X of the Covenant of the League of Nations, which required the United States to subordinate its sovereignty to the league. Utopian Wilson wanted the United States to commit to guiding the nations of the world with good feelings. Wilson was blind to the naked chauvinism of the European powers who wanted to cut up the body of the defeated Axis.

The league critics, using the words of the late Theodore Roosevelt, said that without military arms any such international arbitration was futile. Few Republican politicians trusted Europe to do other than to rearm and go to war again.

Senate Foreign Relations chairman Henry Cabot Lodge of Massachusetts tried to amend the Versailles treaty and the league covenant in concert with other Republicans favorable to a modified league, such as William Howard Taft, Charles Evans Hughes, and Herbert Hoover of California. Other Republicans condemned Wilson's negotiations with such vehemence they became known as the *irreconcilables;* chief among them were the so-called Progressive senators Hiram W. Johnson of California, William E. Borah of Idaho, Philander C. Knox of Pennsylvania, and Robert La Follette of Wisconsin. Prominent Republican contributors such as Henry Frick and Andrew W. Mellon financed a nationwide publicity campaign against the treaty.

Lodge's power overwhelmed the *irreconcilables* in the Senate, and Lodge could have delivered Wilson the votes to pass a modified and cautious treaty and covenant.

Stubborn Wilson had bargained tirelessly with the Europeans; however, he wouldn't negotiate with his own Congress. Instead, in September 1919 Wilson entrained on a coast-to-coast speaking tour to make his case to the public. "What the Germans used," Wilson predicted, "were toys compared to what would be used in the next war."

Wilson coaxed his Republican opponents. "I admit the distinguished history of the Republican party," the president said at Spokane. "I do admit that it has been the creator of great constructive policies, and I should be very sorry to see it lose the prestige which it has earned by such policies."

Wilson even believed he could challenge the courage of the Republicans. "I want to get into any kind of trouble that will help liberate mankind," he said at Reno, Nevada. "I don't want to always be thinking about my skin or my pocketbook or my friendships."

Wilson blasted the German-American influence in the Republican party. It was also true that many German-Americans from all sides felt that the treaty was too harsh on Germany. "Any man who carries a hyphen about him," the president said at Pueblo, Colorado, "carries a dagger which he is ready to plunge into the vitals of the Republic."

Fate plunged into Wilson's life the night after making his fortieth tour speech at Pueblo, Colorado. On September 27, 1919, at 5 A.M. on board the presidential special, the first lady called the president's physician to the president's compartment. What the doctor saw was a wrecked human being—mortally ill with thrombosis and arteriosclerosis.

Presently the presidential special was sidetracked a mile from the station at Wichita, Kansas, where ten thousand admirers were waiting at 6 A.M.

That morning the first lady, Edith Bolling Wilson, and the president's physician, Dr. Cary T. Grayson, began telling lies about Wilson's health to the press and public. "The president has been under such a strain during the last year," Dr. Grayson argued, "and has so spent himself without reserve on this trip, that it has brought on a nervous reaction to his digestive organs." Grayson also blamed the Treaty of Versailles trip, "The trouble dates back to an attack of influenza last April in Paris." Grayson established a careful retreat, "His condition is not alarming, but it will be necessary for his recovery that he have rest and quiet for a considerable time."

Wilson's presidency was finished. His major agenda for the next nineteen months was to deceive the nation that he was healthy enough to discharge the duties of his office.

Wilson's collapse not only ended the Versailles treaty and the league covenant, which were defeated in the Senate in November, but also choked the hopes for a Wilson third term.

In domestic affairs, Wilson's priggish administration successfully pushed through the Eighteenth Amendment for prohibition, leading to a decade of hypocrisy and organized crime. Wilson also engineered the gagging of political dissent in the United States. It was Wilson's administration, with the cooperation of the Democratic congressional majority in the Sixty-fifth Congress of 1917–18, that passed the tyrannical alien and sedition acts, which were used by Attorney General A. Mitchell Palmer, appointed March 1919, to harass Germans, Russians, Jews, socialists, and immigrants. In 1918 longtime Socialist candidate Eugene V. Debs was arrested for resisting the war effort and sentenced to ten years in jail.

The pious, failing Wilson did nothing to answer the epidemic of race riots in 1917–18 that scarred the nation from St. Louis to Washington and New York.

Wilson's administration of the so-called New Freedoms was the highwater mark of racial violence after the Civil War. The Ku Klux Klan was reinvigorated in 1915, and it grew until it was able to elect candidates to

Congress who were open about their Klan sponsorship. The Klan politicians, almost entirely Democrats, spoke against not only Negroes but also Catholics, Jews, and any non-white-Protestant presence. The deceitful Wilson said little of weight against the Klan. The Republican party also stood by in silence at the rot of race war.

The Republicans concentrated on reclaiming all the power. By the spring of 1920, the Republicans were confident that whoever they nominated would win the presidency. Every healthy Republican member of the Senate and most Republican governors of large states threw a hat in the ring.

In June, after all the primaries, there were four credible candidates: Progressive Hiram Johnson of California (Roosevelt's old ally); conservative General Leonard Wood of the Cuban governor-generalship (Roosevelt's Rough Rider pal who had missed out on the European war); Governor Frank O. Lowden of Illinois (the conservative businessman choice); and young, deft wartime food administrator Herbert Hoover of California.

The delegates gathered at Chicago (for the tenth time in seventeen conventions) expecting a fierce fight for the unpledged delegates. Johnson's friends warned against General Wood. Wood's friends warned against Governor Lowden. Governor Lowden's friends warned the Progressives that the governor was the choice of the Old Guard. Everyone warned against a repetition of the convention of 1912, which had shattered the party and elected Wilson.

"I'm going to dig up the vocabulary of 1912," said one senator about the stealing of delegates, "and begin calling these people burglars and second story men. The sooner this convention comes to a realization that it has got to take Wood or Johnson the better."

None of the candidates was shy about coming to Chicago to promote himself to the delegates and the press. Johnson held rallies at the Auditorium Hotel on Michigan Avenue, speaking to crowds as Roosevelt once had and displaying a three-hundred-foot "Johnson for President" banner—behind which was a much smaller "Hoover for President" banner. General Wood, wearing his jodhpurs and riding breeches, strutted along Michigan Avenue like a caricature of a military dictator.

Admired former president William Howard Taft, now a Yale law professor, was hired by a magazine syndicate to analyze the convention fights. Taft most distrusted Johnson of California and wrote, "He is flushed with the [primary] victories in California, Michigan and Nebraska, with the united support of the Sinn Feiners, the Progressives and the radical labor vote, who will not support any state Republican candidate."

Taft also spoke against all the Progressives. "The Future of the Republican party must be unhampered by the paralyzing party membership of Senators Johnson, La Follette, Borah, [Asle J.] Gronna, and [George W.] Norris."

The delegate bickering was so predictable, Old Guard "Stand-Pat" conservatives versus Bull Moose Progressives versus maverick Rooseveltian General Wood, that it moved humorist Heywood Broun to write an "I am for Hiram" march that mocked Johnson's loud patriotism.

> We want a true American
> There in the White House chair
> Just like our old own glory
> Red, white, true-blue and square
> I am for Hiram
> Yes, I am
> He's for the U.S.A.
> Three cheers for Hiram Johnson
> Hip-hip! Hip-hip! Hur-ray!

Hoover was in New York hiding out from the fisticuffs. He predicted trouble in the balloting and warned, "Third parties are not a success"; then he outlined his candidacy: "What will be the big issue in the campaign? The League of Nations or economics, I believe."

The most informed prediction was a *Herald Tribune* headline: "Old Guard Determined to Beat Wood, Hope for Dark Horse."

The gavel (made from the wood of Independence Hall, Philadelphia) opened the wrangling in the Chicago Auditorium on Tuesday, June 8 in the midst of a blistering heat wave, ninety-nine degrees with darting thunderstorms and lightning over the lake.

The treat of the first day was a speech by ancient former senator Chauncey Depew of New York, now eighty-six years old, who had first attended a Republican convention when Lincoln was renominated at Baltimore in 1864.

"My friends," Depew proclaimed, "we all here can say 'Glory, Hallelujah!' We all here are convicted, convinced, and converted. We all here belong not only to the Republican Church, but to that church which means unity, civilization with liberty, and good government." [Applause] "One and all, the whole nation, will stand up for the principles of the fathers, for the principles of Lincoln, for the principles of McKinley, Taft and Roosevelt."

The first woman to address the convention as a voter (the Nineteenth

The hungry candidates before the 1920 convention—Harding in the back with Hughes, Taft, and Coolidge; Johnson in the foreground with Wood, Lowden, Borah, Knox, and Hoover. New York Herald Tribune, *June 2, 1920.*

Amendment would go into effect in August 1920) was Margaret McCarter of Kansas; she was cheered for her remarks: "I stand here as a representative of twenty million women. We are organized, we are trained, we are ready for the duties of citizenship. We stand loyally by the party inaugurated by Abraham Lincoln—the party of liberty and life, of loyalty and love, the party that has never failed the good old stars and stripes."

The first day's rocky incident was when a Wisconsin La Follette supporter tried to read a substitute plank advocating disarmament as well as the nationalization of industries. He was shouted down by the gallery and delegates. "No! No! No! Socialist! No!"

Stately Henry Cabot Lodge spoke that day as permanent chairman of the convention. He was brutal in his partisanship. "Mr. Wilson and his dynasty, his heirs, and assigns, or anybody that is his, anybody who with bent knee has served his purposes, must be driven from all control, from all influence upon the government of the United States. . . . They must be driven from office and power, not because they are Democrats, but because Mr. Wilson stands for a theory of administration and government that is not American."

On the second day, the platform was striking for its emphasis on foreign affairs. A plank declared relations with Mexico a disgrace. Another plank condemned the war powers of the president: "Usurpation is intolerable."

The platform also denounced high taxes and the high cost of living (inflation). Another plank called for tougher standards in immigration and for the "exclusion of mental defects and criminals."

On civil rights, the platform was contradictory. Without much explanation, the Palmer raids were openly supported: "Aliens within jurisdiction . . . are not entitled to the right or liberty of agitation directed to or against the government of the United States." Yet there was an anti-lynching plank—"a terrible blot on our American citizenship"—that underlined how badly frightened the country was by the serial race riots. The party moved to support women's suffrage—"Welcome!"—and to advocate for women in industry with "the principle of equal pay for equal work."

Nominating began on Friday in more waves of heat that exhausted the delegates as the speeches dragged on.

Hiram W. Johnson's name was cheered by the California delegation, while it was jeered from the gallery for California's Wilson majority vote in 1916: "Who put Wilson in the White House?" the gallery demanded.

Governor Frank O. Lowden was advanced as "a Businessman for President."

Brigadier General Leonard Wood, former chief of staff of the army, who had led the Rough Riders up San Juan Hill with Roosevelt, was "a plain, blunt man, with a blunt belief in facts." Wood was praised by Theodore Roosevelt's sister, Corinne Robinson: "I want Leonard Wood not because he was my brother's friend but because he is my brother's type of man."

Popular, granite-handsome Calvin Coolidge, the governor of Massachusetts, was boomed for his Yankeehood: "A boyhood on a lonely farm in Vermont bred him in industry, frugality and self-reliance."

Then there was the bright-eyed dark horse, Senator William G. Harding of Ohio. Harding was a protégé (some said bagman) of the now deceased conservative Senator Joseph B. "Fire-alarm" Foraker of Ohio, who had resigned the Senate in disgrace in 1909 for taking bribes from Standard Oil. "In personal character he has the dignity, urbanity, and breadth of vision of McKinley" argued the nomination speech. "Like that other great Ohioan, he is one of the common folks best loved by those who know him best."

At 7 P.M., after four long-winded ballots of the delegations, there was no winner, nor even a candidate who was dominating. The delegates retired to their hotels to choose sides. Johnson and Lowden were at the Blackstone Hotel; Wood was at Fort Sheridan; Hoover was in New York; Harding was at the Auditorium Hotel. Everyone made frantic telephone calls till well after midnight. The distressing fact was that Roosevelt had gone and left no successor. The party bosses gathered in the famous "smoke-filled room" at the Blackstone Hotel and planned for the next day.

Saturday morning, October 13, was an ironic day that showed a false report of military coup against "Trotzky" and "Lenine" in Moscow. The balloting began in earnest. Lowden and Wood traded the lead for the fifth, sixth, seventh, and eighth ballots. Johnson was never a factor. Maverick La Follette held on to only the grumpy Wisconsin delegates. On the ninth ballot, the anti-Wood and anti-Lowden forces from the "smoke-filled room" launched their assault. The New York delegation bolted with sixty-six votes to dark horse Harding. Before there was anyone to stop the boom, Harding had swept to victory on the tenth ballot.

Harding didn't expect it, and he was caught unaware in a back chamber of the Auditorium. When he learned he'd been chosen, he and his wife dashed to the hotel to prepare themselves. Later, Harding's first recorded remark to the press was a strange and off-key jest. "If you want to make Mrs. Harding looked pleased," he said with his pinch-faced, politically savvy wife, Florence Kling Harding, at his side, "tell her something about the price of millinery coming down."

Hiram Johnson was irked by upstart Harding: "It has been a good fight. We lost, and I don't whine. I take my beatings standing up."

The campaign was a singular beating of the Democrats. Harding stayed home at Marion, Ohio, following the McKinley model of politicking at Canton, Ohio. Harding preached the brilliantly obtuse phrase "a return to normalcy." Meanwhile, the vice presidential nominee, Governor Calvin Coolidge of Northampton, Massachusetts, traveled the country showing off his sincere Yankee nature of flintiness and restraint.

Harding declared that the election turned on just two issues: Article X of the League of Nations covenant; and reform in Washington. "America is not ready to mortgage her conscience to the Old World," he said on election eve, "or agree to send her citizens to engage in European disputes."

The Democratic nominee, Governor James M. Cox of Ohio, was a weak-voiced candidate. In desperation at the close of the campaign, the Ohio Democrats tried a crude trick by circulating the rumor that Harding's grandmother was a "Negress." This lie caused Harding's aged father to get in a fistfight with a Democratic agent the Sunday before the election in Marion, Ohio. "You called my mother a Negro!" old Dr. George Harding cried out.

The grace note of the campaign was the surprise Democratic vice presidential candidate, forty-year-old Franklin Delano Roosevelt of New York. Young Roosevelt had risen in his party through the same patronage assistant secretary post at the Navy Department that his famous cousin had first held. He was as sober, reform-minded, zealous, and well-spoken as his famous older cousin. It was a happy irony of partisan politics that the young Roosevelt prospered in the New York Democracy with the help of his famous family name and that FDR followed many Progressive programs that would later turn up in the New Deal. "If the voters realize that this is a deep-seated struggle between two different conceptions of government," Franklin Roosevelt said on election eve, "—that is, it is the old fight between the progressively minded and the reactionists—the results on Election Day will furnish an overwhelming surprise to the old-fashioned prognosticator."

Wall Street bet on Harding 12–1. Harding won the biggest landslide in Republican history. With women voting nationally for the first time, there were twenty-six million votes. Harding took 60.3 percent and 404 electoral votes, sweeping the North and West and even grabbing Tennessee from the Democratic Solid South.

The Republican majorities grew hugely in both houses of the new sixty-seventh Congress and in all state legislatures in the North and West. The Republicans even won Franklin Roosevelt's Hyde Park. From coast to coast, the Republicans and the "return to normalcy" were in command.

Perennial presidential candidate Eugene V. Debs was still in federal prison in Atlanta for war resistance, but he took 915,490 votes (3.4 percent) for the Socialist ticket. The day after the election, Debs commented darkly on American politics, "I shall not be disappointed over the results of the election, as the people will get what they think they want in so far as they think at all."

Harding vs. Cox, 1920. New York Herald Tribune, *June 2, 1920.*

In New York the confident and dapper Charles Evans Hughes, who would soon be named the new secretary of state in order to repair the war-shattered international relations, remarked on the Republican triumph, "Fine! Fine!"

★ 1924 ★

Charming, chummy Warren Gamiel Harding's brief tenure was blessed by the brilliant Hughes at State and the sagacious Taft as chief justice of the Supreme Court. However, the administration was cursed by naked graft and a bad run of luck that killed the president.

Harding was a man who liked to be liked. The president made many friends when he pardoned Debs from prison in time for him to spend Christmas 1921 with his family.

Secretary of State Charles Evans Hughes was a visionary in world affairs. Throughout his service he refused to trade with Lenin's Bolsheviks, whom he denounced as torturers and tyrants. Hughes formalized the peace treaties with Germany and Austria and began arms limitations talks for both the Pacific basin and Europe. Over many years Hughes negotiated testily with Mexico, where the politicians were toying with Moscow's troublemaking Reds: Hughes managed to avoid the open war that had threatened the Mexican border ever since Taft's administration. Hughes did stumble in Nicaragua, where the rebel Augusto Sandino provoked violence: the only way the Americans could calm the region bordering the critical Panama Canal was to install Sandino's executioner, Anastasio Somoza, in a cynical dictatorship.

Other Harding successes were the president's Cabinet choices of the Pittsburgh banking millionaire Andrew W. Mellon at Treasury and the California mining millionaire Herbert Hoover at Commerce. Banker Mellon and engineer Hoover both sought to boost business by cutting taxes. Wall Street was delighted. Nearly twenty thousand businesses failed in 1921, causing sharp unemployment and broad wage cuts in the major industries. The bull run in the markets that began at the bottom of 1921 was always aided by Mellon's and Hoover's belief that lower taxes were good for big business, and big business was good for government. Mellon was soon enjoying a three-hundred-million-dollar tax revenue surplus on a three-billion-dollar federal budget. Hoover was most busy expanding the 1919 Federal Highway Act and readjusting the protectionist tariff upward to protect American manufacturing and farm goods. The boom got onboard the automobile business and raced ahead.

Harding's personal mistakes soon threatened all the rest. The president's White House was colored by all-night poker games, heavy and open whiskey drinking, and the president's beautiful mistress. Harding's poker party fell apart in the spring of 1923. A Justice Department pal of the president was accused of taking payoffs from bootleggers. Two cronies committed suicide when accused of corruption. Elsewhere, Interior Secretary Albert B. Fall was accused of selling naval oil reserve district Teapot Dome to oilmen. Soon, the Teapot Dome scandal pointed right into the White House.

For the moment, Harding remained most popular. However, in the summer of 1923, with the rumors of spoilsmanship spreading, the president decided to get out of Washington for a vacation. He embarked on a much ballyhooed tour to the West and Alaska. In a special train with a radio-equipped Pullman car, Harding moved across the country making speeches on law and order, on farm aid, and on a proposal to reorganize the railroads. Accompanying him was his now invalid wife, Florence. "I have been looking forward to this trip for six years," said the first lady, "and I am not going to be talked out of it." Also on the trip were several members of the Cabinet, including Commerce Secretary Hoover and his wife who met the embassy at Tacoma, Washington.

The big political controversies that summer, a year from the major scandal investigations by Congress, were how much the United States wanted to help rebuild Europe and how likely it was that millionaire Henry Ford of Michigan was going to try for the presidency on a third-party ticket called the National Move.

On the first controversy, half the Senate went on European junkets to justify their positions that the United States should stay out of European affairs. "Europe wants our purse," said Senator Hiram Johnson of California after he returned on the gigantic liner *Leviathan,* "not our ideas."

On the second controversy, Henry Ford was trying to talk his way out of his reputation for bigotry and anti-Semitism, which had made him a most controversial figure over the last years. The nation was routinely pummeled by the Ku Klux Klan that summer—in July a man was burned at the stake in Yazoo City, Mississippi, in front of half the town—yet even still, Henry Ford's dangerous remarks were startling: "You probably think the labor unions were organized by labor, but they weren't," Ford inanely told a magazine in July. "They were organized by the Jew fi-

Henry Ford

nanciers. The labor union is a great scheme to interrupt work. It speeds up the loafing. It's a great thing for the Jew to have on hand when he comes around to get his clutches on an industry. . . . These Jew financiers are not building anything. They wait until things begin to decay; then they get into them."

The touring Harding did not speak out so foolishly. He boosted the world court; he promoted Mout Zion Park; he extolled the virtues of the Alaska Territory; he shook hands with every farmworker who approached him. On July 5, Harding and his party departed Tacoma, Washington, on board the army transport *Henderson,* and for the next three weeks enjoyed excited greetings at every major settlement along the Gulf of Alaska: Wrangell, Juneau, Seward, Anchorage. After an Alaska Railroad train ride to Fairbanks and an automobile trip to Chitina, the president entrained on the Copper River and Northwestern Railroad to rejoin *Henderson* at Cordova, sailing for Sitka on July 21.

Harding's crisis began at Sitka, where *Henderson* took on board a special dining treat of flavorful Dungeness crabs. The crabs had been cooked at Sitka two days before by two experienced fishermen and then packed for the presidential party. On Monday, July 23, Harding and the seasick first lady, along with personal secretary George Christian and Mr. and Mrs. Herbert Hoover, all enjoyed luncheon on the world-famous crab. That night all the diners experienced extreme discomfort they all associated with the crabs at luncheon. The president's physician, Brigadier General Charles E. Sawyer of Marion, Ohio, declared that the upset was ptomaine poisoning.

Harding recovered with the others. *Henderson* called at Vancouver on Tuesday and Wednesday, and the president played nine holes of golf in a bright sun. He also enjoyed a big luncheon and later a heavy English dinner. At sea again on *Henderson,* Harding was awakened Thursday night when the ship collided with one of the destroyer escorts, *Zeilin 313,* that had come out to greet the president. On Friday, Harding landed at Seattle in another bright sun to the cheers of tens of thousands who had turned out for a presidential motor parade and a stadium speech. The president closed the day at the Press Club, where he joked so long at the podium that he delayed the departure of his special train.

It was not until 2 A.M. Saturday morning, July 28, on board the Harding Special enroute to San Francisco, that the president awoke in extreme distress. Dr. Sawyer treated the president immediately. The next day the doctor gave out the statement that the president was suffering with an "attack of copper-poisoning from eating Sitka crabs."

On Saturday morning, Harding, looking gray and drawn, dressed himself and walked off the train at San Francisco to join the mayor in a car. Harding went immediately to bed in the presidential suite of the eight-story Palace Hotel off Market Street. On Sunday the doctor's reports were not happy. The president's pulse and temperature were high. There was "grave anxiety."

By Monday the thirtieth, the doctors said that Harding was "battling for his life," because of the onset of pneumonia and what was said to be an infected gall bladder. The blame was still fixed on copper poisoning and ptomaine from the crabs. Now there was also mention of the fatigue of the trip and the hot sun in Vancouver and Seattle.

No one panicked. Harding was a good patient. The president told his worried doctors on Monday, "Go ahead, fellows, but when you get through I may have to dismiss the whole lot of you."

By Tuesday the thirty-first, the copper poisoning explanation was dismissed as "buncombe." Harding was still ill but no longer at risk. "I know I am better," he told his doctors. He asked for food. He was given soft-boiled eggs and toast but refused his request for "old-fashioned blackberry juice."

The president was fifty-eight years old. The doctors knew he had a family history of high blood pressure and arterial sclerosis. One of his sisters had died suddenly of an embolism. The doctors also knew that the president had struggled with influenza the previous spring. The doctors worried the president might have badly weakened himself on the trip.

The country was told the president was "on the road to recovery."

Vice president Calvin Coolidge was on vacation at his father's home in Plymouth, Vermont. Coolidge tried to stay in communication with the presidential party. He had stayed up most of Saturday night when the news was negative, but now on Monday he relaxed with the nation. The vice president made plans to go to New Hampshire later in the week.

On New York's popular radio station WOR, three hundred thousand listeners were led in a radio prayer for Harding's recovery, followed by the playing of the president's favorite hymns, "Abide with Me" and "My Faith Looks Up to Thee." In Los Angeles, the war hero General John Pershing spoke for many, "The only thing for Americans to do in this anxious hour is to hope and pray for his speedy recovery."

On Wednesday, August 1, the doctors felt more confident. They joked that they would at last let the president read the newspapers. One doctor did warn, "Don't presume now that there is no danger. We may always expect sideshows."

In Washington the eighty-four-year-old White House gardener Uncle Charles Patten, who had fought in the Civil War alongside the president's father, did tell the press that he was very worried about what he heard. The newspaper photograph of Patten showed a frightened man.

Shortly after seven P.M. San Francisco time, Thursday, August 2, two flower girls knocked on the door of the presidential suite to deliver bouquets to the president. The first lady greeted the children and then went back to her seat beside her husband's bed. She was reading the newspapers aloud. She found her place and continued.

Momentarily the president said, "Read that again." Then with a shudder he collapsed. He was dead where he sat in bed.

The first lady raced to the bedroom door and called out, "Find Dr. Boone and the others, quick!"

The presidential party was scattered at dinner. Hoover was the first to arrive, and when he came out of the suite he told the reporters, "Boys, I can't tell you a thing."

The word spread through the hotel instantly, "Harding's dead." Downstairs in the hotel's Rose Bowl Room, the dancers were told the news and departed in tears. By 7:30 the president's secretary had telephoned Coolidge in Vermont.

Coolidge was asleep when the telephone call came in, and he took the call in his robe. Within moments a car arrived to deliver the formal telegram from San Francisco: "The President died instantly, while conversing with members of his family at 7:30 P.M. The physicians report that death was apparently due to embolism, probably apoplexy."

Coolidge was shaken. He wired Washington immediately for a copy of the oath of office while he dressed and prepared his family for the ordeal.

Coolidge's widower father, farmer-legislator John Calvin Coolidge, was a notary public. At 2:47 P.M., in the most understated oath-of-office ceremony in presidential history, the elder Coolidge swore in his own son as the thirtieth president of the United States.

Calvin "Silent Cal" Coolidge (he was also nicknamed "Red"), of Northampton, Massachusetts, was welcomed by the nation as a port in a storm. The Republican party soon needed all of Coolidge's serenity as the Teapot Dome scandal and the Veterans Bureau scandal broke in Washington. Gone was the talk of a Ford third party or a Hiram Johnson boom. Instead the party committed itself to Coolidge and his sincere, close-lipped dignity. The new president had a beautiful, loyal wife, Grace Goodhue Coolidge, and two vigorous sons, John and Cal Junior, and together they made an attractive and inspiring first family. The nation was pleased and relieved.

By June 1924 and the Republican convention in Cleveland, there was no debate that Coolidge would be the presidential nominee. The party bragged that the convention would finish in three days. "The platform will not be difficult to draft," said a committeeman. "Coolidge is our candidate, and Coolidge will be our platform. This convention is going to cut a garment to fit the man who must wear it."

As it happened, there was a platform debate between the so-called Wets and Drys over the Volstead Act that enforced the Eighteenth Amendment. "We prate of moral leadership of the world," mocked one Wet of the Republican Drys, "while the world laughs at us as the most guileless race of hypocrites ever gathered under one flag."

The first day of the convention, Tuesday, June 9, saw a sea of happy men in bright straw boaters outside Convention Hall. Also notable were the 250 women voting or alternate delegates, including Mrs. Vincent Astor of New York, at the first convention since enactment of the Nineteenth Amendment. The convention was a most fashionable event. Speculators were asking $350 for a ticket. The party paid $20,000 for a motion picture of the proceedings.

Inside Convention Hall, the podium was wired for sound, and two radio networks were broadcasting the proceedings gavel to gavel. After the opening prayer and the "Star-Spangled Banner," delegates were led in a song for Coolidge to the tune of "Marching through Georgia."

> *Hurrah! Hurrah! Oh, Coolidge is the man*
> *Hurrah! Hurrah! We'll boost him all we can.*
> *For no finer citizen for office ever ran—*
> *Help win the country for Coolidge.*

Over at the Wisconsin delegation there was one sour face, Robert La Follette, Jr., who was chief of staff for his longtime maverick father, Senator Robert La Follette. "This convention is more hard-boiled than the 1920 one," the young La Follette complained. "The great issue before the American people today is the control of the government and industry by private monopoly."

The delegates believed the great issue was who would make the best vice president. Coolidge said he'd let the party choose his running mate, and he meant it. A most popular vice presidential choice was the voluble isolationist William E. Borah, the senator from Idaho; there were also booms for the popular Herbert Hoover, the businessman's choice Frank Lowden of Illinois, and the little-known diplomat and former U.S. budget director Brigadier General Charles E. "Charlie" Dawes of Illinois.

The second day provided the platform with its traditional Republican planks for a protective tariff and tax relief. Foreign relations were no longer primary. The party was clear it did not want the British debt canceled. Technological change was featured in the support of expanding federal highways and promoting commercial aviation.

Twenty-second on the list of planks was concern for the Ku Klux Klan's outrages throughout the country and a demand for Congress to enact an anti-lynching law.

Twenty-third on the list was a plank for orderly government: "Dishonesty and corruption are not political attributes," the plank read—meaning that the party promised there would be no more Teapot Dome scandals.

On the third day Calvin Coolidge was nominated by acclamation with a huge cheer that the nation heard on the radio. In Plymouth, Vermont, John Calvin Coolidge's eyes were wet as he plugged one ear to lis-

Coolidge vs. Davis vs. La Follette, 1924. New York Herald
Tribune, *November 3, 1924.*

ten in with the other. Afterward, the president's father walked over to
visit his neighbor E. R. Pike, ninety years old, who had voted for Lincoln
and every Republican since.

The vice presidency was as open as Coolidge wanted it to be. Twenty-
three candidates spanned the breadth of the party. Borah's isolationism
offended too many Easterners. Only three candidates became credible,
Dawes, Lowden, and Hoover, and on the third ballot sixty-year-old
Dawes of Illinois, who had never held an elective office, was named to
the ticket.

The campaign never truly challenged Coolidge. The Democrats, meeting at New York City, tore themselves apart with 103 ballots; yet in the end they bypassed the able governor Al Smith of New York to settle on the unknown John W. Davis of West Virginia. William Jennings Bryan's younger brother, Governor Charles Bryan of Nebraska, was named number two on the ticket.

The surprise of the summer was that Senator Robert La Follette made good on his longtime threat to bolt the party. In July La Follette revived Theodore Roosevelt's Progressive banner, collected Montana's Burton K. Wheeler as vice president, and ran on a platform of honest, paternal, and efficient government that would undo the power of the trusts and corporations.

By fall the campaign came down to rhetorical insults tossed at the Republicans. "The supreme question is whether this nation," La Follette complained, "shall be preserved for its people, or whether it shall be degraded into the mere servant of the monopoly system . . . —an empire, ruled by the servants of the plutocratic system which now control it?"

Democratic nominee John W. Davis complained, "When we talk of corruption in public office they point to the existence of a budget. When we complain that the public treasury has been given away, they cry that the Constitution is in danger. When we point to the unjust burdens that prices artificially raised by law have placed on the consumer, they offer us the comforting reflection that the average America eats 17 pounds of butter a year."

Coolidge said little or nothing in reply. The president let the droll campaign slogan "Keep Cool with Coolidge" carry the argument.

The Republicans swept the nation again, nearly doubling the Democratic vote. Twenty-nine million voted, and Coolidge took 54 percent of the vote for 382 electoral votes. Davis took 28.8 percent for 136 electoral votes, entirely in the South. The brilliant La Follette, while taking nearly five million votes, managed only the 13 electoral votes of his Wisconsin.

The Republicans strengthened their majorities in both houses of the new Sixty-ninth Congress.

Two weeks after the election the Senate leadership took its revenge on La Follette and his allies and declared the Progressives out of the Republican party. Twenty-four years after he had first caused a stir, Robert La Follette was finished as a Republican player. La Follette's unforgivable sin wasn't just that he'd bolted to form a third party but rather that he'd advocated a policy of nationalizing trusts and cleaning up government that turned out to be broadly popular. In several large states such as California, La Follette actually ran ahead of Davis and the Democrats. La Follette had to go—and all the better if he went to the Democrats on his way to blazes.

Coolidge and pachyderm caddie ready to putt-out; Davis and La Follete still in the rough, 1924. New York Herald Tribune, *November 5, 1924.*

★ 1928 ★

Handsome, clever, conventional Cal Coolidge oversaw the most spectacular bull run of the stock market in history, and then, like a wise insider, he got out of the way before the sky fell.

Coolidge made the federal government into the businessman's white knight: high protectionist tariff, lower federal taxes, major capital building projects, and "Silent Cal" Coolidge in the White House. The president coined the bull remark "The business of America is business" and watched the markets take off.

Soon the markets were so robust that the the professionals invented the so-called investment trusts, which functioned as today's mutual funds with the profound distinction that there was no reporting of the holdings and no annual report. The investment trusts worked like catnip on a playful public that liked to throw its quick-inflating currency at whatever promised the highest returns. In the summer of 1924, General Motors was trading at 13 on the New York Stock Exchange. By the summer of 1928, GM was trading at 220 before it split four ways, and it was still far from the top.

Coolidge's domestic policy was to choose an able Cabinet and then step back into the neatness and frugality of his White House, where his wife reigned with warm success.

Tireless capitalist Andrew Mellon continued his reign at Treasury. The exuberant Herbert Hoover carried on with his boosterism at Commerce. At State, the able Hughes was replaced with the silver-haired, open-minded former senator Frank B. Kellogg of Minnesota. Kellogg continued Republican isolationist policies toward Europe and refused to recognize the Stalinist Soviets. Later Kellogg went along with the French to negotiate the clawless Kellogg-Briand Pact that was meant to outlaw war, for which Kellogg received the Nobel Peace Prize in 1929.

American life offered rich paradoxes under Coolidge and the bull market. At the same time the vile Ku Klux Klan could stage a mass march of forty thousand in Washington, and William Jennings Bryan could waste the last days of his life at the bizarre Scopes trial in Tennessee, heroes such as Rear Admiral Richard E. Byrd and Floyd Bennet flew over the North Pole, and the amazing young adventurer Charles A. Lindbergh flew solo across the Atlantic. Automotive, aviation, radio, and construction technology lifted American business up, while social diseases like immigrant-bashing, union-breaking, and race-lynching tormented the most vulnerable in the country.

Coolidge's contribution was to veto veterans' and farm bills as too expensive and to encourage expansion of the merchant marine, commercial aviation, federal highways, the U.S. Navy—and anything else his pal Henry Ford wanted on his way to rolling out the fifteen millionth car.

Coolidge coined aphorisms that remain his legacy, such as "I have never been hurt by what I have not said."

In the quiet summer of 1927, Coolidge stunned the world by issuing his most famous one-liner: "I do not choose to run for President in Nine-teen Twenty-Eight."

The circumstances of Coolidge's bowing out were equally surprising. The president, his family, and entourage were on vacation in the Black Hills of South Dakota, at a game lodge outside Rapid City. On Tuesday, August 2, the fourth anniversary of his sudden elevation to the office, the president donned an overcoat for the cool weather and rode his car over the muddy track into the town. The Summer White House office was in a classroom of Rapid City High School. As soon as the president arrived, he invited all the reporters into his makeshift office. The press corps of newspapermen filed in casually.

"Is everybody here?" Coolidge asked.

The door was then locked, and without ceremony the president handed each correspondent a folded slip of paper with the typewritten statement *"I do not choose to run for President in Nineteen Twenty-eight."* Coolidge never actually said out loud that he was quitting the nomination that was his for the asking.

The stunned reporters asked the president for comment. Coolidge shook his head. The reporters ran for the telephones. Coolidge and his friend Arthur Capper, Republican senator from Kansas, strolled outside.

"You certainly gave the newspapermen a start," said Capper.

"Yes, so it seemed," said Coolidge.

The next day, the world exploded in disbelief. Hiram Johnson, the ambitious senator from California, said, "I'm intensely interested in the president's announcement. It is a most astonishing thing. I do not know what to say at this time."

New York banker Charles E. Mitchell argued that Coolidge might be persuaded to change his mind. "But what is the choice of the people?" Mitchell asked. "May not that be the controlling factor?"

Another Wall Streeter observed that losing Coolidge was no loss. "The 'Coolidge Policies' never existed. They merely represent the opinions of a group of men who believe that employment and prosperity can best be furthered by furthering the interests of the businessman." He added the caveat, "So long as business is kept within reason."

Nicholas Murray Butler, president of Columbia University, held that Coolidge was probably firm about shunning a third term. "President Coolidge has done precisely what I have always thought he would do when he felt the time was ripe. . . . He realizes, as did Theodore Roosevelt in 1904, that in the essence of the matter, and not merely the form, is the point of no third term."

Henry Ford had the most practical word. "No one who knows President Coolidge will doubt his sincerity. For myself I think that Herbert

Hoover is the logical Republican candidate. This is a business generation and he is a businessman."

Not only was Hoover the logical choice, he was also a skillful, talkative, energetic candidate with an attractive family and a million dollars in the bank—the richest man who had ever run for the presidency.

Through the primary season of 1928, Hoover amassed an overwhelming 531½ pledged delegates, led by his primary wins in California, New York, and New Jersey. The lone credible challenger to Hoover was Frank Lowden of Illinois, who was at half of Hoover's strength. There were several tries at a "Draft Coolidge" movement that got no response from the White House. By convention time, the president sat happily and silently on vacation in rustic splendor at Cedar Island Lodge, on an island in the Brule River in the Wisconsin woods.

On Tuesday, June 12, the Kansas City convention hall was dressed in flags and bunting, the two leading radio announcers of the day, Andy White and Graham MacNamee, were on the air live from the floor, and "the greatest show on Earth" was launched with the wit of the greatest showman of the day, movie star and rope-twirler Will Rogers.

"There won't be an original saying or a new passage uttered during the fiesta," Will Rogers remarked of the convention. "But the old Newspaper Boys will 'smoke' it up, and Graham MacNamee will tell it to you over the 'Rodeo,' so that you will imagine Henry Clay, Daniel Webster and Calhoun are there in droves. Its just as I say, one of our Follies that we have built up that no other country in the world would understand or know for what reason it was being held. But we like it, and its distinctly ours. Its the same place where our public men can do foolish things, and due to the surroundings they kinder look plausible at the time."

Efficiently and matter-of-factly the delegates accepted a platform that reproduced all of the aims of the 1924 platform. The frank concern of the platform committee was that to change anything would look like a repudiation of the extremely popular winner Calvin Coolidge, and this would invite defeat at the polls. The party was superstitious about its seven-year run of luck. Planks promoted aviation, transportation, communication, and electrification, while farmers, veterans, sailors, engineers, and industrial workers were promised support. Disarmament was advanced. The Democrats were knocked.

"The reason a thing doesn't look ludicrous to us," reported Will Rogers of the convention, "is that a man at the last one did and said exactly the same thing. If a silk hat blows off at exactly the same place every day, why it ain't near as funny as it is if you wasn't looking for it to happen; so these long-winded silly nominations, and the 'save the country' speeches, you don't laugh at them when they are made, for we

Hoover takes command, 1928. New York Herald Tribune, *June 16, 1928.*

have become so accustomed to them that its like the high hat blowing off, *we know its going to do it."*

Nicholas Murray Butler of New York contributed the best warning on the complacency of the convention. "If, as seems likely, Governor [Al] Smith is nominated by the Democratic Party at Houston, we will have against us one of the most popular figures of our generation. . . . No one can defeat Smith who alienates the agriculture vote of the Mississippi Valley or the liberal vote which is widespread throughout the country."

Herbert Hoover, 1928.
New York Herald Tribune,
June 24, 1928.

Hoover's cockiness, cropped haircut, and fleshy-faced enthusiasm carried all before him. He was nominated on the first ballot to a great demonstration that was mostly for the one-hundred-station radio audience listening in. The majority leader of the Republican Senate, Charles Curtis of Kansas, sixty-eight, was named for the vice presidency to satisfy the shaky farm vote of the Mississippi Valley.

With Hoover of California at the head of the ticket, for the first time since Frémont's peculiar bid the burgeoning Golden State was to lead the Republican party to battle for a nation of 122 million.

Hoover's first challenge was to overcome a revived Democracy. At the end of June at Houston, the Democrats nominated the talented governor Al Smith of New York. Smith enjoyed the brilliant nominating speech of Franklin Delano Roosevelt, who called the governor "the Happy Warrior of the political battlefield." Number two on the Democratic ticket was Senator Joseph T. Robinson of Arkansas, who would after 1932 rise to majority leader of the Senate and shepherd through the bulk of the New Deal.

On the Hoover Special, Hoover's campaign rolled happily against the Happy Warrior. Running between Washington and his home in Palo Alto, California, Hoover preached to the nation from his philosophical and autobiographical book, *American Individualism* (1920).

Hoover was an intellectual speaker, not at all a common man like the Brooklyn-accented Smith. However, Hoover discovered that his wealth was not resented as long as he could talk about his rough, scary, poor childhood. Born the son of an Iowa blacksmith, Hoover had been orphaned early and had gone to live with his uncle in Oregon. He had worked hard at school, worked his way through Leland Stanford University, then worked all over the world, including tsarist Russia, in order to make his fortune as a mining engineer. He had entered public service by happenstance when in 1914 he had organized relief efforts for war-stranded American travelers.

Hoover's crowning campaign speech "The Philosophy of Rugged Individualism" completed his canvass in New York in late October. "When the war closed," Hoover remarked about the success of the Republicans since Wilson's failed administration, "we were challenged with a peacetime choice between the American system of rugged individualism and a European philosophy of diametrically opposed doctrines—doctrines of paternalism and state socialism. The acceptance of these ideas would have meant the destruction of self-government through centralization of government."

Election eve, Hoover knew that his message of "rugged individualism" as opposed to state socialism was a winning argument. Arriving home to vote in Palo Alto, California, Hoover repeated his two major campaign promises. If elected, there would be "a job made secure for every man and woman." And if elected, there would be "a decrease in poverty until we are within hope that it will be abolished from America."

The elder statesman Charles Evans Hughes asserted, "In voting for

Herbert Hoover, we should do our utmost to promote our prosperity, which is the foundation of progress."

A hard, harsh note on election eve came from New York. The eloquent Democrat Franklin Delano Roosevelt was running for governor in New York on a Progressive platform. Angered by the slander spread by the Republican party that he was terminally ill—a coded reference to

Hoover vs. Al Smith, 1928. New York Herald Tribune, *November 5, 1928.*

Roosevelt's polio-crippled legs—Roosevelt snapped, "I am not going to dignify that kind of a story with a denial." Roosevelt then attacked the GOP with a partisan fury: "Our fight, both in the state and the nation, is not against the rank and file of the Republican Party, but it is definitely against *the stupidest and most narrow-minded, most bigoted leadership that we have ever witnessed in this country.*"

Roosevelt also slammed Herbert Hoover: "Hoover's theory is another way of saying that there exists at the top of our social system a very limited group of highly able, highly educated people through whom all progress must originate. Furthermore that this small group, after doing all the thinking, all the originality, is fully responsible for all progress in civilization and government."

(Hoover's theory was more cogent than Roosevelt credited. In August Hoover had outlined his understanding of the American system: "The government is more than administration; it is power for leadership and cooperation with the forces of business and cultural life in city, town and country. The Presidency is more than executive responsibility. It is the inspiring symbol of all that is highest in American purpose and ideal.")

Thirty-six and a half million voted. Hoover won 58 percent and 444 electoral votes—the largest electoral college vote tally in history so far.

Benevolent Al Smith could not even win his home state of New York. However, Al Smith's protégé, Franklin "Frank" Delano Roosevelt, did win the New York governorship over the Republicans, bringing the freshest and most unquestionably honest voice to the battle since his cousin, Theodore Roosevelt.

Elsewhere Smith lost even traditional Democratic strongholds. A Roman Catholic and anti-Prohibition "Wet" could not hold the Klan-dominated Solid South, and for all his exertion on the campaign, Smith gained only 40 percent of the vote for 87 electoral votes.

The GOP increased its majorities in both houses of the new Seventy-first Congress.

Afterward Will Rogers joked about Hoover's virgin win. "You can't lick this Prosperity thing, even the fellow that hasn't got any is all excited over the idea."

Another vote of approval came the day after the election, when Wall Street's new darlings, the investment trusts (mutual funds), joined with the smart moneymen like J. P. Morgan to bull the markets in what was called a "Hoover rally."

General Motors at 220^3/$_4$. Buy GM! General Electric at 170. Buy GE! U.S. Steel at 162. Buy Steel! Just buy! You don't have the cash? No worry, friend. *We'll lend it to you.*

★ 1932 ★

Herbert Hoover was a stag caught in the headlights of the stock market crash.

Hoover would talk and talk about his experience the rest of his long and dignified life, but he never recovered from those black October days when the world according to Wall Street came to an end.

The new president was an astute, honest, perseverant public servant who was well qualified to administer the executive branch of government. He was not a politician, however, not a man who lived on the campaign trail trying to get the people to love him. This fact blinded Hoover to the simple, obvious, inarguable fact that after October 1929, the country's confidence was broken. Once the confidence was gone, there was no stopping the fall into the Great Depression. (Bodies in motion tend to stay in motion until they hit an immovable object that pushes back, such as Roosevelt's New Deal.)

Confidence gone, the American people no longer believed in Hoover's promises of a job for every man and an end to poverty. The market that had raised the Republicans up since McKinley turned out to be a breakable toy. This revelation panicked the nation. And no one, not even the engineer in Herbert Hoover, could fix the crisis that followed once the people started believing that there was *no solution*.

Absent confidence, there is no economy, a political truism that Hoover did not appear to understand.

What did Hoover do when he looked at the smoking ruin of the New York Stock Exchange? He ignored it: "Any lack of confidence in the basic strengths of business," he said in November 1929, "is foolish."

The president denied it: "Business and industry," he said in January 1930, "have turned the corner."

The president declared it over: "We have now passed the worst," he said in May 1930.

Meanwhile, commodity prices spiraled downward with the stocks. The Republicans tried to fight off the collapse with the traditional high wall of tariff protection. In June 1930, the Republican Congress passed the controversial Hawley-Smoot Tariff Bill, intended to raise the protectionist tariff to revive industry. Over one thousand economists urged Hoover to veto Hawley-Smoot. Hoover ignored the advice and signed the bill, a decision hailed by Wall Street as a solution. "President Hoover's signature to the Smoot-Hawley Tariff Bill," said the National Association of Manufacturers, "should result in taking the tariff out of the log-rolling and political maneuvering, and relieve business from the disastrous effects of general revisions for years to come."

The truth was that protectionism no longer worked the way it had since the McKinley days. Regardless of Hawley-Smoot, the farm and equity prices continued to collapse.

The results of the 1930 midterm elections were mixed, but definitely negative for the Republicans. In the new Senate, there were forty-eight Republicans and forty-seven Democrats, with one Democrat-leaning independent. In the new House, the Democrats took over with the pugnacious John Nance Garner of Texas as Speaker of the House.

In December 1930, with unemployment skyrocketing to four million, Hoover was forced to address the crisis as a "depression." The president argued with so many excuses, however, it was clear he was not ready to drop his laissez-faire dutch-unclehood and fight the depression with cash and shovels. "The origins of the depression lie to some extent within our own borders," Hoover wrote in his 1930 annual message to Congress, "through a speculative rather than constructive enterprise. Had overspeculation in securities been the only force operating, we should have seen recovery many months ago." Hoover went on to blame the depression on a grab-bag of troubles: "The political agitation in Asia; revolutions in South America and political unrest in some European states; the method of sale by Russia of her increasing agricultural exports to European markets; and our own drought—all have contributed to prolong and deepen the depression."

A year later, Hoover conceded that business was terrible, but he still tried to distract the nation with a pep talk about the future. "If we lift our vision beyond these immediate emergencies, we find fundamental national gains even amid depression," Hoover wrote in the 1931 annual message to Congress. "Business depressions have been recurrent in the life of our country and are but transitory."

Hoover's refusal to face the facts made him a part of the problem. He rejected direct federal relief to the unemployed—"I am opposed to any direct or indirect government dole"—and chose instead to promote a national voluntary effort that flopped miserably. He vetoed a 1930 veterans' bonus bill that was aimed at helping unemployed veterans. He vetoed the 1931 Muscle Shoals Bill that would have established public power for the Tennessee Valley. In December 1931 he refused to heed a contingent of protesters called the "Hunger Marchers" who were petitioning for a minimum wage.

Finally in January 1932, Hoover moved to relieve some of the nightmare by establishing the Reconstruction Finance Corporation, directed by former vice president Charles E. Dawes; it strived to revitalize industries with huge loans. And yet Hoover would still not act to get direct federal aid to the terrified unemployed and trapped poor.

"The money was all appropriated for the top," Will Rogers joked harshly about the RFC and all of Hoover's ideas, "in the hopes it would *trickle down* to the needy."

While Hoover fussed and fumed—"We must face a temporary increase in taxes," he wrote in December 1931—the markets that failed in New York also pulled down Europe and Asia and made the world vulnerable to wretched tyrannies.

On the same New York *Herald Tribune* front page there was a photograph of the preening, cavalry-booted Adolf Hitler alongside a photograph of the Hunger Marchers moving on Washington in December 1930. Adolf Hitler remarked to the press why he didn't need to bother to lead a protest march on Berlin: "Why should we march on Berlin," he joked about his popularity as he emerged from the Brown House, "when I am here quite as much as I am in other parts of the Reich?" The fifteen hundred Hunger Marchers held signs that read "Hoover's Stagger Plan: Stagnation and Starvation," and "Not a Cent for war, All Funds for the Unemployed."

As unemployment reached fifteen million and the stock market declined 90 percent, Hoover finally seemed to comprehend the depth and breadth of the panic. The president signed the 1932 Glass-Steagall Banking Act in hopes of stopping the run on federal gold by the banks and a vast dollar-hoarding by frightened citizens. Calling Glass-Steagall "patriotic" and "non-partisan" and "a financial bulwark of the national defense," Hoover offered yet another explanation for the prolonged crisis. "The gradual credit contraction during the last eight months," he said in February 1932, "arising indirectly from causes originating in foreign countries and continued domestic deflation, but more directly from hoarding, has been unquestionably the major factor in depressing prices and delaying business recovery."

Hoover's stubborn mistakes did not encourage GOP challengers to the president. By the spring of 1932 the three Republicans who were tempted, Governor Gifford Pinchot of Pennsylvania and the maverick Progressives William E. Borah of Idaho and Hiram Johnson of California, had either fallen in line behind the president or chosen silence.

Hoover's renomination was so certain at the Republican convention in Chicago in mid-June 1932 that the delegates would not address the depression crisis directly, because that would mean having to knock the party's standard-bearer.

Amazing to see, the delegates made the major issue not the worldwide depression but rather the national prohibition. The chief convention contest was between the Wets, who wanted repeal of the Eighteenth Amendment, and the Drys (including President Hoover) who insisted that liquor was the great evil. The Wets won convention publicity by numbers and exuberance. Chicago authorities were warned not to arrest Republicans, so five hundred speakeasies in the Loop welcomed the delegates without fear of raids. "Why should I get myself in bad," argued a federal agent, "by raiding a place now when some senator or other political figure is liable to be there?"

The Chicago weather was unusually cold for June, seventy degrees blowing off the lake and cutting through the linen suits and sheer chiffon dresses of the delegates. The Wets entertained themselves with bootlegged liquor that was priced unusually hot: eleven dollars for a fifth of scotch; thirteen dollars for a quart of champagne; seventy-five cents for a drink of whiskey; twenty-five cents for a gin; fifty cents for domestic beer.

The most popular events of the convention week were the demonstrations by the Wet Warriors. There was a naval parade on the lake led by the yacht *Mizpah,* followed by an air show led by drunken pilots, followed by a horse-drawn Wet Parade on Michigan Avenue that gave out free beer to all comers.

Inside the Chicago Auditorium, no debate was more heated than the five hour floor fight on the second day between the Wets and Drys that resulted in a vote against outright repeal, 690–454. It was a sham victory for the Drys. Wet delegates celebrated their defeat on the floor with buckets of beer the press called "foamy liquid resembling beer from pails."

The fifteen hundred flags hanging gaily on Michigan Avenue, the twenty-three miles of bunting in the Auditorium, the celebratory radio network broadcasts from the convention floor could not camouflage the fact that the delegates knew the country was bitter. The delegates could take their free beer and their free passes to the Chicago White Sox's Comiskey Park or the Washington Park racetrack, and the conventioneers could listen to party ancients like Kansas's Senator Arthur Capper ("History is going to record that Herbert Hoover has done a good job"), but the Republicans could not escape the wretched fact that out there on Chicago's South Side, evicted families lived in open sewers and polio-broken children begged for coins.

The platform was candid. "We meet in a period of widespread distress and of an economic depression that has swept the world. The emergency is second only to the great war. The human suffering may well exceed that of a period of actual conflict."

The platform also promised a crusade. "Republicans collectively and individually, in nation and state, hereby enlist in a war which will not end until the promise of American life is once more fulfilled."

Unfortunately, there were no new ideas in the planks, just the usual calls for high tariff, sound money, immigrant restriction, aid to disabled veterans. The most innovative plank was to urge revision, not repeal, of the Eighteenth Amendment. The Democrats were accused of advocating deficits, heavy public expenditures, and unbalanced budgets. There was the routine plank for the Negro—"For seventy years the Republican party has been the friend of the American Negro"—with no thought that the Negro vote was about to quit the GOP for the Democrats.

Permanent chairman Bertrand H. Snell tried to rally the troops with a nostalgic partisan review that illustrated the absence of new ideas to fight the depression. "The way to resume specie payments after the Civil War was to resume," Snell declared, "and the Republican party accomplished it; the way to restore prosperity following Democratic free trade depression was to open the mills, and the Republican party did it; and now the way to restore good times is to restore them, and the Republican party has set itself resolutely upon that course."

Hoover and Vice President Curtis were renominated on the first ballot in the shortest Republican convention ever gathered. Hoover's acceptance remarks from Washington revealed his defensiveness: "I shall labor as I have labored to meet the effects of the worldwide slump which has devastated us with trials and suffering equaled in but few periods of our history."

The 1932 campaign was ideological and passionate. At their July convention in Chicago, the Democrats nominated Governor Franklin Delano Roosevelt of New York, a man as articulate, passionate, and thoughtfully partisan as Hoover.

Governor Roosevelt, on the attack on radio and in person, crisscrossed the country making an argument for a complete reconstruction of the government and the country which he called the *New Deal*—a conscientious updating of Theodore Roosevelt's famous *Square Deal*. Governor Roosevelt, who the newspapers dubbed FDR, promised that his New Deal would help "the forgotten man at the bottom of the economic pyramid."

Hoover, on the defensive, rode his Hoover Special from city to city trying to explain what a threat he believed Roosevelt's New Deal was to the American way of life.

The last week of the campaign, Hoover amplified his beliefs at a rally of twenty-five thousand loyalists at New York's Madison Square Garden: "This contest is more than a contest between two men. It is more than a contest between two parties. It is a contest between two philosophies of government. Men who are going about the country announcing that they are liberals, they are the reactionaries of the United States."

Hoover continued with partisan fervor, "My conception of America is a land where men and women may walk in ordered liberty, where they may enjoy the advantages of wealth not concentrated in the hands of a few, but diffused through the lives of all." He added with prescience, *"This election is not a mere shift from the ins to the outs. It means deciding the direction our nation will take over a century to come."*

Hoover's Madison Square Garden performance was punctuated by the heckling of one ominous voice. "You're a liar," called a man from the gallery on the Fiftieth Street side, "you've ruined the country!"

The heckler's name was Jack Baron, an unemployed seaman and member of the Marine Workers Industrial Union.

On election eve, Hoover tried to moderate his alarmist rhetoric at St. Paul, Minnesota. "I have made no effort to appeal to the destructive emotion; I have made an endeavor to appeal to reason which I can only hope has been effective. I have fixed my faith upon logical conclusion of the thoughtful people who have never failed the country in any hour of danger."

FDR buried the GOP. Roosevelt voted in Hyde Park and then went to receive the election results at New York's Biltmore Hotel. FDR accepted Hoover's concession telegram at midnight, New York time, and then went home to 49 East Sixty-fifth Street.

More than thirty-nine million voted. Roosevelt won 57.4 percent of the vote and forty-two states for 472 electoral votes, winning North, South, and West. Hoover gained only 39.6 percent of the vote, the second lowest Republican total ever; he held only the four rockbed Republican states of Maine, New Hampshire, Vermont, Pennsylvania, along with the newly wealthy states of Connecticut and Delaware for 59 electoral votes.

The new Seventy-third Congress was a Democratic hurricane sweep. The Senate showed 60 Democrats to 35 Republicans and 1 Democratic-leaning Farmer-Laborite. The House showed 310 Democrats to 117 Republicans with 5 Farmer-Laborites.

Hoover's defeat brought capitulation-selling and price-bottoming in the economy. There was a final spiral in the commodity and equity markets that brought the closing or restriction of nearly every bank in the Union in the four months between the November election and the March inauguration. This was to be the last time there would be such a delay, for the Twentieth "Lame Duck" Amendment shifted the inauguration to January.

Hoover vs. Franklin Delano Roosevelt, 1932. New York Herald Tribune, *November 3, 1932.*

★ 1936 ★

Roosevelt took command for his famous "Hundred Days" with the nation huddling in despair.

Roosevelt's inaugural speech, March 4, 1933, was the most inspiring moment since Lincoln's second inaugural. "This is preeminently the time to speak the truth, the whole truth, frankly and boldly," Roosevelt announced on a sunny, cold day in the nation's capital. "Nor need we shrink from honestly facing conditions in our country today. This great nation will endure as it has endured, will revive and will prosper. So first of all let me assert my belief that the only thing we have to fear is fear itself—nameless, unreasoning, unjustified terror which paralyzes needed efforts to convert retreat into advance."

FDR was as powerful a partisan as his older cousin TR. He used his inaugural address to launch a jeremiad against "the interests" of Wall

After the election, 1932: cleaned out by the New Deal. New York Herald Tribune, *November 9, 1932.*

Street. "The rulers of the exchange of mankind's goods have failed through their own stubbornness and their own incompetence, have admitted their failure and abdicated. Practices of the unscrupulous money changers stand indicted in the court of public opinion, rejected by the hearts and minds of men."

The heart of Roosevelt's address, as well as the central genius of his first term, was one partisan sentence that sounded as bully and evangelical as if it had been declared by the master of the bully pulpit, Theodore Roosevelt, once upon a time. *"They [the Republicans] have no vision, and when there is no vision the people perish."*

FDR was a brilliant vision—a rugged, self-confident, self-sacrificing man of the fundamental New York Democracy, son of a railroad president, fifth cousin of the famous Roosevelt—and what followed his inauguration was a flood of faith, hope, and charity.

"America hasn't been as happy in three years as they are today," Will Rogers wrote just after the inauguration. "No money, no banks, no work, no nothing, but they know they got a man in there who is wise to Congress, wise to our so-called big men. The whole country is with him."

Roosevelt and the Democratic Congress produced quick results in the famous Hundred Days of the Seventy-third Congress: direct relief to the poor, agricultural and manufacturing support, tariff adjustment, labor and banking reforms, securities regulation (designed by the fox in the chicken coop, Joseph P. Kennedy), public power in the Tennessee Valley, repeal of prohibition with the Twenty-first Amendment, and a daring suspension of the gold standard to stop the gold drain followed by a devaluation of the dollar.

Roosevelt built many of his programs around a continuation of Hoover's Reconstruction Finance Corporation. Roosevelt also named a Cabinet with several former Republicans, especially Henry A. Wallace at Agriculture and former Bull-Mooser Harold L. Ickes at Interior. Roosevelt dealt gamely with a Supreme Court dominated by the sagacious chief justice Charles Evans Hughes and other Republicans.

Nonetheless, the Republican party members, in Congress and the state houses, sat on their hands during the first sweep of New Deal legislation.

What the most conservative members of the GOP tried instead was to rant against the New Deal tide with upside-down logic: "We began pulling out of what the Democrats call the Hoover depression just a month or two before the election of 1932," claimed E. Harold Cluett, New York Republican candidate for the U.S. Senate. "Natural recovery took us along upward until July 1933. Then the New Deal hit business like a battering ram, and we have been in the Roosevelt Depression ever since."

Other voices knocked Roosevelt as either a fascist or a communist. Demagogue radio-broadcaster Father Charles E. Coughlin of Detroit, Michigan, used his Shrine of the Little Flower Radio Station to call the New Deal "Jew Deal," and to spread the fairy tale that FDR was descended from an early Hyde Park settler named Rosenveltd. Cranks such as physician Francis E. Townsend of California and novelist Upton Sinclair of California proposed totalitarian income redistribution that made the New Deal look timid. Communist agitators such as Earl Browder of the American Communist party, a paid agent of the mass-murdering Stalin (Dzhugashvili), called Roosevelt a covert fascist and called the New Deal "the death rattle of capitalism." And Southern maverick Huey P. "Kingfish" Long, the Democratic senator from Louisiana, aimed to challenge FDR with a program of benevolent dictatorship he called Share-the-Wealth. Huey Long's murder by a madman bit off his trajectory before it was clear how Roosevelt would have finessed Long's manipulations.

The 1934 midterm elections for the new Seventy-fourth Congress brought marked increases for the New Deal. The Senate became 69 Democrats to 25 Republicans, with 2 Farmer-Laborites. The House became 319 Democrats to 103 Republicans, with 10 others. One peppery new senator was Judge Harry S. Truman, a young, ambitious politician out of the Democratic Missouri machine.

Roosevelt possessed what no president since Grant had enjoyed: a two-thirds majority in Congress, a worshipful citizenry, and the nerve to save the country. Like Horace Greeley and Abraham Lincoln, like U.S. Grant and Theodore Roosevelt, FDR was a miraculous hero who rode to the rescue, and the American people loved him for it.

By the presidential year 1936, the Republicans were scatterbrained up against the FDR juggernaut. Curmudgeons like H. L. Mencken made sour jokes that the president could be beaten by a Chinaman or even a Republican. The truth was that hatemonger Father Charles E. Coughlin was more of a threat to the White House than any member of the Republican remnant.

The shrunken Republican party divided into three camps. The most conservative members wanted to run Hoover again. The most liberal partisans wanted to try one of the old Roosevelt Bull Moose Progressives, such as Senator William E. Borah of Idaho or Colonel Frank Knox, publisher of the *Chicago Tribune*. Other longtime Progressives like Hiram Johnson of California, George W. Norris of Nebraska, and the young Robert M. La Follette, Jr. of Wisconsin, were regarded as ineligible because they were supporting much of the New Deal.

The third Republican camp was uncommitted, and it held the upperhand just because the Hooverites and the Progressives were so laden with problems. The uncommitted camp boomed many new prospects, but none more effectively than former Bull Mooser and Theodore Roosevelt–lover Alf Landon, the forty-eight-year-old governor of Kansas who was being cagily promoted to the party by midwestern newspaper- and radiomen.

By the mid-June convention at Cleveland, there were many delegates willing to announce beforehand that Landon of Kansas would be chosen on the first ballot. Landon represented nothing old and nothing new, just his resourceful self. He was a hardworking governor who agreed with most all of the New Deal, and he was lucky to have a homey style and a beautiful young family. Spry, small, handsome, spectacled Landon did not actually attend the convention, but remained at home in Topeka, Kansas.

The Cleveland convention did not try to hide the frightening depression. The hall itself was left colorless, no bunting, no displays, just a few American flags hung in the gray cavern. On the first night, hooligans cut two main radio cables and tampered with the public announcement system. Delegates were so hard-up that they tried to sell their extra tickets for twenty-five dollars. "Take the boys from the West Coast," a delegate explained. "They had a long way to come, and they had to pay their own expenses. The easiest way to make expenses is to sell a few tickets."

On the second day, prideful Herbert Hoover made a partisan attack on the New Deal as a dictatorship. "In Central Europe the march of Socialist or Fascist dictatorships and their destruction of liberty did not set out with guns and arms," Hoover argued. "Dictatorships began their ascent to the seats of power through the elections provided by liberal institutions. The 1932 campaign was a pretty good imitation of this first stage of European tactics."

Hoover knocked Roosevelt for using class warfare to advance the New Deal. "There are some moral laws written in a great book," Hoover ruminated. "Overall is the gospel of brotherhood. For this first time in the history of America we have heard the gospel of class hatred preached from the White House. That is human poison more deadly than fear. Every reader of the history of democracy knows that is the final rock upon which all democracies have been wrecked." Hoover exhorted, "Stop the retreat. In the chaos of doubt, confusion and fear, yours is the task to command."

The convention sang out the "Battle Hymn of the Republic," and

"We Want Hoover!" and then the campaign theme song, "Three Long Years" to the tune of "Three Blind Mice."

> *Three Long years*
> *Three long years!*
> *Full of grief and tears.*
> *Full of grief and tears.*
> *Roosevelt gave us to understand*
> *If we would lend a helping hand*
> *He'd lead us to the promised land.*
> *For three long years!*

The platform was broad-based negativity, an indictment of a tyrant. "America is in peril." "For three long years the New Deal Administration has dishonored American traditions and flagrantly betrayed the pledge upon which the Democratic party sought and received public aid."

The platform's accusations were dire: "The powers of Congress have been usurped by the President."

"The integrity and authority of the Supreme Court have been flaunted."

"Regulated monopoly has displaced free enterprise."

Worst of all, "appeals to passion and class prejudice have replaced reason and tolerance."

The platform recommended a tepid version of everything the New Deal was accomplishing. It occurred to no one that FDR's New Deal had improved much of the genius of Theodore Roosevelt and his Bull Moose party. The Republican platform's few positive statements, such as a call for a women's wage amendment to the Constitution, and a bill of rights for "our colored citizens," were overwhelmed by the bitterness of defeat.

On the third day, Landon received the nomination on the first ballot. That evening at the Topeka governor's mansion, Landon came out to meet the celebration under bursting sky rockets and to the music of the Christian Endeavor Drum and Bugle Corps of Topeka. "Nothing is more worthwhile than the regard of one's neighbors," Landon said. "Nothing tugs more strongly at one's heartstrings than their good wishes."

The vice presidency was a choice between the conservative senator Arthur H. Vandenberg of Michigan, a sharp-tongued speaker who boasted, "I belong to one bloc and it has one slogan, 'Stop Roosevelt!' and the Progressive candidate, Frank Knox. The convention chose the big, fair-haired, pince-nez-wearing Knox on the first ballot. The Republican National Committee promised an aggressive campaign that would combine the front-porch strategy with a few railroad swings around the country.

The campaign was a one-sided triumph for Roosevelt, despite the fact that the Hearst papers and a vast majority of the press opposed the president every day of the canvass. Roosevelt used his acceptance speech for renomination at Philadelphia to attack his enemies as "economic royalists" who had "created a new despotism and wrapped it in the robes of legal sanctions." Later, Roosevelt opened his campaign by declaring, in Syracuse, "The true conservative seeks to protect the system of private property and free enterprise by correcting such injustices and inequalities as arise from it."

Landon ran on the suggestive slogan "Save the American Way of Life"; in his stiff speeches, however, Landon had little more to offer than traditional GOP planks for sound money and balanced budgets. "This administration boasts that its spending has brought recovery," Landon argued in St. Louis in November. "But it is not a solid recovery. It is a spendthrift delusion, the delusion of a nation that is running through its capital and mortgaging its future."

Landon's best vote getter was his attractive daughter Peggy Anne from his first marriage. *"Our Peggy Anne, pretty sunflower girl,"* crooned an orchestra leader. *"Peggy Anne with eyes of brown / You are the toast of our land and the pride of our town."*

Industrialists backed Landon because he wasn't FDR. The conservative Democrat Lamont Du Pont of E. L. du Pont de Nemours of Delaware chose the day he launched his new ninety-six-foot power yacht, *Marmot,* in Wilmington to attack Roosevelt as a hatemonger. "President Roosevelt has built class hatred. He has engaged one group against another, labor against employer, farmer against the city dweller, on a basis of enmity and distrust."

The reactionary Henry Ford, unapologetic anti-Semite and labor basher, found a way to accuse the New Deal as an international conspiracy. "Industry is opposed to the New Deal," Ford said in Detroit the day before the election. "International finance is for it. The New Deal legislation is compelling all kinds of American industry to become customers of the money lenders. That's right in accord with the basic alien principle behind all New Deal projects."

Du Pont and Ford spoke to an empty room. Elsewhere the wealthy prepared for the worst-case scenario of the redistribution of wealth. The weekend before the election, it took ten armored trucks and forty-two armed guards to transport gold and gems from a dead man's estate to a Boston bank.

A famously wrongheaded pre-election telephone poll made by the

Alf Landon vs. Roosevelt, 1936. New York Herald Tribune, *October 6, 1936.*

Literary Digest declared that Landon would defeat Roosevelt, and this bizarre prediction was accepted by the GOP hopeful without looking at the fact that the people who could afford telephones were dominantly Republican. The first ever presidential poll by the Gallup's Institute of Public Opinion Poll predicted FDR would win with 53.8 percent. Gallup was short by five miles.

More than forty-four million voted. Landon won the first voting town of the tiny Millsfield, New Hampshire, 5–2. Then the rest of the nation weighed in, and Roosevelt took 60.8 percent and forty-eight

After the election, 1936. New York Herald Tribune, *November 4, 1936.*

states for a massive 523 electoral votes. Landon lost his own Kansas by nineteen thousand and won only Maine and Vermont for 8 electoral votes. The joke told against the GOP the next day was, "As Maine goes, so goes Vermont."

There was also a wide field of minor parties that opposed some aspect of the New Deal. Father Coughlin's hate-mongering Union party gained 2 percent and no electoral college votes. Norman O. Thomas's utopian Socialist party and Earl Browder's Soviet-run Communist party polled far behind.

In the new Seventy-fifth Congress, the Democratic two-thirds majority grew, with a Senate of 76 Democrats to 16 Republicans and 4 others, with a House of 331 Democrats to 89 Republicans and 13 others. November 1936 was the high-water mark of the Democratic party after the Civil War.

★ 1940 ★

Roosevelt's Second Administration consolidated the New Deal and prepared for war.

The president challenged Charles Evans Hughes's Supreme Court over the Court's decisions to declare unconstitutional the National Industrial Recovery Act and other projects. Roosevelt threatened to undo the independence of the judiciary by increasing the Supreme Court from nine to fifteen members and packing it with his own partisans. The battle spread to Congress, where the sudden death of Senate majority leader Joseph T. Robinson weakened the president's hand. The 1936 Judicial Procedure Reform Act made changes in lower courts but left the Supreme Court alone. In the end, fate intervened on Roosevelt's side as seven vacancies opened on the Court in the next few years. The president nominated, among others, the accomplished Hugo Black of Alabama (1932), Felix Frankfurter of Massachusetts (1938), William O. Douglas of Connecticut (1939).

By 1938 the Republican party was a dried-up lemon. The La Follette family of Wisconsin might have been able to revitalize the GOP, but it had spun off into the National Progressives of America. Herbert Hoover still led a call for "rugged individualism" that pleased the party conservatives. The defeated Alf Landon joined with the party's national chairman to urge social reforms most similar to the New Dealers', though Landon also agreed with the GOP plank for a balanced budget.

New Republican blood appeared suddenly in New York, where crusading young New York City district attorney Thomas E. Dewey waged a fierce gubernatorial campaign against Roosevelt's handpicked successor in Albany, Governor Herbert Lehman. Sadly, Dewey's campaign was marred with anti-Semitic tricks by Republican campaigners. "Whispers concerning racial or religious preferences have been injected into this campaign on both sides," Dewey said on election eve at his East Forty-fourth Street headquarters. "The man or woman who votes for a candidate because of his race or religion, or votes against him for such a reason, is a disgrace to American citizenship. . . . There are some things more important than being elected governor, and one is the spirit of religious and racial good will. I would rather go down to defeat than be elected by any vote based on race or religion."

FDR took note of the rough GOP tactics in his home base of New York. In a fireside chat on election eve, 1938, the president pushed back at the Republicans with rhetorical fire. "As of today, Fascism and Communism—and old-line Republicanism—are not threats to the continuation of our form of government," Roosevelt observed. "But, my friends, I venture the challenging statement that if American Democracy ceases to move forward as a living force, seeking day and night by peaceful means to better the lot of our citizens, then Fascism and Communism, aided, unconsciously perhaps, by Old-line Tory Republicanism, will grow in strength in our land."

The class and tribal hatred worsened. There was a photograph of German Nazi potentate Hermann Goering's new daughter on the front pages of American newspapers at the same time there was a photograph of the smiling cinematographer Leni Riefenstahl, who was visiting New York and denying she was Nazi dictator Adolf Hitler's girlfriend. Meanwhile in the New York gubernatorial campaign, there circulated an incredible falsehood and slander with regard to Benjamin Franklin: that Franklin had made a speech to the 1789 Constitutional Convention in Philadelphia calling for a constitutional ban on Jews before they took over the young country. The source of this smear was supposedly an entry in the 1789 diary of constitutional convention delegate Charles Pinckney.

New York voters held their nose at the bad smell as they returned Lehman over Dewey by a seventy-thousand plurality.

Nationally in the midterm elections, the Republicans won back rockbed Pennsylvania and Ohio, where the deceased William Howard Taft's tall, balding son, Robert A. Taft, won a seat in the U.S. Senate. The GOP gained sufficiently in the new Seventy-sixth Congress that, even though it was still a woeful minority in the Senate, 69 Democrats to 23 Republicans and 4 others, the House was no longer monolithic, with 261 Democrats to 164 Republicans and 4 others.

By the presidential year 1940, the Republicans were no better organized against FDR.

Just before the Republican June convention in Philadelphia, with a national military draft of forty million men imminent, Roosevelt stunned the GOP by picking off two of its stars for his War Cabinet. Veteran New York diplomat Henry L. Stimson, who had first walked with Theodore Roosevelt in the failed gubernatorial election of 1910, accepted appointment as secretary of war. And Frank Knox of Illinois, 1936 candidate for vice president, accepted the post of secretary of the navy.

The Republicans showed their hurt surprise. "Having entered the Cabinet, Stimson and Knox are no longer qualified to speak as Republicans or for the Republican party," announced the party's national chairman, John D. Hamilton. "Both men have long desired to intervene in the affairs of Europe, and the Democratic party now becomes the war party."

New York district attorney Thomas Dewey commented from New York City, "The president has taken from the Republicans two leading interventionists. This can only be interpreted as a step toward war."

The German News Agency in Berlin called Stimson and Knox "warmongers."

In reply, lifelong Republican Knox argued, "National defense is not a partisan question. It should have the united support of the people regardless of party."

The war in Europe divided the country as well as the Republican party, and as the convention gathered at the Philadelphia Auditorium in late June, there was no unanimity toward the burning threat of Hitler.

There was no unanimity toward a candidate, either, with eleven names tossed up as possible. From the East there was Governor Earle Baldwin of Connecticut, Senator H. Styles Bridges of New Hampshire, newspaperman Frank E. Gannet of New York, Governor Arthur H. James of Pennsylvania. From the West there were senators Charles L. McNary of Oregon, Arthur Capper of Kansas, Hanford MacNider of Iowa, Arthur H. Vandenberg of Michigan, and Robert A. Taft of Ohio.

Against all these party regulars there was the bizarre boom of a complete outsider, Wendell Willkie of New York City, a forty-four-year-old president of an electric utility company who had been a Democrat as recently as 1938.

Incredibly, Willkie was the popular darling of the press as he strode up Philadelphia's Market Street the day before the convention opened. The photograph showed a clean, broad, happy-faced man in a trim white suit with a boater in hand.

"Dewey has most of the delegates," observed a Kansas delegate, "Taft has most of the king-makers, but Willkie has most of the enthusiasm."

Willkie sounded his naïveté about the ways of the nomination process. "Things couldn't be better," he said on Monday of convention week. "Things are getting better right along. I will have delegates from all of the country, from Maine, Minnesota, California, Washington, Pennsylvania, to mention a few. This will be the most independent Republican convention in history, with no bosses."

The Philadelphia convention was the first to use the new television technology. The National Broadcasting Company had four cameras (two at the podium, one at the entrance, one in an interview room) connected by coaxial cable 108 miles to W2BXS in New York. The television signal was also broadcasted by radio wave over the Philco Station in Philadelphia and the GE station in Schenectady, New York. Reception was reported excellent at the various screens set up at New York department stores, bars, hotels, and at the RCA exhibit at the New York World's Fair.

Other aspects of the convention were old hat. Herbert Hoover appeared to make another attack on the New Deal. "That brings me to the restoration of morals in government," Hoover argued. "Does anyone in the United States doubt that the New Deal has built up the most gigantic political machine to control the vote that was ever known in this country?"

The permanent chair of the convention warned, "For seven anxious years we have seen this march toward one-man government."

The platform was uniformly negative about the New Deal: "The New Deal Administration has failed America. The zero hour is here." And just as alarmed about American involvement in the European and Asia wars: "The Republican Party stands for Americanism, preparedness and peace. We accordingly fasten upon the New Deal full responsibility for our unpreparedness and for the consequent danger of involvement in war."

Significantly, the platform warned of "un-American activities" in the New Deal—the first time this construction had appeared in a GOP platform.

Elsewhere, a young Democratic voice and future president, John F. Kennedy, twenty-three, son of Roosevelt's ambassador to Great Britain, commented upon the occasion of his first book publication, *Why England Slept*: "I do not believe that in fighting a Fascist country, you have to set up Fascism, but I do believe that certain aspects of democracy and capitalist economy must go when a country is at war with a totalitarian nation."

There were many fresh aspects of the convention, such as the keynote address by thirty-three-year-old Governor Harold Stassen of Minnesota. The nominating speech for Robert A. Taft of Ohio—"No Glamour, No Sarong, Just A Man Who Won't Go Wrong: Bob Taft"—extolled his freshness: "Ohio, Mother of presidents, brings to their convention its distinguished son. He is easy and approachable. His farm and city neighbors say he is the most unselfish man they know. He hates a high hat, literally and spiritually."

The nominating speech for Wendell Willkie was free of all cant since Willkie wasn't even a registered Republican. He had been brought along by an overnight boom in the Republican newspapers after distinguishing himself by fighting a letter-writing battle with New Dealers over the regulations of the Tennessee Valley Authority. Willkie was a new sort of politician to the Republicans, a well-spoken, optimistic, up-to-date corporation man whose devotion was to the bottom line of a company's books. "If you want things nice and silky," read a banner, "go ahead and vote for Willkie."

The most exciting part of the convention was the demonstration by the Willkie supporters that followed Willkie's name being placed into nomination. The Willkie forces had hoarded tickets to the Auditorium gallery, and they packed it with supporters. When Willkie's name was mentioned, ten thousand exploded with a rhythmic chant, "Willkie! We want Willkie!" that overwhelmed the delegates on the floor.

The balloting began amid all the excitement. Dewey led handily on the first, second, third ballots, with Taft of Ohio trailing strongly. But then the Stop-Dewey forces bolted for Willkie, including 27 delegates from New York and 28 from Massachusetts. Michigan senator Vandenberg had predicted beforehand that he would win on the sixth ballot. Eerily it was Willkie who carried the nomination on the sixth ballot with 998 delegates.

The Willkie boomers were ecstatic, singing to the air of Walt Disney's new hit movie *Snow White and the Seven Dwarfs,*

> *Heigh-ho! Heigh-ho!*
> *It's back to work we go*
> *With Wendell Willkie leading us*
> *The jobs will grow!*
> *Heigh-ho, heigh-ho—heigh-ho!*
> *We've all been feeling low.*
> *But Willkie's hand will save the land*
> *Heigh-ho Heigh-ho.*

"I'm very appreciative," Willkie said afterward at the Benjamin Franklin Hotel alongside his wife and son. "I'm very humble. I'm very proud. It's going to be a great battle."

The campaign was no battle whatsoever. Frustrated Republicans had turned to an amateur politician as they had once turned to Horace Greeley. Though Willkie traveled widely and spoke with vigor, he was a lightweight in an arena of giants.

Willkie did flail gamely. He warned that the New Deal had reduced the Constitution to a "scrap of paper." He claimed that the New Deal was going to socialize medicine. He tried repeatedly to make FDR's un-

Wendell L. Willkie captures the GOP. Omaha World-Herald. *Repr.*
New York Herald Tribune, *July 7, 1940.*

precedented campaign for a third term into a crisis. "Our unwritten law
against granting a third term to any president is not even mentioned by
the third-term candidate," Willkie said at Newark, N.J. in November.
"He doesn't even attempt to justify his violation of that principle against
a third term which has been established in these United States for more
than 150 years."

Elsewhere, Willkie conducted himself with alarmist cant: "I feel a
deep sense of humility that I've been called to lead this sacred cause, a
cause so sacred that if I do not win, liberty must pass from this world.
We must win, we are going to win."

Willkie vs. Roosevelt, 1940. New York Herald Tribune, *October 24, 1940.*

Hoover worked for Willkie against FDR's foreign policy. "If we look back over the whole record of Mr. Roosevelt's relations with Europe and Asia," Hoover remarked in Lincoln, Nebraska, during election week, "there is not one act which has substantially contributed to peace. There are hundred of acts which tend to drag us into war."

The infamous bullish economist Irving Fisher of 1929, now professor emeritus at Yale, popped up to knock FDR's domestic policy. "President Roosevelt would have little chance today were it not because of two sinister facts—the political machines which he has created, and the millions of people on relief or employed by him, who he has put under personal obligation."

FDR's old mentor, Al Smith, appeared in Boston to support "No Third Term—Democrats for Willkie." "The third term candidate declared that 'we have the greatest fighting equipment in the world,' " Al Smith broadcasted wearing a Willkie button. "So we have, but the trouble is that we have so little of it."

The Democrats replied hotly. Henry A. Wallace, FDR's vice presidential running mate and former secretary of agriculture, a wild-eyed, lank-haired speaker, accused Willkie of Nazification. "Millions of Americans who hear me tonight," Wallace said at Madison Square Garden, "know from personal observation that there is Nazi propaganda and Nazi pressure for the election of the Republican candidate." Wallace called Willkie, "the man Hitler wants."

New York mayor Fiorello LaGuardia, a Republican who had joined forces with the New Deal, called Willkie's campaign prediction of war by springtime, "reckless and unpatriotic behavior." "The utility candidate," LaGuardia said at St. Louis, "will wind up his campaign bewildered and in despair, driving home the war scare."

FDR's son, Franklin Delano Roosevelt, Jr., then twenty-six, addressed the issue of Al Smith's defection. "Wall Street got Al Smith. Wall Street will never get my father."

A wry controversy occurred during election week when heavyweight champion Joe Louis announced he was voting for Willkie. Former heavyweight Jack Dempsey was shocked, and from his restaurant in New York reminded, "As for Joe Louis—by coming out for Willkie he's talking against his race and his people. He should remember he was a poor man himself. He used to pick cotton. Mr. Roosevelt is the poor man's friend."

Joe Louis countered sharply from Chicago, "If you're going to vote Democratic just go South and see how those Democrats work. Don't help the South. Every Democratic vote is for the South."

Nearly fifty million voted. The first town to report was the small Sharon, New Hampshire, with twenty-four votes for Willkie and seven votes for FDR.

Roosevelt won 54.7 percent and thirty-nine states for 449 electoral votes. Willkie made a weak showing in traditional Republican neighborhoods in New England and through the Great Plains states to Colorado for 82 electoral votes.

The new Seventy-seventh Congress was a copy of the Seventy-sixth, with Democrats in command as the war in Europe crashed into American politics.

Roosevelt's fund-raiser and ambassador to Great Britain Joseph P. Kennedy commented on the gloom. "People call me a pessimist," he said in Boston. "I say, 'What is there to be gay about?' Democracy is all done. Democracy is finished in England. It may be here."

★ 1944 ★

Roosevelt's third administration went to war.

After Pearl Harbor, December 7, 1941, the Republicans fell in line and shouldered the war effort along with Democrats and socialists. Partisan politics disappeared from the front page in the black tide of war news.

The 1942 midterm elections were quiet, and significant in that the country seemed to turn away from the polarizing differences between the parties. The new Seventy-eighth Congress was almost evenly divided in the House, 218 Democrats to 208 Republicans and 4 others. The Senate continued lopsided, 58 Democrats to 37 Republicans and 1 other.

In New York Thomas Dewey—who had distinguished himself by raising millions for philanthropy in 1941—won the governorship in 1942 over a newcomer (Herbert Lehman had retired). This time Dewey ran a solemn campaign against the so-called bosses. "Being governor is pretty sober business in these times," Dewey remarked. The GOP was cheered by the gubernatorial victories of three other newcomers: Edward Martin in Pennsylvania, Harry F. Kelly in Michigan, and Earl Warren in California.

Longtime Republican maverick senator George W. Norris of Nebraska, now eighty-one, was defeated after thirty-nine years in Congress. Norris had broken with the party years before over conservation issues and other Progressive planks, and had supported Al Smith in '28 and FDR since '32. Norris asked tearfully, "Why are the voters so mad at me?"

For the next two years, the American war effort continued bipartisan. The sour-faced Harry S. Truman of Missouri distinguished himself by conducting popular investigations of waste and mismanagement in government housing, and politicians from all sides used the war to demonstrate their zeal for cost cutting and reform.

By June of 1944 the Republicans faced a convention in which they had to find a way to challenge Roosevelt even while the president was conducting the massive June 6, 1944, D-Day invasion in France. Under impossible conditions, the party gathered at Chicago to go through the ceremony.

"Conventions are like relatives," observed a Chicago policeman. "You're glad to see the people come. You're glad to see them go."

There were no primaries of note nor any genuine jawboning. The party indicated early that dapper, mustached Thomas Dewey of New York, forty-two, was the unanimous favorite. A Stop-Dewey movement fizzled quickly, leaving iconoclast Harold Stassen the only favorite son who wouldn't drop out.

Twenty thousand crowded into the Chicago auditorium for what proved to be one of the hottest sessions ever staged. The television networks had set up four ten-thousand-watt and five-thousand-watt klieg lights above the podium. Every speaker at the podium and every delegate up front on the floor was bathed in sweat for three days. The joke was that the GOP didn't have enough clean shirts to get anyone nominated.

New governor Earl Warren of California gave the keynote address while human steam rose from the pit of sweltering delegates in front of the stage and Warren's red jowls rained sweat on the pages of his speech.

"We believe the New Deal is destroying the two party system," Warren complained. "The New Deal is no longer the Democratic Party. It is an incongruous clique within that party. It retains its power by patronizing and holding together incompatible groups. It talks of idealism and seeks its votes from the most corrupt political machines in the country. The leaders of its inner circle are not representative of the people. They are the personal agents of one man." Thick-necked, big-shouldered Warren exhorted, "Over all this—and over all of us—is the ominous, gargantuan figure of an arrogant, power-intoxicated bureaucracy."

Meanwhile at Albany, New York, Dewey made sure he was photographed going in and going out of his offices while he waited for the word. His promoters made sure the press knew that a plane was ready to carry Dewey to Chicago to accept the nomination in person.

A spectacular event at the convention was the appearance of "General" Jacob S. Coxey of Ohio. Now ninety years old, Coxey had been the leader of Coxey's Army in 1894 when it marched on Grover Cleveland's Washington (during the dire depression of 1893–96). Coxey was now campaigning for a universal currency that he claimed would bring peace. He wore a Lincoln penny that dangled a bell that he said he would ring when the nation was free.

The platform was anti–New Deal. The Republican party was for total victory and for a permanent peace. The party approved of the establishment of a United Nations, but it would not support the United States joining a world state. There was a plank calling for a constitutional amendment that would place a two-term limit on the presidency. Another plank called for lower taxes as soon as the war ended.

Hoover spoke in order to offer a vision of the future of the party. "America needs a change in Administration to get out of personal power diplomacy," he said. He added that the party must prepare for the return of "12 million younger men matured far beyond their years under the supreme test of war."

On Wednesday, June 28, with the temperature at ninety-nine degrees on the floor, the delegates didn't slump, they slushed as Dewey was chosen the nominee on the first ballot. In New York Dewey boarded a United Airlines flight, "State of Ohio," and flew four hours to Chicago with his family, aides, and press photographers. Dewey's appearance at the podium that evening was delayed by the governor's need for a fresh shirt change.

For the vice presidency, the delegates couldn't have their first choice, Earl Warren, and reached instead for the log-cabin-born senator from Ohio, John William Bricker.

From a distance Democrats looked over the new ticket, Dewey and Bricker, and shrugged off the threat. "The shoving of Willkie into the background and the bringing of Hoover and Dewey into the front," said Senator Ebert D. Thomas, Democrat of Montana, "means that the Republican Party will remain the GOP of the 1920s."

Dewey proved an able, eloquent campaigner who made attacks on FDR and the New Deal the only issue.

"Let us again make getting ahead a vital part of our American speech and thought," Dewey said at Buffalo in late October. "For years the New Dealers have sneered at the old American idea of 'getting ahead.' Let us make sure that our children can again believe that there is room for every one to get ahead. Let us nail that principle to our masthead as we set out on a sure course for the future."

Falling farther and farther behind, Dewey tried hard partisanship. He accused Roosevelt and the New Deal with alarmist red-baiting rhetoric that would well up again years later during the Cold War. "In Russia a Communist is a man who supports his government," Dewey said at Boston in November, his tenth major speech of the campaign. "In America a Communist is a man who supports the fourth term so our form of government may be more easily changed. Nazism and Fascism are being crushed out of the world. But the totalitarian idea is very much alive and we must not slip into its other form—Communism."

Harold L. Ickes, Roosevelt's longtime ally and Interior secretary, fired back at Dewey with equally hard partisanship. "The campaign of Mr. Dewey has become a sly, but deliberate effort to encourage and to capitalize upon the anti-labor and anti-Semitic feeling which he believes exists within the United States."

New York senator Robert F. Wagner, a Roosevelt loyalist, hit Dewey harder. "A Republican victory would put in the White House a man

Dewey vs. Roosevelt, 1944: Smoking out the New Deal. New York Herald Tribune, *October 24, 1944.*

whose blushing falsifications sought to impair the morale of our fighting forces, to satisfy his uncontrolled craving for political advancement."

Dewey was unruffled and increased his anti-Communist attack. "The Democratic party is now weakened by twelve years of one-man rule," Dewey said at Baltimore. "It has been taken away from the Democrats. It is now being captured by a coalition of subversive forces, including New Dealers, members of the Political Action Committee and the Communists."

Roosevelt was profoundly tired, obviously sickly, shrunken inside his coat. He could hardly move from his car when he traveled. Since Roosevelt had suffered polio in 1924, no news organization had ever broken the unspoken pact that the press would not speak of the president's disability or even photograph the president being moved in or out of his wheelchair. No one now broke the pact, but in 1944 no photographer could any longer conceal the severe aging in the president's face.

At Boston the Sunday before the election, Roosevelt was a shadow of the man who had first won in '32. Yet he found the strength in his excellent voice to slam back at Dewey's charge of communism and totalitarianism. "Everybody knows I was reluctant to run for President this year," Roosevelt said. He spoke from the back of his open-topped limousine that had been parked on a ramp at second base at Fenway Park. "But since this campaign developed, I tell you frankly that I have become most anxious to win—and I say that for the reason that never before in my lifetime has a campaign been filled with such misrepresentation, distortion and falsehood." Roosevelt then showed his temper. "Never since 1928 have there been so many attempts to stimulate in America racial or religious intolerance. When any politician, any political candidate stands up and says that the government of the United States—your government—could be sold out to the Communists—then I say that candidate reveals, and I'll be polite, a shocking lack of trust in America. He reveals a shocking lack of faith in democracy—in the spiritual faith of our people."

Roosevelt regained his temper in order to review the achievement of his twelve-year New Deal administration. "Then, if ever there was a time in which the spiritual strength was put to the test, that time was in the terrible depression of 1929 to 1933. Our people in those days might have turned to alien ideologies—like Communism or Fascism. But—our democratic faith was too sturdy. What the American people demanded in 1933 was not less democracy—but more democracy—and that is what they got. Yes, the American people proved in those black days of depression—as they have proved again in this war—that there is no chink

in the armor of our democracy. On this subject—and on all subjects—I
say to you, my friends, what I said when first you conferred upon me the
exalted honor of the Presidency: 'We have nothing to fear but fear itself.'
And today I can add a corollary to that. And I do not think you will ever
cast the majority of your votes for fearful men."

Fearful men.

Roosevelt had thrown his last solid partisan punch and had hit
Dewey and the Republicans square. Roosevelt had called the GOP *fear-*
ful men, and nothing that was said in the last moments of the campaign
could blunt the potency of this charge.

Nearly forty-eight million voted on Tuesday, November 7, 1944.

Roosevelt voted at Hyde Park's Town Hall and then, as was his custom, went on to his mother's house to await results. "We have been
through so many campaigns," said Sara Delano Roosevelt, the president's mother, "that one really just waits for the results, with confidence
that whatever the people decide will be good for the nation."

The crusading, clean-up-the-waste senator Harry S. Truman of Missouri was the surprising replacement for Vice President Henry A. Wallace on the ticket. Truman voted with his wife in his hometown of
Independence, Missouri. Truman's mother, ninety-one-year-old Martha
Truman, was a lifelong Democrat. She sprang from the car and addressed her son, "Which way, Harry?"

"This way, Mama," Truman answered.

While his mother went inside to vote for him, Truman spoke to the
press with his newfound stature. "I am sure the President and I have the
support of the nation."

Roosevelt and Truman took 53.3 percent of the vote and forty states
with 432 electoral votes. Dewey won 45.9 percent of the vote and took
99 electoral votes.

The Democrats retained the new Seventy-ninth Congress comfortably.
Of note was the first-time election of Democrat Helen Gahagan Douglas
from California's Fourteenth Congressional District. Wife of the actor
Melvyn Douglas, Douglas would go on to retain her seat until 1950,
when she would try for the Senate by going up against a Republican congressman from the Twelfth California District, Richard M. Nixon.

In New York at the Roosevelt Hotel, Governor Dewey took heart
from the fact that he had scored a better percentage of votes against
FDR than any previous candidate—Hoover, Landon, Wilkie. At a
press conference the day after the election, before he left for Albany,
Dewey argued that the war and not Roosevelt was the major issue of
the campaign. Dewey also argued that the GOP was in the most unified shape it had been since 1928. He noted that he was happy to see

After the election, 1944. New York Herald Tribune, *November 8, 1944.*

the defeat of arch isolationist Republicans such as Senator Gerald P. Nye of North Dakota and Representative Hamilton Fish, Jr., of New York.

"Next time, Governor," a policeman called to Dewey on his way out.

"It's been a lot of fun this time," Dewey yelled back with a smile and wave.

Dewey had most enjoyed his campaign. Up against one of the conquering Allied commander in chiefs, Dewey had demonstrated that he could punch and counterpunch with gusto.

Significantly, Dewey had identified a campaign theme of *the Com-*

munist threat that would grow to become the defining issue of the post-war era.

Before there was a Cold War, there was the Republican 1944 Dewey campaign warning of the Communist party's threat to the American way of life. Before there were Eisenhower, Nixon, Ford, Reagan, and Bush, there was Thomas E. Dewey making anticommunism into the rallying battle cry of the Grand Old Party. Dewey's partisan genius would rattle American politics and change the world for the next fifty years.

☆ 5 ☆

Cold Warriors—I Like Ike!
Nixon's the One!
The Great Communicator!

1946–1992

It's so unfortunate and disappointing," Rose Kennedy said of the Watergate scandal. The occasion was an interview for Mrs. Kennedy's eighty-fourth birthday at her Hyannis Port, Massachusetts, home.

The date was Sunday, July 21, 1974.

These were the last days of Richard Nixon's presidency. After sixty-seven months in office, Nixon's second-term administration was on the brink of failure as the Congress and the Supreme Court closed in with recommendations and rulings that would soon end the Watergate debacle with the president's resignation from office.

In those overheated summer days in the United States, there was only the obsessive topic of the last days of Richard M. Nixon wherever two or more newspaper readers or television watchers gathered. Birthdays, weddings, ball games, delivery rooms—it didn't matter what else was going on, everyone had an opinion and everyone wanted to know what other folks thought.

It was the same for Rose Kennedy. Daughter of a famous Boston Democratic politician, Representative John F. "Honey Fitz" Fitzgerald, who had survived Theodore Roosevelt's Republican hegemony era; widow of Ambassador Joseph P. Kennedy, who had served Franklin Delano Roosevelt's four administrations; and mother of a president and two senators, Rose Kennedy was the reigning queen mother of Democratic politics. Not surprisingly, the press wanted to know what she thought of the tragedy of President Nixon. What was fresh was that Mrs.

Kennedy responded compassionately of a man who was so widely decried as a liar, crook, and bully.

Mrs. Kennedy did not venture into the legalistic tangle of special prosecutors, Supreme Court arguments, plea bargaining, and constitutional interpretations that were all giving the country a collective headache. Instead she said she found the day-to-day maneuvering of attorneys and Congress and White House spokesmen "so confusing."

Mrs. Kennedy's candor was liberating. After two years of revelations and crises, the Watergate scandal had turned into an endless series of press conferences and legal gymnastics on all sides. To call Watergate "so confusing" was generous.

The truth was that Watergate was a mess that made little sense outside of the 120-year-old battle between the Grand Old Party and the Democracy.

Drive a sitting Republican president out of office because of a failed burglary of the Democratic National Committee headquarters in the Washington, D.C., Watergate Hotel complex on June 17, 1972? Impeach and remove with trial by Senate the thirty-seventh president because he may have ordered a cover-up of the links between the nabbed burglars

Watergate, May 1973. New Yorker, May 19, 1973.

and the reelection campaign at the White House? Put the nation through a constitutional crisis because the Republicans had hammered the Democrats with every resource—including laundered money, spying, bugging, sabotage, and overall rascalry—in the 1972 presidential election, and had been rewarded for all-out partisan combat with a staggering 60 percent of the popular vote?

Because Nixon beat the pants off a weak-willed rival, Senator George McGovern of South Dakota, whose nomination fractured the Democracy into potato chips, you're going to run the president out of town? Because Nixon of California was great at defeating the Democrats—was the master of hammer-and-tong electioneering—was he going to be destroyed by his lifelong enemies, the Democrats?

Mrs. Kennedy knew all about the partisan battle between the Republicans and Democrats that had darkened her life for forty years. She had watched her father and husband use generously funded persuasion to make sure FDR of New York got on the 1932 Democratic ticket and then defeated Herbert Hoover of California in the general election. She had also watched her father and husband use more generously funded persuasion in 1960 to make sure her second son, John F. Kennedy, outlasted Senator Hubert Humphrey of Minnesota and Senator Lyndon B. Johnson of Texas in the primaries to win the Democratic presidential nomination at Los Angeles. And she was certainly aware that her father and husband and sons had fought the 1960 presidential contest against Vice President Richard M. Nixon down to the last electoral college vote—and that there was ample evidence that the 1960 general election had been badly tainted by Mayor Richard M. Daley's Chicago machine and Lyndon B. Johnson's South Texas machine.

Later, darkly, Mrs. Kennedy had watched how the savage partisanship of Texas had poisoned the air that her second son, President John F. Kennedy, had charged into that day of his assassination in Dallas, November 22, 1963. More recently, she had watched how partisanship had ripped apart the Democratic party in the 1968 primary season so that when her third son, Senator Robert F. Kennedy of New York, had entered the nomination race, he had walked into a gloomy fatalism that extended into that Los Angeles hotel kitchen where he was murdered by a Palestinian anarchist.

Mrs. Kennedy had even had to stand by and watch agents from the White House's flying security and enforcement squad, known as the Plumbers, attack and humiliate her fourth son, Senator Edward M. "Teddy" Kennedy of Massachusetts, after his troubled conduct in the drowning death of his campaign worker, Mary Jo Kopechne in 1969.

More than any other living American citizen, Mrs. Kennedy knew partisanship when she saw it. Instead of debating the double-talk of the scandal, Mrs. Kennedy spoke of Richard Nixon as a man who deserved understanding. Mrs. Kennedy said that Mr. Nixon had done well for himself to have reached the presidency "without advantages." Mrs. Kennedy noted that her son John F. Kennedy, a graduate of Choate and Harvard, had enjoyed the love and support of his wealthy father and beloved grandfather in his march into the House in 1946, the Senate in 1954, and the White House in 1960.

"I don't believe there was anyone like that for Mr. Nixon," Rose Kennedy added.

The truth was more severe. No one had ever supported Richard Nixon more than expediency required. He was profoundly a self-made man. Born poor on a small citrus grove farm in the sandy hills of Southern California, Richard Nixon had pulled himself up by his own bootstraps, without family fortune or paternal oversight, to put himself into the House, the Senate, the vice presidency, and now the presidency. Nixon's entry into politics in 1946 was an accident of history—he had been invited to compete for a party primary with dozens of others, like a spelling bee contestant—and ever since that day Richard Nixon had invented and reinvented himself, had driven himself beyond all expectations, had held himself up with only the backbone God gave him.

Yet in her remarks, the graceful Rose Kennedy offered a hand to Richard Nixon. She spoke of him not as a Republican but as a man—as a suffering human being. She spoke of him with the love of a mother for a son. Mrs. Kennedy's loving concern was not disproportionate. Her slain son John F. Kennedy had crossed paths so often with Richard Nixon that they seemed twinned in their fates from their first entrance on the political stage. One of the strangest ironies in the whole of Richard Nixon's spectacular career was that in his freshman year in the Eightieth Congress, 1947–49, one of the first other freshmen he had encountered was Representative John F. Kennedy of Massachusetts.

In his memoirs written years after the Watergate crisis, Nixon recalled some of those early days with Rose Kennedy's son. In the spring of 1947, Nixon and Kennedy were picked by a senior congressmen as bright prospects in their respective parties. Mr. Baby-faced Republican versus Mr. Baby-faced Democrat. They were sent to McKeesport, Pennsylvania, to debate the controversial Taft-Hartley Bill on labor relations before an aroused union audience—the first Nixon-Kennedy debate, with Nixon for and Kennedy against the measure.

"We took the Capital Limited back to Washington after the debate," Nixon recalled in 1978. "We drew straws for the lower berth, and—this time—I won. We sat up late, talking far more about foreign policy than about domestic issues. Kennedy and I were too different in background, outlook, and temperament to become close friends, but we were thrown together throughout our early careers, and we never had less than an amicable relationship. We were of the same generation—he was only four years younger than I; we were both Navy veterans; we both came to the House the same year; and we were both committed to devoting enormous energy to our work. Our exchanges in committee meetings and our discussions in the cloakrooms were never tinged with personal acerbity that can make political differences uncomfortable."

Nixon summarized the parallels he felt he shared with Kennedy. "In those early years we saw ourselves as political opponents but not political rivals. We shared one quality which distinguished us from most of our fellow congressmen: neither of us was a back-slapper, and we were both uncomfortable with boisterous displays of superficial camaraderie. He was shy, and that sometimes made him appear aloof. But it was a shyness born of an instinct that guarded privacy and concealed emotions. I understood these qualities because I shared them." *

After Rose Kennedy's kindness, there was no generosity from anyone for Richard Milhous Nixon.

Those last three weeks in office were a ceaseless barrage of facts and findings aimed at him. The Democrats were ganging up for the coup de grâce. The Democrats were going to get Nixon with the same partisan tactics of leak, smear, innuendo, subpoena, court ruling, arrest warrant, secret transcript, eavesdropping, and just general divide-and-conquer manipulation of the press and public that the president had perfected against his opponents.

A quick survey of Richard Nixon's record shows what a master of partisanship he was. The red-baiting tactic that Nixon used to defeat Democrat Jerry Voorhis for Congress from California's Twelfth Congressional District in 1946; the red-baiting tactic that Nixon used to defeat Democrat Helen Gahagan Douglas in the California senatorial race of 1950; the red-baiting tactic that Nixon used to attack the Democratic opposition in the service of Eisenhower's presidential tickets in 1952 and 1956; the red-baiting tactic that Nixon used in his hard losses to Democrat Kennedy in the 1960 presidential race and to Democrat Harold Brown in the 1962 California gubernatorial contest; the red-baiting he used to win a plurality victory in the 1968 presidential race over liberal Democrat Vice President Hubert Humphrey and segregationist Democrat George Wallace, governor of Alabama; and the ruthless red-baiting

*Richard Nixon, *The Memoirs of Richard Nixon* (New York: Grosset & Dunlap, 1978), p. 43.

he used for his massive majority victory over liberal Democrat Senator George McGovern of South Dakota in 1972—all this brilliant Democrat-bashing had helped to construct a record unequaled in modern politics.

In the summer of 1974, the decades of electioneering came back on Richard Nixon as if the tsunami of defamation that Nixon had always been able to launch against the other guy had gone all the way around the world to fall back on Nixon. The strange justice of it was that all those Democrats whom Nixon had accused as reds and *pinkos* and fellow travelers and bums now rose up to unseat him like the mob at the Winter Palace.

On Wednesday, July 24, the Supreme Court ruled unanimously, 8–0, that President Nixon had to hand over to Special Prosecutor Leon Jaworski certain tape recordings made in the Oval Office of conversations between the president and his aides on the Watergate scandal. The same day the House Judiciary Committee, composed of twenty-one Democrats and seventeen Republicans (Nixon had carried twenty-nine of the thirty-eight districts in the '72 election), began a nationally televised debate on the recommendation that President Nixon be impeached by the House and sent to the Senate for trial.

On Saturday, July 27, the House Judiciary Committee voted 27–11 to approve the first article of impeachment—accusing the president of "a course of conduct or plan" to obstruct the investigation of the Watergate break-in and to cover up the obstruction. Later, Senate majority leader

Watergate, June 1973. Richmond News Leader. *Repr.* Washington Post, *June 5, 1973.*

By MacNelly in the Richmond News Leader

"Quick, Lillian . . . We're Missing the Start of 'Truth or Consequences!'"

Mike Mansfield, a Democrat from Montana, who had to prepare for a trial of the president by Senate, remarked sullenly, "The line of demarcation has been reached."

On Friday, August 2, former White House special counsel John W. Dean III was sentenced to prison for his part in the Watergate break-in and cover-up. Dean, whose testimony to the Senate Watergate Hearings in June 1973 had broken open the scandal, was contrite and grim faced about his serial roles as White House agent and then White House accuser. "What bothers me most," Dean said, "is that I was involved in corruption of government and misuse of a high office."

The same day, the head count for and against the president in the Senate was said to be well short of the two-thirds majority needed for conviction of the president. Nevertheless, the support for Nixon was soft. Senator Bob Dole, a Republican from Kansas and former GOP national chairman, remarked, "I've been hearing 60 to 40 against the President. I'm not certain it's accurate and don't know what the mood of the country will be in a few months when we get to a vote. Suppose inflation improves and people get tired of the impeachment issue—maybe he'll come up in the polls."

Dole was echoed by Republican national chairman George Bush, who argued that, polls aside, the GOP would surprise everyone in the fall midterm elections. Yet Dole's and Bush's wishfulness about markets and polls was hopeless. The bond and stock markets had already voted their decision by selling off sharply not only to year lows but also to decade lows. The Watergate crisis had started bleeding the markets in the spring of '73. The triple blow in October of the Arab oil embargo over the Yom Kippur War, the Saturday Night Massacre when Nixon had fired special prosecutors and his own Justice Department in order to protect his tapes, and the resignation of the disgraced graft-taking vice president, Spiro T. Agnew, had accelerated the market sell-off. By the summer of '74, the long crisis in presidential leadership combined with the oil-shocked inflation in the economy were more than enough to crush the stock and bond markets with a recession that would later be measured as the worst since the end of the Second World War. The president's approval ratings had been plunging since October. By July '74 the Gallup and Harris opinion polls reported new lows in support for Nixon, with a crushing 70 percent disapproval rating.

The final blow came on Monday, August 5, when the White House obeyed the Supreme Court ruling and released three critical tape recordings of conversations on June 23, 1972, between the president and his aides. The remarks on the tapes made it clear that President Nixon had known about the Watergate break-in from the first instance and had ag-

Watergate, August 1974. From Herblock Special Report (W. W. Norton & Co., Inc.).

gressively participated in the obstruction of justice and the cover-up ever since. The tapes made it obvious that the president had lied repeatedly to the nation for over fifteen months. The tapes guaranteed that the president would be impeached and removed from office, unless he first resigned.

No mercy would be shown Richard Nixon. No one would help Richard Nixon. He had raised himself up "without advantages," and he would be broken down "without advantages." The president's resignation on August 9 and flight from the White House in *Marine One* was staged for national television in the most humiliating fashion possible. Nixon knew his resignation was a victory for the Democrats. He knew he was beaten by those he had long beaten. He knew he also had been abandoned by the GOP that he had worked since the Second World War to raise up. He knew that the famous conservative senator Barry Goldwater of Arizona, whose 1964 presidential defeat had badly weakened the Republican party, had carried the message to him from the Senate that the president of the United States did not have more than six votes for acquittal, and Goldwater's wasn't one of them.

The president's last comments to his White House Staff displayed his fury at what was being done to him. "And so I say to you on this occasion," Nixon remarked in the East Room of the White House on the morning of August 9, "we leave proud of the people who have stood by us and worked for us and served this country. We want you to be proud of what you have done. We want you to continue to serve in government if that is your wish. Always give your best. Never get discouraged. Never be petty. *Always remember others may hate you. Those who hate you don't win unless you hate them. And then you destroy yourself.*"

What was it about Richard Nixon that made Washington hate him to the point of destroying him? Why was it that for the nineteen years after his resignation Richard Nixon had to sneak in and out of ceremonial events that other former presidents were welcomed to? What about Nixon moved the television networks to cover his spectacular state funeral in 1993 with a cannonade of disapproval?

Why does Richard Nixon remain the most controversial president of the twentieth century?

The answer is Nixon's genius for partisanship—his skill at gnashing and slashing the Democrats at election time. The irony of his genius is that what made him great also made him reviled by his opponents and feared by his fellow Republicans. Nixon learned early in his career to win elections by polarizing the electorate, usually on the issue of anti-communism. Nixon would never let anyone forget that J. Edgar Hoover had congratulated him personally for pursuing and breaking Alger Hiss as a communist agent. And then two decades later Nixon stunned and confounded all of his critics—whom he had pummeled for decades as communist sympathizers—by opening relations with the People's Republic of China in 1971 as well as by advancing détente with the Soviet Union in 1972.

Richard Nixon was a partisan fighter and a partisan trickster whom no one ever trusted, just as he never trusted anyone. He was a giant of political intrigue. He was a Shakespearean-scaled creation of ambition and dare and suspicion. The answer to all the enmity in 1974 was the plain fact that Richard Nixon was just tougher than everyone else in American politics. Tougher than all the other Republicans. Tougher than every Democrat. So rough and tough that when Richard Nixon showed weakness, both Democrats and Republicans were quick and eager to turn on him with long knives.

"I know these people," Nixon said of his enemies in the final days in the White House. "When they detect weakness somewhere they would not hesitate to harden their position. If they want to put me behind bars, let them."*

This talent of Nixon's to be tougher-than-tough, a partisan's partisan, the last best GOP heavyweight, was nowhere better demonstrated than in an infamous recording tape from the Watergate scandal—the so-called smoking gun that destroyed the presidency. It was recorded by the voice-activated eavesdropping system in the Oval Office that Nixon had ordered installed in 1971.

The date was Friday, June 23, 1972, six days after the Watergate break-in by a team of White House operatives known as the White House's Special Investigation Unit, or the Plumbers.

In the privacy of the Oval Office, the president was discussing the Watergate break-in with his chief of staff, H. R. "Bob" Haldeman, a Los Angeles advertising executive who had joined Nixon's '68 campaign staff.

"Of course, this Hunt, this will uncover a lot of things," Nixon said to Haldeman. E. Howard Hunt, fifty-two, was a CIA agent who had co-led the Plumbers along with former FBI agent G. Gordon Liddy. Hunt and Liddy as well as several CIA-affiliated Cubans and a CIA stringer named James McCord had been arrested and charged with the break-in the week before. "You open that scab," the president continued about Hunt, the Plumbers, and the White House involvement, "there's a hell of a lot of things and we feel just that it would be very detrimental to have this thing go any further."

Nixon was rehearsing out loud what his aides might be able to say to the CIA bosses Richard Helms and General Vernon Walters to convince them to stop the FBI's ongoing investigation of the break-in. In other words, the president was looking for a way that he could order his aides to persuade the CIA to persuade the FBI to obstruct justice.

Nixon qualified, "This involves these Cubans, Hunt, and a lot of

---

*Stephen E. Ambrose, *Nixon: Ruin and Recovery, 1973–1990* (New York: Simon & Schuster, 1991), p. 419.

hanky-panky that we have nothing to do with ourselves." Nixon listened to his own fabrication and didn't much like it. The president changed his tone, "Well, what the hell, did [Attorney General John N.] Mitchell know about this?"

Haldeman answered, "I think so." Haldeman knew the truth was that Mitchell, now running the Committee for the Re-Election of the President, had known well beforehand about G. Gordon Liddy's plans to harass the Democratic National Committee. "I don't think he knew the details," Haldeman tried, "but I think he knew."

"He didn't know how it was going to be handled, though," asked Nixon, "with Dahlberg and the Texans and so forth?" Nixon immediately conceded the worst. "Well, who was the *asshole* that did? Is it Liddy? Is that the fellow? He must be a little nuts?"

"He is," said Haldeman.

G. Gordon Liddy, forty-three, Fordham law graduate, army veteran, FBI veteran, ex-prosecutor, and failed GOP congressional candidate in '68, was then just beginning his rise to national prominence as the most outlandish patriot in the Republican party.

"I mean," the president tried, "he just isn't well screwed on is he? Is that the problem?"

"No, but he was under pressure apparently," Haldeman explained, "to get more information, and as he got more pressure, he pushed the people to move harder—"

"Pressure from Mitchell?" the president asked.

Haldeman said, "Apparently."

"Oh, Mitchell," said Nixon. "Mitchell was at the bottom of it."

"Yeah," said Haldeman.

"All right, fine, I understand it all," said Nixon.

The president understood it all profoundly. He had just unpacked the contents of an attack launched by his reelection campaign against the Democrats. Everything Nixon had learned in thirty-eight years in contest with the Democrats was contained in the simple remark, "All right, fine, I understand it all."

Nixon added, "We won't second guess Mitchell and the rest. Thank God it wasn't Colson."

White House special counsel Charles W. Colson was the president's hardheaded partisan point man to get things done against the president's enemies. Colson knew all about the Plumbers, but Colson had not been primarily involved with the Watergate break-in.

Haldeman answered about Colson and the ongoing FBI investigation of the Watergate break-in: "The FBI interviewed Colson yesterday. They determined that would be a good thing to do. To have him take an interrogation, which he did, and that—the FBI guys working the case concluded that there were one or two possibilities. One, that this was a White House—they don't think that there is anything at the election committee [Committee for the Re-Election of the President]—they think it was either a White House operation and they had some obscure reasons for it—non-political, or was it a—Cuban and the CIA. And after their interrogation of Colson yesterday, they concluded it was not the White House but are now convinced it was a CIA thing, so the CIA turnoff would—"

"Well," interrupted the president, "I'm not sure of their analysis, but I'm not going to get that involved. I'm staying away from it."

"No, sir, we don't want you to," said Haldeman.

Nixon ordered, "You call them in." The president meant that Haldeman should call in the CIA and the FBI and lie to them about the origin of the Watergate break-in.

Haldeman agreed. "Good deal."

Nixon emphasized, "Play it tough. That's the way they play it and that's the way we are going to play it."

"OK," said Haldeman.

"Play it tough. That's the way they play it and that's the way we are going to play it." Here in one bitten-off order from the leader of the Free World was the naked truth of Nixon's amazing success—why Richard Nixon dominated fifty years of American politics, from the Second World War to the end of the Cold War.

Richard Nixon *played it tough*. Richard Nixon did not want it any other way. Nobody helped him. He helped himself. From the first moment he appeared on the political landscape in 1946 to the last moment he mounted *Marine One* on the White House South Lawn and waved one last stiff-arm farewell to the camera, *Richard Nixon was tough*.

Richard Nixon did not stop being tough in August 1974. Nixon was tough enough to ride out a life-threatening phlebitis attack soon after his resignation. He was tough enough to outlast the toxic enmity and disrespect of the American press for the next two decades in order to write books and travel widely and counsel five more presidents. He was tough enough to refuse life-support systems that would have prolonged his life some weeks in 1993. He was tough to the finish to make certain that his remains were to lie within a dozen yards of the humble little farmhouse in Yorba Linda, California, where he was born.

"My first conscious memory is of running," Nixon remembered of his childhood. "I was three years old, and my mother was driving us in a horse-drawn buggy, holding my baby brother Don on her lap while a neighbor girl held me. The horse turned the corner leading to our house at high speed, and I tumbled onto the ground. I must have been in shock, but I managed to get up and run after the buggy while my mother tried to make the horse stop. The only aftereffect of the accident was that years later, when the vogue of parting hair on the left side came along, I still had to comb mine straight back to hide a scar caused by the fall."*

★ 1948 ★

Roosevelt's sudden death in the spring of 1945 transformed the political landscape of the United States. Gone was the depression. At the door was the frightening Cold War.

On the afternoon of Thursday, April 12, 1945, at approximately 4:35 P.M. Eastern War Time, Franklin Delano Roosevelt died of a cerebral hemorrhage in a small room at the so-called Little White House in Warm Springs, Georgia.

Two and a half hours later Vice President Harry S. Truman, sixty, took the oath of office in the Cabinet Room of the White House—the seventh vice president in American history to succeed on the death of a president. "The world may be sure that we will prosecute the war on both fronts, east and west," Truman said, "with all the vigor we possess, to a successful conclusion."

From Albany, New York, Governor Thomas E. Dewey contributed his own opinion: "In building for the future peace of the world, even as the war progressed, Franklin Roosevelt made his final and perhaps his greatest contribution. With that work coming to its first fruition in the near victory, his loss is indeed irreparable."

Dewey and the GOP set quickly to work to repair the Republican party after the long FDR suzerainty.

Immediately at the end of the fighting in Europe and Asia, the Cold War emerged as the battleground between partisan camps. Democratic confusion over the Soviet Union made the Republicans the easy winners of the early Cold War debate. In the winter of 1946 Truman's secretary of state warned about Soviet aggression. Within a week former British prime minister Winston Churchill made his famous "Iron Curtain" speech in Missouri that was understood by all sides as the opening of the Cold War. Soon came a huge embarrassment for the Democrats when Henry A. Wallace, the commerce secretary and former vice president,

*Nixon, *Memoirs*, pp. 3–4.

made a bizarre pro-Stalin speech in New York in September 1946. Truman was obliged to fire Wallace within a week and bring in Averell Harriman of New York (heir to his father E. M. Harriman's railroad trusts) as the new secretary of commerce.

By November 1946 it was clear the Democrats were troubled with domestic as well as foreign issues, and the GOP opposition was gaining in the polls. Truman, surprisingly, did not fight hard, and the week of the election he entrained for Missouri without any plans to speak out during his train tour.

Governor Dewey, campaigning for reelection in New York, took advantage of Truman's silence by hammering the Democrats. "The Republican Party has given teamwork government in our state, and by that we mean progressive government that goes forward upon the firm foundation of sound finance and repudiates the philosophy of debts, deficits and day dreams." Dewey also attacked the Democrats as communist sympathizers. "They have the support of a fifth party which is the appointed agent of totalitarianism in this country," he said at the Cooper Union, "and whether they disavow that support or not, they have it."

Dewey won a massive plurality victory in New York to lead a national sweep for the GOP. The new Eightieth Congress completely reversed sixteen years of Democratic rule. The Republicans won the Senate, 51 Republicans to 45 Democrats; in the House it was 246 Republicans to 188 Democrats. Republicans also won twenty governorships, including the unopposed reelection win of Governor Earl Warren in California.

In House races in California, Republicans won fourteen of the twenty-three seats, including the first victory of political newcomer Richard M. Nixon, forty-three, of the Twelfth Congressional District of Orange County.

The Republican victory was so massive that Democratic senator William J. Fulbright of Arkansas suggested that Truman resign office after he named Republican senator Arthur H. Vandenberg secretary of state. Fulbright said he feared a stalemate with a Democrat in the White House and a total Republican Congress, so his solution was constitutional juggling. "By appointing a Republican Secretary of State and then resigning, he will be acting in a perfectly legal, constitutional matter," Fulbright said, interpreting the contemporary presidential succession law. "The Constitution provides for the Secretary of State to succeed the President when there is no Vice-President."

Truman did not resign. However, Fulbright was right in predicting a standoff in the Eightieth Congress between the Democratic executive and the Republican legislative. Of note was that the GOP had to pass the landmark Taft-Hartley Labor Bill over Truman's veto in June 1947.

Presidential year 1948 began with the wide assumption that the Republican party nominee would be the new president.

In January General Dwight David Eisenhower announced that he would not accept the Republican nomination if offered. The Eisenhower boom failed as the general announced he would accept the presidency of Columbia University in New York.

By the June convention in Philadelphia, the Dewey friends had an advantage over all rivals. The Stop-Dewey forces had several good candidates, including conservative Senators Robert A. Taft of Ohio and Arthur H. Vandenberg of Michigan, and also Governor Earl Warren of California and former governor Harold A. Stassen of Minnesota. None of these men could combine to advance a single choice against Dewey. The convention was declared wide-open for politicking and deal making.

Pundit Walter Lippmann remarked about Republican Speaker of the House Joseph W. Martin's goals at the convention: "The Martin-Taber-Allen-Halleck junta believe that any Republican can be elected in November, that they do not, therefore, have to think about defeating the Democrats, and can concentrate on a fight to control the Republican party."

Pundits Joseph and Stewart Alsop saw the convention not as a place to pick a winner, since any Republican could whip Truman, but rather as a battle over foreign policy. "The stage is set at Philadelphia for the final struggle between the isolationists and men of the Vandenberg school, between the backward looking and the modern minded Republicans."

The ordinary delegate understood the convention as a good excuse for a week of celebration and loose living. Signs such as "Who But Taft" and "Man the Oar. Ride the Crest. Harold Stassen. He's the Best" greeted conventioneers as they arrived at the very popular Bellevue Stratford Hotel. A four-foot-high elephant stood by quietly in the lobby. Everyone hoped that there would be no balloting until after Wednesday, because everyone wanted to see the Joe Louis vs. Jersey Joe Walcott heavyweight prizefight on television on Wednesday evening.

State-of-the-art television technology dominated Convention Hall. Four networks, ABC, CBS, NBC, and the Dumont, occupied broadcast booths built above the platform. Television cameras were set up at the gallery level to sweep over the floor and provide a dramatic glimpse of the action. There were interview rooms at the Bellevue Stratford set aside for chats with candidates and VIPs. For the first time the politicians had to carry on their arguments both on the floor and on national television.

Governor Dwight H. Green of Illinois was the keynote speaker on Monday, June 21. He aimed to define the differences between the parties. "The Republican party, today as always, is the party of faith in the individual American—of faith in the great destiny of our Republic. We are not going back to any yesterday. All our yesterdays have taught us that we have a duty tomorrow." Green emphasized that "the New Deal Party can have no real program, because it is no longer a real party. It mustered its majorities from a fantastic partnership of reaction and radicalism. For years, this strange alliance was held together by bosses, boodle, buncombe and blarney."

Representative Clare Boothe Luce of Connecticut, wife of the *Time* magazine boss, spoke of the bravura confidence in the hall. "Let's not waste time measuring this unfortunate man in the White House against our specifications. Mr. Truman's time is short. His situation is hopeless. Frankly, he is a gone goose."

Dewey did not wait for his nomination to attack Truman. In New York he gave a television interview that knocked Truman as a naïf against the communists for having recently said that Stalin was a prisoner of the Politburo. "Stalin is the boss of Russia," Dewey said on NBC. Dewey added he would meet with Stalin only if he had to, and that he distrusted everything Stalin said or did.

President Truman, watching on TV from the White House, reported that he regarded Dewey as the hardest Republican candidate to beat in the fall.

On the second day, seventy-four-year-old Herbert Hoover addressed the confident, gleeful delegates. Hoover, putting aside the old class-warfare issue, plunged eloquently into the threat of communism. "Liberty has been defeated in a score of nations. They have revived slavery. They have revived mass guilt. They have revived government by hatred, by torture, by exile. Today the men in the Kremlin hold in their right hands the threat of military aggression against all civilization. With their left hand they work to weaken civilization by boring from within." Hoover turned his wrath on communist sympathizers in the United States. "Our difficulty lies not so much with obnoxious Communists in our midst as with the fuzzy-minded people who think we can have totalitarian economics in the hands of a bureaucracy, and at the same time have personal liberty for the people and representative government in the nation. Their confused thinking convinces them that they are liberals— but if they are liberals, they have liberalism without liberty. Nor are they middle-of-the-roaders as they claim to be: They are a halfway-house to totalitarianism."

The Republican platform opposed national economic problems such as the unbalanced budgets, the high cost of living, the high tax burden, and overlapping regulation.

What the platform relished was foreign policy. "We dedicate our foreign policy to the preservation of a free America in a free world of freemen." The platform called for a crusade against communism. "We pledge a vigorous enforcement of existing laws against Communists and enactment of such new legislation as may be necessary to expose the treasonable activities of Communists and defeat their objective of establishing here a Godless dictatorship controlled from abroad."

Nominations began on Wednesday and continued amid a rancorous marathon session that didn't adjourn until 4:02 A.M. Thursday morning—wrecking everyone's plans to watch the Louis-Walcott fight in peace. Throughout the session the Dewey managers—"Clean Up with Dewey"—were in control of the majority of delegates. All the Taft and Stassen forces could do was fight a delaying action against the inevitable. Earning his baptism by fire that night was Stassen's young chief of staff, future Supreme Court chief justice Warren Burger of Minnesota.

The session was dragged out by nomination speeches for dark horses such as General Douglas MacArthur of Wisconsin. "Douglas MacArthur is not actively seeking the presidency of the United States," declared nominator Harlan Kelley of Milwaukee, Wisconsin, "but he has stated in no uncertain terms that if the people of America call upon him to serve he would accept."

On Thursday the Republicans chose Thomas E. Dewey. Dewey led easily from the first ballot over Taft and Stassen, and by the second ballot he was only a handful of votes short for a majority. The pro forma third ballot made the choice unanimous.

For the very first time the Republicans had named a previously defeated candidate to be the standard-bearer. Dewey addressed the convention on live television at 9:17 P.M.: "To me, to be a Republican in this hour is to dedicate one's life to the freedom of men. As long as the world is half-slave and half-free, we must peacefully labor to help men everywhere to achieve liberty."

Later, back at the Bellevue Stratford, Dewey used a loudspeaker from the balcony of his room to address a huge crowd that was blocking Broad Street. "I want to tell you how I happened to be delayed. I was delayed because I finally got through a long distance call to my mother."

The final day, Earl Warren of California accepted the vice presidential nomination after a unanimous ballot. Warren had turned down the same spot four years before, and this time he explained that he felt he had been "hit by a street car."

On the same day a half world away, the two-day-old Soviet blockade of Berlin, until then a hazy affair, tightened and deepened. The Soviets cut the power and blocked all food and supplies into the city by land route from West Germany. The American forces announced emergency plans to begin an airlift of food into the surrounded city. The convention ended with a jolt at the first big battle of the Cold War.

Dewey did not press his immediate huge advantage on the Berlin crisis. Instead, with the Allied Air Forces beginning what would be one of the most heroic victories over the Stalinist tyrants in East Germany, Dewey chose to talk about electioneering. He announced his sunny expectations that millions of Democrats would join him in ending the Republican party's sixteen-year "drought."

Dewey's campaign remained buoyant and lofty. The Democrats had done the GOP the apparent favor of breaking apart like an angry family: Harry Truman won the Democratic nomination at the July convention. But then Democratic senator J. Strom Thurmond of South Carolina broke off to form a segregationist third party called the States Rights party, or the Dixiecrats. Also, the cranky former vice president Henry A. Wallace declared himself a candidate for president on the Progressive party ticket with a platform of undisguised appeasement toward Stalinism.

By October Dewey commanded a huge lead in the opinion polls. George Gallup's poll showed well over 50 percent for Dewey to a shaky 37 percent for Truman.

Dewey enjoyed strength in all the traditional Republican sections, New England, the East, the Midwest, and the West. The only part of the country that was identified as anti-Dewey was the traditionally Democratic Solid South, which was said to be leaning to the Dixiecrats. States' rights candidate Thurmond underlined this interpretation when he attacked Dewey: "The record of the Republican candidate in opposition to Southern progress is well known. I do not see how such a man can claim a single vote in the South."

Two weeks before the election, Dewey maintained his lofty tone at the Alfred E. Smith Dinner at the Waldorf-Astoria in New York. "For much of humanity this is an age of inhumanity; not inhumanity of nature or of machine, but of man's inhumanity to man. On much of the face of the earth no human being draws a free breath. He lives in constant fear of the heavy tread upon the stair or the knock at night upon his door. He lives in constant fear of the secret police. That is a fear even worse than poverty or sickness for it warps the mind and freezes the soul."

The final week of the campaign, freshman congressman Richard M.

"We Got To Burn The Evil Spirits Out Of Her"

Richard Nixon's debut in a Herblock cartoon, May 1948 during the House Un-American investigations by the Eightieth Congress. From Herblock Special Report (W. W. Norton & Co., Inc.).

Nixon of California joined in the Dewey parade as well as advancing his own recent notoriety as a member of the House Un-American Activities Committee. In a radio broadcast debate with Truman administration spokesmen over the question of loyalty oaths in government service, Nixon defended his August espionage investigation of State Department official Alger Hiss based on the allegations of *Time* writer Whittaker Chambers. "I must admit I have been very close to the case," Nixon said carefully. "From the testimony that we have heard to debate, the credibility of Mr. Hiss has been substantially impaired; the credit of Mr. Chambers has stood on the items where corroborative testimony was available. That is the conclusion I would reach on the testimony to date." (Within a month, Chambers would produce the Pumpkin Papers that documented Hiss's espionage and condemned Hiss to years in jail and a lifetime of contretemps.)

The Tuesday before the election, Dewey enjoyed a ticker tape parade on La Salle Street in Chicago, where he aimed to boost the tough reelection campaigns of Governor Dwight H. Green and Republican senator Wayland Brooks. Asked about the taunting and mocking attacks Truman was making on him on the president's whistle-stop swing around the country—"We all know," Truman had joked in Cleveland, "that for twelve years the Republicans have been poll happy"—Dewey responded, "Nobody believes that stuff anyway, do they? Including the people who are saying it."

Election eve, the polls remained Dewey's best friend. The lone worry in the Dewey camp was whether the Republicans could retain control of the Senate. Dewey traveled from his Pawling, New York, farm to speak on a national radio broadcast. His tone was confident to the end, "I believe with all my heart that we Americans have made up our minds we are going to have a strong, united nation."

From Independence, Missouri, Truman broadcasted a partisan radio warning. "Tomorrow you will be deciding between the principles of the Democratic party—the party of the people—and the principles of the Republican party—the party of privilege." Truman underlined his class-warfare theme, "I believe that a Democratic administration, pledged to continue the present policies of our country, is our best insurance against going back to the dark days of 1932."

Nearly forty-nine million voted. Nationwide there were five hundred thousand television sets to watch the network election broadcasts. The counting continued long after the networks went off the air. By dawn in New York the newspapers declared that this was the closest election since the Wilson-Hughes 1916 race. The doubtful states of Ohio and Illinois went Democratic after breakfast. In New York Dewey at his Roosevelt Hotel headquarters conceded defeat at 11:15 A.M., Wednesday, November 3.

The Republican party was dumbfounded. Dewey had gained only 45.1 percent of the vote for 189 electoral votes. Sixty-four-year-old Truman and his seventy-year-old running mate, Senator Alben W. Barkley of Kentucky, had won 49.6 percent of the vote for 303 electoral votes. The Dixiecrat Thurmond took 2.4 percent of the vote and 39 electoral votes

Truman beats the polls and Dewey, 1948. New York Herald Tribune, *November 6, 1948.*

entirely in the Old Confederacy. The feisty Progressive Wallace took 2.4 percent but won no states.

The Democrats recaptured both houses of the new Eighty-first Congress, reversing all the GOP gains from '46. Truman had argued shrewdly on the campaign trail, "We don't need a new president, we need a new Democratic Congress!" The new Senate would show 54 Democrats and 42 Republicans; the new House would show 263 Democrats and 171 Republicans and one other.

On Wednesday, heavy selling hit the New York Stock Exchange in the sharpest break since the summer of 1946.

At New York Democratic headquarters at the Biltmore Hotel, the victorious celebrated with champagne and a satirical chorus about the wrongheaded pollsters.

We are poor little lambs who were led astray
Bah! Bah! Bah!
Little black sheep who will miss our pay,
Bah! Bah! Bah!
Gentlemen pollsters up in a tree,
Bah! Bah! Bah!
Damned from here to eternity,
God please save us from Tom Dew-Wee
Bah! Bah! Bah!

★ 1952 ★

Truman's second administration stumbled and fell before the propaganda assaults of the Soviets and then the sneak attack by the Soviet-backed tyrants in North Korea.

The propaganda blows were serial, and Truman did little to fight back. In January 1949, the United States recognized the Republic of (South) Korea; however, new secretary of state Dean Acheson failed to identify Korea as included inside the sphere of American military protection. In August 1949, the State Department blamed the Nationalist Chinese of Formosa for losing China to the communists and argued that the United States was not ever at fault for the success of mass-murdering Mao Tse-tung. In September 1949, Truman told the American people that the Soviet Union had tested an atomic bomb; he hinted that the Soviet weapon was probably built with atomic secrets stolen by Soviet agents. In March 1950, State Secretary Acheson claimed that the United States and the Soviet Union could coexist in reasonable security. On June 25, 1950, Stalin's Korean puppets in North Korea invaded South Korea and attacked American and Korean forces in the dead of night.

Washington was stunned. Truman rushed back by plane from a weekend in Independence, Missouri. Democratic House leader John W. McCormack of Massachusetts warned, "This one thing is certain—it shows that you cannot trust the Communists. Stalin and his gang are out to control the world."

Republican Senate minority leader Kenneth S. Wherry of Nebraska was angry: "You couldn't expect anything else with the China policy we've got of waiting till the dust settles. The Administration should stand up and do something and then we'll stop these Commies."

The war in Korea dominated partisan politics for the next four years. Korea validated the Republican party's anticommunism for the rest of the Cold War. Predawn sneak attack by murderous, godless puppets was understood to justify every dollar spent on national defense and every paragraph of anti-communist rhetoric directed at those who wanted appeasement with Moscow.

The midterm elections of November 1950 were hit by spectacular shocks. On November 1 the advancing American forces in Korea came within thirty miles of the Manchurian border, where they captured Red Chinese soldiers who admitted they were awaiting an attack on the United Nation Forces. On November 2 two assassins, Griselio Torresola and Oscar Collao, both of the Bronx, New York, were shot down at the steps of the Blair House in Washington in a failed attempt to murder President Truman, who was napping upstairs. On election eve General Douglas MacArthur told the United Nations assembly in New York that the Red Chinese were a "new foe" in Korea. The stock market sold off on the new war scare.

On election day, November 7, Republicans were badly disappointed that they failed to take either the Senate or the House; however, several significant players strengthened their bases. Dewey won reelection in New York; Taft won reelection in Ohio; Warren won reelection in California (the same day his youngest daughter was stricken by polio). Newcomer Republican Everett M. Dirksen defeated Democratic Senate majority leader Scott W. Lucas in Illinois.

In California Richard M. Nixon defeated Representative Helen Gahagan Douglas to win the open Senate seat.

By the presidential year 1952, the Korean War still dominated the national news. Those with foreign policy experience became the darlings of the Republican party. Dewey had long made it clear that he would not run again. Dewey had also let it be known since the Korean outbreak that he aimed to be a kingmaker for General Dwight David Eisenhower. The only question for the Eisenhower boom was whether Eisenhower could be persuaded to give up his NATO tour in Paris, to declare himself a Republican, and to come home to run for the presidency.

Senator Robert A. Taft of Ohio was the other credible nominee. Taft represented deep conservative GOP traditions reaching back to his father and the golden TR era. He also stood out as a rough critic of the Truman administration, which he called a "socialistic planned economy." Taft also enjoyed wide support among the labor forces in the Midwest.

In preconvention maneuvering, Eisenhower resigned his army command and traveled to Denver, Colorado, as a temporary headquarters for his campaign to win the Republican nomination over the well-organized and delegate-rich Taft.

A week before the gavel, Eisenhower used his strength as a foreign policy expert to speak against Taft as an isolationist: "Those who assert that America can retire within its own borders," argued Eisenhower in Texas, "those who seem to think that we have little or no stake in the rest of the world and what happens to it; those who act as though we had no need for friends to share in the defense of freedom—such persons are ignorant or irresponsible or they are taking an unjustified gamble with peace."

Taft replied archly a few days later that the United States could not afford to run the world, that a "New Deal" for the whole world would make the United States into an imperialistic bankrupt.

The Chicago convention at the International Amphitheater was anticipated as a toe-to-toe showdown between two well-organized and well-financed contenders. Spoilers Earl Warren and Harold Stassen argued that a deadlock would make their candidacies viable. From the outset the opponents showed that there would be no standoff. Eisenhower, arriving on a special train from Denver, promised his enthusiastic fans "a slugging match from beginning to end." The general was open about his approach to the week: "I don't believe you can take these people and manipulate them around like a regiment. You can't tell them to file right and have them do it."

Taft, riding in an open green Cadillac convertible to greet his supporters in front of the Conrad Hilton Hotel, described his approach to the convention: "There is only one thing to do and that is to present the Republican principles without any moderation to catch the Left-Wing voters. They are the principles the great majority of the American people believe in."

When it came time to fight, the general and the senator were ready to get tough. For example, the first contest of the week was at the Credentials Committee over many contested Southern delegations. "The Taft group act like a bunch of thieves who returned half the loot," remarked an Eisenhower supporter from Texas about his split state delegation, "in the hope of escaping indictment." Taft responded to the delegate fights by calling the whole maneuvering "empty," but only after his forces had lost their arcane ploy in a floor fight.

Retired general MacArthur opened the convention on television (Walter Cronkite was in the CBS booth) with a sentimental keynote speech that was most partial to the Eisenhower sense of global mission. "I speak with a sense of pride that all my long life I have been a member of the Republican party, as was before me my father, an ardent supporter of Abraham Lincoln. I have an abiding faith that this party, if it remains true to its great traditions, can provide a leadership which, as in the days of Lincoln, will bring us back to peace and tranquillity." MacArthur was also blunt about his belief that the Truman administration was a treacherous disgrace: "By exhaustive taxation which withers initiative, reduces energy and, in the end, destroys the spirit of enterprise; by spendthrift policies which stagger the imagination; by discouraging adherence to the principle of private ownership of property, they have established the prerequisites to a socialistic or even a Communistic state."

The first day's true gravity was provided by Mamie Eisenhower. A reporter asked her if, as a soldier's wife, she was worried about her son, Captain John Eisenhower, who was soon returning to combat in Korea. Mrs. Eisenhower looked hard at the reporter. "That's a strange question to ask a mother," she replied. "Soldier's wife or not—*I'm still very much a mother.*"

On the second day, with the bickering Taft and Eisenhower forces all around him, seventy-eight-year-old Herbert Hoover spoke to the Republican ages. "This election may well be the last chance for the survival of freedom in America," he warned. "In a time of confusion and crisis the action of a Republican convention ninety years ago saved this nation for free men. The Whig party temporized, compromised upon the issue of freedom for the Negro. That party disappeared. It deserved to disappear. Shall the Republican party receive or deserve any better fate if it compromises upon the issue of freedom for all men, white as well as black. If you make free men your issue, you can revive the call which your and my ancestors issued ninety years ago when this party was born to make all men free."

The Eisenhower forces had such good momentum that rumors grew hot about the second place on the ticket. The two California Republican senators, William F. Knowland and Richard M. Nixon, were the leading names. A MacArthur boom was fading. The Taft forces let out that they favored Knowland. The Eisenhower friends said the general favored the young, energetic navy veteran Nixon.

On the third day Taft battled back by picking up the sentimental endorsement of Herbert Hoover. Taft also attracted the unwelcome compliment of retiring president Truman. "I am afraid," Truman said about Taft with a smile in Washington, "that my favorite candidate is going to be beaten."

The third day featured a dark speech by freshman senator Joseph R. McCarthy of Wisconsin, who had vaulted to national power by leading a witch-hunt for communist agents in the United States, McCarthy accused the Truman administration of "a combination of abysmal stupidity and treason." McCarthy said that Korea was the great issue of 1952: "Shall America continue to squander her blood, waste her resources and sacrifice her position of world leadership." McCarthy mocked Secretary of State Dean Acheson, who, he said, "hit the communists with a perfumed handkerchief at the front door while the communists batter our friends with blackjacks at the back door." The band played "On Wisconsin," and McCarthy's aroused supporters on the floor paraded with cardboard "red herrings" on poles, a sarcastic reference to Truman's 1948 put-down of the Hiss investigation.

The platform contained both denunciations of Truman's "Fair Deal" administration as graft-ridden and promises of hard fighting against Communists. The prominent foreign policy planks were written by Dewey adviser John Foster Dulles, a fastidious New York lawyer who had worked for the Truman State Department and who now threw his prestige to Eisenhower. "We charge that the leaders of the administration in power lost the peace so dearly earned by World War II," declared the platform. "The moral incentives and hopes for a better world which sustained us through World War II were betrayed, and this has given Communist Russia a military and propaganda initiative which, if unstayed, will destroy us."

For the first time since Theodore Roosevelt's campaigns, the Republican platform pounded the Democrats on civil rights. "We deplore the duplicity and insincerity of the party in power in racial and religious matters. Although they have been in power for many years, they have not kept nor do they intend to keep their promises." And the platform promised specific civil rights remedies, including an end to lynching, an end to segregation in the District of Columbia, and an end to poll taxes.

Of note, the platform called for statehood for Hawaii, Alaska, and Puerto Rico, and self-government and suffrage for the District of Columbia.

The platform also reminded the public that the GOP was prepared to stand by the red-witch-hunting by McCarthy of Wisconsin. "There are no Communists in the Republican party. We have always recognized Communism to be a world conspiracy against freedom and religion. We never compromised with Communism and we have fought to expose it and to eliminate it in government and American life."

Wednesday evening, the nominations and wild demonstrations— forty minutes for "Big Bob Taft" and forty-three minutes for "Ike's Peak or Bust"—dragged out the session until after the networks went off the air. The Taft forces danced to "Four Leaf Clover," and the Eisenhower friends danced to "Deep in the Heart of Texas." The organists in the amphitheater were forbidden from playing two songs, "Marching through Georgia" and "Donkey Serenade."

Balloting was set for Thursday noontime, July 10. Early that morning there appeared on the front pages of newspapers a photo of Eisenhower breakfasting with Stassen of Minnesota, while Taft was pictured shaking hands with Warren of California.

Like Eisenhower's Operation Overlord invasion of France, the Eisenhower ballot battle was so carefully planned and executed, it was all over on the first try. At the end of the roll call of states, Taft had 500 votes while Eisenhower had 595—just 9 votes short of the nomination. A sudden rush to change votes led by Stassen's Minnesota soon permitted the convention to make Eisenhower's nomination unanimous on the first full ballot.

In the flush of victory, the convention then moved to make Richard M. Nixon, in a white suit, the vice presidential nominee by acclamation—the youngest man in American history, at thirty-nine, to be nominated on a ticket. "I pledge to you," Nixon told the delegates, "that I'll put on a fighting campaign for a fighting candidate—Dwight D. Eisenhower."

Eisenhower's decision to choose Nixon as a running mate was hailed as the general's first brilliant political decision. Nixon was measured by the pundits as a middle-of-the-roader who had stayed out of the party's fights between liberal Deweyites and conservative Taftites. Eisenhower's campaign manager, Massachusetts Senator Henry Cabot Lodge, Jr., praised Nixon generously, "He is a fine young man and an outspoken foe of communism. He is a splendid leader. He is a young man, but not too young."

An exultant Eisenhower addressed the convention on live television that evening. "Our aims—the aims of this Republican crusade—are clear: to sweep from office an Administration which has fastened on every one of us the wastefulness, the arrogance, and corruption in high places, the heavy burden and the anxieties which are the bitter fruit of a party too long in power."*

Years later in his diary, Eisenhower reviewed his decision to seek and accept the nomination. "I think the argument that began to carry for me the greatest possible force," Eisenhower wrote at the close of his second administration in 1959, "was that the landslide victories of 1936, 1940 and 1944 and Truman's victory over Dewey in 1948 were all achieved under a doctrine of 'spend and spend, and elect and elect.' It seemed to me that this had to be stopped or our country would deviate badly from the precepts on which we had placed so much faith—the courage and self-independence of each citizen, the importance of opportunity as opposed to more material security, and our belief that American progress

---

*Dwight David Eisenhower, *The Eisenhower Diaries,* ed. by Robert K. Ferrell (New York: W. W. Norton, 1981), p. 376.

depended upon the work and sweat of all of our citizens, each trying to satisfy the needs and desires of himself and his family—and that instead we were coming to the point where we looked toward a paternalistic state to guide our steps from cradle to grave."*

Eisenhower also recalled for his diary the whole convention process. "As time for the convention approached, I told my friends that I did not want to go to Chicago. I felt that the business of nominating a candidate belonged to the convention and its delegates. The whole process was completely distasteful to me. But all the friends that I have mentioned and hundreds more kept hammering that it was my duty to allow myself to be seen, to receive visitors at my hotel suite, and to chat with them on a friendly basis. This I did. By the time the voting for candidates rolled around I was completely worn out and heartily sick of the whole business."†

The Eisenhower-Nixon campaign was energetic and most shrewd about the power of the television camera. It also produced a magnetic advertising slogan, "I Like Ike." Eisenhower was an iron man on the road, visiting forty-five states by rail and air. Nixon easily doubled the general's itinerary. The Democratic opponent, Governor Adlai E. Stevenson of Illinois, a grandson of Bryan's 1896 running mate, was an able campaigner as well. The speeches from both sides were well crafted. Publicity stunts still dominated the discussion, however, and in September Nixon was knocked by the charge that he had taken eighteen thousand dollars from a Senate campaign slush fund for his private expenses.

Nixon's response was to ask for television time to explain his chagrin. In the famous "Checkers" speech, he admitted that, among other gifts from friends over the years, he had been given a small dog named Checkers. Nixon also mentioned his wife Pat Nixon's "good Republican cloth coat." At first, Nixon's confession was regarded as a body blow that would get him kicked off the ticket by the virtuous Ike. Eisenhower saw more clearly that Nixon's personality was winning: not larger-than-life but rather comfortable inside that small, wavy, black-and-white image. Calling Nixon "courageous and honest," Eisenhower announced that he would rather have Nixon than "a boxcar full of pussyfooters."

The last weeks of the campaign, Eisenhower emphasized his military genius when he promised in Detroit that, if elected, "I shall go to Korea." Carrying the tactic to Stevenson's Illinois, Eisenhower enjoyed a ticker tape parade on Chicago's La Salle Street and then underlined his ambition to visit the battlefront: "I have no magic wand to bring that war to

---

*Eisenhower, *Diaries*, p. 376.
†Ibid., p. 377.

Nixon's "Checkers" speech. From Herblock Special Report
(W. W. Norton & Co., Inc.).

an end. But I know that on the spot I can learn something that will be
helpful in serving the American people in the cause of peace."

Election week was marred for the Republicans by a telephone interview with McCarthy, who was running hard for reelection in Wisconsin.
"This is the most frantic lying spree upon which a Presidential campaign
has ever embarked," McCarthy said of the Democrats. "What makes the
lying doubly viscious and doubly revealing is that it is for the purpose of
hiding the Communist-line thinkers and writers selected by the Demo-

Eisenhower vs. Stevenson, 1952. New York Herald Tribune, November 1, 1952.

crat candidate to do his speech writing and thinking for him. They, of course, will remain at his left-hand if Stevenson were elected."

A happy note on election week was that Hollywood actress Jane Wyman, ex-wife of actor and screen union politician Ronald Reagan, had married the composer from her movie *Love Song*.

Election eve, television took over the process. Tom Dewey performed a superman feat by staying on the air on New York's WOR television for an eighteen-hour national hookup to answer phoned-in questions about why Eisenhower should be elected. Eisenhower spent part of the evening in a Boston studio for an hour-long national broadcast. The general was badly bruised on the forehead when a wall clock prop fell on his head at midnight.

This man can save

American lives

Dwight David Eisenhower: political advertisement, 1952.
New York Herald Tribune, *November 4, 1952.*

More than sixty-one million voted in a nation of 150 million. Eisenhower won a landslide, gaining 55.1 percent and carrying thirty-nine states for a massive 442 electoral votes. Eisenhower, the fifth Republican general to be elected president (after Grant, Hayes, Garfield, and Harrison), had brought together the traditional GOP bulwark of the North, Midwest, and West. Stevenson, conceding defeat at 1:45 A.M. Wednesday morning, managed to hold only the South, absent Tennessee and Virginia.

Eisenhower's victory speech at New York's Hotel Commodore was generous and modest. "I am indeed as humbled as I am proud that the American people have made this decision." The next day the president-elect departed for the Augusta National Golf Club in Georgia for the first of his trademark golfing holidays.

The Republicans gained control of the new Eighty-third Congress, though barely and shakily: Senate, 48 Republicans and 47 Democrats and one other; House, 221 Republicans and 212 Democrats and one other.

The best note for the Democrats in the country was the surprising upset victory in Massachusetts, where two-term representative John F. Kennedy defeated Republican brand-name Henry Cabot Lodge, Jr., for a U.S. Senate seat.

★ 1956 ★

Eisenhower's first administration featured two profound successes: the 1953 armistice in Korea that ended the fighting and exposed the international lie that the Soviets wanted friendship; and the Supreme Court's 1954 *Brown v. Board of Education* decision that finished the national lie that there was "separate but equal" education for white and nonwhite Americans.

Eisenhower's Cabinet choices reversed the New Deal appetite for "experts" and turned the executive over to Republican businessmen, one of them a General Motors president and two of them former car dealers. The Democrats joked that the Cabinet included "eight millionaires and a plumber." The plumber was the lone Democrat in the group, Labor Secretary Martin Durkin, former president of the Journeymen Plumbers and Steamfitters Union.

Secretary of State John Foster Dulles became the major Cold Warrior of his generation, and he soon secured the CIA directorship for his pipe-smoking younger brother, Allen Foster Dulles. At Justice, Eisenhower named Dewey aide Herbert Brownell, whose job was complicated by the manias of FBI boss J. Edgar Hoover. The profound choice for the new president was naming Governor Earl Warren of California in 1953 to become the new Supreme Court chief justice. It was the Warren Court's 1954 *Brown v. Board of Education* decision that reversed the infamous 1896 *Plessy v. Ferguson* decision that had gutted the Fourteenth and Fifteenth Amendments and sanctioned the apartheid jim crow laws. "We conclude," read the majority decision, "that in the field of public education the doctrine of 'separate but equal' has no place. Separate education facilities are inherently unequal."

Eisenhower's administration prospered in foreign affairs. In January 1953 Dulles announced the "Captive Peoples" Resolution that declared the United States was a friend to all people held in captivity behind the Iron Curtain by Stalin and his lackeys in Eastern Europe and Asia. A disarmament deadlock followed. Eisenhower and Dulles pursued an aggressive program of communist containment and nuclear preparedness that led to the creation of the largest peacetime military in history and transformed the American economy into what Eisenhower later called a military-industrial complex.

The McCarthy debacle grew to a scandal in 1954 when the reckless senator turned his witch-hunting on Eisenhower's United States Army. McCarthy's aide Roy M. Cohn tried to investigate the senator's false claim that the army was covering up communist espionage at Fort Monmouth, New Jersey. Army Secretary Robert T. Stevens fought back and helped break McCarthy's support in the Senate. McCarthy was condemned by the Senate, if not censured, in December, 67–22.

At the 1954 midterm elections Vice President Nixon attempted to use partisan tactics to stigmatize the Democrats as Communist sympathizers. Nixon warned the nation of "the Stevenson-Truman campaign to elect an anti-Eisenhower, A.D.A. left-wing Congress." He argued, "I know that millions of Democrats will resent the tactics of this left-wing group whose standards of honesty, security, and morality are not representative of the great traditions of the Democratic Party."

The election results were a disappointment. The Democrats regained both houses of Congress for the new Eighty-fourth Congress. The Democrats would hold the House for the next forty years and hold the Senate for all but Ronald Reagan's first term.

In the fall of 1955 Eisenhower suffered a serious heart attack that frightened the country. He recovered slowly, without moving to pass power to Nixon. Again in the spring of 1956 Eisenhower suffered a serious setback with a bout of ileitis that put into question his ability to run for reelection.

The GOP deliberately postponed the national convention to August to give Eisenhower the longest possible time to heal and the shortest possible campaign season. During the delay the Democrats meeting at Chicago again nominated the once-beaten Stevenson on a platform that disgraced itself with a weakened civil rights plank. Eisenhower's Warren Court had left the Democrats, by far the majority party in the country, in the weak position of having to speak against *Brown v. Board of Education* in order to hold the votes of their Southern base.

By mid-August, Eisenhower was repaired, the Northern Democrats were heartbroken, and the Republicans were eager to meet in a love fest at San Francisco's Cow Palace.

"The Republicans stormed this graceful city today," wrote the young Republican pundit Rowland Evans, Jr., to begin convention week, "to nominate President Eisenhower for a second term amid reports that several names will be placed into nomination for the vice-presidency along with that of Vice-President Richard M. Nixon, the almost certain winner."

Nixon demonstrated his showmanship by inviting members of the Young Republican Club along with their mascot, a three-foot-high elephant named Dolly, to his San Francisco headquarters. Among others challenging Nixon for the number two position was Governor Goodwin J. Knight of California, who controlled half the huge California delegation. Diplomat Harold Stassen of Minnesota was backing Governor Christian A. Herter of Massachusetts. The Maine delegation advanced Senator Margaret Chase Smith, the only woman in the Senate, as a vice presidential candidate.

The crucial news the first day of the convention, Monday, August 20, was that the president's health was much improved. Former New Hampshire governor Sherman Adams, Ike's de facto chief of staff, admitted that the president would probably not recover his strength until at least October. Adams conceded that the president's color was not good and his diet was weak. Adams warned that the Democrats were sure to claim that Eisenhower's health problems made him a "part-time" president. Adams wanted the GOP to reply vigorously to the charge.

Dutifully, Governor Arthur B. Langlie of Washington gave a keynote speech that mocked the Democrats as divisive, deceitful, equivocating weaklings and that declared the goal of the second Eisenhower administration: "We are here to pledge to the American people four more years of honest, efficient administration of our government by the fine men and women who have been called to serve them at Washington—four more years of a crusade for a finer and better world under the competent, steadfast forthright leadership of Dwight D. Eisenhower."

The Republican National Committee listed the three finalists in a contest to write the '56 campaign slogan. A Pennsylvania man tried, *"No trenches, but work benches,"* and a D.C. woman offered, *"A bright to-morrow with Eisenhower."* The winner was a New Jersey man who proposed

> Peace, prosperity, and progress
> If you want all three
> Vote G.O.P.

On the second day the platform was accepted without debate. It promised faith and determination in leadership; a dynamic economy of lower taxes, a balanced budget, and sound money; a federal government of integrity and efficiency.

The platform featured a statement of principles written by the president himself: "The individual is of supreme importance. The spirit of our people is the strength of our nation. America does not prosper unless all Americans prosper. Government must have a heart as well as a head. Courage in principle, cooperation in practice make freedom possible. To stay free, we must stay strong. Under God we espouse the cause of freedom and justice and peace for all peoples."

The platform emphasized how the Eisenhower administration had improved national immigration policy from the xenophobic 1950 McCarran Act. The planks called for the United States to remain "a haven for oppressed peoples."

Tuesday evening, the president arrived at San Francisco airport and was welcomed by Nixon and a crowd of five thousand shouting "Ike!"

Rumors surrounded the event because of the talk that Eisenhower was open to a groundswell to dump Nixon from the ticket. While the president went on to his suite at the St. Francis Hotel, Nixon and his wife attended a champagne celebration for eight thousand at the Civic Auditorium, hosted by California governor Knight. Entertainment was provided by opera star Helen Traubel, singing "I Could Have Danced All Night," and TV star Leo Carrillo, who hugged the vice president while calling him "DEECK!" Nixon, in formal dress, was careful to shake hands with his nemesis Harold Stassen of Minnesota as well as Governor Knight of California.

The president soon stopped the behind-the-scenes maneuvering for the vice presidential nomination. Eisenhower was annoyed at Stassen's game playing, and generally tired of Stassen always boasting of his critical role in the '52 nomination. The president directed Sherman Adams to

Eisenhower vs. Stevenson, 1956. New York Herald Tribune, *August 24, 1956.*

shut Stassen down. Adams called Stassen's candidate, Governor Christian Herter, who would later serve as secretary of state, and told him to back Nixon. Herter quickly called a press conference and obeyed.

On the third day the convention came to its feet and jubilantly renominated Eisenhower and Nixon for another term. Party discipline required Herter of Massachusetts to deliver the nomination speech for Nixon. "A hard fighter in partisan contests, the Vice-President has been equally effective in advancing bipartisan causes," Herter argued. "One reason why the Vice-President has been such an effective member of Ike's team is because he shares the same conviction as the President himself. . . . In votes, in speech, in deeds, in thoughts, he has been—he is—he will continue to be an Eisenhower man all the way, all the time."

At a press conference after the nominations, the president was asked if there was any truth in the rumor that he had come to San Francisco to interview alternatives to Nixon. "Not the slightest," replied Eisenhower.

Nixon was not at the Cow Palace to hear his renomination. Wednesday morning the vice president had flown suddenly to Whittier with his wife and brothers to be at the bedside of his failing seventy-seven-year-old father, Frank A. Nixon. All three Nixon brothers gathered for a photograph in the living room. Nixon's obvious pleasure with his family reinforced the argument that he was in touch with the common man. The next day Nixon greeted reporters at the door with a wave. "He cannot talk too much," Nixon said of his father's condition. "He just put out his hand and shook hands."

Frank Nixon died within a week, on September 4, 1956. Years later in his memoirs Nixon remembered the ordeal: "The doctor told me that it was only [my father's] determination to see me defeat Stassen and be renominated that had kept him alive this long. Now his condition was rapidly worsening. He knew that the end was near, so he gave my mother instructions for his funeral and asked to be allowed to die at home rather than in the hospital."*

The Stop-Nixon whispering campaign had failed. The explanation at the time was that the Stop-Nixon forces had been driven not by any GOP dissent but by the enmity the Democrats felt for Nixon because of the Hiss case—in other words, Stassen was a pointy-headed intellectual Stevensonite. Others said that Nixon was just too much of an anti-communist zealot ever to make a statesman. The fact that Nixon had been opposed by Knight of California revealed that Nixon did not enjoy a natural sectional base, like Herter of Massachusetts or Stassen of Minnesota. The result was that Nixon was left a winner alone atop his own party—no permanent allies, no permanent friends, just a God-given talent to get knocked around and yet still to do what was necessary to get votes.

"He has come very far since the day he entered politics," wrote Stewart and Joseph Alsop after Nixon's renomination, "by answering a newspaper advertisement placed by a group of rich California Republicans, inviting applications from young war veterans who might wish to run for the Congressional seat of Jerry Voorhis. Clearly, he saw politics then as a sort of jungle, in which advancement was the prize, and the prize was won by the simple rule of dog-eat-dog by any means available."

"Courage is one of Nixon's conspicuous qualities," the Alsops con-

---

*Nixon, *Memoirs*, p. 75.

tinued. "Another is his ability to face hard facts, instead of shoving them under the rug: and still another is his willingness to deal with hard facts when that is necessary, even if the price and risk are considerable. And as the foregoing implies, yet another conspicuous Nixon quality is a strong, inquiring, absorptive and analytical intelligence."

Nixon returned to the Cow Palace on Thursday to make his acceptance speech. "No man could be more greatly honored," he told the convention. "Our party, I say to you, is not a party of drift and self-satisfaction. The greatest moments of the Republican party have been those many years in which it was progressive and forward looking. We are conservative only in the sense that we keep what is sound and proven from the past, and of that we are certainly proud."

Eisenhower celebrated his renomination by getting up early Friday morning for eighteen holes of golf at Pebble Beach, California. For the first time in American history, a man was going to demonstrate he was fit and firm enough for the presidency by teeing off.

The campaign used a two-tier strategy: The president would take it easy and make speeches on statesman issues such as peace and disarmament and technology—Ike advocated an atomic-powered merchant ship. Meanwhile, the vice president would show partisan vigor while hammering at the Democrats with controversial issues such as anticommunism and class warfare.

"Mr. Stevenson has implied again and again that the rich are getting richer and the poor are getting poorer," Nixon argued at Youngstown, Ohio, during an October swing through the heart of labor territory in the Midwest. "What he fails to point out is that labor's share of the national income during the Truman administration was 65 percent. It has increased to 69 percent after four years of the Eisenhower administration."

Stevenson, unable to make headway against the grandfatherly Eisenhower, struck back at the vulnerable Nixon. "We keep hearing of a 'new Nixon' and an 'old Nixon.' We hear that one day his campaign is on the high road and the next day is on the low road. We hear him described as the very model of an Eisenhower Republican and then we hear him described as the darling of the reactionary Old Guard. The *Wall Street Journal* called him a *conservative Republican,* while another newspaper called him a *liberal Republican.* There is no man who can safely say he knows where the Vice-President stands. Who can say they have seen his real face?" Reminding people that Eisenhower's uncertain health could well mean Nixon would become president, Stevenson pounded, "It is impossible to think in these terms of a man whose greatest political talent is a mastery of personal innuendo, who cries 'treason' and spreads fear

Eisenhower vs. Stevenson, 1956. New York Herald Tribune, *August 24, 1956.*

and doubt, a man who uses language to conceal issues rather than ex-plore them, a man whose trademark is slander."

Foreign crises in Poland, Hungary, and the Mideast colored the last weeks of the campaign and reminded voters of Eisenhower's role as Free World leader. With Soviet tanks outside Warsaw, Soviet tankers opening fire on Hungarian protesters in Budapest, British jets pounding the Egyptians, and the Israelis driving onto the banks of the Suez, the president did not have to say very much to receive the tense admiration of the public.

The final campaign strategy was to declare the president's health excellent. Nixon kept attacking the Democrats to the end, logging two hundred speeches and forty thousand miles in a superhuman effort to carry the GOP banner to all sections of the country.

Election eve, the headlines from Europe and the Mideast promised catastrophe and defeat for the Free World. The polls showed Eisenhower so far ahead that the pollsters doubted themselves. John Foster Dulles was in the hospital to have a cancerous growth removed from his large intestine. The television news routinely mentioned a Third World War.

More than sixty-one million voted. Eisenhower took 57.4 percent of the electorate and all sections of the country for 457 electoral votes. Stevenson gained 42 percent and only pieces of the old Confederacy, including Missouri, for 73 electoral votes.

What soured the Eisenhower landslide was that the Democrats retained control for the new Eighty-fifth Congress. Eisenhower was the first Republican president since Hayes to win the White House and yet not bring along with him a new Republican Congress.

The day after the election, the president thanked the electorate and went back to the National Security briefings on the Hungarian and Suez disasters. On Saturday Eisenhower flew up to his farm in Gettysburg, Pennsylvania, to look over his Black Angus herd. "We ought to hold onto that one," the president remarked of a small bull, "until we see how he develops."

The high irony of election week was that the Nobel Peace Prize Committee in Oslo announced that it could find no one worthy of the Peace Prize.

★ 1960 ★

Eisenhower's second administration continued the military buildup against the Soviet Union and People's Republic of China and then launched troops against Southern segregationists in Little Rock, Arkansas.

Eisenhower retained the cancer-survivor Dulles at the State Department until 1959. John Foster Dulles and his brother at the CIA set about combating the Soviet threat everywhere in Latin America, Europe, Asia, the Middle East, and Africa. Dulles's *domino theory*, that if one regime fell to the Soviets the rest could follow like dominoes, directed foreign policy; while the military doctrine of *brinksmanship*, that is, daring the Soviets to the brink of nuclear war, guided the enormous overseas commitment of American troops, planes, and ships.

Back home the Eisenhower administration encouraged the expansion of what was then called the "supercorporation" that dominated Wall

Street. Choice corporate names included Standard Oil and Shell Oil, United States Steel, Reynolds Aluminum, General Motors, First National Bank, International Business Machines, United Fruit Company. The stock markets rewarded bigness with high prices. After the recession of '57, the stock market rallied from October 1957 to a new all-time high on the Dow Jones Industrial Average in 1960. After thirty years, October 1929 was finally a floor and not a ceiling to prices.

The autumn of 1957 saw a major civil rights crisis that was exacerbated by a major foreign policy embarrassment over the Soviet Sputnik launch. In early September, Congress passed the Civil Rights Act—the first civil rights legislation since Reconstruction—which expanded the federal powers to stop racial discrimination in the states. Weeks later the Arkansas government, led by the Klan-sponsored Democrat Orval E. Faubus, openly encouraged racial discrimination at Little Rock High School. Eisenhower sent in the 101st Airborne and the Arkansas National Guard to restore law and order. "Failure to act in such a way," said the president, "would be tantamount to acquiescence in anarchy and the dissolution of the Union."

The next month, Eisenhower did not so easily answer the Sputnik crisis, when the Soviets launched an artificial satellite that was feared as a new weapon. Panic led to the sudden aggrandizing of the National Aeronautics and Space Administration and the sudden discovery of a so-called missile gap with the Soviets. Soviet dictator Nikita Khrushchev taunted the administration about Sputnik when he told two visiting British politicians, "We have even more up our sleeve." The truth was that the Sputnik launch was a publicity stunt by a slave labor state. Nonetheless, the great Cold War battle of space travel began with a slapdash Republican response. "Nobody is going to drop anything down on you from a satellite while you are sleeping, so don't worry about it," argued the secretary of defense, who added without much conviction that any bomb from space "would burn up before it could reach you."

The civil rights crisis accelerated again in 1960 when the National Association for the Advancement of Colored People and other civil rights groups moved to integrate lunchrooms in the South with so-called sit-ins at dining counters and drugstores. Southern states arrested the protesters. The Supreme Court quickly voided these arrests in *Garner v. Louisiana*. Eisenhower backed the law. "There must be no second-class citizens in this country," said the president.

The 1958 midterm elections frustrated the GOP. The Democrats deliberately took advantage of the civil rights crisis to expand their control of the new Eighty-sixth Congress. The new Senate was 62 Democrats to 34 Republicans; the House, 280 Democrats to 152 Republicans.

The Democrats also prospered when young, glamorous John F. Kennedy, the senator from Massachusetts whose national stature had grown atop his 1956 best-seller, *Profiles in Courage,* won a smashing re-election. Other significant Democratic winners were the new governor Edmund G. Brown of California and new senators Robert C. Byrd of West Virginia and Eugene McCarthy of Minnesota.

The GOP plum was that young, glamorous Nelson Rockefeller, son of the famous John D. Rockefeller of Standard Oil, defeated the railroad scion and New Dealer Averell Harriman for the governorship of New York.

The tired, discouraged Nixon was quick to call Rockefeller to congratulate him on his victory as "one of the brightest spots on the national scene." The press asked Rockefeller whether he had ambitions for the GOP presidential nod. "That has absolutely no meaning to me," said Rockefeller. "I have no other interest but to be governor of this state."

Nixon recalled the 1958 midterm elections in his memoirs. "The defeat was massive, and November 4, 1958, was one of the most depressing election nights I have ever known. The statistics still make me wince. . . . The defeats in crucial states, among them California and Ohio, meant that the party would have to face the formidable task of rebuilding its state organization if I was to have any hopes of carrying them in 1960. . . . The next morning I heard that one television commentator had told his viewers that the big winner of 1958 was Nelson Rockefeller—who had been elected governor of New York by a wide margin—and the big loser was Richard Nixon. It seemed to me that the worst fears of my friends and advisers had been realized. My campaigning had had little visible effect, had gained me little thanks or credit, and had tarred me with the brush of partisan defeat at a time when my potential rivals for the nomination, Rockefeller and Barry Goldwater, were basking in the glory of victory. Perhaps Dewey had been right: I should have sat it out."[*]

The presidential year 1960 opened with the curious irony that Eisenhower was healthier and more popular than ever, but the Twenty-second Amendment (passed by the Republicans in 1951) limited the presidency to two full terms and thereby made Ike ineligible for a third term he probably could have had for the asking.

Vigorous Richard M. Nixon, forty-seven, was the logical heir apparent. Nixon worked and traveled hard during the second term to make certain he was the first thought in the party's mind. Rugged trips to Moscow, where he spontaneously sparred with Khrushchev at the fa-

[*]Nixon, *Memoirs,* p. 200.

mous "Kitchen Debates," and to Poland, where he received the adoration of large crowds crying, "Long live America!" demonstrated that Nixon was the supreme Cold Warrior of his generation. Nixon was never ambiguous about his anticommunism and was quick to spot and denounce tyrants like Fidel Castro and Nikita Khrushchev. At the Kitchen Debates, Nixon listened coolly to the translation of a Khrushchev threat, "We are strong, we can beat you!" Nixon responded, "No one should ever use his strength to put another in the position where he in effect has an ultimatum. For us to argue who is the stronger misses the point. If war comes, we both lose."*

In July, the Democrats anticipated Nixon's campaign by nominating for president the startling senator John F. Kennedy of Massachusetts two weeks before the Republican convention. Kennedy was a clear speaker with an extremely telegenic personality, his brilliant smile and relaxed manner contrasting greatly with Nixon's heavy-bearded, slow-spoken, and oddly ungainly presence. Kennedy used his acceptance speech before seventy-five thousand at Los Angeles's mammoth Coliseum to strike at Nixon's character. "All over the world, particularly in the newer nations, young men are coming to power," said Kennedy on July 15, "men who are not bound by the traditions of the past—men who are not blinded by the old fears and hates and rivalries—young men who can cast off the old slogans and delusions and suspicions. The Republican nominee-to-be, of course, is also a young man. But his approach is as old as McKinley. His party is the party of the past. His speeches are generalities from 'Poor Richard's Almanac.' Their platform, made up of left-over Democratic planks, has the courage of old convictions. Their pledge is a pledge to the status quo—and today there can be no status quo."

The preconvention maneuvering of the Republicans included another Stop-Nixon movement, this time advancing Nelson Rockefeller as a liberal alternative or perhaps Senator Barry Goldwater of Arizona as a conservative alternative. Rockefeller played along with the Stop-Nixon forces by announcing a week beforehand that he would not second Nixon's nomination. What Rockefeller did not mention that day was that he had refused Nixon's offer of the second spot on the ticket.

Nixon recalled the setback in his *Memoirs:* "The obvious Republican equivalent of the Kennedy-Johnson ticket would have been the Nixon-Rockefeller ticket. I made the gesture of offering him the position when we met in New York on July 22. As I expected, he declined. I was not altogether sorry, because Rockefeller's despondent temperament would have made him a much more difficult running mate for me to deal with

*Nixon, *Memoirs,* p. 209.

than Johnson would be for Kennedy. But his refusal left me without the option of the kind of finely balanced ticket the Democrats had achieved" (p. 218).

Eisenhower was not comfortable with or adept at partisanship. He seemed to hold back from outspoken support of Nixon, and this was understood as a call to cast around for a challenger. The truth was that Eisenhower disliked the convention process and hated the bizarre public ceremony. The president did agree that it was necessary for him to come to the convention to receive acclaim on national television. However, Eisenhower did not go along with the idea that there should be something left to chance or dicker at the convention. Eisenhower inadvertently took away from Nixon the power to name his own running mate when he announced the weekend before the convention that he wanted his United Nations envoy, Henry Cabot Lodge, Jr., of Massachusetts, the man Kennedy had whipped for the Senate in '52, to be vice president.

The Republican convention in Chicago (July 25–28) was as well orchestrated as the '56 San Francisco gathering. Without a ballot contest for the top or bottom of the ticket, there was little drama to tempt the now omnipresent television networks. Instead the Nixon forces offered a clockwork pageantry.

"The Vice-President will arrive at 11:15 A.M. at O'Hare Airport," announced the briefing paper to the television producers the day before. "He will go by helicopter to Meigs Field, arriving at noon. His motorcade will leave at 12:05 P.M. for the Blackstone Hotel, his headquarters. As the Vice-President passes the Drake Hotel about 12:15 P.M., the Californians staying there will give him a rousing welcome, backed up by a large band. He will stop and stand up and wave, but he will not leave his car."

The briefing paper argued, "You had better have plenty of cameras at the Blackstone. Will you have a camera on the roof of the Hilton? Because you will need it to catch the drama when he arrives at Blackstone, at approximately 12:30 P.M."

Tuesday, the party welcomed Eisenhower with a ticker tape parade through the Loop on live television. Later the president took the podium to defend his record to the adoring delegates. The president's hardest slap at Kennedy was that "we shall do nothing here to serve the cult of pessimism, to spread false gospel among our allies or create misunderstanding among yourself." A glitch came when Dirksen of Illinois drank the glass of water on the podium after introducing the president, so that Eisenhower had to deliver his long speech dry. Afterward the convention chanted, "We want Ike" and "We want Mamie," as the bands played on. The President returned thumbs-up and held wide his arms with V-for-Victory signs.

On the third day the platform was accepted by voice vote. Many conservative Southern delegates yelled "No!" The Nixon forces had avoided a floor fight by adjusting the civil rights plank in the Platform Committee both to satisfy Rockefeller-backed liberal demands for immediate desegregation and to blunt Southern demands for the status quo. The final plank gave something to both sides. It pledged full use of federal power, resources, and leadership to eliminate discrimination; at the same time the plank refused language that would have given the federal government three years to construct and implement desegregation plans.

In foreign affairs and national defense the platform called for aggressive, expansive, and boundless military efforts against the Soviet threat. The platform addressed the so-called missile gap by noting that the submarine-launched Polaris missile, tested a week before, was proof of American technological mastery in the Cold War. The platform opposed Red China's entry into the United Nations.

After the platform's acceptance, a Southern Republican boss remarked of the controversial civil rights plank, "We think we have a moderate program we can sell in the South. It leaves a lot to be desired. We're not elated, but we do not plan to appeal."

Looking in from Denver, the Democratic vice presidential nominee, Senator Lyndon Baines Johnson of Texas, aimed to cause trouble with a clever partisan quip. "I think the Republicans are real desperate. Rocky is going one direction. . . . Goldwater is going the other direction. And Nixon doesn't know where he is going."

Nixon was going to the top. The third evening of the convention celebrated Nixon's nomination on national television. Senator Mark Hatfield of Oregon used only 290 words in his nomination speech, "The White House is not for sale—its lease is up for renewal." And then the bands played "California Here I Come" and "Anchors Aweigh," and the choreographed fifteen-minute demonstration was led by a huge photograph of Nixon wagging a finger at Khrushchev at the Moscow Kitchen Debates. The roll call followed dutifully. A slight mar was that ten delegates from Louisiana refused to make the ballot unanimous and gave their votes to conservative darling and states rights advocate Barry Goldwater of Arizona.

The best partisan moment of the evening was provided when Tom Dewey attacked Kennedy in his prenomination speech. "He modestly announced that like Abraham Lincoln, he was ready," Dewey said of Kennedy's Los Angeles acceptance speech. "With further modesty he then proceeded to associate himself with George Washington, Thomas Jefferson, Alexander the Great and Napoleon. Just about the only kindred spirits he left out were Julius Caesar and Hannibal."

Nixon wins the nomination, 1960. New York Herald Tribune, July 24, 1960.

On the fourth day United Nations envoy Henry Cabot Lodge, Jr., famous for his televised rhetoric against Soviet dirty tricks on the U.N. Security Council, was nominated unanimously for the vice presidency on the first ballot. The Republican ticket was now entirely weighted on foreign policy.

Nixon's acceptance speech on national television was long, articulate, and devoted to the Cold War. "I have seen hate for America, not only in the Kremlin but in the eyes of Communists in our own country, and on the ugly face of a mob in Caracas. I have heard doubts about America expressed, not just by Communists, but by sincere students and labor leaders in other countries searching for the way to a better life and wondering if we had lost the way." Nixon appealed, "My fellow Americans, I know that we must resist the hate, we must remove the doubts, but above all we must be worthy of the love and the trust of millions of this earth for whom America is the hope of the world."

Lodge's acceptance speech underlined the fears of the Cold War. "My fellow Americans, the basic contest in the world is no old-fashioned traditional partisan rivalry between the Republicans and the Democrats. The basic contest is the life and death struggle between the Communists on the one hand and those who insist on being free on the other. This is what gives this election of 1960 its compelling, overwhelming importance to us and the world."

The campaign began that night when the three television networks, led by NBC, offered time and facilities to Nixon and Kennedy for the first Republican-Democratic presidential debates ever—not just on television or radio, but ever. From Hyannis Port, Kennedy accepted "wholeheartedly." In Chicago Nixon aides also accepted, though Nixon reserved the right to review the format.

Quickly, the prospect of television debates overwhelmed the summer and fall campaigning. Nixon and Kennedy traveled and talked heroically to huge crowds with elaborate staging. On the stump Nixon held back his rhetoric to avoid his label as a slasher, while Lodge emphasized the Soviet threat. On the stump Kennedy capitalized on his glamorous wit, while leaving partisan counterpunching to the rough Johnson. However, this routine campaigning could not match the thrill of the two young candidates face-to-face on live television. It was as if television became the theme of the campaign, while the two candidates were just the actors for the shoot-out in the high noon of the autumn.

There were four hour-long debates in the television studio. The first three debates were careful standoffs, each candidate stating familiar positions of foreign and domestic issues. Both men were polite, and the questioners were obsequious. Meanwhile, the incredible opera of America kept spilling events that always threatened to steal the spotlight: the Pirates beat the Yankees in seven games, and the Yankee skipper Casey Stengel was fired; Eisenhower became the oldest sitting president at seventy; the visiting Khrushchev traveled from the Soviet compound at Glen Cove, Long Island, to the United Nations Assembly for his daily antics, later promising at the steps of the plane that took him back to Europe, "If you want war, keep provoking it and you'll get it," and still the campaigners kept punching and counterpunching each other coast to coast.

The fourth and what became final debate (a fifth was fumbled) was the crowning moment of the most expensive campaign so far in American history, Friday evening, October 21, 1960. The questioners were as famous as the candidates: Quincy Howe and John Edwards of ABC; Walter Cronkite of CBS; Frank Singiser of Mutual Broadcasting System; John Chancellor of NBC. The candidates were comfortable with the format, and remarks were sharp though familiar about the Soviets, Cuba, China, Formosa, civil rights, summit conferences, disarmament. The closing statements were eloquent partisanship.

Kennedy argued against the Republican party's self-satisfaction. "My judgment is that the Republican party has stood still here in the United States and has also stood still around the world. . . . If we stand still here, if we appoint people to ambassadorships and positions in Washington who have a status quo outlook, who don't recognize that this is a revolutionary time, then the United States will not maintain its influence."

Nixon argued against Democratic anxiety. "We're on the side of free-

Nixon and Lodge vs. Kennedy and Johnson, 1960. New York Herald Tribune, *October 3, 1960.*

dom. We're on the side of justice, against the forces of slavery, against the forces of injustice. But we aren't going to move forward and we aren't going to be able to lead the world, to win this struggle for freedom, if we have a permanent inferiority complex about American achievement."

The black-and-white cameras showed each man at his best, but the camera's clear favorite was Kennedy. The camera loved his flashing eyes and smart smile—the best presidential smile since TR. Nixon's posture was weary, his smile was brief, his eyes were heavy-lidded. Worse, the camera showed that Nixon perspired heavily under the makeup. On the radio Nixon's sonorous baritone projected confidence, while Kennedy's Boston accent was jarring. In the small TV screen, however, Nixon remained the common man, while Kennedy appeared larger-than-life like a TV star.

Election week the final Gallup poll found a statistical dead heat, Kennedy 49 percent and Nixon 48 percent. The nation was so tired of the campaign zeal that the news of Clark Gable's heart attack was the

Nixon vs. Kennedy, 1960. Algemeen Hadelsblad. *Rpr.* New York Herald Tribune, *October 30, 1960.*

lead story the day before the election. Nixon was so weary that at Los Angeles on television he called his running mate "Cabot Liar" before he corrected himself to "Lodge." Kennedy showed his exhaustion when he was three hours late for a rally at Newark, New Jersey; he recovered by promising, "I offer you my regrets for being late. But I haven't been playing golf."

Election eve, Nixon topped his campaign with a four-hour telethon from Detroit, moderated by two real TV stars, Robert Young and Lloyd Nolan. Kennedy closed his campaign at a frantic rally at the Boston Garden. The Republican National Committee reported that the party had spent $1.1 million buying time on nationwide television; it had spent an additional $2.4 million on the campaign. The Democrats did not release figures.

More than sixty-eight and a half million voted. Three of the early voters in New York, at the Sixty-sixth Election District of the First Assembly District, were voter no. 44, Herbert Hoover; voter no. 63, James A. Farley, FDR's 1932 campaign chairman and postmaster general; and voter no. 88, Cardinal Francis J. Spellman.

The three networks boasted that they were devoting computer machines both to summate the vote and to project winners as early as possible. CBS chose an IBM RAMAC 305 to tabulate votes at the studio; while at IBM headquarters an IBM 7090 mainframe giant would project the outcome with less than 1 percent reporting—perhaps as early as 7 P.M. EST. NBC chose an RCA 501 computer to project the winner with only 5 percent counted. ABC planned to use a Remington Rand Univac "computer-projector" to predict the election before the East Coast polls closed.

The twist was that the election turned out to be too close to call. The newsmen could only make guesses until well after midnight in New York. Three hours later, at 12:15 A.M. Los Angeles time, Nixon spoke to his supporters in the Ambassador Hotel ballroom: "If the present trend continues, Senator Kennedy will be the next President of the United States." Three hours later, however, one of Nixon's daughters awoke him to report rumors of vote fraud in Illinois and Texas. Dirksen urged Nixon to refuse to concede and to demand a recount.

Nixon kept his own counsel and decided to concede defeat. Still, there was a queasy uncertainty about the returns.

For four days the nation watched as Kennedy's electoral college count bobbed, from 274 to 273 to 332. Republican national chairman Thruston B. Morton of Kentucky asked Republican leaders in eleven states to recheck the vote. Nixon did not change his mind about refusing to ask for a recount.

Identified at the time and debated for decades afterward were the returns from Illinois, Missouri, and Texas, especially from the Cook County Democratic machine, the East St. Louis Democratic machine, and the Democratic machine in South Texas.

A week after the election, Kennedy and Nixon met at the Key Biscayne Hotel in Florida to shake hands and share laughs for the cameras. "I asked him how he took Ohio," Kennedy quipped.

The final official results showed Kennedy with 49.7 percent for 34.2 million votes and 303 electoral college votes. Nixon gained 49.5 percent for 34.1 million votes and 219 electoral college votes. The Dixiecrat segregationist candidate, Senator Harry F. Byrd of Virginia, took half a million votes from the South and gained 15 electoral votes.

The official result would show that Kennedy won Illinois by the 4,500 plurality he received from Chicago; Kennedy won Missouri by the 5,000 plurality he gained from East St. Louis; Kennedy won Texas by 50,000 plurality, chiefly from the South Texas border.

In his *Memoirs,* Nixon reviewed his decision not to ask for a recount and rather to concede to Kennedy the day after the election. "We [the Republican party] had made a serious mistake in not having taken precautions against such a situation, and it was too late now. A presidential recount would require up to half a year during which time the legitimacy of Kennedy's election would be in question. The effect could be devastating to America's foreign relations. I could not subject the country to such a situation. And what if I demanded a recount and it turned out that despite the vote fraud Kennedy had still won? Charges of 'sore loser' would follow me through history and remove any possibility of a further political career. After considering these and many other factors, I made my decision and sent Kennedy a telegram conceding the defeat" (p. 224).

★ 1964 ★

John F. Kennedy proved an agile politician and a convincing Cold Warrior, and his brief administration was marked by spectacular crises in Cuba and by more sensational resolutions.

By the 1962 midterm fall elections, the world was on the brink of war over the Cuban missile crisis. Kennedy threatened to invade and bomb Cuba unless the Soviets withdrew their secretly deployed ICBMs. Elsewhere the president had thrown military resources into the smoking crises in Southeast Asia, especially in South Vietnam and Laos. By comparison, the GOP could offer no stronger defense of freedom.

In civil rights, Kennedy had outmaneuvered Southern segregationists in both parties to support the civil rights crusader Dr. Martin Luther King, Jr., of Georgia. Also, the president's brother Robert F. Kennedy had demonstrated an activist fervor against the rot in the labor movement, especially the International Brotherhood of Teamsters led by Jimmy Hoffa, as well as against the shenanigans in big industry, especially the alleged price fixing by the big steel and big aluminum makers.

Also, the president had committed to NASA and the astronauts to beat the Soviets to a manned moon landing.

The result of the president's energy was a broad-based Democratic lead in the polls across all sections of the country. The final midterm Gallup poll cited the Cuban crisis as the reason for a sharp Democratic surge. Nationwide, 55 percent of Americans favored the Democrats, while 45 percent supported the Republicans. In New York, Republican Rockefeller's lead was said to be insurmountable; in Michigan, however, gubernatorial Republican challenger George Romney had dipped in his lead over the incumbent Democrat.

In California, gubernatorial challenger Richard Nixon slipped badly in his lead over pallid incumbent Edmund G. Brown. The last California poll listed 8 percent now undecided because of the Cuban crisis. After the missile blockade in October, Governor Brown had directed his banners painted with the slogan "Our President's Choice," whereas before the Cuban crisis Brown had avoided even the word *Democrat* in his ads.

Eisenhower, at the age of seventy-two now breaking eighty on the links, was urged to write an appeal to get out the Republican vote. The president still could not enjoy partisanship, so he apologized: "In urging the election of Republicans on Tuesday, I am fully aware that neither party is the sole repository of virtue or evil."

Election eve, the hottest race in the country was Nixon versus Brown. Nixon was gambling his career on the governor's race as the way back to the presidential track. He decided to go on statewide television to make a grim attack on Brown for what Nixon called "a smear campaign unprecedented in the history of American politics." Nixon's fury lit up the black-and-white screen and surged into every living room. He said he had been attacked since 1948 because of the Whittaker Chambers–Alger Hiss case. He said his opponents had defamed him with "the most vicious barrage of attacks on any man, any public figure of our time. The charges included everything from bigamy to perjury to forgery, all the malicious things that can be brought up, habitual drunkenness, even insanity." Nixon asked, "How do I answer the charge that has been made over and over again that I'm anti-Negro, anti-Semitic, or anti-Catholic? In my years in Washington, Cardinal Spellman, Jackie Robinson, and

General David Sarnoff were among my closest friends. One is a Negro, another a Jew, and the other a Catholic."

Election night, the television coverage dominated the events with the state-of-the-art of national live reporting. From New York City, Walter Cronkite and Eric Sevareid anchored CBS on Madison Avenue; Chet Huntley and David Brinkley led NBC coverage at Rockefeller Center; Ron Cochran, Howard Smith, and William K. Lawrence were the ABC anchors from West Sixty-sixth Street. The local competition was the *Phil Silvers Show,* an episode entitled "Bilko's Black Magic," and a sadomasochistic war movie with Jack Palance, Eddie Albert, and Lee Marvin, *Attack.*

The networks declared the critical Republican races to be Rockefeller and veteran senator Jacob K. Javits in New York, fifty-five-year-old auto executive Romney's challenge in Michigan, Representative William W. Scranton's run for an open governorship in Pennsylvania, and Nixon's challenge in California.

There was an unusually heavy voter turnout of forty-five million nationwide. Surprise winners included new Democratic senator Daniel K. Inouye of Hawaii, also the reelected Republican senator Everett McKinley Dirksen of Illinois. New Republican governors included Scranton of Pennsylvania and Romney of Michigan. Reelected in a redistricted seat was Representative Bob Dole of Kansas, forty-one, slim, and attractive.

The surprise loser was Richard M. Nixon. The election was so close that Nixon delayed his concession until 10 A.M. on Wednesday morning, when an aide, Herbert G. Klein, read the concession telegram to Brown to the press at the Beverly Hilton headquarters. Nixon then stunned the reporters by appearing in person to deliver a bitter, seventeen-minute soliloquy.

"Now that Mr. Klein has made his statement," Nixon began, "and now that all the members of the press are delighted that I have lost, I want to make one myself." Standing alone at the microphone, exhausted from a night of defeat, Nixon continued, "I believe Governor Brown has a heart even though he believes I have not. . . . I believe he is a good American, even though he believes I am not. . . . I want it to be known that I never during the course of the campaign raised a personal consideration against my opponent. I never accused him of a lack of heart, of a lack of patriotism. You gentlemen didn't report that I defended his patriotism, that I said he was a man of good motives. For once, gentlemen, I would appreciate that you write it that way."

Nixon coolly criticized the press: "My philosophy of the press has never gotten through. . . . I think a reporter has the right, if he thinks one

NBC news anchors Chet Huntley and David Brinkley, 1962. Advertisement in New York Herald Tribune, *November 6, 1962.*

candidate ought to win, then he should say so. I might say that I wish you had given my opponent the same going over you gave me. You've had the opportunity to attack me. I've given as good as I've taken. You've had a lot of fun."

Nixon closed with a dramatic farewell to politics: "The last play. I leave you gentlemen now and you will now write it. You will write and interpret it. That's your right. But as I leave you I want you to know—just think how much you're going to be missing. You won't have Nixon to kick around anymore. . . . This is my last press conference."

Nixon walked through the lobby, got into a rented Buick with an aide, and drove home.

Sunday night following the defeat, ABC aired a network special entitled "The Obituary of Richard Nixon," hosted by Howard K. Smith. Principal guests included former congressman H. Jerry Voorhis, whom Nixon had defeated in 1946, and Alger Hiss, now fifty-eight, who maintained his innocence of the perjury charges stemming from Nixon's 1948 investigation. Also featured was Representative Gerald Ford of Michigan.

Nixon's rough departure left the Republican party searching for a front-runner for the 1964 nomination. Within weeks the friends of Senator Barry Goldwater of Arizona and the friends of Governor Nelson

Rockefeller of New York were maneuvering for Nixon's discarded crown. In early 1963 Rockefeller undermined his own chance by divorcing his wife and marrying a divorced mother of four. Goldwater, without collecting a vote, stood tall.

The Kennedy assassination in the fall of 1963 (by an inarticulate anarchist, Lee Harvey Oswald) rocked all partisan forces. Just after the murder, new president Lyndon Baines Johnson was considered unknown and vulnerable outside of the Democratic South. Worse, Kennedy's death exposed the White House to all the simmering crises around the globe.

Johnson's foreign policy stumbled and staggered at the outset. In Vietnam, where two weeks before Kennedy's death the CIA had murdered Catholic dictator Ngo Dinh Diem and replaced him with army dictator General Douong Van Minh, the Johnson decision was to resupply and to increase the number of American military advisers. An American observer commented ruefully about the communist insurgents, "The Viet Cong is fighting harder than ever, they've made some big gains—and it's going to be a tough fight." Elsewhere an American H-1 helicopter pilot observed about the fighting in the Mekong Delta, "They hold their fire until the critical moment when the chopper has dropped the troops and must regain altitude. There are unconfirmed signs they have anti-aircraft weapons with 12-man gun crews."

Johnson rallied his party by moving on domestic affairs. The 1964 Civil Rights Act was passed with Johnson's heroic lobbying and presented the president as a statesman. Johnson grandly announced his plans for a federally funded "Great Society."

The GOP was game for frantic party politics. Nixon chose not to reenter the race. The Republican contest was now between the Goldwater conservatives from the West and South, who advocated states rights and strenuous anticommunism, and the Rockefeller forces, who advocated civil rights. The heart of the matter was that Goldwater had voted against the 1964 Civil Rights Act, making him unacceptable to the Republican liberals and moderates from the East.

The March New Hampshire primary startled the party when an organized write-in vote put Henry Cabot Lodge, Jr. ahead of Goldwater and Rockefeller. Goldwater rallied his forces and swept primaries in Illinois, Texas, and Indiana. Rockefeller threw himself into Oregon and won a plurality over Lodge, Goldwater, and a 17 percent write-in vote for Nixon. (Nixon's quiet strategy was not to campaign but rather to wait for a possible deadlock among rivals.) California on June 2 was the last primary prize, and Goldwater won 51 percent over the combined Rockefeller-Lodge Stop-Goldwater movement.

Stop-Goldwater now turned to boom neophyte Governor William W.

Scranton of Pennsylvania, forty-six years old, a former ambassador to the still little known South Vietnam. Scranton spent weeks signing up support from Lodge, Rockefeller, Romney, Senator Hugh Scott of Pennsylvania, and also President Eisenhower.

Convention week, Eisenhower admitted the inevitable: "It looks like Goldwater. I think Goldwater will get the nomination, and it will be up to him to pick his own running mate." Dirksen of Illinois, who would nominate Goldwater, was more blunt: "There are no 'ifs' about it. It's settled, in my judgment."

Goldwater captures the GOP, 1964. New York Herald Tribune, *July 18, 1964.*

Civil rights leaders announced they were going to lead a protest in San Francisco against Goldwater to "show the world that the Negro people are vigorously opposed to the nomination of Barry Goldwater."

Goldwater was said to be maneuvering to win the support of Governor George C. Wallace of Alabama, a segregationist who held control of the Dixiecrat vote from 1960.

The San Francisco Convention opened Monday, July 13 in the aging Cow Palace. The event was a full-scale television special, with gavel-to-gavel coverage and huge teams of reporters from all three networks roaming the convention floor in search of controversial interviews. The popular NBC *Today Show* offered morning coverage. There were complaints that television was changing the kind of candidate that could be chosen and the way the party could conduct its business. On the other hand, the network anchors Cronkite, Reasoner, Sevareid, Huntley, Brinkley were promoted more aggressively than the politicians. The result was a vanity previously practiced only by candidates. "Neither David or I take many notes into our Convention booth," Chet Huntley wrote in a publicity release, "because we've found it easier to rely on our memory than to ruffle through piles of printed matter."

"Anti-Goldwater" rallies dominated the first day of the convention. Fifty thousand civil rights protesters marched to the Civic Auditorium to hear speeches by Rockefeller, Lodge, and New York's two Republican senators, Jacob K. Javits and Kenneth B. Keating. Also present were civil rights leaders Jackie Robinson, the Reverend Ralph Abernathy representing Martin Luther King, and James Farmer of CORE. Signs in the crowd included, "I'd rather have the scurvy than Barry-Barry," and "Goldwater is a rat fink." Rockefeller told the protest crowd, "I am deeply concerned that the convention may not recognize the problem facing this country today." A labor official predicted that Goldwater was "a great danger to the political future of Negro America." Scranton-supporter and athlete Jackie Robinson observed, "Goldwater's emergence as a possible candidate has encouraged the bigots in the South."

At the convention Scranton sent a slashing letter to Goldwater that ignited the delegates. "You have too often casually prescribed nuclear war as a solution to a troubled world," Scranton wrote. "You have too often stood for irresponsibility in the serious question of racial holocaust." Scranton also accused Goldwater of rigging the convention. "With open contempt for the dignity, integrity and common sense of the convention," Scranton wrote, "your managers say in effect that the delegates are little more than a flock of chickens whose necks will be wrung at will."

Goldwater refused to accept the letter. He was said to be "hopping mad," yet he was so completely in control of the delegations that he did not reply.

The platform was released early in hopes of calming the civil rights upset. The "Discrimination" plank equivocated: "We recognize that any such discrimination is a matter of heart, conscience and education as well as equal rights under the law."

The platform also included the traditional Republican planks for tax reduction, balanced budget, repayment of the public debt, conservation, and a smaller federal government. The document was remarkable for introducing social and cultural issues under headings such as "Faith in Individuals," "Faith in the Competitive System," "Faith in Limited Government."

The platform was adamant about the Cold War. "We Republicans, with the help of Almighty God, will keep those who would bury America aware that this nation has the strength and also the will to defend its every interest. Those interests, we shall make clear, include the preservation and expansion of freedom—and ultimately its victory—every place on earth."

On the second day, the Stop-Goldwater forces tried one last time. Scranton supporters put forward a more liberal substitute civil rights plank that condemned extremists such as the John Birch Society. Scranton demanded a floor vote on his substitute plank. Representative Melvin R. Laird of Wisconsin, a Goldwater backer who served as chairman of the platform committee, had the entire 8,500-word platform read aloud in order to delay the roll call vote on the Scranton plank until after the television audiences in the East, Midwest, and South had gone to bed. Scranton lost.

Eisenhower's speech Tuesday night tried to lift the convention above the wrangling. "We can—and we should—compete vigorously and honorably among ourselves. But never can we afford to permit ourselves to be led astray by meaningless slogans, labels, preconceived notions and prejudice; we shall not be, if we cleave to the straight path of principle and common sense." Eisenhower then joined in denouncing the press: "My friends, we are Republicans. If there is any finer word in the entire field of partisan politics, I have not heard it. So let us particularly scorn the divisive efforts of those outside our family, including sensation-seeking columnists and commentators, who couldn't care less about the good of the party."

Right after Eisenhower's peace-making, Nelson Rockefeller took the podium to denounce extremism and to urge an anti-extremist amendment to the platform. The California delegation was deployed just in front of the podium and its Goldwater supporters glowered and hissed at Rockefeller. A chant started in the gallery and spread across the floor, "We want Barry! We want Barry!" Rockefeller kept talking, and he caused an eruption of boos and catcalls when he referred to "Republican liberals." The outcry "We want Barry!" drowned out the governor. Rockefeller grinned nervously and tried mockery, "It's still a free country, ladies and gentlemen."

The anti-extremist amendment was voted down by voice vote. "No!" When the nays were asked to stand, a solid wall of fervent Republican conservatives stood up across the Cow Palace. The party and the television audience could see that the party was now in the hands of the Goldwater conservatives.

Pundit Joseph Alsop stated the Republican problem starkly. "The practical politics of this year's election consequently differs from the politics of any past election in this century. In the person of Senator Goldwater, the Republicans seem to be about to nominate a candidate whose views of war and peace and other subjects have alarmed and alienated great numbers of people in his own party."

Pundit Walter Lippmann wrote bluntly, "Senator Goldwater has a passion to divide and dominate."

On Fisherman's Wharf the nondelegate Richard Nixon gave a press conference to announce his support for Goldwater, calling the senator "a reasonable man and a moderate man." When an ardent Republican tried to put a "Goldwater for President" cowboy hat on the former vice president's head, Nixon removed it before the photographers could click.

On the third evening Barry Goldwater, a trim, silver-haired fifty-five-year-old, was easily nominated on the first ballot. Goldwater's choice for running mate was the party national chairman, Representative William E. Miller of Lockport, New York. The dapper and diminutive Miller, forty-nine, was accepted uniformly. Goldwater candidly remarked, "One of the reasons I chose Miller is that he drives Johnson nuts."

Goldwater watched the nomination ceremony on television from his hotel suite. He turned to the press in the room to go on the attack against President Johnson. "He's the phoniest individual whoever came along," Goldwater said. "He opposed civil rights until this year. Let them make an issue of it. I'll recite the thousand of words he has spoken."

On the fourth and final night, Thursday, July 16, Goldwater's acceptance speech rocked the party and the country. The text was generally a boost for freedom and a knock against communism. One line burned into the television sets and newspaper editorials afterward. "Extremism in the defense of liberty is no vice. Moderation in the pursuit of justice is no virtue." The Cow Palace exploded in cheers for Goldwater's assertion. Delegates celebrated not only for their candidate but also against the defeated Rockefeller-Scranton liberal forces.

Rockefeller left the convention before Goldwater's acceptance speech. The next day the governor issued an angry denunciation of the candidate. "To extol extremism—whether 'in defense of liberty' or in 'pursuit of justice'—is dangerous, irresponsible and frightening. Any sanction of lawlessness, of the vigilantes and of the unruly mob can only be deplored. The extremism of the Communists, of the Ku Klux Klan, of the John Birch Society—like that of most terrorists—has always been claimed by such groups to be in the defense of liberty." Rockefeller closed, "I shall continue to fight extremism in the Republican Party. It has no place in the party. It has no place in America."

The campaign was a tempest. Without the support of Rockefeller's New York party apparatus and Scranton's Pennsylvania party apparatus, Goldwater had no credible chance to defeat Johnson in the electoral college.

Goldwater was a stern, determined politician. He led the Republicans with a new ideological style of conservatism that resembled an inheritance of traditional party platform issues on taxes, government activism, military preparedness, fiscal policy. Goldwater's opposition to the 1964 Civil Rights Act was the one component of his philosophy that departed from historical GOP platforms and collided with the Eisenhower administration's civil rights emphasis.

Goldwater's campaign slogan was deliberately contentious: "In Your Heart, You Know He's Right."

The Goldwater campaign strategy concentrated on the so-called Sun Belt of the Southwest as well as on the old South and Midwest. Goldwater forces invented a new kind of Republican electioneering called "the Southern Strategy"—based on a 1961 Goldwater speech in Atlanta: "We're not going to get the Negro vote as a bloc in 1964 and 1968, so let's go hunting where the ducks are."

Thanks to Goldwater's anti–civil rights posture, Johnson enjoyed the unprecedented advantage of being a Southern Democratic politician who could campaign and win New York City. Election week, long ahead in the polls, Johnson spoke at a giant rally in Madison Square Garden. "This is not a conservative philosophy," Johnson said of Goldwater's "extremism" remark. "This is not a Republican philosophy. This is not a philosophy ever before embraced by a major American leader. 'Conservative' may be written on their banner. But 'radical' is in their hearts."

Goldwater, campaigning before segregationists in South Carolina, could only rail on against the 1964 Civil Rights Act and Johnson's Great Society. "That way lies destruction," said Goldwater.

An infamous detail of the campaign was a Democratic television commercial that was nicknamed the "Daisy Spot." Brief, crude, facile, the commercial showed a small girl picking the petals off a daisy while a speaker counted backward, "Ten, nine, eight . . ." and then a mushroom cloud covered the screen. The last detail was a logo for the Johnson campaign. The commercial fed the fantasy that the reserve air force general Goldwater would start a nuclear war with the Soviets as soon as he was in the White House.

Election eve, with the Gallup poll giving Johnson 61 percent and Goldwater 32 percent, there was dark foreshadowing about Vietnam. Vietcong mortars killed four Americans and wrecked twenty-one B-57 bombers at the Bien Hoa airbase. Johnson immediately promised Ambassador Maxwell Taylor a new supply. Goldwater remarked, "The Communists are scared stiff that you will elect me."

Goldwater vs. Johnson, 1964. New York Herald Tribune, *November 2, 1964.*

More than seventy million voted out of eighty-eight million registered voters. Johnson took 61.1 percent and forty-four states for a massive mandate of 486 electoral votes. Goldwater, who went to bed without conceding, took only 38.5 percent and won only Arizona and four Dixiecrat-dominated Southern states (Alabama, Mississippi, Georgia, and South Carolina) for 52 electoral votes.

The worst aspect of the Republican defeat was in the new Eighty-ninth Congress. The Senate would show 68 Democrats to 32 Republicans. The House would show 295 Democrats to 141 Republicans.

In New York, Rockefeller's break with Goldwater gave Johnson a 2.5 million plurality and helped elect to the Senate Democrat Robert F. Kennedy over Republican incumbent Kenneth B. Keating. Republican John V. Lindsay held on to his seat in the House for the Seventeenth Congressional District.

From the links in Augusta, Georgia, Eisenhower commented dourly on the party's defeat and division. Asked about the future for Republicans, the president added that Richard Nixon was a man "of great ability and great astuteness who would play a great part in unifying the party."

★ 1968 ★

Lyndon Baines Johnson's landslide quickly turned to mud when he lied to the nation over a minor naval confrontation in the Tonkin Bay off Vietnam in the fall of 1964 and thereby won congressional approval to commit U.S. ground forces to the bottomless pit of the undeclared Vietnam war.

Johnson boasted of his masterful management of Congress to construct his Great Society, such as the social innovations of Medicare for the elderly and Medicaid for the disadvantaged and the 1965 Voting Rights Act passed over the race-baiting of the president's own Texas party. Johnson did not look closely at the dangers in the fact that the Great Society produced a drastic 300 percent increase in federal welfare (AFDC) checks, rising from three million recipients in 1960 to ten million recipients by 1970, when the number would level off until it took off again in 1990.

It would be Johnson's ugly manipulation of Congress to go along with the Vietnam war that cursed the Johnson administration, the Democrats, and the country for the rest of the Cold War.

Johnson sent the first marines to provide ground protection for American air forces in March 1965. By April Fool's Day American bombers were dropping napalm on nineteen thousand acres of jungle in order to destroy Vietcong bases fifty-five miles northeast of the capital of Saigon. The official term was *defoliation*. The American air force general in charge commented, "I hope it will keep burning for some time."

By the midterm elections of 1966, the burning had spread to American political campaigns. The debate was played out with slang words such as *antiwar doves* versus *prowar hawks,* regardless of party.

Governor Mark Hatfield of Oregon, a Republican dove, was running for a Senate seat against a Democratic hawk. "The government must be honest with the people," said Hatfield in Portland, Oregon, days before the election. "That's the only reason I talk about Vietnam. I'm told it's dangerous to talk as I do. But I believe the American people have the right to know what our goals and objectives are."

Nixon went back on the campaign trail for Republican candidates, and he used the Vietnam war to score the Johnson administration and the Democrats. Nixon was no dove, but he did fault Johnson for unclear war aims. A peeved Johnson, facing surgery on his gall bladder and throat, took a shot at Nixon: "It is his problem to find fault with his country during a period of October every two years."

Nixon enjoyed the partisan duel and responded to Johnson from Manchester, New Hampshire. "We can all have a fit of temper now and then," he said, smiling about his 1962 display of temper at the Beverley Hills Hilton. "But we mustn't allow a fit of temper to have any effect on developing the policy America needs to save lives in Vietnam." Nixon added sharply, "It is my duty as the spokesman of the loyal opposition in a political campaign to raise questions about a policy which I do not believe is the best policy to achieve America's goal of peace without appeasement."

Election week, both Johnson and Nixon appealed for a large turnout. Nixon predicted that Johnson's outburst at him about Vietnam would boost GOP chances in the close contests. These included four Senate races—of Republican Edmund Brooke in Massachusetts, Republican Charles Percy in Illinois, Republican Howard Baker in Tennessee, Republican John Tower in Texas. Also critical was one gubernatorial race— of Republican and Hollywood favorite Ronald Reagan against incumbent Edmund Brown in California.

Election eve, at elitist Harvard, home base of the Kennedy Democrats, the campaign fever ran hot over the Vietnam war when Kennedy's "Whiz-Kid" defense secretary Robert S. McNamara was mobbed by students in crewcuts. "Murderer!" the Harvards accused. "How many civilian casualties have there been in South Vietnam?"

A ruffled McNamara, straightening his wire-rimmed glasses, replied, "We don't know."

In a heavy turnout the Republican party posted modest gains across the nation. The new Ninetieth Congress remained solidly Democratic. However, many of the new faces were fresh Republicans, and the party felt exultant. Hatfield, Brooke, Percy, Tower, Baker all won for the first time in the Senate; Republican Winthrop Rockefeller of Arkansas and Republican Spiro T. Agnew of Maryland won first-time governorships. Governor Rockefeller of New York was easily returned for a third term.

Democratic segregationists held off Republicans in the South. Segregationist Lester Maddox won election as governor of Georgia. Segregationist George Wallace placed his wife, Lurleen Wallace, in the governorship of Alabama to satisfy state law that he could not succeed himself.

The major Republican victory was Ronald Reagan's in California. A veteran actor and former president of the Screen Actors Guild, Reagan was a favorite of Goldwater's and the conservative wing of the party. Reagan had survived Brown's late attempts to smear him as racist. Election night, the victorious, handsome, eloquent Reagan used his superb baritone to declare that Californians should no longer be divided by "labels." Reagan said, "Partisanship ends as of today."

The maneuvering for the GOP nomination began the next day and continued full force into the presidential year 1968. Conservative Nixon and liberal Rockefeller were the favorites, followed by conservative Reagan and liberal Romney.

A dark fate ruled the year. In early March, with the Tet offensive massacring tens of thousands in Vietnam, Johnson was shocked by the New Hampshire presidential primary strength of dove Democratic senator Eugene McCarthy of Minnesota. Late March the humiliated president dropped out of the race: "I shall not seek and I will not accept the nomination of my party for another term as your President."

Johnson's surrender shocked both parties. Nixon gained all the advantage, since he had already won the GOP New Hampshire primary and forced Rockefeller out of the race. The day before Johnson's speech, a national Harris poll put Nixon within two points of President Johnson.

After Johnson's surrender, Nixon carefully constructed a Vietnam position somewhere between hawks and doves: "Like every American," he said in early April, "I hope for an early and an honorable settlement of this war."

One week later the nation was stunned again by the murder of Martin Luther King, Jr., in Memphis, Tennessee. Rioting and mass protests in many major cities obliged Johnson to use federal troops to restore order. Army combat engineers were pictured playing cards while on sentry duty at Washington's Fifteenth Street and M Street. King's funeral in Atlanta attracted all the major politicians except Johnson, who sent Vice President Hubert Humphrey of Minnesota in his place.

Immediately after the service, Rockefeller declared that he had changed his mind again and was available for another try at the nomination. Nixon ignored Rockefeller's new boom and pushed ahead through primary season, keeping his fire on the Johnson administration and potential general election rivals Hubert Humphrey and Robert Kennedy. Late in the primaries there was a sudden boom for the reluctant hawk Reagan of California, darling of the veteran Goldwaterites: "I would favor a step-up of the war," Reagan said of Vietnam.

Dark fate came again in early June with the assassination of Robert F. Kennedy of New York just after he won the Democratic California primary. Another national funeral, and another gathering of the major politicians in tribute, left Nixon standing above his old competitors like a man winning at musical chairs.

In midsummer a defeated, dejected Rockefeller tried to cobble together a Stop-Nixon movement, substituting Romney for himself. Eisenhower weighed in by endorsing Nixon. By the Miami Beach convention in early August, Nixon had control of the party and the nomination process.

The Cold War dominated the news. In Vietnam 4,500 army soldiers from Fort Carson, Colorado, arrived to bring U.S. military strength to 540,000. In Eastern Europe, Soviet puppet states denounced anti-Soviet developments in Czechoslovakia as "counter-revolutionary." The secret Soviet plot to invade and subjugate Czechoslovakia was at T-minus-fifteen days.

Meanwhile in Miami Beach's Convention Hall, the confident Republicans came to terms with the platform's controversial Vietnam plank. "We have come as close to satisfying any candidate we nominate as anything we could reduce to writing," said Dirksen of Illinois of the Vietnam plank after working hard to make it acceptable to all three credible nominees, Nixon, Rockefeller, and Reagan. "All three candidates," said House minority leader Gerald R. Ford of Michigan, "have taken a position that a platform fight [on Vietnam] will hurt them."

The Vietnam plank read like a mind twister of caveats: "We pledge a program for peace in Vietnam—neither peace at any price nor a camouflaged surrender of legitimate United States or allied interests—but a positive program that will offer a fair and equitable settlement to all, based on the principle of self-determination, our national interests, and the cause of long-range world peace."

Nixon was a confident front-runner. He announced before the opening gavel that he would defer his VP choice until after he had heard from the delegates.

Joseph Alsop admired Nixon's mastery. "There are plenty of indications here at Miami that a big rightward jump is already under consideration by the former Vice-President," Alsop wrote on opening day of the convention. "The Nixon people on the Resolutions Committee are taking a near-Goldwater line. Nixon himself has been talking up the so-called 'Southern strategy,' even to some Northern delegates, as though George Wallace did not exist. Above all there is a clear possibility that if nominated Nixon will then choose Gov. Ronald Reagan of California as his running mate."

Nixon's "Southern Strategy" was a clever update of Goldwater's "Southern Strategy." Nixon asserted that he would campaign in the Southern states where Goldwater had performed well in 1964. Nixon knew that third-party candidate George Wallace would likely win the Southern states. However, Nixon's effort in the South would oblige the Democratic campaign to devote time and money to try to hold on to the Solid South electoral base.

A small surprise the first day of the convention was Ronald Reagan's bold declaration that he was finally a declared candidate. "It certainly makes life easier," a beaming Reagan said of his decision. A Georgia delegate observed that Reagan's candidacy was "our answer to George Wallace in the South."

Nixon forces were nonplussed. Nixon delegate counter Richard G. Kleindienst said he had over six hundred votes; when challenged, Kleindienst remarked, "Well, those other guys are wrong."

Nixon was correct all week. He departed from his Montauk, Long Island, seclusion to fly by chartered jet to Miami airport, where he was greeted by former Dixiecrat now Republican senator Strom Thurmond of South Carolina as well as by the Republicans governors of Alaska, Montana, Idaho, and Massachusetts. Nixon's headquarters at the Miami Beach Hilton Plaza Hotel was overrun with aides, press, and a small elephant that misbehaved in the crowd. Nixon put out the rumor that he was considering Rockefeller of New York, Mayor John V. Lindsay of New York, or Senator Charles Percy of Illinois as his choice for vice president.

The second day of the convention was darkened by fate when Eisenhower suffered a grave heart attack in his hospital suite at Washington's Walter Reed Hospital. Eisenhower had addressed the convention by telephone on the first night, and news of his sudden turn worried the evening session.

Tom Dewey, a cheery sixty-six, delivered a passionate partisan attack on the Democrats for the television cameras. Permanent convention chairman Gerald Ford of Michigan promised the TV audience, "We will free the American people from the Vietnam war. We will free the American people from the inflation that pinches their pocketbook."

By the third day the single alarming development of the convention was that the network anchors were bored by the lack of confrontation and tension. An outburst by a few civil rights protesters on the second night, while Ford was speaking, had been the only unscripted event so far. Walter Cronkite was reduced to mentioning that the thousands of red, white, and blue balloons held in a net above the convention floor cost thirty-three cents each.

The third night, Nixon's name was placed into nomination by the photogenic new governor of Maryland, Spiro T. Agnew, who had a reputation as a poor speaker. This night Agnew proved eloquent. "When a nation is in crisis," Agnew argued, "and when history speaks firmly to that nation that it needs a man to match the times, you don't discover such a man, you recognize such a man." The dove Hatfield of Oregon seconded Nixon's nomination: "He is not bound by the mistakes of the past."

Rockefeller was nominated by Governor Raymond P. Shafer of Penn-

Nixon wins his second presidential nomination, at Miami Beach, 1968. Washington Post, *August 11, 1968.*

sylvania. Reagan was nominated by California state treasurer Ivy Baker Priest.

At 5:33 P.M., in time for the evening network audience, Gerald Ford called upon the first delegation to vote: "Alabama?" The roll call was swift. Wisconsin's 30 votes gave Nixon the nomination plurality, and he finished with 692 total on the first ballot. Rockefeller polled 272, chiefly from New York, Pennsylvania, and Massachusetts. Reagan polled 182 delegates, almost entirely from California and the South.

At the same time in the city of Miami, ten miles from the posh seaside hotels and Convention Hall, there was a riot in the Liberty City ghetto. A planned civil rights rally had exploded after police turned up with shotguns and newsmen turned up with cameras. A police spokesman said at 10 P.M., "There is either a lull or we have contained it."

Later that night, Nixon chose Agnew of Maryland for the second spot, and the convention approved. Agnew had attracted attention as a *liberal* Republican who had been tough on criminals and rioters in Maryland. Nixon called Agnew "a man of inner strength." Nixon also knew that Agnew brought strength in the traditional Border states to offset the loss of the South to Wallace.

On the last night, Nixon's acceptance speech on national television was brilliant craftsmanship, the sum total of his twenty-year education as a partisan and his lifelong pursuit of glory. He was most proud later of the autobiographical finale. "I see another child," he spoke of his childhood in Yorba Linda. "He hears the train go by at night and dreams of faraway places he would like to go. It seems an impossible dream. But he is helped on his journey through life. A father who had to go to work before he finished the sixth grade, sacrificed everything so that his sons could go to college. A gentle, Quaker mother with a passionate concern for peace, quietly wept when he went to war but understood why he had to go. A great teacher, a remarkable football coach, an inspirational minister encouraged him on his way. A courageous wife and loyal children stood by him in victory and defeat. In his chosen profession of politics, first scores, then hundreds, then thousands and finally millions worked for his success. Tonight he stands before you—nominated for President of the United States."

The campaign started that night, when Humphrey of Minnesota, with a strong hold on the Democratic convention in Chicago in a week's time, commented to the press that a Humphrey-Nixon race presented the nation with "a clear choice."

Wallace told the press that night that the Nixon-Agnew ticket would lose Maryland and the entire South. "The people are going to elect a new

Richard Nixon's trademark salute vs. Hubert Humphrey's hopes.
Greensboro Daily News. *Repr.* Washington Post, *October 28,*
1968.

party in November," Wallace boasted of his segregationist American
party.

The first postconvention Gallup poll showed Nixon leading
Humphrey 45 percent to 29 percent. Nixon's rueful jest about himself
and his early lead was to quote a *New York Times* columnist, Tom
Wicker, "No Republican, as has often been said, unites the Democrats
the way Nixon does."

Nixon opened his campaign by stopping over at LBJ's Texas ranch
outside Houston for a ceremonial intelligence briefing on the state of the
world. "As I started to board the helicopter," Nixon recalled about his
departure from the Johnson ranch, "Johnson's dog darted past my legs
into the cabin. There was a great deal of laughter, and I practically had

to pick the animal up and carry him down the steps. Johnson shouted in mock anger, 'Dick, here you've got my helicopter, you're after my job, and now you're gonna take my dog.' "

For the next three months, there was little humor in the campaign and a great deal of hard electioneering. Nixon said he had to win three of the seven large electoral states of California, Illinois, Michigan, New York, Ohio, Pennsylvania, and Texas. There were no televised or public debates between the three candidates. Instead the campaigns spent tens of millions for television advertising. The Nixon campaign chose a simple slogan for buttons and banners, "Nixon's the One."

With two weeks to go, all three candidates were spinning around each other like prizefighters, concentrating their appearances and television-time firepower in the crucial big states.

In New York City, Nixon was hawkish, charging the Democrats with a "security gap" in strategic weapons that undermined the country's ability to negotiate with the Soviets from a position of strength.

In Los Angeles, Humphrey was dovish, "I favor worldwide—supervised, and carefully safeguarded—reductions in arms and military expenditure. The next President of the United States must have the courage to dare to seek worldwide reductions."

In Madison Square Garden in New York, George Wallace and his running mate, retired air force general Curtis LeMay, were ebullient before a throng. Wallace accused former defense secretary McNamara of using "computerized defenses" that undermined U.S. security.

A week later in Michigan and New York, Nixon repeated his security gap charge. Humphrey in Pennsylvania announced he was endorsed by the dove Eugene McCarthy. Wallace in Michigan claimed that he would get taxpayers earning fifty thousand dollars or more per year "to pay their tax at the actual rate called for in the tax structure."

The candidates' continental footwork quickened in the last days: Nixon in Los Angeles, where he promised to go to Saigon if it would bring peace and repeated that he had a plan to end the war; Humphrey in Houston, where he promised to bring peace in Vietnam; and Wallace in the Deep South, where he promised to enforce all laws. Vietnam and civil rights were the issues at the start and at the finish. Nixon supporters repeatedly emphasized a news photograph of the candidate standing near a rally sign that read "Bring Us Together."

Election eve, the Gallup and Harris polls rated the election a dead heat between Nixon and Humphrey. Nixon led in the Midwest and West, while Humphrey led in the East. The South was given to Wallace. A final Harris poll found Humphrey had a slight lead, though the race was still "too close to call."

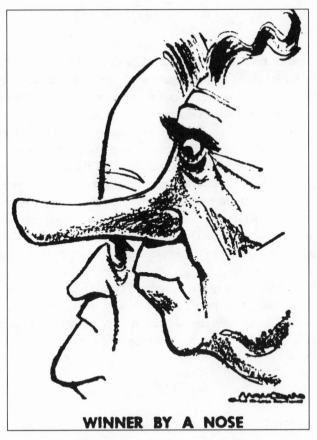

WINNER BY A NOSE

Nixon vs. Humphrey, 1968. Chicago Sun-Times. *Repr.*
Denver Post, *November 10, 1968.*

Election day, the news media speculated about a constitutional crisis if no candidate gained a majority in the electoral college and the decision was moved to the Democrat-controlled House of Representatives. The New York stock market hedged its bets with a sluggish volume of ten million shares on Monday close. From Paris came the news that a poll at Harry's New York Bar gave Nixon 149 votes, Humphrey 148 votes, and Wallace 11.

Nearly seventy-three million voted. The networks were unable to predict the winner until well into Wednesday morning. Nixon later recalled that he did not relax until he saw he'd taken Ohio and California and probably Illinois, around 3 A.M. New York time. When Illinois was declared to Nixon at noontime Wednesday, Chicago time, Humphrey conceded from his Minneapolis hotel: "According to unofficial returns," read Humphrey's telegram to Nixon, "you are the winner of the election. My congratulations."

The final results would take more than a week to tabulate. Nixon's electoral majority bobbed between 276 and 300. Mayor Richard J. Daley of Chicago, charging "irregularities," refused to concede Illinois to Nixon for four days, despite the fact that Nixon held a 135,000 plurality.

In the end Nixon won 43.4 percent for 31.785 million votes and 301 electoral votes, including Illinois. Humphrey won 42.7 percent for 31.275 million votes and 191 electoral votes. Wallace won 13.5 percent for 9.9 million votes and 46 electoral votes, all from the deep South.

In the new Ninety-first Congress, the Democrats retained firm control. In the Senate, there were 58 Democrats to 42 Republicans; in the House, 243 Democrats to 192 Republicans. Notable Republican victories included the young Bob Dole of Kansas to the Senate, and the return of Goldwater of Arizona to the Senate after his hiatus since the '64 presidential defeat.

The New York stock market accepted Nixon's victory with a modest uptrend. "We have two priorities," a Nixon financial aide told the financial press. "The first is the balance of payments, and the second is to handle inflation. Both concern the integrity of the dollar."

★ 1972 ★

Richard Nixon's first administration stressed a pragmatic integrity in foreign and domestic affairs.

Cabinet appointments emphasized Nixon's experience in fighting the Cold War. Secretary of State William P. Rogers, National Security Adviser Henry Kissinger, and Defense Secretary Melvin R. Laird supervised the president's aggressive policy toward the Soviets. In strategic arms, Nixon prevailed upon the Senate to approve the ABM (Anti-Ballistic Missile) Treaty with Moscow that began the move toward détente with the Soviets that would eventually include strategic arms limitation. In the Middle East, Nixon committed the United States to Prime Minister Golda Meir and the Israelis. In Southeast Asia, he turned away from an armistice and ordered massive B-52 bombings in March 1969 that would lead to increased ground fighting and eventually to massive antiwar protest in America.

Nixon handled the antiwar unrest with a masterful 1969 speech called the Silent Majority speech. "And so tonight—to you, *the great silent majority* of my fellow Americans—I ask for your support," the president told the television audience on November 3, 1969. "I pledged in my campaign for the presidency to end the war in a way that we could win the peace. I have initiated a plan of action which will enable me to keep the pledge. The more support I can have from the American people, the sooner the pledge can be redeemed; for the more divided we are at home, the less likely the enemy is to negotiate at Paris. Let us be united for peace. Let us also be united against defeat. Because let us understand: North Vietnam cannot defeat or humiliate the United States. Only Americans can do that."

In domestic affairs, Nixon's critical decision was to fill vacant Supreme Court posts. First was to find a replacement for seventy-seven-year-old Earl Warren of California, who was retiring as chief justice. After asking Tom Dewey, who declined for reason of age, Nixon turned to Warren Burger of Minnesota, a veteran Harold Stassen supporter. Burger would soon be joined by two more Nixon appointments, attorney Lewis Powell of Virginia, sixty-four, and Assistant Attorney General William Rehnquist of Arizona, forty-seven. The Burger Court would soon rule on controversies such as school busing, abortion, and eventually the White House tapes on the Watergate scandal.

The most spectacular Cold War achievement in Nixon's presidency was the American victory in the moon race. Apollo XI landed on the moon in August 1969, followed by five more moon landings by 1972.

At the midterm election in 1970, Nixon was in command of national integrity. The president represented pragmatic, even liberal domestic policies that stressed his agility and experience. However, the Vietnam war remained unsolved, and antiwar protest after the May Cambodia incursion was ruinous. In answer to the civil unrest, the theme of the midterm campaign was "law and order." The president campaigned in hopes of winning the Senate for the GOP.

A Nixon favorite was the handsome and Yale-educated Representative George Bush of Texas, then forty-six, who was challenging Democrat Lloyd Bentsen for a Texas Senate seat. Nixon traveled to rural Longview in East Texas to boost Bush's standing among the conservative Texans outside Houston and Dallas. Bush addressed the issue of antiwar protests: "The way to turn the kids off is to tell them you have to do it just the way it's always been done. You shouldn't write off an entire generation."

Election eve, Nixon pounded his message that he wanted the public "to vote for those men who will vote for the President not against him." Violent antiwar protests in California boosted the reelection chances of Governor Ronald Reagan.

Of note, House minority leader Gerald Ford of Michigan did not seize upon the law-and-order theme. "Return a man of peace to Congress," urged Ford's television ad. "Support Jerry Ford. He gets things done."

The Republicans fell short. The Democrats kept control of the new Ninety-second Congress. In large state governorships, the Republicans retained Reagan in California but lost Pennsylvania, Ohio, and Illinois to the Democrats.

Nixon began the second half of his administration with a bold move to open diplomatic relations with Red China. Nixon secretly sent his envoy Kissinger to China in July 1971, and several days later the president stunned the world and his own anti-Communist party by announcing that he would visit Peking the next year.

Nixon's domestic boldness in 1971 was his ordering of a wage and price freeze in late summer. The markets rewarded the decision by rallying stocks on heavy volume; however inflation eventually returned and skyrocketed in 1974, plunging the country into a deep recession. Later, Nixon recalled the decision ruefully. "The piper must always be paid," he wrote, "and there was an unquestionably high price for tampering with the orthodox economic mechanisms."* Nixon chose to intervene in orthodox economic mechanisms at other moments in his administration, such as when he devalued the dollar against foreign currencies, and when he took the United States off the gold standard. Nixon speechwriter and later pundit William Safire wrote of the failure of Nixon's economic policies to control inflation, stabilize the dollar, or assure the markets that "the fault, dear Brutus, lies not in the actions of our leader, but in ourselves, when we demand that the government regulate our working lives without intruding on our freedom."†

By the presidential year 1972, Nixon still could not find an end to the Vietnam war. The president did have a Cold War strategy—détente with Moscow, normalization with Peking—and yet neither of these achievements offset the wide antiwar protest. Nixon was harried not only by critics from the Democratic party but also by leaks to the media from inside his administration. The 1971 unauthorized release of the Pentagon Papers (confidential government documents critical to the Vietnam war) and many additional leaks moved Nixon to approve the establishment of the White House's Special Investigation Unit, called the Plumbers.

The Plumbers later moved to the reelection campaign staff, where their illegal activities became the germ of the Watergate scandal.

The mystery of Nixon's presidency was why a politician so in command of his policies would allow his loyal aides to act so out of control. Attorney General John Mitchell's Committee for the Re-election of the President became a loony, sloppy, cash-drunk organization that encour-

---

*Nixon, *Memoirs*, p. 521.
†William Safire, *Before the Fall* (New York: Doubleday, 1975), p. 528.

aged lawless behavior by lawyers and cronies. Yet the president stood by and not only approved but also comforted the foolish and felonious.

The fact was that the president had no credible partisan opposition from the Democrats or any other group. The Democratic party had wrecked itself in 1968 over the Vietnam war. Through the 1972 primary process the Democrats could find no potent candidate. Neither Humphrey, nor Humphrey's 1968 running mate, Senator Edmund Muskie of Maine, nor Senator George McGovern of South Dakota were anything but limp challenges to Nixon's popularity. In the winter, polls momentarily showed Muskie with some sectional currency, but his dovishness undermined his ability to appeal to the large conservative bloc of the Democracy.

The best that can be said of the Plumbers' break-in of the Democratic National Committee Headquarters in the Watergate Hotel complex, June 17, 1972, was that it was a clumsy attempt to eavesdrop on a party that had already given up hope against the GOP. The burglars were even carrying out-of-date bugging equipment.

Within a week of the break-in, Nixon was fully apprised of the Watergate incident. The president was ready to cover it up with lies and deceptions. There was no hesitation, and the proof of this conduct was the darkest moments in the June 23, 1972 reel-to-reel tapes, the so-called smoking gun. Strangely, the president knew that every word he spoke about the obstruction of justice and cover-up was being recorded by a taping system, since he had ordered the system installed in the Oval Office in the winter of 1971.

"The existence of the tapes was never meant to be made public," Nixon later recalled, "—at least not during my presidency. I thought that afterward I could consult the tapes in preparing whatever books or memoirs I might write."*

The content of the White House tapes of June 1972 would not be revealed for more than two years. By the mid-August Republican convention, the news flap over the Watergate break-in seemed to be fading despite continued alarm in the press.

For example, the *Washington Post*'s young reporters Bob Woodward and Carl Bernstein, directed by their editor Ben Bradlee, remained in pursuit of a link between the Watergate burglars and the Nixon White House; in mid-August, just prior to the convention, Woodward and Bernstein reported that former commerce secretary Maurice Stans, the reelection finance chairman, had denied to investigators that the reelection campaign had financed the break-in.

*Nixon, *Memoirs*, pp. 500–502.

At the same time *Time* magazine reported that the three men who had been arrested by the police as accomplices to the Watergate burglars were all "members of the Securities Intelligence Squad of the Committee for the Re-Election of the President." *Time* named G. Gordon Liddy, E. Howard Hunt, and Robert Maridian.

The public shrugged. Convention week opened with Nixon's approval rating at a new high of 59 percent. A Chicago poll showed the president leading Democratic nominee George McGovern, who had already stumbled by shuffling his vice presidential choices, by 23 percent.

Confident Republicans, gathering on the latest convention date in the party history, August 21–24, devoted the week in Miami Beach to tailoring a platform and party to Richard Nixon. There was no drama whatsoever to report, so the media gave its time to pageantry and protests. Three hundred antiwar protesters boiled into the Fontainbleu Hotel lobby chanting, "Nixon, Agnew, you can't hide! / We charge you with genocide!" and "Run, Nixon, run, Nixon, run-run-run-run! / People of the world are picking up the gun!"

In nearby Flamingo Park, a protest group led by famous dissidents such as Rennie Davis and David Dellinger provided colorful theater for the touring reporters. A tent called a *vomitorium* encouraged visitors to express their opinion of the GOP. "If you can't throw up for Nixon, vote for him," announced a barker.

The Republicans issued the platform before the first day of the convention. Richard Nixon's reelection was the crowning plank; however, there was attention to controversial social issues that would bedevil the party for decades. The platform opposed school busing and teacher hiring quotas, while it called for income tax credits for private school bills, mandated national health care insurance for all employees, voluntary prayer in school, and passage of a women's equal rights amendment.

The only shadow on the day was a newspaper column by longtime GOP watchers Rowland Evans, Jr., and Robert Novak, who wrote from Miami Beach about "the specter of the Watergate Caper" that was spooking Republican's leaders about the reliability of reelection figures such as John Mitchell, Maurice Stans, former assistant attorney general Robert Maridian—and an unknown White House counsel named John Dean.

The Nixon campaign had written a script for the convention that included the time-outs for television commercials. TV was now reporting on what amounted to a Republican-produced TV special about Richard Nixon. For example, on the second night, Gerald Ford was scheduled to announce at 9:14 P.M. that a resolution seating all the delegates had been accepted "by a chorus of ayes."

"I'm as aware of the evils of Communism as anyone, but good God, when you think of eight hundred million Chinese in terms of _franchises_..."

Nixon vs. McGovern, 1972. New Yorker, _August 5, 1972._

The second night, the convention renominated Nixon in speedy fashion. On the roll call, Missouri's thirty votes gave Nixon the majority. A two-minute demonstration followed. On the floor White House domestic aide John Ehrlichman commented, "A mere bagatelle." Later that night, the president went out visiting, and a famous photograph showed

Nixon vs. McGovern, 1972. Denver Post, *November 1, 1972.*

him on the stage of Miami Marine Stadium being hugged by Las Vegas entertainer Sammy Davis, Jr.

Longtime Nixon loyalist Murray Chotiner reflected afterward on the president's public stature. "Let's face it, for years Mr. Nixon has been an individual you either liked or disliked. Now there are many who never liked him but who have come to admire him and to respect the job he's done. He's never going to be thought of as a father figure like Ike. No matter what his age, he's always thought of as a young man, because his early rise in politics was rapid. But now there is more intelligent respect for him than there's ever been."

The Nixon reelection campaign was effortless. McGovern and his final choice for running mate, Kennedy relative Sargent Shriver, never rallied more than the liberal wing of the Democrats. Nixon led the polls from wire to wire. There were no presidential debates. An important new development was that the '72 campaign was the first application of the 1971 Federal Election Campaign Act, which regulated campaign financing and provided federal funds for media advertising. The unexpected result was that the public funds swelled the campaign coffers without slowing the traditional desire to raise as much money as possible from influential private donors.

On election day, the American population stood at an unofficial 210,002,963. Seventy-seven million voted. Nixon's landslide was astonishing. The president gained 60 percent and won every state except Massachusetts for 520 electoral votes, the second greatest total in American history. McGovern held only Massachusetts for 17 electoral votes. A Libertarian candidate received 1 electoral vote.

The Republican disappointment was that the Democrats easily remained in control of the new Ninety-third Congress. The single GOP surprise was new senator Jesse Helms, fifty, of North Carolina.

"The election was sort of a standoff," commented Senator Bob Dole of Kansas, the Republican party chairman. "After you take the President's personal landslide, there wasn't any landslide at all."

★ 1976 ★

Nixon's second administration collapsed under the twin burdens of Vietnam and Watergate.

Nixon's failure to win either house of Congress left him vulnerable to a well-organized and hostile majority who had the tools to undo and wreck his presidency.

Nixon's decision to send the B-52 bombers over North Vietnam in the infamous Christmas Bombing of 1972 enraged the antiwar factions in the Congress and press. The apparent peace accord in Vietnam in January—"Peace is at hand," said Secretary of State Henry Kissinger—did nothing to appease Nixon's partisan foes. The American POWs were returned, and still the war in Vietnam continued with a small American ground force and a massive American aid program.

Henry Kissinger. Washington Post, *September 12, 1974.*

Also in January the Burger Supreme Court offered a decision, *Roe v. Wade,* that undid all state prohibitions on abortion. This ruling alarmed Nixon's most socially conservative supporters and began a GOP-led crusade for an anti-abortion amendment to the Constitution.

Most damaging to Nixon was that in January several of the Watergate burglars, including CIA agent and "Plumber" E. Howard Hunt, pled guilty in John J. Sirica's federal court. Two other burglars, G. Gordon Liddy and James McCord, remained on trial. Judge Sirica was not fooled by the tactic of pleading guilty to avoid a fact-finding trial. "Well I'm sorry," Sirica told the felons, "I don't believe you." Immediately the court intensified the demand for the whole truth of the episode.

The Watergate scandal was now a permanent part of the daily news. The mass media chipped away at the White House cover-up. Later, the White House tape recordings would show that Nixon's White House staff was obsessed by the cover-up from January 1973 until the President's resignation the following year. In April, Nixon's aides Haldeman, Ehrlichman, and Dean were obliged to resign to continue the cover-up. In June, disgraced White House counselor John Dean, then thirty-four, began his testimony to Senator Sam Ervin of North Carolina's Senate Select Committee investigating Watergate. Dean pointed fingers and named names, and the first and most important name he accused of complete responsibility for the Watergate break-in and cover-up was Richard Nixon. For the next fourteen months the fall of the presidency followed like a slow-motion avalanche.

Nixon did not acknowledge his part in the scandal other than as a partisan battler who was giving as good as he got—tit-for-tat electioneering.

Years later, Nixon recalled his meeting with Haldeman right after the June 1972 burglary. "At the end of our discussion I came back to the frustrating situation concerning the break-in. I told Haldeman that it seemed that the Democrats had been doing this kind of thing to us for years and *they* never got caught. Haldeman agreed that the Democrats always seemed to get off easier. He said the press just never went after them the way they went after us. Later in the same day [Wednesday, June 21, 1972], I said that every time Democrats accused us of bugging we should charge that we were being bugged and maybe even plant a bug and find it ourselves!" *

The catastrophe of the Watergate scandal was that the profound policy achievements of Richard Nixon's presidency were canceled out in the political memory. The Cold War strategy that led to détente, arms limi-

*Nixon, *Memoirs,* pp. 634–46.

tation, China relations; the liberal and experimental social programs in welfare, education, health care, and civil rights; the moon landings and establishment of the space shuttle program; the adamant defense of Israel from sinister Soviet plots with Arab clients—all that work was overshadowed by the scandal.

Certainly the blackest hole in the Nixon presidency was October 1973. In the same month the Egyptians launched a Soviet-backed sneak attack on the Israelis, supported by Soviet clients in Syria and Lebanon. At the same time, Nixon was attempting to protect the cover-up by firing his entire Justice Department in order to fire the first Watergate Special Prosecutor Archibald Cox. In addition, Vice President Spiro T. "Ted" Agnew, who had been under investigation since summer for graft while in the Maryland governorship, walked into Nixon's office and resigned his post before pleading no contest to felony corruption charges in federal court.

Nixon solved the Mideast crisis with genius, tact, toughness, and luck. Nixon handled Agnew's disgrace with calm resolve by turning to choose the popular minority leader Gerald Ford as the new vice president. However, Nixon used none of these skills to solve the Watergate crisis, and the result was a doomed presidency.

The midterm elections year 1974 began a severe economic slowdown that would become the worst recession since the Second World War. Public confidence in the president plunged in October 1973 and never recovered. Inflation skyrocketed. The bond market collapsed. The stock market continued a bear cave retreat. The press called for Nixon's ouster every day. By summer Nixon tried to run away from his problems with a dashing trip to the Mideast to open relations with Egypt and woo it away from the Soviets, and then with a dashing trip to Moscow to press détente on the jowly, drunken Soviet dictators.

There was nowhere to hide from a Congress and Supreme Court that aimed to remove a deceitful, unpopular president. The last weeks of the Nixon presidency were a sad cycle of deceptions, denials, defiance, defeat. Nixon resigned rather than watch the House of Representatives pass a bill of impeachment and send it to the Senate for trial.

August 9, 1974, Richard Nixon mounted the steps of the presidential helicopter, *Marine One,* waved good-bye to the specter of Watergate over the White House, and flew to California to begin a nineteen-year ordeal of disgrace. The president who had once boasted, "I believe in playing politics hard, but I am also smart," was brought down by other men who played politics hard and who were, at the end, smart, too.

Gerald R. Ford. Washington Post, *August 18, 1976.*

The new thirty-eighth president, Gerald R. Ford of Grand Rapids, Michigan, was a modest, well-educated, long-patient Republican politician from the industrial heartland. He was the fourth vice president (Arthur, Roosevelt, Coolidge), to succeed a Republican president, and he was the first man to gain the chief executive without standing for a national election beforehand.

Importantly, Ford was well-liked. "He'll be all right," said an intuitive Grand Rapids woman on the day Ford took the oath of office. "He won't be exciting like Kennedy, but he'll be O.K."

Immediately following his swearing-in ceremony in the East Room of the White House, at noon, August 9, 1974, Ford addressed the excitement of the Watergate crisis. "I believe that the truth is the glue that holds government together, and not only government but civilization itself. That bond, though strained, is unbroken at home and abroad. In all my public and private acts as your president, I expect to follow my instincts of openness and candor with full confidence that honesty is always the best policy in the end."

Ford's decision to name Nelson Rockefeller as vice president (before resigning, Nixon had urged Ford to choose Rockefeller), as per the Twenty-fifth Amendment, was a widely popular decision that helped build public confidence in an administration that enjoyed no electoral mandate.

Ford dropped much of his hold on public confidence in September when he pardoned Richard Nixon of all possible prosecution for the Watergate scandal. Ford knew the pardon was a risk. He told Democrat Tip O'Neill of Massachusetts beforehand. The future Speaker of the House responded candidly, "Jesus, don't you think it's kind of early?"

The public agreed with Tip O'Neill. Ford's pardon of Nixon ended the honeymoon with the press and public and derailed his presidency. Ford recalled the hubbub in his autobiography. "I wasn't prepared for the allegations that the Nixon pardon prompted. What I had intended to convince my fellow citizens was necessary surgery—essential if we were to heal our wounded nation—was being attacked as a 'secret deal' that I had worked out with Nixon before he resigned. And the timing of the

'Now to shut the book on Watergate . . .

Ford pardons Nixon, 1974. Philadelphia Inquirer. *Repr.* Washington Post, *September 13, 1974.*

announcement—eleven o'clock on a Sunday morning—was being touted as 'proof' of the conspiracy."*

Two months later at the fall midterm elections, the GOP was reeling on the defensive for the Watergate scandal and the pardon. There was no sympathy for Nixon, who was severely ill in California with internal bleeding. There were calls for Ford's impeachment, too.

The Democrats won a landslide in both houses of the new Ninety-fourth Congress, including achieving a veto-proof two-thirds majority in the House, 291 Democrats to 144 Republicans. The Democrats won or retained governorships in the critical big states New York, Pennsylvania, Florida, Texas, and California and dominated all governorships: 36 Democrats to 13 Republicans with one independent.

The severe bear of a stock market had discounted the Democratic triumph beforehand. Reaction to the election was muted on modest volume, leaving the Standard & Poor 500 index at 75.21.

The Ford administration did not recover. The following spring, 1975, the sudden collapse of the South Vietnamese government ended the United States' twenty-year debacle in Southeast Asia. At the same time, the Democratic-dominated Congress passed the largest peacetime budget deficit in American history in hopes of spurring growth out of the recession. Ford was seen as powerless to more than tinker with the Demo-

*Gerald R. Ford, *A Time To Heal: The Autobiography of Gerald R. Ford* (New York: Harper & Row and the Reader's Digest Association, 1979), p. 179.

cratic tax-and-spend ambition to expand the federal government into all aspects of American life.

In the fall of 1975 Republican dissatisfaction with the administration forced the president to let Rockefeller withdraw from any possible future candidacy.

Soon after, former California governor Ronald Reagan, a strong conservative voice in the party, telephoned Ford to alert him that he was going to challenge him in the primaries. "Hello, Mr. President," Reagan told Ford, "I am going to make an announcement, and I want to tell you ahead of time. I am going to run for president. I trust we can have a good contest, and I hope it won't be divisive."

"Well, Governor," said Ford, "I'm very disappointed. I'm sorry you're getting into this. I believe I've done a good job and that I can be elected. Regardless of your good intentions, your bid is bound to be divisive. It will take a lot of money, and it will leave a lot of scars. It won't be helpful, no matter which of us wins the nomination."

Reagan returned, "I don't think it will be divisive. I don't think it will harm the party."

"Well, I think it will," tried the president.*

Ford and Reagan were both right. The challenge did divide the party. The challenge also strengthened the party, because the primary fight in the winter and spring of 1976 restored much of the morale broken in the Watergate scandal.

Ford defeated Reagan in New Hampshire and then continued to score heavily with the party faithful in the big states such as Michigan, Illinois, and Ohio.

Reagan kept his bold candidacy alive by winning North Carolina in March and going on to take the crucial states of Texas, Georgia, and California. The primary challenge gave Reagan the opportunity to establish his vivid personality and to extol the conservative philosophy.

"Under Kissinger and Ford, this nation has become Number Two in a world where it is dangerous—if not fatal—to be second best," Reagan told a Florida audience. "All I can see is what other nations the world over see: collapse of the American will and the retreat of American power. There is little doubt in my mind that the Soviet Union will not stop taking advantage of détente until it sees that the American people have elected a new President and appointed a new Secretary of State."†

In mid-August, the Republican Convention promised a week of televised battles between Ford's apparent majority and Reagan's devoted

---

*Ford, *A Time to Heal,* p. 333.
†Ibid., pp. 373–74.

mavericks. Ford prepared for the contest by working on his acceptance speech at the White House. Reagan, who had already named moderate senator Richard S. Schweiker of Pennsylvania as his choice for VP, stayed on the attack by demanding that Ford indicate his running mate ahead of time.

Kansas City was in a festive, cleaned-up mood for the thirty-thousand guests expected for its first GOP convention since 1928. The two-year-old Kemper Arena was decorated and up-to-date, with seats for seventeen thousand.

Kansas also featured its proud former presidential candidate, Alf Landon, now eighty-nine and most witty. The former Kansas governor astonished everyone by riding his horse for the cameras on his farm in Topeka. Landon was solidly behind the president. "Ford did exactly the right thing [in pardoning Nixon]," he told the press; "it had nothing to do with Nixon personally." Landon also dismissed the Democratic nominee, former governor James E. Carter of Georgia, "Do you know anyone who has figured him out?" And Landon was happy with his long life in Kansas. "We preferred the simple but more intelligent life of Kansas to Washington. There are some intelligent people in Washington, but there are more of 'em in Kansas."

The Republican delegates were surveyed just prior to convention week. The striking details were that 85 percent had held party office, that 76 percent were Protestant, that 62 percent described themselves as conservative or very conservative.

Reagan's challenge was most persuasive to the uncommitted delegates. "I'm not quite sure how I find myself in this position," Reagan said in Los Angeles. "But if it's the Lord's will—that's all I ask—to do what I can to serve and to serve Him."

A sixty-two-year-old president who had never run for national office and who had spent his political career dreaming about becoming Speaker of the House was in a fight to the finish with a sixty-five-year-old former governor who had spent most of his life as a Democrat. The battle was heavily weighted toward the president from the first clash, when Ford won a Rules Committee decision that he did not have to name his running mate before he was nominated. The history of contested GOP conventions suggested that the candidate who won the first procedural question, however small the issue, was usually the winning candidate.

Reagan fought on. Upon arrival at the airport, he was asked if he could still win on the first ballot. He replied, "Yes," and then he joked, "Easier on the second."

On the first night, retiring vice president Nelson Rockefeller, sixty-six, and Senator Barry Goldwater, sixty-seven, appeared together on the podium. The intention was to show that old adversaries could walk together.

Nonetheless, the fight had moved past the old warriors to the hotel lobbies where Reagan was politicking in earnest. "There is no way I will consider being the Vice President on a ticket at this convention," Reagan told Indiana delegates. "I have not come here for that purpose. If I fail in the bid I am making, I will return to the position of an independent commentator and critic of the political scene."

The platform was written by the Goldwater-Reagan conservative wing of the party. The party opposed affirmative action as a quota system, opposed a national health insurance, opposed forced busing, opposed deficit spending and the unbalanced federal budget, opposed wage and price controls, opposed federal welfare, opposed amnesty for Vietnam protesters.

On foreign policy, the party was an unbowed Cold Warrior, calling for "superior national defense," and declaring "commitment to Israel is fundamental and enduring." The Soviet Union was anathema. The party wanted the army increased to sixteen divisions.

The platform also attacked the Democrats. "The Democrats' [1976] platform repeats the same thing on every page: more government, more spending, more inflation. . . . The Republican platform says the opposite—less government, less spending, less inflation. In other words, we want you to retain more of your money, money that represents the worth of your labors." In an echo of McKinley days, the platform crooned, "We do care about your getting paid in *sound dollars.*"

Reagan's boom surged and then fell short. The mood of the convention, still wounded by Watergate revelations, was to choose a moderate standard-bearer. Ford was nominated on the first ballot on Wednesday evening, August 18. The contest between Ford and Reagan was the closest first ballot vote in modern party history—1,187 for Ford, 1,070 for Reagan. On the alphabetical roll call of states, Ford was not over the top until West Virginia at 1:30 A.M. Eastern Standard Time.

A relieved president announced that he would not press Reagan to accept the second spot. Ford met with advisers late in the night to whittle the choices to four names, including party vice chairman Anne Armstrong of Texas. "But what a gamble it would be!" Ford later recalled thinking at the time.*

Ford chose Dole of Kansas. "A man with whom I felt very comfortable," Ford later recalled. "We had been friends for years in the House. He had supported my effort to become Minority Leader, and I had re-

*Ford, *A Time to Heal,* p. 402.

turned the favor in 1971 when he wanted to be named chairman of the Republican National Committee.*

At 10:30 A.M. Thursday, the president called Dole's hotel suite. "We'll be a great team," Ford told Dole, who accepted cheerfully.

That evening on live national television the president used his acceptance speech to challenge Democratic candidate Carter to several televised debates. Ford also made the best speech of his career. "We will wage a winning campaign in every region of this country, from the snowy fields of Minnesota to the sandy plains of Georgia. We concede not a single state. I speak not of a Republican victory but a victory for the American people. You at home listening tonight, you are the people who pay the taxes and obey the laws. You are the people who make our system work. You are the people who make America what it is. It is from your ranks that I come and on your side that I stand. Having become Vice President and President without expecting or seeking either, I have a special feeling toward these high offices. To me the Presidency and Vice Presidency were not prizes to be won but a duty to be done."

Ford was regarded a hardworking man with limited electioneering gifts. He surprised the party by conducting a skillful campaign against a well-financed majority party with an attractive candidate in Carter. The three televised debates were such a success that they established the event as a tradition of subsequent campaigns.

By November the polls showed that Ford had pulled even with Carter in the big electoral college states. There was no overriding issue of the campaign, so the candidates talked about themselves. The television advertising on both sides was nonconfrontational and tended to level the differences between the parties.

In Texas Carter tried a weak attack, "Gerald Ford has been in the White House as long as John Kennedy was President. Can you think of a single program that he's put forward that's been accepted?"

The same day in New York Ford appeared with New York Yankee stars and avoided any talk about Carter at all.

Senator Dole was assigned the old Nixon role of Republican partisan, and election eve he stayed on the attack in St. Louis: "[The Democrats] can't talk about their programs because they don't have any, so [their vice presidential nominee Walter] Mondale says Watergate, Watergate, Watergate." Dole accused Carter of America-bashing. "I remember Governor Carter saying America is weak, America is not respected. But there's a lot right about America. And American voters are going to stand up for America tomorrow."

*Ford, *A Time to Heal*, pp. 403–404.

Eighty million voted. Carter won the closest electoral college contest since the 1916 election between Wilson and Hughes.

The Ford-Dole ticket gained thirty-eight million votes and twenty-seven states, including Illinois, Michigan, and California for 241 electoral votes. The Carter-Mondale ticket gained forty million votes and twenty-three states, including the Solid South, for 297 electoral votes. The Republican inability to hold retiring vice president Rockefeller's New York gave the election to the Democrats. A poll showed that of the voters who decided in the last days of the contest, 60 percent voted for Carter.

The Democrats retained their power in the Congress. The new Ninety-fifth Congress would show a House of 292 Democrats to 145 Republicans. In the Senate the Democrats retained the power, 62–38. The worst Republican defeat was in Ohio, where Democrat challenger Howard Metzenbaum defeated incumbent senator Robert Taft, Jr., grandson of the president and son of Senator Robert A. Taft. There was now total Democratic rule in Washington.

Jimmy Carter told Speaker of the House Tip O'Neill of Massachusetts, "I'll be calling you soon and we'll sit down and talk about Congress.

★ 1980 ★

James Earle Carter's majority administration was threatened by foreign affairs in the Middle East and Latin America, and was weighed down by the treachery of the Soviets.

The Republicans were now such a minority in Congress and in the state houses—the weakest numbers since the New Deal—that the party was free to develop aggressive philosophical arguments and to engage charismatic ideological candidates. The question was which way would the GOP go in the face of a Democratic power base that favored the liberalism of big government? The conservatism of less government and aggressive military preparedness was regarded as failed after the 1976 defeat. Republican pundit George F. Will even wrote, "Ronald Reagan has run his last race."

Ronald Reagan had campaigned hard for Ford in the general election and was urged by loyalists after the election to declare his candidacy for 1980. "I wasn't the reluctant candidate I'd been in 1965 and 1976," Reagan later recalled. "I wanted to be president. But I really believed that what happened next wasn't up to me, it was up to the people: If there was a real people's movement to get me to run then I'd say I'd do it, but I was going to wait and see."*

On midterm election day, 1978, the Carter administration was faced with the sudden, violent collapse of the government of Iran, an event that would trouble American foreign policy for decades. Carter held emergency meetings on Iran the weekend before the election. Secretary of State Cyrus Vance commented, "We fully support the efforts of [Shah Mohammad Reza Pahlavi, head of Iran] to restore order while continuing his program of liberalization."

Also on election day, in Paris, exiled Iranian opposition leader the Ayatollah Ruholla Khomeini, accused America of backing the shah with forty-five thousand American advisers. Khomeini said that his followers were hostile to the United States.

The midterm elections did not reflect the deteriorating situation in the Mideast. Republicans made modest gains in the new Ninety-sixth Congress, including thirty-four-year-old newcomer Newt Gingrich of Georgia in the House.

In Arkansas state attorney general Bill Clinton, thirty-two, defeated GOP state chairman A. Lynne Lowe for the governorship, making Clinton the youngest governor since Republican Harold Stassen of Minnesota was elected at thirty-one in 1938.

Two days after the election, Harold Stassen of Minnesota, now seventy-one, declared that he would be a candidate for the Republican presidential nomination in 1980. Stassen said he would run on a platform "to clean out the corruption in Washington" and to "overcome inflation with full employment."

Over the next year the Carter administration struggled and failed in Iran. On November 4, 1979, Khomeini agents overran the American Embassy in Teheran, Iran, and took more than one hundred American citizens hostage. Khomeini rebuffed all attempts to negotiate a quick end to the crisis, including rejecting the pope's intercession on November 10.

Three days later in New York, Ronald Reagan, now sixty-eight, announced his candidacy for the White House, joining a field of ten announced GOP hopefuls. Reagan's theme was the restoration of American greatness at home and abroad. "I don't agree that our nation must resign itself to inevitable decline, yielding its proud position to other hands," Reagan declared. "I am totally unwilling to see this country fail in its obligation to itself and to the other free peoples of the world." On the issue of the inflation-wracked economy, Reagan tearfully recalled his childhood, when his father had been fired at Christmastime in the mid-

---

*Ronald Reagan, *An American Life* (New York: Simon & Schuster, 1990), p. 205.

dle of the depression. "I cannot and will not stand by while inflation and joblessness destroy the dignity of our people."

The same day Reagan announced his candidacy, there was a widely used Associated Press photograph of two unshaven Iranians using an American flag to haul away trash at the U.S. Embassy compound in Teheran. In December the Soviets invaded Afghanistan. Carter's flaccid response was to cancel grain sales to the Soviet Union and to cancel the American participation in the Moscow Olympics.

The presidential year 1980 opened with a January Republican caucus vote in Iowa that surprised the press when former Republican National Committee chairman George Bush of Texas outpaced Ronald Reagan. The New Hampshire primary in late February was the first serious contest for the huge Republican field—in addition to Bush and Reagan were Representative Phillip M. Crane of Illinois, former treasury secretary John B. Connally of Texas, Representative John B. Anderson of Illinois, Senator Howard Baker of Tennessee, and Senator Bob Dole of Kansas.

Debates in New Hampshire illustrated the colorful range of political opinions. In domestic affairs, Bush favored indexing tax rates. Baker and Dole wanted a balanced budget amendment to the Constitution. Anderson supported freedom of choice on abortion. Crane wanted a return to the gold standard. Connally wanted a moratorium on taxing interest in savings accounts. Reagan called for a freeze on federal hiring and a 30 percent federal tax cut over three years.

The most important event in the New Hampshire primary was the famous debate at Nashua High School on the Saturday before the election. The unwieldy format of seven candidates on a dais led the Reagan and Bush forces to propose a debate just between their two candidates. Federal election agents ruled that Editor Jon Breen's *Nashua Telegraph* newspaper could not sponsor the debate unless all candidates were included. Reagan solved the dilemma by putting up the seven thousand dollars needed to rent the facility. Eventually Reagan extended invitations to the other candidates. The night of the debate, six candidates arrived (Connally stayed away) to find on the stage one table and two chairs. Bush and Reagan sat down, leaving Dole, Baker, Crane, and Anderson milling behind. The confusion led to jeers from the two thousand in the audience.

"I decided I should explain to the crowd," Reagan later recalled in his memoirs, "what the delay was all about and started to speak. But as I did, an editor of the Nashua newspaper [Jon Breen] shouted to the sound man, 'Turn Mr. Reagan's microphone off.' Well, I didn't like that—we were paying the freight for the debate and he was acting as if his newspaper was still sponsoring it—and so I turned to him, with the microphone still on, and said the first thing that came to my mind: *'I am* *paying for this microphone, Mr. Breen!'* Well, for some reason my words hit the audience, whose emotions were already worked up, like a sledge-hammer. The crowd roared and just went wild. I may have won the debate, the primary—and the nomination—right there. After the debate, our people told me the gymnasium parking lot was littered with Bush-for-President badges."*

Under chilly, cloudy skies Reagan did win the New Hampshire primary. Reagan scored so heavily, with 50 percent of the vote, that he ended all but the most splinter challenges. Reagan told the press of his victory, "When we go to Vermont tomorrow, we won't need an airplane. We'll fly over there on what happened tonight." Reagan celebrated his win by reorganizing his staff and naming New York lawyer and former CIA agent William J. Casey as his new campaign director.

Dole said of his defeat, "Obviously there's not much of a campaign out there." Dole also suggested there might be room for a Ford boom: "I would guess you'll be hearing from President Ford."

Ford stayed out. Reagan swept through the rest of the primaries to gather a mountain of delegates by the July convention.

As the Republicans gathered in Detroit, the national news was alarming to the Reagan conservatives. Overseas, the hostage crisis continued in Iran while the Soviets continued a belligerent stance throughout the Mideast. At home, inflation was soaring while the stock and bond markets were crushed. And the Supreme Court handed down a decision, *Fullilove v. Klutznick,* that permitted Congress to impose racial quotas in awarding money to federal projects.

The tasks for the Detroit convention were to write a strong social conservative platform and to choose a virile, viable vice president. An early casualty of the platform debate was the co-chair of the party, Mary Crisp, who argued over feminist themes. "Our party has endorsed and worked for the ERA [Equal Rights Amendment] for forty years. Now we are reversing our position and are about to bury the rights of over 100 million American women under a heap of platitudes. Even worse is that our party is asking for a constitutional amendment to ban abortions."

Detroit's Joe Louis Arena, named for the man who'd backed Willkie in 1940, was tailor-made as a soundstage for a Republican-produced live television special on Ronald Reagan. The theme of the week was written across the face of the podium, "Together . . . a New Beginning."

Before leaving California for the convention, Reagan used the popular Sunday television show *60 Minutes* to launch a partisan attack on Carter. "I think very definitely the Soviet Union is going to throw a few

*Reagan, *An American Life,* p. 213.

bones to Mr. Carter during the coming campaign in order to help him continue as president. I would be very worried about me if the Soviet Union wanted me to be president."

The first day of the convention brought the astonishing news that President Carter's brother, Billy Carter, had registered as a foreign agent and disclosed that over the past two years he had received hundreds of thousands of dollars from the Soviet-backed and anti-Israeli Libyan government headed by dictator Muammar Qaddafi.

At the convention Gerald Ford appeared on the podium with his popular wife, Betty. Ford began the evening's attacks on Carter. "Last November 4," Ford said of the Iran hostage crisis, "more than 50 of us were taken hostage in Iran. This November 4, with their tragedy burning in our conscience, we will vote to elect a new American president."

Senator Richard Lugar of Indiana was cheerful. "Thank goodness for an election year in this country. We will soon have in Ronald Reagan a president who is prepared to kick out the blocks and let the productive wheels of the great economy roll once more."

Former defense secretary Donald H. Rumsfeld, a dark horse for the second spot on the ticket, blasted Carter as "perhaps the most naive president in modern times" and added, "You have heard of the proposals to change a president's term to six years. The best argument I know against the six-year term is sitting in the White House today."

The Republican platform was released on the first day without any

Ronald and Nancy Reagan vs. Jimmy Carter, 1980. Denver Post, July 1, 1980.

serious controversy. Planks called for large tax cuts, shrinking the size of the federal payroll, restricting federal support of health care including abortions, and school tuition tax credits.

"Properly informed," the platform argued, "our people can make the right decisions affecting personal or general welfare, free of pervasive and heavy-handed intrusion by the central government into the decision-making process. This tenet is the genius of representative democracy."

On the second day, Ford removed his name from consideration for the vice presidency and urged Reagan to choose George Bush. Reagan commented, "I'm getting the same advice from everyone—I ought to go with Bush."

Bush, waiting to be called upon, gave a witty, candid remark, "I don't like this waiting. [It's] giving me peristaltic contractions in my lower colon. We'll have some X-rays soon, in keeping with my policy of full disclosure."

Reagan was nominated unanimously and chose Bush as expected. Reagan recalled in his memoirs about telephoning Bush after Ford had left his suite. "George," Reagan began on the phone, "it seems to me that the fellow who came the closest and got the next most votes for president ought to be the logical choice for vice-president. Will you take it?"*

Bush also later recalled the telephone call. "It came out of the clear blue sky. He was most gracious in the invitation, and, of course, I was very pleased."

Reagan's commanding acceptance speech emphasized that the Reagan administration would deliver a 30 percent tax cut and would challenge the Soviet Union with an aggressive buildup of American arms. Reagan's speech held up the superb metaphor of making America into "a shining city on a hill." However, Reagan also used his speech for a knock on Carter and the Democrats: "The major issue of this campaign is the direct political, personal and moral responsibility of the Democratic party—in the White House and in Congress—for this unprecedented calamity which has befallen us."

Reagan closed by departing from his prepared speech on the TelePrompTer to call for a silent prayer by the delegates. "Can we doubt that only a divine providence placed this land, this island of freedom here as a refuge for all those people who yearn to breathe freely: Jews and Christians enduring persecution behind the Iron Curtain, boat people of Southeast Asia, of Cuba and of Haiti, the victims of drought and famine in Africa, the freedom fighters of Afghanistan and our own countrymen held in savage captivity. I'll confess that I've been a little afraid to sug-

*Reagan, *An American Life,* p. 216.

gest what I'm going to suggest. I'm more afraid not to. Can we begin our crusade joined together in a moment of silent prayer? God Bless America."

The campaign was a seamless triumph for Ronald Reagan. There were two debates; however, the first from Baltimore included only Reagan and independent candidate John B. Anderson. Stubborn Carter finally agreed to the lone presidential debate in late October.

Meanwhile, Reagan kept up the attack, especially on the endless hostage crisis in Iran. "I believe that this [Carter] administration's foreign policy helped create the entire situation that made their kidnap possible," said Reagan in Kentucky. "And I think the fact that they've been there that long is a humiliation and disgrace to this country."

The presidential television debate on Friday, October 28 at Cleveland's Convention Center established that Reagan was a complete master of the audience. During a temperamental exchange between the two candidates, President Carter claimed that Reagan had started his career by opposing Medicare.

"There you go again," responded a grinning Reagan, winning a loud roar of laughter from the audience. Reagan countered Carter's charge by saying that he had opposed one Medicare bill and supported another, and that he supported medical care for the elderly.

Long after the debate, it was suggested that Reagan's campaign director, William Casey, had obtained a copy of President Carter's briefing book in preparation for the debate, and that this, rather than Reagan's quick wit, explained why Reagan was able to blunt so many of Carter's points. What is usually not mentioned about this scandal is that at the time the media pundits declared that Carter had won the debate "on points."

Election eve, Reagan and Bush campaigned together in Reagan's birth state of Illinois. A sign held up behind the picture of them read "Reagan Plays Well in Peoria." Reagan flew on to California, where he closed his campaign with a nationally televised speech in which he pounded the hostage issue: "I know that tonight the fate of America's 52 hostages is very much on the minds of all of us."

Eighty-six million voted. Reagan took nearly forty-four million votes (51 percent) and forty-four states for 489 electoral college votes, including every large state. Reagan won California by one and a half million votes. Carter took thirty-six million votes (42 percent) and six states for 49 electoral votes. Third-party candidate John B. Anderson attracted five and a half million votes (5 percent) for no states or electoral votes.

Reagan's victory was called a tidal wave for conservatism. Impor-

Reagan vs. Carter, 1980. Providence Journal-Bulletin. *Repr.* Denver Post.

tantly, in the new Ninety-seventh Congress, the Republicans won control of the Senate for the first time since Eisenhower's administration: fifty-three Republicans to forty-seven Democrats. The Democrats remained in control of the House, but it was a shaky hold that depended upon Southern districts that had voted heavily for Reagan.

Notable Republican victories included several Senate newcomers, including Alfonse D'Amato of New York, Dan Quayle of Indiana, and Arlen Specter of Pennsylvania. Democratic survivors of the Reagan landslide included the reelection of Gary Hart of Colorado and John Glenn of Ohio.

The stock market's reaction to Reagan was explosive. The day after the election was the heaviest trading day in history at 92.64 million shares on the New York Stock Exchange. The threat to the stock and bond markets remained hyperinflation. The Federal Reserve discount rate, then at 11 percent, was expected to tighten to 12 percent momentarily. The Standard & Poor 500 index stood at 131.29, and bellwether growth stock IBM traded at 68. Commented General Electric president Reginald H. Jones, "With this landslide sweep of a more conservative economy stance, you're going to see a considerable encouragement of the private sector."

An unusual detail of the election was that Carter conceded the contest so early on election night that when Reagan got the congratulatory telephone call from the president, about 7:30 P.M. Los Angeles time, the West had not yet finished voting.

★ 1984 ★

The Great Communicator Ronald Reagan delivered on his promises to cut the income tax and to push back at the "evil empire" of the Soviet Union.

Fate nearly stopped the president only seventy days into his office. Monday afternoon, March 30, 1981, President Reagan addressed a grumpy audience of AFL-CIO members at the Hilton Hotel in Washington, D.C. "Together we will make America great again," the president closed.

Reagan was not wearing a bulletproof vest that day. He left the hotel by the T Street exit, heading for his limousine at the curb. The president waved to a small crowd of spectators and press personnel. There was a quick series of gunshots from the direction of the sidewalk. Secret service agent Jerry Parr yanked the president from the action and shoved him head first into the open limo door and onto the floor of the rear seat. Parr jumped on top of the president, the door closed, and Parr ordered the driver to get to the White House.

Behind them, wounded on the ground with bullets meant for Reagan, were White House press secretary James Brady, secret service agent Timothy J. McCarthy, and D.C. police officer Thomas K. Delhanty.

The shooter was a twenty-six-year-old Colorado man named John W. Hinckley, Jr., who presented nothing more than the anarchy of previous presidential assassins such as Guiteau, Czolgosz, Oswald.

In the speeding-away limousine, the president did not realize he had been shot. A .22-caliber bullet had deflected off the armored limousine and penetrated Reagan under the left armpit. It struck the top of the seventh rib, deflected three inches into the lower left lung. It stopped approximately one inch from the heart.

Reagan thought the pain in his side was because he'd broken a rib when the agent had landed on top of him. "But when I sat on the seat," Reagan later recalled, "and the pain wouldn't go away and suddenly I found that I was coughing up blood, we both decided that maybe I had broken a rib and punctured a lung." In the car, Reagan joked to Parr about their cinematic escape. But then, at Dupont Circle, Parr realized that the red blood meant a lung injury, and he ordered the car to George Washington University Hospital.

"By then," Reagan recalled, "my handkerchief was sopped with blood and [Parr] handed me his. Suddenly, I realized I could barely breathe. No matter how hard I tried, I couldn't get enough air. I was frightened and started to panic a little. I was just not able to inhale enough air."*

The president was badly hurt and didn't know it. At the hospital, there was no stretcher waiting. Reagan got out of the car and was helped by secret service agents to the hospital door. After fifteen yards, the president started to collapse. A paramedic helped Reagan into the emergency room, where the president fell to one knee.

"I can't breathe," Reagan whispered.

They carried the president to a stretcher and cut away his clothes. "The first we knew about his chest wound," recalled a doctor, "was when they cut off his thousand dollar suit and we saw a few drops of blood on his shirt. I had been really afraid that we had a very serious situation on hand. I figured that if he had been shot, that was something that could be taken care of. But if he looked that bad after a coronary thrombosis, I would have feared for his life."†

The president was taken immediately into surgery. Four hours later in the recovery room Reagan was alert enough from the anesthesia to visit with the first lady, Nancy Reagan. In the middle of the night, the doctors judged the president improved enough to allow him to breathe on his own. As a medical worker pulled the endotracheal tube from the president's mouth, he said, "Well, this is it."

Reagan overheard in alarm, and, because he could not speak, he reached for a notepad to write to the nurse, "What does he mean—this is it?" The nurse explained all was well. Reagan wrote a note, "Where am I?"

He was told, "You're in the recovery room."

Reagan wrote, "How long have I been here? How long will I have to stay here?"

Meanwhile back at the White House, there was an unhappy constitutional controversy about the chain of command with the president wounded. Vice President Bush was aboard *Air Force 2* enroute from Dallas–Ft. Worth to Austin when he was telephoned at 2:40 P.M. and told the initial inaccurate report that the president was unhurt in the shooting.

Secretary of State Alexander Haig arrived at the White House at 3:02 P.M. When Haig learned that the vice president had not been properly informed that the president had been hit by a bullet, contrary to the first

---

*Herbert L. Abrams, *"The President Has Been Shot": Confusion, Disability, and the 25th Amendment in the Aftermath of the Attempted Assassination of Ronald Reagan* (New York: Norton, 1992), p. 56.
†Ibid., p. 59.

Alexander Haig, Washington Post, *September 12, 1974.*

reports, he personally telephoned Bush in *Air Force 2.* The connection was poor. Bush said he would return to Washington as soon as possible. *Air Force 2* had to set down in Austin to refuel before leaving for Washington.

With Bush airborne and not easily accessible, there was general confusion at the White House Situation Room in the basement of the West Wing with regard to what to tell the press about the profound issue of succession in the event of catastrophe.

What happened was that at 4:14 P.M. deputy White House press secretary Larry Speakes, just back from the hospital, was grabbed by a frantic press corps and asked, on live TV, if the vice president was assuming emergency powers. Speakes, unaware of the planning by Haig and others in the Situation Room, answered evasively, "We just haven't crossed those bridges yet."

An alarmed Haig, watching Speakes' uninformed performance on the lone TV in the Situation Room, said "We've got to get him off," and then charged upstairs to take the podium.*

What the public next saw was handsome, grim-faced and winded Secretary of State Haig trying to correct the record himself. "We are in close touch with the vice president," he said helpfully. The trouble came when Haig was asked who was making decisions for the government right now?

"Constitutionally speaking, gentlemen," said Haig, "you have the president, the vice president, and the secretary of state, in that order, and

---

*Alexander Haig, *Caveat: Realism, Reagan and Foreign Policy* (N.Y.: Macmillan, 1984), p. 159.

should the President decide to transfer the helm, he will do so. As of now, I am in control here, in the White House, pending return of the vice president and in close touch with him. If something came up, I would check with him, of course."

Haig's representation was particular to the details of the moment—in the Situation Room, where senior members of the Cabinet were assembled—however it was inexact with regard to the 1947 Succession Act. Haig was fifth in line, not third.

When Haig returned to the Situation Room, he sparred with Defense Secretary Caspar Weinberger and White House chief counsel Fred Fielding over the ambiguity of his television statement. More significantly, Haig's use of the clause "constitutionally speaking," had been instantly misunderstood by the television audience. Subsequently, Haig has written that he was "guilty of a poor choice of words, and optimistic if I would be forgiven the imprecision out of respect for the tragedy of the occasion." Haig has conceded, "I ought to have said 'traditionally speaking' or 'administratively speaking' instead of 'constitutionally.' "*

At the time of the shooting, however, Haig's imprecision was only part of the larger confusion about the president's capacity to govern. Paragraph 3 of the Twenty-fifth Amendment, Presidential Succession, Disability, and Inability, was applicable at that moment and for some weeks afterward. The controversy over whether George Bush should have invoked Paragraph 3, as it was his power to do so, remained a sore point for the participants.

At 8:20 P.M. the vice president went on television to assure the nation. "The American government is functioning fully and effectively," he said, without answering the problem of the Twenty-fifth Amendment: Who decides capacity to govern? When?

Ronald Reagan's strength and luck outlasted the crisis of the shooting. Like a storybook hero, the president recovered his health presently, and for the next two years he demonstrated commanding leadership. The press had dubbed Reagan the Great Communicator, and the president used his power at full volume.

In domestic affairs, Congress gave Reagan the tax-cutting budget he asked for—thanks to the votes of Southern Democrats called the Boll Weevils who joined with minority leader Bob Michel of Indiana and the Republicans. In foreign affairs, Reagan joined with Prime Minister Margaret Thatcher of Great Britain and eventually Prime Minister Helmut Kohl of West Germany to strengthen NATO and to intimidate the Soviet Union. Reagan's budgets backed up his bully pulpit rhetoric by provid-

*Haig, *Caveat*, p. 164.

ing the American military with a variety of aggressive weapons, including the new MX missile, the B1 bomber, a six-hundred-ship navy with new aircraft carriers, and secret programs such as the Stealth aircraft.

The cost of defense buildup moved the United States from the world's largest creditor nation in 1980, with a national debt of one trillion dollars, to the world's largest debtor nation a decade later, with a national debt of four trillion dollars by 1992.

The buildup also meant that the Soviets were beggared in competition and reeling in retreat from the American technological onslaught. The Kremlin panicked right away. In May 1981 the decrepit dictator Brezhnev, the bloody-minded KGB chief Yuri Andropov, and the cunning future dictator Mikhail Gorbachev attended a secret Moscow confab to discuss the likelihood of an American nuclear first strike. The Soviets were falling down on their own bayonets. Desperate endgame measures included a Moscow-ordered Polish military crackdown on dissidents in December 1981. The Soviets also increased the KGB's disinformation campaigns against the popular American president.

The president's response in 1982 was to make a famous speech in which he labeled the sixty-five-year-old Soviet dictatorship "the evil empire." The president followed this accusation by announcing that he was going ahead with a massively expensive space- and ground-based antimissile and antisatellite screen, the Strategic Defense Initiative, nicknamed Star Wars.

By the midterm elections in 1982, Reagan wanted a Republican increase in the Congress to enable his tax cutting and defense buildup. The battle was uphill, however, owing to a drawn-out economic recession that had led to a swelling budget deficit (for fiscal year 1982, the deficit was $110 billion). Reagan would not raise taxes, nor would he cut back on defense expenditures. The election result was a standoff. The Democrats picked up twenty seats in the House—following a tradition dating back to the Civil War that the president's party would lose an average of nineteen seats in the midterm elections. The GOP did retain control in the Senate, including newcomer Pete Wilson of California.

Despite the costs, Reagan did not back off on his Cold War strategy. He simultaneously pressed the Soviets at the bargaining table over armament levels in Europe, while under the table the president unleashed William Casey's CIA in Afghanistan, Lebanon, Central America. Eventually, Reagan launched a military strike against the Soviet puppet Grenada in the Caribbean and approved a massive secret war against the Soviet puppet Nicaragua. In Europe, Reagan ordered the deployment of deadly Cruise and Pershing missiles.

Reagan's Cold War risks were great. The terrorist bombings in

Lebanon that destroyed the American embassy and then massacred a peacekeeping marine contingent were shocks to the country. Reagan wrote in his diary the night of the 1983 Lebanon embassy bombing, "Lord forgive me for the hatred I feel for the humans who can do such a cruel but cowardly deed."*

The Soviets' fear of Reagan's aggression was inept as well as cowardly—leading to their shooting down of an off-course Korean airliner over the Sakhalin peninsula in September 1983.

Presidential year 1984 began with the death of the new Soviet dictator Yuri Andropov and a full-scale disintegration of the Soviet economy. Meanwhile, Reagan traveled to Beijing to reinforce relations with the People's Republic of China. Reagan made certain that Moscow understood his antagonism. On August 11, 1984, just before the GOP convention in Dallas, Reagan underlined his Cold War temper when he made a half-mocking remark during a sound check for a radio broadcast from his California ranch. The president joked wryly, "My fellow Americans, I'm pleased to tell you today that that I've signed legislation that would outlaw Russia forever. We begin bombing in five minutes." The press overheard and hurriedly reported the president's remarks as a gaffe.

Coming in a presidential year, there was a momentary flap over the bombing remark. A brief bump in the polls for Democratic challenger Walter Mondale of Minnesota made a Reagan supporter joke, "If you had a significant Democrat candidate, this would be a dogfight. Then people could vote Reagan out of office, still liking him. But they also sense the incompetence on the other side. People who know Mondale like him, but very few know him. To others he comes across as whiny. People think they know Reagan. If you had someone else with hero worship, the election would be a question."

Within days of the bombing remark, a network poll showed Reagan had regained his gigantic lead over Mondale, 58 percent to 35 percent.

Mid-August, Vice President Bush led the first rush of 4,424 delegates and alternates into one-hundred-degree Texas weather to open the convention in Dallas. Republican National Committee chairman Frank J. Fahrenkopf remarked, "The biggest fear I have is overconfidence on the part of the activists we depend on as a minority party to go out and do our missionary work. I hope the convention will serve as an energizer for them."

The *energizer* the convention needed was the unmistakable evidence of a burgeoning American economy. The Standard & Poor 500 index

*Reagan, *An American Life,* p. 443.

closed the afternoon of the first day at 164.94, with bellwether IBM at 123. After a wearying bear market in the recession of '82, the Reagan Revolution was well begun with the first leg of a powerful bull market.

A Republican survey of the delegates and alternates produced unsurprising generalizations of the convention. Eighty-seven percent were white. Sixty-three percent were conservative or very conservative. Sixty-eight percent were against a tax increase. Sixty percent were Protestant. Sixty percent were college graduates. Forty-nine percent were female. Forty-six percent believed that abortions should be restricted. Twenty percent had annual incomes over one hundred thousand dollars.

The platform was accepted with cheers on the second night. It was a serene conservative document—anti-tax, anti-discrimination, anti-abortion, anti-Communist, anti-gun control, anti-welfare, anti public housing; pro death penalty, pro tuition tax credits, pro savings, pro growth, pro defense. In foreign affairs, the platform saluted the Grenada invasion and the support of freedom fighters (Contras) in Nicaragua.

The best partisan moment of the evening was when Housing Secretary Jack Kemp, a longtime Reagan loyalist, used the Republican platform's foreign policy plank to attack the Democratic party: "Millions of Americans no longer feel at home in a party whose leaders see no difference between the Soviet invasion of Afghanistan and the American liberation of Grenada." Kemp charged, *The leaders of the Democratic party aren't soft on communism. They're soft on democracy.*

The platform was blunt about the Soviets. "We hold a sober view of the Soviet Union," read a foreign affairs plank. "Its globalist ideology and its leadership obsessed with military power make it a threat to freedom and peace on every continent."

Reagan and Bush were nominated without opposition on the third night during a tightly scheduled, purposely routine television broadcast. The all-seeing television technology, with its mobile cameras and instant communications between performers, had now driven out all candor, risk taking, and spontaneity from the convention. The Republican party would never again permit the shocking confrontation of the 1964 convention to appear on live TV. What was left, forty-four years after the first experiment with television at the 1940 convention, was a four-day infomercial.

The nostalgic moment of the evening was when Senator Barry Goldwater of Arizona, now seventy-five, repeated his famous extremism remark at the podium to the cheers of the faithful. Goldwater also provided a passionate burst by accusing the Democrats of being war makers. "Every war in this century began and was fought under Democratic administration. You doubt me? World War I—Woodrow Wilson,

Democrat. World War II—Franklin Roosevelt, Democrat. Korean War—Harry Truman, Democrat. Vietnam—Jack Kennedy and Lyndon Johnson, both Democrats."

Ronald Reagan's last campaign began with his acceptance speech on August 23, 1984. The strength of the speech was an assault on the Democrats that would have pleased William McKinley, Theodore Roosevelt, William Howard Taft, Charles Evans Hughes, William Harding, Calvin Coolidge and Herbert Hoover: "The choices this year are not just between two different personalities, or between two political parties. They are between two different visions of the future, two fundamentally different ways of governing—their government of pessimism, fear and limits, or ours of hope, confidence, and growth. Their government sees people only as members of groups. Ours serves all the people of America as individuals. Theirs lives in the past, seeking to apply the old failed policies to an era that has passed them by. Ours learns from the past and strives to change by boldly charting a new course for the future."

George Bush vs. Geraldine Ferraro, 1984. Buffalo News. *Repr.* Washington Post, *October 20, 1984.*

The campaign was brief and one-sided. Reagan needed only to cite the gross national product—up 10 percent in the first quarter and 7 percent in the second—and the fact that inflation had shrunk to 4 percent per annum. On the other hand, Mondale had not only promised to raise taxes, then he'd also chosen Geraldine Ferraro as his running mate. Ferraro's tangled family finances dragged the Democratic ticket from behind to far behind.

There were two televised debates. Reagan delivered the most successful argument in all the presidential TV debates so far when he joked about Mondale, "I will not make age an issue in this campaign. I am not going to exploit for political purposes my opponent's youth and inexperience."

The polls never wavered in Reagan's commanding lead. The party hoped to ride the president's coattails to boost Republicans in Congress and the state houses.

Election eve, Reagan closed his campaign in California with GOP Governor George Deukmajian in Sacramento and later, in San Diego, with entertainer Wayne Newton leading "America the Beautiful."

George Bush closed his vice presidential campaigning in Houston, where he was greeted with placards such as "Baseball, Hot Dogs, Apple Pie and Reagan-Bush" and "Kick Ass George." After his single debate with Democrat Ferraro, Bush had remarked that he had "kicked some ass."

(Geraldine Ferraro's candidacy was not the first female run for the White House. In 1884, Washington attorney Belva Lockwood ran for president against Republican James G. Blaine and Democrat Grover Cleveland. Lockwood ran on a National Equal Rights party ticket and received 4,149 votes.)

More than ninety-two million voted. Reagan won the greatest electoral college landslide in GOP history, gaining 54.45 million votes (58 percent) and every state but Minnesota for 525 electoral votes. Mondale took 37.57 million votes (41 percent) and only his home state and the District of Columbia for 10 electoral votes. Exit polls showed that Reagan won 81 percent of conservatives, 68 percent of the self-employed, 67 percent of Protestants, 62 percent of males, 61 percent of whites, and 61 percent of independent voters.

Reagan's coattails were the question: The GOP retained control of the Senate, fifty-three Republicans to forty-seven Democrats, losing two Republican incumbents from the Midwest. In the House, however, the GOP picked up a few seats but remained in the distinct minority.

In Houston, Vice President Bush was interrupted in an election night thank-you speech by a supporter crying, "Bush in '88." The vice president tried to ignore the charge, but the crowd of supporters cheered loudly. At Andrews Air Force Base later, Bush remarked on his future, "I'm really not decided whether I'm going to do it or not, and I have the luxury of plenty of time to make up my mind."

★ 1988 ★

Reagan's second administration continued the pressure on the despotic and beggarly Soviet Union and its puppets even while the president suffered a partisan drubbing at the hands of the Democratic Congress—the infamous Iran-Contra scandal.

Reagan's State of the Union address in 1985 established the Reagan Doctrine of the Cold War. "We must stand by our democratic allies," the president declared. "And we must not break faith with those who are risking their lives—on every continent from Afghanistan to Nicaragua—to defy Soviet-supported aggression and secure rights that have been ours from birth." Reagan mentioned his concerns about the hostile Democrats in the House and Senate: "It is essential that the Congress continue all facets of our assistance to Central America. I want to work with you to support the democratic forces whose struggle is tied to our own security."

In April yet another new Soviet dictator, Konstantin Chernenko, died, and young dictator Mikhail Gorbachev was installed at the Kremlin. Gorbachev was a Communist party zealot, and at first he pretended he had other things to do besides negotiate with the United States. By the fall of 1985, Reagan and Gorbachev had met at Geneva to begin work on a strategic arms reduction treaty. The Soviets were failing, and they aimed to use arms reduction as camouflage for the weakness of their armed forces and rot of their system.

In mid 1985, Reagan underwent surgery to remove a cancerous growth in his colon. Again the president and his staff did not follow the instructions of the third paragraph of the Twenty-fifth Amendment and transfer the presidency to Bush until Reagan was fully recovered.

Late in 1985, Reagan, worried by the growing budget deficits, urged Congress to give him the Gramm-Hollings-Rudman Bill to control federal spending—the first attempt to return to the longtime GOP plank for a balanced budget. Reagan's diary on December 10 mentioned his negotiations about the spending bill: "Began the day with a meeting, the Dem and Republican Congressional leadership. Spent most of our time on the Gramm Rudman Hollings bill which later in the day I found had made its way out of the conference. Not as good as we would have wanted but still a bill I'll have to sign." At the bottom of the entry Reagan added mention of a landmine that would damage his administration: "Bud M back from England and his meeting with the Iranian 'go between' [Iranian arms merchant Mnucher Ghorbanifar] who turns out to be a devious character. Our plan regarding the hostages is a 'no go.' "*

What the president was short-handing in his diary was the tangled web of counterterrorism, guerrilla warfare, and arms dealing that would become the Iran-Contra scandal a year later. Reagan had signed on to the deal while he was recovering from cancer surgery at Walter Reed the summer before. In December 1985 White House national security aide Robert "Bud" McFarlane had traveled to Europe to propose a deal in which American-backed Israel would sell anti-Western Iran powerful weapons systems in hope that this would aid release of American hostages in Lebanon held by Iranian-backed militias. Later this deal would include a component that skimmed cash off the arms sales and diverted it to financing the American-backed Contra guerrilla force fighting to bring down the Soviet-backed Nicaragua Sandinista government.

Republican defeats in the 1986 midterm elections were the backdrop for the Iran-Contra scandal. Reagan and Bush campaigned hard for both houses. Tradition was against them, for the six-year mark in every two-term presidency saw a sharp loss for the president's party. The Republicans lost six Senate seats and control of the Senate. Losses in the House expanded the Democratic control. The new 100th Congress would show a strong, spirited Democratic majority that was moved to advance many of its members as candidates for the 1988 presidential race.

An ominous coincidence was that on election day the first story appeared about White House aide McFarlane's clandestine meetings with the Iranians about the hostages. Revelations followed quickly from many news sources in the Mideast. On November 13, the president went on television to deny the rumors of arms-for-hostages shenanigans. "We did not," Reagan said, "repeat, did not trade weapons or anything else for hostages, nor will we."

The president was speaking with superficial accuracy. The Israelis, acting for the United States, had sold Iran arms in hope of freeing hostages. The whole truth about the Iranian arms shipments was far more dangerous to the administration than a swap for hostages. Days later, the president met with chief of staff Don Regan and Attorney General Ed Meese and learned what Reagan later called "a bombshell." The National Security Council Director, Admiral John Poindexter, and his assistant, Colonel Oliver North, had diverted part of the money the Iranians paid the Israelis to support the Contras in Nicaragua.

*Reagan, *An American Life*, p. 510.

Reagan's diary entry that day illustrated his shock to the point of using the Watergate term *smoking gun.* "After the meeting in the Situation Room, Ed. M and Don R. told me of a smoking gun. On one of the arms shipments the Iranians had paid Israel a higher purchase price than we were getting. The Israelis put the difference in a secret bank account. Then our Col. North (N.S.C.) gave the money to the 'Contras.' . . . North didn't tell me about this. Worst of all, John P. found out about it and didn't tell me. This may call for resignations."*

The president ordered an investigation, but the damage was done. Resignations did indeed follow from Don Regan, John Poindexter, Oliver North, Robert MacFarlane (who attempted suicide), and a bevy of shadowy players in the tangled deals. Eventually the scandal would sweep to CIA director Bill Casey, who died of brain tumor before he could be questioned about the extent of his role in the scandal.

The Democratic Congress, dominated by young, ambitious Democrats such as Senator Joe Biden of Delaware and Senator Gary Hart of Colorado, did not hesitate to blast the Reagan administration for the Iran-Contra scandal. The summer of 1987 saw a televised Joint Congressional Committee investigation that at once dazzled and confused the public. The chief Democratic charge was that the administration had lied to Congress about the Contra war in Nicaragua. Lesser charges were that Casey, Poindexter, and North had created a secret operation that ran wild inside the government, without any congressional oversight.

Through 1987, President Reagan was hard-pressed to handle the damage to his authority by both the secret the Nicaragua war and the secret arms deals with the Iranians. The president brought in a new chief of staff, former senator Howard Baker of Tennessee, to restore confidence in the White House. Vice President Bush was also pulled into the scandal by charges that his staff was intimately involved in the Contra effort.

In his memoirs years later, the president confessed his frustration with the scandal. "If I could do it over again," Reagan wrote of the days following his learning of the illegal diversion of funds to the Contras by Poindexter and North, "I would bring both of them into the Oval Office and say, 'Okay, John and Ollie, level with me. Tell me what really happened and what is it that you have been hiding from me, Tell me everything.' If I had done that, at least I wouldn't be sitting here, writing this book, still ignorant of some of the things that went on during the Iran-Contra affair."†

---

*Reagan, *An American Life,* p. 530.
†Reagan, *An American Life,* p. 543.

Presidential year 1988 began with a donnybrook for the Republican presidential nomination between Reagan's heir apparent, Vice President Bush, and a field of deft hopefuls. Chief challenger was Senate minority leader Bob Dole of Kansas, who campaigned as a moderate. Also contending were Reagan loyalist Jack Kemp of New York, who sought the conservative vote; former governor Pete Du Pont of Delaware; television evangelist Pat Robertson, who emphasized anti-abortion and school prayer; and maverick former secretary of state Alexander M. Haig.

The primary campaign began with a scare for front-runner Bush when Dole took the tiny Iowa caucus. The vice president's campaign staff, led by prominent aides Roger Ailes, Lee Atwater, Peggy Noonan, responded with aggressive advertising in New England—what was called negative advertising because it included attacks on rivals. Bush demonstrated electioneering skill the last snowy week before the New Hampshire vote by shedding his image as Yankee statesman and turning to handshaking confession.

"They say I was born comfortable," Bush told a breakfast meeting in Nashua, New Hampshire, while a blizzard raged outside the building, "and they're right. Not fabulously wealthy, but even they have their trials. John Kennedy once said to a friend, 'You don't know how hard it was growing up in that house.' His parents made demands. Mine [Bush's deceased father was Senator Prescott Bush of Connecticut] did too."

Famous midnight voters at Dixville Notch, New Hampshire, gave Bush the early lead with eleven votes to Dole's six. The full New Hampshire result showed Bush with 38 percent to Dole's 29 percent and the others trailing badly.

Bush was relieved. "I have a lot in common with Mark Twain," he said on election night. "Reports of my death were greatly exaggerated."

Dole was miffed, and he revealed his reputation for testy rejoinder when he told a television interviewer that Bush should "stop lying about my record."

Three weeks later Bush prevailed in the so-called Super Tuesday primary that grouped large Southern states together on the same day. By spring the vice president was completely in control of the nomination.

Preparing for the New Orleans convention in mid-August, George Bush continued his confessional style to the press. He reflected about his political education in his adopted state of Texas, where he had once courted and won LBJ's approval. Later Bush had courted and won Richard Nixon's support. Bush's failure to win a Senate seat in '64 and again in '70 left him available to his mentor, Nixon, for appointed jobs in Washington, and Bush served Nixon as chairman of the GOP, envoy to Red China, and director of the CIA.

The New Orleans convention in the huge, dazzling Sugardome opened with a spectacular farewell night to Ronald Reagan. As with Eisenhower, there was the irony that the Twenty-second Amendment was the only thing that stopped Reagan from a third term in the White House—and there were placards recommending "Reagan for VP '88."

Reagan responded to the affection with a valedictory speech the first night of the convention. "Many's the time I've said a prayer of thanks to all Americans who placed this trust in my hand, and tonight please accept our heartfelt gratitude, Nancy's and mine, for this special time you've given in our lives. Just a moment ago, you multiplied the honor with a moving tribute. And being only human, there's a part of me that would like to take credit for what we've achieved. But tonight, before we do anything else, let us remember, that tribute really belongs to the 245 million citizens who make up the greatest, and first three words of our Constitution: We the people . . ." Reagan also contributed his partisan wit by endorsing Bush with a reference to his famous movie role of George Gipp, the Notre Dame football star: "So, George, I'm in your corner. . . . But George, just one personal request: Go out there and win one for the Gipper."

The Republican platform was devoted to winning with the ideas of the Reagan Revolution. On foreign policy, the platform was definitive that the Soviets must quit all support of communist regimes, particularly in Nicaragua. The party opposed a Palestinian state and insisted that Jerusalem remain an undivided city.

In domestic affairs, the platform was traditionally antitax and in favor of cutting many taxes restricting capital growth. There were planks calling for a balanced budget, a two-year budget cycle, a presidential line-item veto, a required supermajority in Congress to raise taxes, and a toddler tax credit for preschool children to offset child-care costs.

In social policy, the platform opposed abortion and insisted on a human life amendment to the Constitution. For the first time there was an Acquired Immune Deficiency Syndrome (AIDS) plank: "AIDS education should emphasize that abstinence from drug abuse and sexual activity outside of marriage is the safest way to avoid infection with the AIDS virus."

The platform argued: "This election will bring change. The question is: Will it be change and progress with the Republicans or change and chaos with the Democrats?"

George Bush contributed a deal of controversy the second day when, in the heat at dockside before the Mississippi riverboat *Natchez*, he announced his choice for his running mate, Senator Danforth J. "Dan" Quayle of Indiana, a handsome young conservative first elected with

Reagan in '80 and now in his second term in the Senate. No one had placed Quayle as more than a dark horse on the list of possible choices, and the party was unsure how to respond. 'All I know is that he's 41, from Indiana and seems attractive," said a West Virginia delegate. "He looks like one of George Bush's sons."

Other Bush loyalists were pleased. "He's an excellent choice," said Representative Dick Cheney of Wyoming, future defense secretary. "There are a lot of us in our 40s who are happy to see a colleague, a peer, become part of the leadership."

Quayle's credentials as a Reagan conservative were not at issue, rather his age, his wealth, and the obvious fact that, though he was telegenic and cheerful, he did not present what detractors called an intellectual weight on camera. Quayle was married to an attractive and articulate attorney, Marilyn Tucker Quayle, and had three healthy children. "Life has been very good to me," Quayle admitted. "I never had to worry about where I was going to go." Other reservations about Quayle included a notorious Florida incident with a Playboy model, and then there were the foggy details of his avoiding the draft with an appointment to the National Guard.

Quayle was the first Republican national candidate from the postwar baby boom generation that was heavily colored by the Vietnam War crisis. Quayle defended his non-combat service record on television: "Let's remember, you're going back 20 years in my life. I was at DePauw, and when we were making those decisions in my senior year, there were a number of us at DePauw that filed applications for the National Guard or the Army reserves. And recollections based on 20 years ago—many of us got in, so it wasn't just a random example."

Quayle did provide a self-deprecating esprit. While making remarks to the press, instead of saying that the Democrats would lead "backwards to the past," he said they would lead "past backwards." Smiling, Quayle corrected himself by saying this was an example of a "Hoosierism."

Bush moved past the negatives about the Quayle surprise and won the nomination unanimously on the third night. On the fourth night the Bush acceptance speech called for a "kinder, gentler nation." Bush was firm about Cold War aims to resist Soviet aggression and negotiate arms control cautiously: "I'll continue our policy of peace through strength."

Bush also made a smart partisan pledge on taxes that was most popular at New Orleans but that would haunt and eventually end the Bush presidency. "My opponent [Governor Michael Dukakis of Massachusetts] now says that he'd raise taxes as a last resort or a third resort. When a politician talks like that, you know that's one resort he'll be

"*George Bush says he will not raise taxes. That's all I know. That's all you need to know.*"

Bush inherits the GOP, 1988. New Yorker, *October 31, 1988.*

checking in to. My opponent won't rule out raising taxes, but I will, and the Congress will push me to raise taxes, and I'll say no, and they'll push, and I'll say no, and they'll push again, and I'll say to them, Read my lips: no new taxes."

The cheers were tumultuous, and George Bush, never a Reagan conservative, left the New Orleans convention with the trust of the right wing of the party. Trailing in the early polls to the colorless Dukakis, Bush went on the attack with television advertising and speeches that emphasized Republican strength against the Soviets while calling attention to Democratic flimsiness on social issues such as crime and patriotism.

Quayle quickly emerged as the vulnerable member of the GOP ticket. Bush was irked by having his first decision questioned by his own party faithful. The vice president, a hero of the Second World War, explained, "We've had a lot of unfounded rumors. . . . [I] looked at [Quayle's] whole record, and there was nothing dishonorable in it. There was nothing done that gave me any feeling anything was done against the rules, and I'm convinced that's the fact."

There were two televised debates between Bush and Dukakis, and one debate between Quayle and the Democratic nominee for vice president, Senator Lloyd Bentsen of Texas.

The Quayle debate proved damaging to the party when Quayle argued that his record of public service was as long as John F. Kennedy's when he ran for the White House. Senator Bentsen's ad-libbed response was nasty: "Senator, I served with Jack Kennedy. Jack Kennedy was a friend of mine. And Senator, you're no Jack Kennedy."

Quayle replied, "That was uncalled for, Senator."

Bush rides Reagan to victory, 1988. Washington Post, *October 27, 1988.*

The last two weeks of the campaign were a slugging match between the tops of the ticket. Bush continued to score with paid advertisements that attacked Dukakis on partisan issues such as pollution in Boston harbor and the governor's furlough program that had released a criminal who had subsequently committed more felonies. Bush dominated foreign affairs by insisting on modernization of U.S. nuclear forces and deployment of Star Wars anti-satellite defenses.

Bush led in the polls in all the large states. With a week to go, a weary

Dukakis made the fatal tactical error of declaring in Fresno, California, "Yes, I am a liberal in the tradition of Franklin Roosevelt and Harry Truman and John Kennedy."

Bush responded gleefully, "Miracle of miracles—headlines—read all about it—he's using the liberal label again!"

A sunspot on the future appeared when Bush was asked in Pennsylvania about the Bob Dole remark that taxes might have to be raised in the next administration. Bush equivocated, "I'm just going to do my best. [Dole] knows what I've said and what I believe. First, I've got to win this election."

Election eve, Bush commented on his political grittiness. "[The Democrats] thought they were going to kick my brains out and get away with it," he said in New Jersey. "They can dish it out but they can't take it."

More than ninety million voted (less than in 1984). Bush-Quayle won solidly, gaining 48.8 million votes (54 percent) and forty-two states with 426 electoral votes, taking all the large states except Governor Mario Cuomo's New York. Dukakis-Bentsen gained 41.8 million votes (46 percent) and eight states with D.C. for 112 electoral votes—though this included one West Virginia elector who insisted on voting for Bentsen alone.

The Republicans did not prosper in the new 101st Congress, which would remain firmly Democratic. The new Senate would have 55 Democrats and 45 Republicans; the House, 262 Democrats and 173 Republicans. Of the governorships, the Democrats held twenty-eight and the Republicans twenty-two.

Once again, a new Republican president faced a hostile Congress dominated by the very liberal ideology he had just campaigned against and defeated. "I've served in the Congress," remarked Bush in a post-election press conference. "And so, I don't think it will be, you know, that they'll do everything my way, and, but I will try very hard because I started with respect for the institution in which I serve."

The Democrats looked at Bush's feisty victory—the seventh time since FDR that a conservative Republican had defeated a liberal Democrat—and plotted for the next election. "No matter how popular your programs may be," remarked Democratic governor and future president Bill Clinton of Arkansas the day after the election about the Dukakis failure, "you must be considered in the mainstream on the shared values of the American people, the ability to defend the nation and the strength to enforce its laws. We have yet to learn that lesson."

★ 1992 ★

Ronald Reagan's chosen successor, George Bush, was the last Cold War president.

Bush pushed Moscow and its puppet states, including the Iraqi tyranny, into the dustbin of history. Yet at the same time the president discarded his own "no new taxes" pledge in pursuit of a so-called bipartisan governance, and the result was that he was thrown out of office by his own Republican party.

Bush's January 1989 inauguration speech, delivered on a windy, cloudy day in the nation's capital, held out the hope of the end of the Soviets. "A world refreshed by freedom seems reborn," declared Bush. "For in a man's heart, if not in fact, the day of the dictator is over. The totalitarian era is passing, its old ideas blown away like leaves from an ancient lifeless tree."

Bush also looked to what he called a "new bipartisanship" with the Democrats. "The old bipartisanship must be made new again. To my friends—and yes, I do mean friends—in the loyal opposition—and yes, I mean loyal—I put out my hand. I'm putting out my hand to you, Mr. Speaker [Jim Wright of Texas]. I'm putting out my hand to you, Mr. Majority Leader [George Mitchell of Maine]. For this is the thing: This is the

George Bush stalked by recession. New York Post, *October 16, 1992.*

age of the offered hand. And we can't turn back clocks, and I don't want to."

The president chose a Cabinet that illustrated his sense of bipartisanship, including his campaign manager and Texas friend James A. "Jim" Baker III at State, Representative Richard "Dick" Cheney of Wyoming at Defense, and Wall Street financier Nicholas F. Brady at Treasury. The president also moved to fill a Supreme Court vacancy with the noncontroversial choice of David Souter of New Hampshire.

Bush also defined bi-partisanship by choosing diverse symbols. He chose George Washington's Bible for his swearing-in, and within months he remarked that he was "an Oyster Bay kind of man," meaning Theodore Roosevelt.

In foreign affairs, Bush was a steady-eyed Cold Warrior, no bipartisanship to be seen. He negotiated arms reductions with Soviet dictator Gorbachev even while he worked to push the "evil empire" into failure. The president treated the Asian powers with caution yet did not permit enmity between giant trading partners. He helped the Berlin Wall fall and then helped powerhouse Germany to reunite. He ordered a military invasion of Panama against narco-terrorists and pressured Colombian drug cartels with American intervention. The president continued the CIA-backed arms shipments into Afghanistan and Central America until all the Soviet puppets had surrendered and only Cuba and North Korea were left like shanties to mark seventy-five years of red malevolence.

Most ably, Bush prepared for the last battle of the Cold War when Soviet puppet Saddam Hussein, tyrant of Iraq, invaded the oil-rich Arab state of Kuwait in August 1990. Bush understood that with the oil prices skyrocketing to forty dollars a barrel, the United States had to secure the Gulf oil fields. The 1991 Gulf War was a proof of the Reagan years of military preparedness; it was also a vindication of the diplomacy of Bush and Baker. The hapless Soviet military stood on the sidelines watching the American display of weapon systems in the attack on Soviet-supplied Iraqi forces. Ground force success in a matter of days was demonstration of American supremacy in the Cold War.

In domestic policy, Bush did try his "new bi-partisanship." He abandoned his "no new taxes" campaign pledge in late June 1990 during the budget negotiations with the Congress on the federal deficit. The Republican party howled in anger.

"I knew I'd catch some flak on this decision," Bush explained at the public outcry. "But I've got to do what I think is right, and then I'll ask the people for support." Asked if he would blame people for concluding that he had mislead them with his no-new-taxes pledge and had never really meant it, Bush responded, "I can understand people saying that. I think it's wrong, but I can understand it. I'm presented with new facts. And I'm doing like Lincoln did, 'think anew,' and I'm thinking anew."

Republican conservatives replied that Bush had lied to them and failed the party. In October Republican minority whip Newt Gingrich of Georgia rejected the tax-raising, deficit-reducing budget package, "It is my conclusion it will kill jobs, weaken the economy," said Gingrich, "and that the tax increase will be counterproductive and that it is not a package I can support. We need to do better than this."

"I cannot and will not support the proposed budget agreement," said Representative Lynn Martin of Illinois, who was campaigning for the U.S. Senate. "It's bad for seniors, bad for taxpayers, bad for the state of Illinois."

In October, a defensive Bush went on national television to argue for his tax increases. After quoting Thomas Paine—"These are the times that try men's souls"—he admitted, "This agreement will also raise revenue. I'm not and I know you're not a fan of tax increases. But if there have to be tax measures, they should allow the economy to grow. They should not turn us back to higher income tax rates, and they should be fair."

The 1990 midterm elections did not reward Bush for his bi-partisan-ship or the dropped no-new-tax pledge. However, the ongoing Gulf cri-sis, and Bush's tough talk against Saddam Hussein as a "brutal dictator," did mask the public disgust at the tax increases. The Democrats ad-vanced in both houses of the new 102nd Congress and in the state houses. In the new Senate, the Democrats picked up one seat, making a total of 56 Democrats and 44 Republicans. In the House, Democrats gained eight seats, so the new breakdown was 267 Democrats, 167 Re-publicans, with 1 independent. House minority whip Gingrich barely survived his race in the Georgia Sixth Congressional District, winning by less than 1,000 out of 150,000 votes.

Importantly for the forthcoming presidential race, the Democrats now held the governorships in four big electoral college states, New York, Pennsylvania, Florida, and Texas.

Following the Gulf War victory in the winter of '91, Bush surged in approval rating to 91 percent. But the recession that followed the oil price shock and the tax increases sliced into Bush's approval for the rest of his term. The scalding partisan battle in 1991 over the Clarence Thomas Su-preme Court confirmation hearings, and the repeated erroneous rosy eco-nomic scenarios from Bush's advisers ("The Treasury Department is not serving the interests of the president," commented the critical Gingrich) made the president vulnerable to Democratic challenge.

The dissolution of the Soviet Union in December 1991 did little to boost Bush's standings in the polls. When Federal Reserve chairman Alan Greenspan cut the discount rate by a full point just before Christmas, Bush was blamed for having let the economy drift into severe slowdown. Wall Street launched a new leg of a bull market with a post–Cold War rally that would eventually carry the Standard & Poor 500 index from 300 through 600. Nevertheless, the president received minimal credit from Wall Street and none from Main Street.

In the 1992 primary season, Bush was challenged by maverick GOP pundit (and former Nixon and Reagan aide) Patrick Buchanan, who ran against the president's broken tax pledge. Buchanan scored well enough in New Hampshire to shake the White House's confidence. "From dawn to dusk, Buchanan brigades met King George's army," boasted the gleeful Buchanan after the New Hampshire vote. "And I'm here to report they're retreating back into Massachusetts."

Buchanan's boom played well in the media but could not unseat the president. At the opening of the Houston convention in mid-August, Bush was in command of a well-financed but dispirited party. The polls showed Bush's approval rating had plunged to 33 percent; in the presidential preference poll he was trailing the Democratic candidate, Governor Bill Clinton of Arkansas, by 25 percent.

The Houston convention was a circus of controversy. The first trouble was a vice presidential boom to replace the controversial young Quayle with more seasoned candidates such as Jack Kemp, Dick Cheney, or the chairman of the Joint Chiefs of Staff, Colin Powell. There was also turmoil when Bush shuffled his old friend Baker from State to the White House as chief of staff and eventually to his old '88 role as Bush campaign manager.

Additional trouble came from the moderate wing of the party, which complained that the platform was in the hands of the conservatives. "If I didn't know better," said one observer, "I would assume the platform was written by the religious right." A survey of the delegates found that 70 percent were conservative, 71 percent were non-Catholic Christian, 80 percent were employed, and 89 percent were white.

Ronald Reagan was the featured speaker the first night of the convention. Again he asked the party to win one for the Gipper. "What we should change is a Democratic Congress," Reagan declared to cheers. "To hear the Democrats talk, you'd never know that the nightmare of nuclear annihilation has been lifted from our sleep." Reagan also used his wit against Democratic candidate William Jefferson Clinton. "I knew Thomas Jefferson," joked Reagan. "Thomas Jefferson was a friend of mine. And governor, you're no Thomas Jefferson."

The television networks, worried about ratings, were trying a new policy to skip coverage of election events that were judged too staged or unnewsworthy. One result was that the first night the networks chose only to encapsulate George Bush's surprise appearance at the convention just before Reagan's speech. Bush promised the delegates that he was going to make "the most stirring political comeback since Harry Truman gave 'em hell in 1948." No one remarked publicly the fact that 1948 was a *Democratic* victory.

The hottest moment of the whole convention was Patrick Buchanan's speech on the first night. The articulate columnist and speechwriter displayed the power and risk of partisan language. Buchanan mocked the Democrats: "The agenda Clinton & Clinton would impose on America—abortion on demand, a litmus test for the Supreme Court, homosexual rights, discrimination against religious schools, women in combat units—that's change all right. But it is not the change America needs." Buchanan also called the July New York Democratic convention "a giant masquerade ball," where "twenty thousand radicals and liberals came dressed up as moderates and centrists in the greatest single exhibition of cross-dressing in American political history."

The Republican platform was confident conservatism. Planks called for a repeal of the "recessionary" 1990 tax increases, a reduction of the capital gains tax to 15 percent, the creation of enterprise zones, tax credits for homeowners, a balanced budget, and a line-item veto.

The social planks were organized around the new Republican theme of "family values." The platform called for an anti-abortion amendment, strengthened border patrol against illegal immigration, and welfare reform: "Today's welfare system is antiwork and antimarriage. It taxes family to subsidize illegitimacy." Most controversial were the plank advocating prayer and pledge of allegiance in the classroom, and the plank on homosexuality—opposing homosexuals in the military and opposing laws permitting "same-sex marriages." On AIDS, the platform argued, "Prevention is linked ultimately to personal responsibility and moral behavior."

In foreign affairs, there was a plank for the building of Stars Wars. For the first time in fifty years, there was no mention of the now defunct Soviet Union or the disgraced, deceitful, withered Communist party.

The second and third days of the convention advanced the Republican argument that Bill Clinton was an untrustworthy liberal and that George Bush could be trusted this time not to raise taxes. The second-night keynote speaker, Senator Phil Gramm of Texas, a former Democrat who had switched parties in 1983, appealed, "It's not that the president did not ask for changes but that the Democrats who run Congress killed these changes."

There was no change in Bush's decision to keep Dan Quayle on the ticket. A popular campaign for sale on the floor was in support of Quayle's "family values" speech in which he had criticized a make-believe television heroine Murphy Brown for having a child out of wedlock. The button read, "Dan is right. Murphy's a tramp."

Bush and Quayle were renominated on the third night after speeches by three vivid Republican voices: First Lady Barbara Bush, Marilyn Quayle, and Cabinet member Lynn Martin.

"Not everyone demonstrated, dropped out, took drugs, joined in the sexual revolution or dodged the draft," the sharp-tongued Marilyn Quayle mocked Bill and Hillary Clinton. "I sometimes think that the liberals are always so angry because they believe the grandiose promises of the liberation movements. They're disappointed because most women do not wish to be liberated from their essential natures as women. Most of us love being mothers or wives, which gives our lives a richness that few men or women can get from professional accomplishment alone."

Also speaking the third night was Mary D. Fisher, a Republican woman who was infected with the HIV virus and who addressed the criticism that the party was insensitive to AIDS. "They are human," Fisher said of AIDS sufferers. "They have not earned cruelty, and they do not deserve meanness."

Bush's acceptance speech on the final night worked to reestablish the president as a candidate the party could trust. No one doubted his Cold Warrior achievements; however, the Soviets were gone and with them all the electioneering advantages of anti-communism. The president declared that he was a leader for the postwar years. He chose to promote himself by using the "superpower" rhetoric that had lost much of its potency in the post–Cold War lexicon.

"The world is in transition," the president said. "And we are feeling the transition in our homes. The defining challenge of the '90s is to win the economic competition—to win the peace. We must be a military superpower, an economic superpower, and an export superpower."

Bush's speech did not apologize for or explain his 1990 tax increase.

The convention closed with a spat between the Virginia and Massachusetts delegations over which state has had more presidents. During the balloting, Massachusetts, birthplace of George Bush, claimed it was home to more chief executives than any other. The facts were Massachusetts four, Ohio seven, Virginia eight. If you counted only the Republican presidents, the clear leader was Ohio: Grant, Hayes, Garfield, Harrison, McKinley, Taft, Harding.

The campaign was a struggle by Bush to win back the loyalty of the Grand Old Party. The party's conservatives charged that Bush's decision to raise taxes had revealed that he was out of touch with the wage earner and taxpayer. The hostile media pundits claimed without evidence that he was a sixty-eight-year-old Cold Warrior who watched the world go by from a limousine window.

Democratic candidate Clinton was a weak challenger who had little appeal to the disaffected Republican and independent voters who had backed Reagan and Bush before. Clinton's negatives were layered—infidelity, draft evasion, campaign financing irregularities in Arkansas, travels in Moscow during the Cold War, a most liberal wife who was said to be running for "copresident." There was little Clinton could do to boost his longshot chances besides choosing the young Democratic loyalist Senator Al Gore, Jr., of Tennessee as a running mate and then hope to get lucky against a well-financed but not widely loved incumbent.

The critical turn in the campaign came when Texas billionaire Ross Perot of Dallas, Texas, decided to get back in the race as an independent candidate. Perot had gone on cable television to declare his candidacy in the spring but then dropped out oddly in July. The Texan changed his mind later in the summer. Diminutive, witty, old-fashioned Perot was a colorful television presence who used the prestigious CNN network to advance his focused agenda of deficit reduction, strong defense, conservative social values. Bush could not easily counter a billionaire who en-

Bush vs. Clinton vs. Perot, 1992. New York Post, *October 16, 1992.*

THE DEBATE THAT WASN'T

dorsed almost all of the GOP platform without the burden of having broken the no-new-tax pledge.

There were three televised debates between all three candidates. The first, October 11 in St. Louis, showed confident men with appeal to different kinds of voters. Though they had a variety of positions on domestic and foreign policies, the so-called character issue was the telling distinction among them. Bush, sixty-eight, and Perot, fifty-seven, were virtuous husbands and fathers, while Clinton, at forty-six, was notorious for extramarital and drug-related incidents.

Bush highlighted the concerns about Clinton's reputation by questioning the report that Clinton protested the Vietnam War in 1969 while he was a Rhodes Scholar in Britain. "Some say, 'Well, you're old-fashioned,' " Bush remarked. "Maybe I am, but I just don't think that's right. Now, whether it's character or judgment, whatever it is, I have a big difference on this issue. And so we'll just have to see how it plays out, but I—I couldn't do that, and I don't think most Americans could do that."

Perot dominated the evening with his homey wit. "If people don't have the stomach to fix these problems," he opined, "I think it's a good time to face it, November. If they do, then they'll have heard the harsh reality of what we have to do. I'm not playing Lawrence Welk music tonight."

The second debate in Richmond, Virginia, October 15, experimented with a freewheeling talk-show format that discarded the traditional podiums for tall chairs and used so-called independent voters in the audience to ask questions of the candidates. In his closing remarks, Bush listed his opposition to new taxes and his intention to cut the deficit by cutting mandatory spending in the budget. Then the president underlined his vast foreign policy experience while mentioning the character issue again. "Now, let me pose this question to America. If in the next five minutes a television announcer came on and said, there is a major international crisis—there is a major threat to the world or in this country a major threat—my question is, who, if you were appointed to name one of the three of us, who would you choose? Who has the perseverance, the character, the integrity, the maturity, to get the job done?"

The third debate in East Lansing, Michigan, was promoted by the major liberal media as Bush's last chance. Beforehand *Newsweek* magazine printed a Clinton cover and speculated how Clinton would govern. *Time* magazine ran the quip, "The Democrats: Measuring the Drapes."

The president used the third debate to counterpunch hard against Clinton's vacillating tax policies and promises of a so-called middle-class tax cut. "So when you hear 'tax the rich,' Mr. and Mrs. America, watch your wallet. Lock your wallet because [Clinton's] coming after you just like Jimmy Carter did."

Bush closed with a rapid-fire Republican flourish. "The other night on character, Governor Clinton said it's not the character of the president but the character of the presidency. I couldn't disagree more. Horace Greeley said the only thing that endures is character. And I think it was Justice [Hugo] Black who talked about great nations, like great men, must keep their word."

Election eve, Clinton in Texas introduced his controversial wife, Hillary Rodham Clinton, as "the next first lady of the United States." The same day Perot in Texas joked about his partyless campaign being labeled crazy: "We're all crazy again now! Don't worry, folks. We've got buses lined up outside to take you back to the insane asylum when all this is over!" And the president in Texas promised "the biggest come-back in American history."

A final poll of registered voters showed Clinton 43 percent, Bush 35 percent, Perot 16 percent. The final lineup of celebrities showed Clinton with Hollywood liberals Glenn Close, Michael Bolton, Kathleen Turner, and Richard Gere, while Bush stood with the conservative national radio talk show host Rush Limbaugh. Bush jested, "Well, here's a good deal for you. Let Governor Clinton have Richard Gere, and I'll take Rush Limbaugh any day!"

Nearly ninety-four million voted, the highest total in history. The re-sult was almost identical with the final polls. Bush lost with 39.1 million votes (35 percent), carrying eighteen states for 168 electoral votes, in-cluding seven states of the old Confederacy but only the large states of Florida and Texas. Clinton won with 44.9 million votes (43 percent), carrying thirty-one states for 370 electoral votes, including the large states New York, Pennsylvania, Ohio, Illinois, and California.

Perot's candidacy brought down the Bush presidency. Perot took 19.7 million votes for no states and no electoral votes. However, the Perot voters made the difference on the five of the eight big states that went to the Democrats with less than a majority. Perot had split the Republican party in much the same fashion that Theodore Roosevelt had divided the party in 1912. The harshest irony was that Perot outpolled Bush by 316 votes in the rockbed Republican state of Maine, so that Clinton won Maine.

In the new 103rd Congress the Democrats retained solid control. The new Senate would stand Democrats 56, Republicans (after a runoff in Georgia) 44. The new House would show 258 Democrats, 176 Republi-cans with one independent. The Democrats won all seven of the House districts that had been redrawn after the 1990 census according to the

1982 amendments to the Voting Rights Act mandating redistricting on the basis of ethnic and racial categories. Notable Republican survivors were senators Al D'Amato of New York, Arlen Specter of Pennsylvania, and Bob Packwood of Oregon.

In defeat the party was combative. "The ultimate betrayal of Bush," said a moderate Republican, "will be to say he wasn't conservative enough. It was in fact the embracing of this platform at the convention that sealed the president's doom."

Ralph Reed of the conservative Christian Coalition countered, "Blaming the evangelicals for this defeat is like blaming the sinking of the *Titanic* on a waiter who dropped some dishes." In fact the Christian Coalition contributed passion and workers to Republican causes across the country. The evangelicals were spirited new blood for a minority party that dearly needed to expand its appeal to voters other than the grandsons of Hooverites.

Bush Cabinet member William J. "Bill" Bennett was a wry critic of the party, and he summed up the collective weariness after the defeat. "We've been in 12 years," said Bennett. "We've been running out of steam."

The Bush presidency closed just as the United States closed down the Cold War. The goal was reached, the race was won, the party stood accomplished even in defeat. In November 1992, what the Republican party needed was not just a new head of steam but also a new destination and a new engineer.

Postscript: Republican Sunrise

★ 1994 ★

The Sunday before the 1994 midterm elections, Ronald Reagan surprised the nation when he revealed that he was suffering from Alzheimer's disease, an incurable brain disorder. Reagan's handwritten letter immediately became the most dignified and heartbreaking document in the history of the Republican party.

> My fellow Americans. I have recently been told that I am one
> of the millions of Americans who will be afflicted with
> Alzheimer's Disease. Upon learning the news, Nancy and I
> had to decide whether as private citizens we would keep this a
> private matter or whether we would make this news known
> in a public way.
>
> In the past Nancy suffered from breast cancer and I had
> my cancer surgeries. We found through our open disclosures
> we were able to raise public awareness. We were happy that
> as a result many more people underwent testing.
>
> They were treated in early stages and we were able to
> return to normal, healthy lives.
>
> So now, we feel it is important to share it with you. In
> opening our hearts, we hope this might promote greater
> awareness of this condition. Perhaps it will encourage a

clearer understanding of the individuals and families who are affected by it.

At the moment I feel just fine. I intend to live the remainder of the years God gives me on this earth doing the things I have always done. I will continue to share life's journey with my beloved Nancy and my family. I plan to enjoy the great outdoors and stay in touch with my friends and supporters.

Unfortunately, as Alzheimer's Disease progresses, the family often bears a heavy burden. I only wish there was some way I could spare Nancy from this painful experience. When the time comes I am confident that with your help she will face it with faith and courage.

In closing let me thank you, the American people, for giving me the great honor of allowing me to serve as your President. When the Lord calls me home, whenever that may be, I will leave with the greatest love for this country of ours and eternal optimism for its future.

I now begin the journey that will lead me into the sunset of my life. I know that for America there will always be a bright dawn ahead.

Thank you, my friends. May God be with you. Sincerely, Ronald Reagan.

The whole of the Republican party read Reagan's letter in shock and prayer. The most successful Republican since Theodore Roosevelt was now faced with a living death in which he would no longer be able to use his magical voice and spectacular brand of *luck* to fight for the party. "I will now begin the journey that will lead me into the sunset of my life," Reagan wrote. Ronald Reagan's sunset was a shadow falling across a party that passionately desired a new dawn.

With two American dawns to go until election day, Republican candidates across the country felt themselves on the edge of a breakthrough in Congress. But every Republican since Dewey knew that the race was not won in the opinion polls but rather in the last hours before the voting polls opened for business. Every candidate also knew that a little of Ronald Reagan's *luck* would be a lot to have this close to the finish.

Minority leader Newt Gingrich of Georgia's Sixth District was looking for the old Reagan luck ceaselessly the last two days. Eight-term veteran Gingrich of Marietta, Georgia, an army brat and former history professor, had been traveling for weeks in pursuit of his ambition to overcome the forty-year Democrat stranglehold on the House and to make the Republicans the majority party and himself Speaker of the House. By election week he had visited 125 congressional districts; everywhere Gingrich went he offered an unusual campaign document called the "Contract with America"—a list of ten pieces of legislation that if elected Gingrich promised to bring to the House floor for a vote within the first one hundred days of the new term.

What was most appealing about the "Contract with America" was that it took many traditional conservative planks from Republican presidential platforms and presented them in the form of a business plan. Ten goals. A timetable. An agenda. For example, traditional planks calling for a balanced budget, tax cuts, and a line-item veto for the president were called the proposed Fiscal Responsibility Act. Traditional planks calling for law and order were grouped under the proposed Taking Back Our Streets Act. Customary Republican support for the military and opposition to any reduction in preparedness was called the proposed National Security Restoration Act. And the long Republican opposition to taxes and support for tax credits and a reduction in the capital gains tax was grouped under several items such as the proposed Job Creation and Wage Enhancement Act and the American Dream Restoration Act. The most unprecedented element in the contract was the proposed Citizen Legislature Act that called for term limits on members of Congress—a most popular theme across the country that had long been opposed by the ruling Democrats.

Gingrich brought more to the districts he visited than missionary zeal for the "Contract with America"; he also brought a drive and talent at phrasemaking that made him a charismatic leader for the party. His standard stump speech was a tony but colloquial argument for what he called "renewing American civilization" and "redirecting the course of human history." Gingrich aimed to appeal to the voters who were alarmed by the collapse of comity and decency in American life. "It is impossible to maintain a civilization," he told audiences again and again in a passionate cadence, "with 12 year olds having babies, 15 year olds killing each other, 17 year olds dying of AIDS, and 18 year olds getting diplomas they can't read."

When criticized on the stump for his extreme partisanship in pursuit of the Speaker's office, Gingrich had a standard reply: "I've been seen as a partisan, and I am a partisan, obviously, because (a) I've been trapped in the House, which is a very partisan environment, for my entire public career in Washington, and (b) because under Reagan and Bush, it was their job to do the vision and it was my job to be a partisan soldier. That era is over."

Election eve, Gingrich kept up the attack on the Democrats in telephone conference calls he held with Republican candidates nationwide. "We're prepared to place our trust in the people to reshape the government," Gingrich argued. "Our liberal friends place their trust in the government to reshape the people."

Republican hopefuls used a clever banner to express their devotion to the minority leader. "Newt Wants You!"

Election day was a Republican sunrise. November 8, 1994, brought Ronald Reagan's famous luck one more time.

The Grand Old Party won an old-fashioned hurricane sweep that was spookily similar to the great Republican victory in the new Fifty-fourth Congress of exactly one hundred years before. Not a single Republican incumbent lost from coast to coast, and more often than not Republican challengers knocked Democratic incumbents out of office.

The Republicans gained control of both houses of the new 104th Congress for the first Republican majority on Capitol Hill since the Eighty-third Congress in Eisenhower's first term.

In the House new Speaker of the House Newt Gingrich and new majority leader Dick Armey of Texas and de facto budget boss John Kasich of Ohio would have 229 Republicans and 206 Democrats. The net pickup of over fifty seats was most striking in the Democratic Solid South base. In Gingrich's Georgia, the eleven congressional seats in the 103rd Congress had been held by 10 Democrats and 1 (Gingrich) Republican; in the new 104th Congress Georgia would send 10 Republicans and 1 Democrat. Commented a Republican agent in Atlanta, "This is the culmination of a political revolution in the South. What's happened is that young, aspiring white politicians will now see their route to positions of power in the Republican party rather than in the Democratic party."

The new Senate with majority leader Bob Dole of Kansas and majority whip Trent Lott of Mississippi would have 56 Republicans and 44 Democrats. Notable young new faces included Rick Santorum, thirty-six, of Pennsylvania; Bill Frist, forty-two, of Tennessee; Spencer Abraham, forty-two, of Michigan; Rod Grams, forty-six, of Minnesota; Mike DeWine, forty-seven, of Ohio; Olympia J. Snowe, forty-seven, of Maine.

Republican victories in the states were also astonishing. New governors included Thomas Ridge of Pennsylvania, George Pataki of New York, and George W. Bush of Texas. In Ohio incumbent Republican George Voinovich won with a 72 percent majority, and in Michigan incumbent Republican John Engler gained a 61 percent majority. The Republicans now held the governor's chairs in six of the seven big electoral college states.

"It's Speaker of the House, not speaker of the party!" joked a joyful Newt Gingrich in Marietta, Georgia, on election night.

The GOP triumphant, 1994. © 1994 by Herblock in the *Washington Post.*

Wednesday dawn brought sober remarks from the two leading Republicans. Bob Dole told the television audience: "We intend to work with the president. We only have one president and that's President Clinton and we are going to do the best we can." Asked if the surprising election results meant that the electorate was angry at Washington, Dole cleverly turned the tables. "Well, I must say not many Republicans lost. I don't know who they're angrier at. I think they're angry at the Democrats. They lost. We won. But we've got our work cut out for us. The American people have given us an opportunity and the responsibility. We're not going to get it done in one year or two years, but we're going to start work on it."

Newt Gingrich's remarks to the morning television audience were more philosophical than Dole's. There was also no suggestion that the new Republican House was going to go slow on the "Contract with America" or any other ambition. "There are profound things that went wrong with the Great Society and the counterculture and until we address them head-on we're going to have these problems." Gingrich the history teacher reflected, "Until the mid 1960's there was an explicit long-term commitment to creating character. It was the work ethic. It was honesty, right and wrong. It was not harming others. It was being vigilant in the defense of liberty."

Asked whom he regarded as obstacles to his vision of America, Gingrich was pointed about his distaste for liberalism in government and the media. "There's only a very small counterculture elite, which is terrified of the opportunity to actually renew American civilization."

Gingrich closed with an optimistic turn of phrase that contained a show of partisan muscle to get things done the Republican way. "I think the Republican Party has an obligation to be positive, but I think it is an obligation to be positive on behalf of the values of the American people."

No bipartisanship. No nonpartisanship. No accommodation. No wait-and-see. *"An obligation to be positive on behalf of the values of the American people."*

ONE HUNDRED AND FORTY YEARS after the party's foundation, the old rules of American politics remained the new rules of American politics.

The power went to the party that won the next new election, time after time.

The power went to those who claimed *an obligation to be positive on behalf of the values of the American people,* whether on the question of liberty, or sound money, or trust-busting, or anti-Communism, or family values.

The power went to the Grand Old Party as long as it kept to Abraham Lincoln's advice that *"a nation of the people, by the people, and for the people shall not perish from this earth,"* as long as it kept to Theodore Roosevelt's advice that *"to our people is given the right to win such honor and renown as has never yet been granted to the people of mankind,"* and as long as it kept to Ronald Reagan's advice, *"You ain't seen nothing yet."*

Index

About the Author

John Calvin Batchelor was born in Bryn Mawr, Pennsylvania, in 1948. He is the author of seven novels, most recently *Father's Day*. He lives with his family in Maine and New York. This is his first work of history.